Reason and Analysis in Ancient Greek Philosophy

PHILOSOPHICAL STUDIES SERIES

VOLUME 120

Founded by Wilfrid S. Sellars and Keith Lehrer

Editor

Stephen Hetherington, *The University of New South Wales, Sydney, Australia*

Senior Advisory Editor

Keith Lehrer, *University of Arizona, Tucson, AZ, U.S.A.*

Associate Editor

Stewart Cohen, *University of Arizona, Tucson, AZ, U.S.A.*

Board of Consulting Editors

Lynne Rudder Baker, *University of Massachusetts, Amherst, MA, U.S.A.*
Radu Bogdan, *Tulane University, New Orleans, LA, U.S.A.*
Marian David, *University of Notre Dame, Notre Dame, IN, U.S.A.*
John M. Fischer, *University of California, Riverside, CA, U.S.A.*
Allan Gibbard, *University of Michigan, Ann Arbor, MI, U.S.A.*
Denise Meyerson, *Macquarie University, NSW, Australia*
François Recanati, *Institut Jean-Nicod, EHESS, Paris, France*
Mark Sainsbury, *University of Texas, Austin, TX, U.S.A.*
Stuart Silvers, *Clemson University, Clemson, SC, U.S.A.*
Barry Smith, *State University of New York, Buffalo, NY, U.S.A.*
Nicholas D. Smith, *Lewis & Clark College, Portland, OR, U.S.A.*
Linda Zagzebski, *University of Oklahoma, Norman, OK, U.S.A.*

For further volumes:
http://www.springer.com/series/6459

Georgios Anagnostopoulos • Fred D. Miller, Jr.
Editors

Reason and Analysis in Ancient Greek Philosophy

Essays in Honor of David Keyt

 Springer

Editors
Georgios Anagnostopoulos
Department of Philosophy
University of California, San Diego
La Jolla, CA, USA

Fred D. Miller, Jr.
Social Philosophy and Policy Foundation
Bowling Green, OH, USA

ISBN 978-94-007-6003-5　　　ISBN 978-94-007-6004-2 (eBook)
DOI 10.1007/978-94-007-6004-2
Springer Dordrecht Heidelberg New York London

Library of Congress Control Number: 2013940872

© Springer Science+Business Media Dordrecht 2013
This work is subject to copyright. All rights are reserved by the Publisher, whether the whole or part of the material is concerned, specifically the rights of translation, reprinting, reuse of illustrations, recitation, broadcasting, reproduction on microfilms or in any other physical way, and transmission or information storage and retrieval, electronic adaptation, computer software, or by similar or dissimilar methodology now known or hereafter developed. Exempted from this legal reservation are brief excerpts in connection with reviews or scholarly analysis or material supplied specifically for the purpose of being entered and executed on a computer system, for exclusive use by the purchaser of the work. Duplication of this publication or parts thereof is permitted only under the provisions of the Copyright Law of the Publisher's location, in its current version, and permission for use must always be obtained from Springer. Permissions for use may be obtained through RightsLink at the Copyright Clearance Center. Violations are liable to prosecution under the respective Copyright Law.
The use of general descriptive names, registered names, trademarks, service marks, etc. in this publication does not imply, even in the absence of a specific statement, that such names are exempt from the relevant protective laws and regulations and therefore free for general use.
While the advice and information in this book are believed to be true and accurate at the date of publication, neither the authors nor the editors nor the publisher can accept any legal responsibility for any errors or omissions that may be made. The publisher makes no warranty, express or implied, with respect to the material contained herein.

Printed on acid-free paper

Springer is part of Springer Science+Business Media (www.springer.com)

Acknowledgments

Preparing this *hommage* to David Keyt has been a labor of love for the editors and contributors alike. The volume contains fifteen essays by sixteen scholars including students, colleagues, and friends (the latter category being all inclusive!). All of the authors make important original contributions to the study of ancient Greek philosophy, and we wish to thank them all for agreeing to participate in this project, for their cooperation with the editing, and for the high quality of their essays. We are also grateful for their patience and good cheer throughout an unexpectedly protracted publication process.

The papers by Gerasimos Santas, Nils Rauhut, Mark McPherran, Charles Young, and Fred D. Miller, Jr. were delivered originally at a conference (aka "the Keytfest") held at the University of Washington in Seattle in 2007 commemorating David Keyt's fiftieth year as a professor of philosophy. Kenneth Clatterbaugh, Chair of the Department of Philosophy at the University of Washington, was very supportive of the program, and Bev Wessel provided valuable administrative assistance. Daniel Fisher, a student of David Keyt, offered generous financial support. Richard Parker, another former student, served as quipster and consummate master of ceremonies.

We are pleased to thank a number of people who have been very helpful with the editing and publication of this volume including Professor Stephen Hetherington, the editor of Springer's Philosophical Studies Series; Ingrid van Laarhoven; Christi Lue; Ties Nijssen; Hendrikje Tuerlings; Professor Nicholas D. Smith, who helped to find a suitable publisher for the volume; and an anonymous reviewer who provided helpful comments. James Dabgotra ably assisted with the first round of editing, and Pamela Phillips did an excellent job copyediting the entire typescript and preparing it for the publisher. We also gratefully acknowledge financial support from the Social Philosophy and Policy Foundation for the original conference and for the editing of the volume.

Finally, we thank David Keyt for his assistance throughout the planning and preparation of the volume and especially for his willingness to contribute a fascinating memoir of his academic career which, in addition to delightful anecdotes about his encounters with notable scholars, offers illuminating insights into his own work and also into the recent history of the subdiscipline of ancient philosophy.

With affection and admiration, we the editors and all the contributors dedicate this volume to David Keyt, in recognition of his major contributions to the study of ancient philosophy, and on behalf of the many students, colleagues, and friends whose lives he has touched and enriched over the past half century.

Del Mar, California
Bowling Green, Ohio

Georgios Anagnostopoulos
Fred D. Miller, Jr.

Contents

Introduction 1
Georgios Anagnostopoulos and Fred D. Miller, Jr.

A Life in the Academy 11
David Keyt

Moral Psychology in Plato's *Apology* 45
Thomas C. Brickhouse and Nicholas D. Smith

Socrates, the Athenian 55
Jean Roberts

Socrates on the Impossibility of a Reasonable Politics 67
Stephen M. Gardiner

Retaliation in the *Crito* 91
Merrill Ring

How Virtuous Was Socrates? 109
Nils Ch. Rauhut

Plato's *Republic* as a Vocation 125
Allan Silverman

Soul, Soul-Parts, and Persons in Plato 147
C.D.C. Reeve

Just City and Just Soul in Plato's *Republic* 171
Gerasimos Santas

Virtue, Luck, and Choice at the End of the *Republic* 197
Mark L. McPherran

The Grounds of *Logos*: The Interweaving of Forms 211
Christopher Shields

Accidental Beings in Aristotle's Ontology 231
S. Marc Cohen

Is There Room for Plato in an Aristotelian Theory of Essence? 243
Frank A. Lewis

***Metaphysics* Z.11 and Functionalism**.. 271
Cass Weller

Aristotle on Belief and Knowledge 285
Fred D. Miller, Jr.

Aristotelian Grace... 309
Charles M. Young

The Works of David Keyt 317

Index.. 321

Contributors

Georgios Anagnostopoulos is Professor of Philosophy at the University of California, San Diego. He has authored *Aristotle on the Goals and Exactness of Ethics* (1994); edited *A Companion to Aristotle* (2009), *Law and Rights in the Ancient Greek Tradition* (2006), and *Socratic, Platonic and Aristotelian Studies: Essays in Honor of Gerasimos Santas* (2011); and has published a number of articles on ancient Greek philosophy, medicine, and culture.

Thomas C. Brickhouse is Professor of Philosophy at Lynchburg College. He is the co-author (with Nicholas D. Smith) of six books and numerous articles on Socratic philosophy, most recently *Socratic Moral Psychology* (2011). In addition to his work in Socratic studies, he has published a number of articles on Plato and Aristotle.

S. Marc Cohen is Professor Emeritus of Philosophy at the University of Washington, where he taught courses in the history of ancient Greek philosophy, logic, and the philosophy of language. He has also taught at the University of Minnesota, Rutgers University, the University of California, Berkeley, and Indiana University. His publications have primarily concerned the metaphysics and epistemology of Plato and Aristotle. He is co-editor of *Readings in Ancient Greek Philosophy* (2011) and co-author of *Ammonius: On Aristotle's Categories* (1991). Recent publications include "Substances," a chapter in *A Companion to Aristotle*, ed. G. Anagnostopoulos (2009), and "Alteration and Persistence: Form and Matter in the *Physics* and *De Generatione et Corruptione*," a chapter in *The Oxford Handbook of Aristotle* (2012).

Stephen M. Gardiner is Professor of Philosophy and Ben Rabinowitz Professor of Human Dimensions of the Environment at the University of Washington, Seattle. In ancient philosophy, he has previously published on Aristotle's ethics and Stoic ethics and is the editor of *Virtue Ethics: Old and New* (2005). He is also the author of *A Perfect Moral Storm: The Ethical Tragedy of Climate Change* (2011) and the coordinating co-editor of *Climate Ethics: Essential Readings* (2010). His articles have appeared in journals such as *Ethics*, the *Journal of Political Philosophy*, *Oxford Studies in Ancient Philosophy*, and *Philosophy and Public Affairs*.

Frank A. Lewis is Professor of Philosophy at the University of Southern California. He is the author of *Substance and Predication in Aristotle* (1991) and *Form, Matter, and Mixture in Aristotle* (1997) as well as many articles on Aristotle's metaphysics.

Mark L. McPherran is Professor of Philosophy at Simon Fraser University. He is the author of *The Religion of Socrates* (2003) and *The Cambridge Critical Guide to the Republic* (2010) and is editor of collections of essays on Socrates and Plato, most recently *Recognition, Remembrance, and Reality: New Essays on Plato's Epistemology and Metaphysics* (1999). He is also the author of numerous papers on Socratic and Platonic philosophy of religion.

Fred D. Miller, Jr. is Professor of Philosophy and Executive Director of the Social Philosophy and Policy Center at Bowling Green State University. He is author of *Nature, Justice, and Rights in Aristotle's Politics* (1995) and many articles concerning ancient Greek philosophy. He is also co-editor with David Keyt of *A Companion to Aristotle's Politics* (1995) and *Freedom, Reason, and the Polis: Essays in Ancient Greek Political Philosophy* (2007) and co-editor with Carrie-Ann Biondi of *A History of the Philosophy of Law from the Ancient Greeks to the Scholastics* (2007). He is Eexecutive Editor of *Social Philosophy & Policy*. He is currently preparing a translation of Aristotle's *De Anima* and *Parva Naturalia* for Oxford University Press. He is a former president of the Society for Ancient Greek Philosophy.

Nils Ch. Rauhut is Professor and Chair of the Department of Philosophy and Religious Studies at Coastal Carolina University. He served as president of the American Association of Philosophy Teachers (AAPT) from 2010 to 2012, and he is author of *Ultimate Questions: Thinking about Philosophy* (3rd edition 2010) and editor of *Readings on the Ultimate Questions* (3rd edition 2009).

C.D.C. Reeve is Delta Kappa Epsilon Distinguished Professor of Philosophy at the University of North Carolina at Chapel Hill. He works primarily on Plato and Aristotle but is interested in philosophy generally and has published on film and on the philosophy of sex and love. His recent books include *Substantial Knowledge: Aristotle's Metaphysics* (2003); *Love's Confusions* (2005); *Action, Contemplation, and Happiness: An Essay on Aristotle* (2012); *Blindness and Reorientation: Problems in Plato's Republic* (2012); and *Aristotle on Practical Wisdom* (forthcoming 2013). He has translated Plato's *Euthyphro, Apology, Crito, Meno, Cratylus* and *Republic* (2005) as well as Aristotle's *Politics*. He is working on a translation of Aristotle's *Nicomachean Ethics*.

Merrill Ring is Professor Emeritus of Philosophy at California State University, Fullerton. His publications in Greek philosophy are a book, *Beginning with the Pre-Socratics* (2nd edition 2000), and a paper "Aristotle and the Concept of Happiness" (1980) in *The Greeks and the Good Life* (ed. David Depew). He is also the author of a number of essays on modern epistemology and philosophy of language.

Jean Roberts is Professor of Philosophy at the University of Washington, Seattle. She has written primarily on Plato's and Aristotle's moral and political theory and is most recently the author of the *Routledge Philosophy Guidebook to Aristotle and the Politics* (2009).

Gerasimos Santas is Professor of Philosophy Emeritus at the University of California, Irvine, where he taught from 1969 until 2008. He also previously taught at Hamilton College, University of California, Berkeley, Brandeis University, Wellesley College, and Johns Hopkins. He has held visiting positions at Stanford University and the University of Salzburg. In addition to many articles on Plato and Aristotle, he is author of *Socrates* (1979), *Plato and Freud* (1988), *Goodness and Justice* (2001), and *Understanding Plato's* Republic (2010) and is the editor of *The Blackwell Guide to Plato's Republic* (2006).

Christopher Shields is Professor of Classical Philosophy and Fellow of Lady Margaret Hall at the University of Oxford. He is the author of *Multiplicity: Homonymy in the Philosophy of Aristotle* (1999) and *Classical Philosophy* (2003). He is also editor of *The Blackwell Guide to Ancient Philosophy* (2003) and *The Oxford Handbook of Aristotle* (2012) and has published many articles on Plato and Aristotle.

Allan Silverman is Professor of Philosophy at the Ohio State University. He is the author of *The Dialectic of Essence* (2002) and numerous articles on Plato and Aristotle. In addition to his research in ancient philosophy, metaphysics, and ethics, he is a Fellow of the Mershon Center for International Security Studies, where he works on the topic of citizenship.

Nicholas D. Smith is James F. Miller Professor of Humanities in the Philosophy Department at Lewis and Clark College in Portland, Oregon. He has collaborated extensively with Thomas C. Brickhouse on several topics in ancient Greek philosophy. His most recent book (with another co-author, Ian Evans) is titled *Knowledge* (2012).

Cass Weller is Associate Professor of Philosophy at the University of Washington. He has published on Plato, Aristotle, and Hume. His recent publications include "Fallacies in the *Phaedo* Again" (reprinted in *Essays on Plato's Psychology*, ed. Ellen Wagner, 2001).

Charles M. Young is Professor of Philosophy at Claremont Graduate University. He has published a number of essays on Aristotle's ethics and is currently working on a book titled *Aristotle on Virtue and the Virtues*.

Abbreviations of Plato's Works

Ap.   *Apology*
Cra.   *Cratylus*
Cri.   *Crito*
Euthd. *Euthydemus*
Grg.   *Gorgias*
Lg.   *Laws*
Phd.   *Phaedo*
Phdr.   *Phaedrus*
Phil.   *Philebus*
Pol.   *Politicus (Statesman)*
Prm.   *Parmenides*
Prt.   *Protagoras*
Rep.   *Republic*
Smp. *Symposium*
Sph.   *Sophist*
Tht.   *Theaetetus*
Ti.   *Timaeus*

Abbreviations of Aristotle's Works

An	*On the Soul (de Anima)*
An. Post	*Posterior Analytics (Analytica Posteriora)*
Cael	*On the Heavens (de Caelo)*
Cat	*Categories (Categoriae)*
EE	*Eudemian Ethics (Ethica Eudemia)*
GA	*Generation of Animals (de Generatione Animalium)*
GC	*On Generation and Corruption (de Generatione et Corruptione)*
HA	*History of Animals (Historia Animalium)*
Insomn	*On Dreams (de Insomniis)*
Int	*Interpretations (de Interpretatione)*
Mem	*On Memory (de Memoria et Reminiscentia)*
Met	*Metaphysics (Metaphysica)*
Meteor	*Meteorology (Meteorologica)*
MM	*Magna Moralia*
NE	*Nicomachean Ethics (Ethica Nicomachea)*
PA	*Parts of Animals (de Partibus Animalium)*
Phys	*Physics (Physica)*
Poet	*Poetics (Poetica)*
Pol	*Politics (Politica)*
Rhet	*Rhetoric (Rhetorica)*
SE	*Sophistical Refutations (Sophistici Elenchi)*
Sens	*Sense and Sensibilia (de Sensu et Sensibilibus)*
Top	*Topics (Topica)*

Introduction

Georgios Anagnostopoulos and Fred D. Miller, Jr.

During the latter half of the twentieth century in the wake of the rise of analytic philosophy, there was also a revival of the study of ancient Greek philosophy. This tandem development was no coincidence. Historians of philosophy came to realize that the new methods of philosophical analysis and criticism could be put to use in uncovering lost treasures in ancient Greek philosophical texts. Plato, Aristotle, and other classical thinkers had themselves used sophisticated techniques of analysis, definition, and argumentation to grapple with fundamental issues and to make important theoretical contributions. Even the apparent missteps committed by the ancients might prove to be instructive. David Keyt's memoir, "A Life in the Academy," which is the first essay in this volume, sheds valuable light on this history.

David Keyt is widely acknowledged as a master in applying philosophical analysis to the interpretation and criticism of ancient texts and the demonstration of their relevance to modern philosophical issues. The following is a brief overview of his most influential contributions to the study of ancient philosophy.

Keyt's early work was devoted to Plato's metaphysics and epistemology. In "The Fallacies in *Phaedo* 102A-107B" (Keyt 1963), he contended that Plato's culminating argument for the immortality of the soul commits basic logical fallacies overlooked by earlier commentators. This essay has continued to be a provocation and a stumbling block for more sympathetic interpreters. Keyt also concentrated on Plato's conception of a Form: If a Form is an entity distinct from sensible particulars,

---

G. Anagnostopoulos (✉)
Department of Philosophy, University of California, San Diego, Gilman Dr. 9500,
La Jolla, CA 92093-0119, USA
e-mail: ganagnostopoulos@ucsd.edu

F.D. Miller, Jr.
Social Philosophy and Policy Foundation, 1616 E. Wooster St., Ste. 24,
Bowling Green, OH 43402, USA
e-mail: fmiller@sppfbg.org

what sort of properties is it supposed to possess? In two articles, he argued that the failure to distinguish between the different types of properties belonging to the Forms leads Plato into serious difficulties: "Plato's Paradox that the Immutable is Unknowable" (Keyt 1969) and "The Mad Craftsman of the *Timaeus*" (Keyt 1971). These finely crafted early works exhibited traits for which Keyt's work has become renowned: concision, originality, and trenchant argumentation, sparkling with flashes of wit. Though better known as a scholar in ancient philosophy, Keyt early on wrote a series of articles on the philosophy of language, and in particular on Wittgenstein. He brought this scholarship to bear in "Plato on Falsity: *Sophist* 263B" (Keyt 1973), where he showed that Plato's analysis of falsity is open to competing interpretations, which in fact correspond to different modern theories of predication.

David Keyt's attention turned to ethics and politics, partly as a result of his experiences in the academy during the tumultuous era of the Vietnam War. The study of the moral and political philosophy of Aristotle (and of Plato to a lesser extent) has continued to be a major focus of his scholarly work. He addressed a fundamental question concerning Aristotle's ethics: What is the best life for a human being? In "Intellectualism in Aristotle" (Keyt 1978, revised 1983) and "The Meaning of *Bios* in Aristotle's *Ethics* and *Politics*" (Keyt 1989), he challenged the view, dominant at the time, that the best life for Aristotle consists exclusively of philosophical activity. Keyt defended an alternative interpretation, moderate intellectualism, according to which, although the philosophical life is best, human happiness also includes the moral and political life. Keyt's interpretation continues as a major force in the treatment of Aristotelian *eudaimonia*. Keyt subsequently turned to Aristotle's *Politics* where he has had his greatest influence on classical scholarship. "Three Fundamental Theorems in Aristotle's *Politics*" (Keyt 1987, revised and published in 1991a) was vintage Keyt, offering a critical analysis of Aristotle's theorems that the polis exists by nature, that man is by nature a political animal, and that the polis is by nature prior to the individual. Keyt argued that all of Aristotle's arguments, however charitably reconstructed, fail and that Hobbes was right to reject these theorems. This essay threw down the gauntlet to all scholars aspiring to defend Aristotle's political naturalism and thus served as a major stimulus to serious scholarship on this issue. Keyt adopted a much more sympathetic stance toward Aristotle's political theory in "Distributive Justice in Aristotle's *Ethics* and *Politics*" (Keyt 1985, revised as 1991b). Here he explicated Aristotle's general concept of distributive justice and showed how it serves as a unifying theme in his constitutional theory, in that the justifications of different constitutions, including democracy and absolute kingship, are all variations on a common theme. This brilliant essay has had an enormous influence on subsequent scholarly work on Aristotle's political theory. Important further work on the *Politics* includes "Aristotle and the Ancient Roots of Anarchism" (Keyt 1993, revised as 1996) and "The Four Causes in Aristotle's *Politics*" (1995). In recognition of his scholarly achievements, he was invited by J. L. Ackrill to contribute a volume to the distinguished Clarendon Aristotle series. His translation and commentary on the *Politics* Books V and VI (Keyt 1999) demonstrated the relationship of Aristotle's account of revolution with his theory of justice and thus the overall unity and coherence of Aristotle's political philosophy. Over the past decade, Keyt has continued to be an active scholar publishing essays on the ethics and politics of Plato, Aristotle, and ancient political thought. Finally, he has made important contributions as an editor. *A Companion to Aristotle's Politics* (Blackwell, 1991c), coedited by David Keyt and Fred Miller, was the first anthology to demonstrate the philosophical importance of the *Politics*. *Freedom, Reason, and the Polis: Essays in Ancient Greek Political Philosophy* (Cambridge University Press, 2007), also coedited with Miller, included recent contributions by leading scholars.

In conclusion, David Keyt's published works have established the highest standards of originality, rigor, and clarity combined with close and faithful exegesis. In all of his scholarship, he has sought to lay bare the logical structure of crucial arguments, employing the tools of modern analysis but eschewing anachronism. In view of his many valuable contributions to the field of ancient Greek philosophy, it is fitting to honor David Keyt with this collection of essays by his students, colleagues, and friends on the themes of analysis and reason in Socrates, Plato, and Aristotle. The essays explore the central role of the concept of reason in metaphysics, moral psychology, epistemology, ethics, and political philosophy. They should be of great interest to contemporary philosophers who recognize that these ancient Greek thinkers discovered many of the analytical methods which continue to be applied today and that they remain a valuable source of theoretical insights.

Reason and analysis form a fitting and unifying theme for this collection. The first five essays dedicated to David Keyt are devoted to the central role of reason in the philosophy of Socrates as presented in Plato's earlier dialogues. Socrates is generally held to espouse intellectualism, the thesis that reason is and ought to be the ruler of the soul. Thomas C. Brickhouse and Nicholas D. Smith, in "Moral Psychology in Plato's *Apology*," consider what implications this has for the place of desire and emotion in Socratic moral psychology. They argue that several passages in Plato's *Apology* cannot be appropriately understood by what has come to be the most widely accepted interpretation of Socratic intellectualism. According to this view, Brickhouse and Smith explain, Socrates saw no role in the explanation of human behavior for such psychological factors as appetites or passions/emotions. They claim, on the contrary, that certain passages in Plato's *Apology* actually reveal that Socrates was quite ready to explain human behavior in precisely the way this interpretation claims he would not (or could not) do. Brickhouse and Smith then provide an understanding of what Socrates is saying in these passages that makes much better sense of them but also continues to depict Socratic moral psychology as intellectualist. They conclude that Socrates does subscribe to an intellectualist moral psychology insofar as it remains true that all human agents always act in ways that reflect their beliefs about what is best for them at the time of action.

In Plato's *Crito,* Socrates offers a famous and much criticized argument that he has a moral obligation to obey the laws of Athens. Three essays examine what Socrates intends to prove with this argument and whether it is defensible. In the first of the these essays, "Socrates, the Athenian," Jean Roberts argues that although the speech that Socrates gives in the *Crito* in the voice of the Laws of Athens claims that an Athenian citizen owes absolute obedience to them, the speech does not articulate Socrates' full and considered judgment about his moral obligation to act in accordance with Athenian law. She argues that the speech articulates Socrates' conception of his legal obligation, an obligation that is, in the broader context of the argument in the *Crito*, carefully subordinated to his broader moral obligations. In this way, the otherwise curious feature of Socrates speaking as the Laws of Athens is explained. The Laws are made to describe their understanding of a citizen's commitment, an understanding that Socrates endorses as such in speaking for them. Nevertheless, she argues, just as any other commitment or agreement in Socrates' view, this one should only be kept as long as doing so does not require doing injustice, a principle enunciated immediately before the speech of the Laws. She concludes that since the situation in which Socrates finds himself in the *Crito* is not one in which he is ordered to do anything unjust, he is bound to obey.

In the next contribution to the collection, "Socrates on the Impossibility of a Reasonable Politics," Stephen M. Gardiner argues that while Socrates comes across as a heroic figure on the one hand, his political theory can seem extreme, myopic, and dangerously naïve, on the other hand. Gardiner contends that Socrates appears paradoxical because he fails to appreciate the need of citizens for protection from the city, he is insensitive to the importance of standard forms of political discourse, and he characterizes himself as the only true politician because of the nature of the political dialogue in which he engages. Gardiner considers possible routes to resolving the paradoxical portrait of Socrates and concludes that Socrates is a pessimist about politics and that this pessimism both explains the apparently troubling features of Socrates' political theory and preserves the understanding of him as heroic.

In "Retaliation in the *Crito*," Merrill Ring suggests that Socrates has two major lines of argument in the *Crito* concerning a possible escape: that retaliation is wrong (and that by escaping he would be retaliating against Athens for its judgment at his trial) and that he has a legitimate agreement with Athens that he will abide by its laws and judgments (and that escaping would be violating that agreement). Ring notes that the second of those arguments has received the major attention in commentaries on the *Crito*. But the retaliation topic, though significantly overlooked, is equally important and equally connected to Athenian thought in the fifth century.

Ring argues that Socrates attempts two distinct arguments to show that, contrary to orthodox Athenian public opinion, retaliation is wrong. However, upon critical examination, both of those arguments fail. The consequence is that one half of Socrates' case for not escaping cannot stand.

Socrates is depicted as the unalloyed embodiment of rationality and virtue in Plato's *Phaedrus*. Nils Ch. Rauhut, in "How Virtuous Was Socrates?" wonders whether there might not be a degree of irony in Plato's portrait. He begins by arguing that the moral character of the historical Socrates plays a role in our understanding of Socrates' philosophy. He then examines a key passage that has shaped understanding of Socrates' moral character: Alcibiades' speech in Plato's *Symposium*. Rauhut considers three different approaches to Alcibiades' speech and argues that all three of them fail to explain the humor in the speech. Based on this result, he develops and defends a new interpretation, arguing that the key to understanding the speech is Alcibiades' use of irony. Rauhut concludes that if readers pay attention to the ironic elements in the speech, Alcibiades' "praise" of Socrates turns out to be a witty deconstruction of Socrates' self-image. Socrates emerges not as an otherworldly saint who has acquired all the cardinal virtues but rather as a human who tries to integrate *eros* within his life.

The next group of essays turns to Plato, who famously argued in the *Republic* and other dialogues that reason is the natural ruler over the soul as well as over the city. The *Republic* advances the controversial thesis that in the best city, the rulers should be philosophers. This thesis is often taken to be deeply anti-egalitarian. Allan Silverman, in "Plato's *Republic* as a Vocation," offers a different interpretation of the role of reason in politics. He offers a revisionary account of Plato's theses that each person should do one job, and that this job is one she is suited by nature to perform. Starting from reflections on Max Weber's and Sheldon Wolin's respective accounts of politics and political theory as vocation, he examines the institutional design of the *Kallipolis* and the implications of Plato's various remarks about how, when, and who is educated in Plato's ideal city. The aim of the *Kallipolis* and its structures is to promote the betterment of all the citizens, as opposed to the promotion of a select few in order to establish a secure, stable polis. Silverman contends that if we consider how we the readers are to regard the differences between those who complete the entire prescribed fifty years of education and those who "drop out" to pursue a calling in geometry, astronomy, the law, or public administration, the notion that each person, especially each "golden-souled" person, is born to do one task seems less and less plausible. Rather than relying on a principle of antecedent nature, Silverman argues that provided that some citizens become philosophers, it makes little difference what even most of the golden and silver do.

C. D. C. Reeve, in "Soul, Soul-Parts, and Persons in Plato," examines the related thesis that the rational part of the soul is the natural ruler over the nonrational parts. In Book IV of the *Republic,* Socrates argues that the soul has an appetitive element, a spirited element, and a rational element. Reeve discusses each of these elements arguing that the rational element alone is *a* soul or *a* person, capable of having fully autonomous propositional attitudes, while the other elements are sub-personal accretions to it, resulting from its embodiment. By distinguishing between sublunary and superlunary embodiment, Reeve shows that this view is present not just in the *Republic* but in the *Phaedo*, *Phaedrus*, and *Timaeus* as well.

Gerasimos Santas, in "Just City and Just Soul in Plato's *Republic*," examines the analogy between the soul and the city and considers whether Plato's argument supports an anti-democratic stance. He argues that the analogy between just city and just soul is a basic building block of Plato's theory of justice. He adopts David Keyt's recent illuminating reading of the analogy and shows how it can be used with a faculty interpretation of the second building block of the theory, Plato's analysis of the human soul. He also argues that Plato's functional theory of good and virtue is a third building block of the theory. Santas brings together these three building blocks of Plato's theory to try to resolve two important interpretive controversies. The first controversy concerns whether the parts of the soul are faculties or agents. While the agent interpretation has been recently well developed, Santas suggests that it is paradoxical and argues both that there is strong evidence for the faculty interpretation and that Plato's theory of justice is better with it. The second controversy concerns whether, in Plato's ideal city, it is true that only the philosophers can be just. A positive answer has had strong supporters in recent literature, but Santas concludes that this is an unnecessarily extreme interpretation of Plato's theory of justice, and that it undermines Plato's main argument that we are better off being just rather than unjust.

Mark L. McPherran, in "Virtue, Luck, and Choice at the End of the *Republic*," considers the famous choice of lives in the Myth of Er. McPherran investigates the tensions between the thought that leading a just life has postmortem rewards and the apparent role of various elements in the Myth, such as luck, that would seem to distance individuals from moral responsibility for their character and their lives after death. McPherran develops the idea that the nature of the choice of lives in the Myth of Er is impacted by luck, providence, and constraints imposed by individuals' previous life experiences and deliberative capacities in a way that seems to undermine their consequentialist reasons for being just. Nonetheless, McPherran contends, Plato's intention seems to be to leave readers with the impression that they are able to make morally significant choices in life and that those who act justly do enjoy better results than those who act unjustly. McPherran concludes that Plato leaves the problems raised by the Myth of Er unresolved but that the Myth serves well to clarify the nature of the problems it exposes.

The argument of the *Republic* is founded upon Plato's theory of Forms and his thesis that reason and knowledge must have the Forms as objects. Plato's *Sophist* contains an even more radical thesis, namely, that *logos* (intelligible speech or language) is possible only because the Forms are "interwoven" with each other. Christopher Shields, in "The Grounds of *Logos*: The Interweaving of Forms," offers a new interpretation of Plato's reasoning and argues that it anticipates an influential modern theory of language. Shields notes that Plato's contention that *logos* is possible only because the Forms are interwoven with each other has excited and perplexed Plato's readers. He suggests that many readers suppose that Plato has, in one way or another, overstated the role of Forms in the generation of *logos*—especially if *logos* is to be understood in narrow semantic terms as "statement" and if we are to take Plato's plurals seriously, so that when he says "Forms" he means *Forms* and not merely *a single Form*. Shields contends that, after all, one can utter a statement without referring to more than one Form; indeed, one can utter an identity statement such as "Paracelsus is Theophrastus Bombastus von Hohenheim" without overtly mentioning even one Form. According to Shields, this has led some to undertranslate or underinterpret Plato's dictum. In fact, Shields concludes, Plato's point is stated carefully and uncompromisingly and Plato means, roughly, that *logos* is impossible without the existence of a freestanding intensional sense structure. His remark is thus the basis of an indirect existence argument for Forms.

The final five articles in the collection consider Aristotle's philosophy. A nice transition is provided by S. Marc Cohen, in his contribution to the volume, "Accidental Beings in Aristotle's Ontology." Cohen argues that along with substances and their properties, Aristotle includes in his ontology such curious entities as *the pale man* and *seated Socrates*, entities he holds to be intermediate between and hence distinct from both the properties (pallor, being seated) and substances (man, Socrates) of which they are composed. Cohen notes that these "accidental beings" (or "kooky objects," as they have been called) have been the cause of perplexity or even dismay in many of Aristotle's readers. Following the lead of Gareth Matthews, among others, Cohen investigates the role of accidental beings in Aristotle's thought in hopes of making them seem a little less strange. He contends that these entities make their first appearance in Aristotle's corpus not in the *Physics* and *Metaphysics* (where their presence has long been noted) but as the non-substantial particulars of the (presumably earlier) *Categories*. He argues that this identification of accidental beings with non-substantial particulars helps to resolve a long-standing dispute about the nature of the particulars in the non-substance categories. Finally, Cohen proposes that the identity conditions of accidental beings suggest that they are best thought of as states or events—the particular states of (or particular events involving) particular substances. An accidental being thus owes its particularity to the particular substance with which it coincides, not to the (universal) property that is one of its constituents.

Frank A. Lewis, in "Is There Room for Plato in an Aristotelian Theory of Essence?" examines the relationship between Plato's theory of Forms and Aristotle's essentialism in the *Metaphysics*. Lewis notes that Aristotle's discussion of essence in *Metaphysics* Z.6 continues his interest in earlier chapters in distinguishing different levels of things that *have* an essence. The basic argument that Aristotle offers at the beginning of the chapter is based on "received" views and makes no distinction in levels. The pale man arguments immediately following, Lewis explains, deal with entities that are not primary and so have an essence in only a reduced sense; Aristotle argues (as he admits) unsuccessfully that such entities are not identical with their essence. Lewis notes that in the elaboration of the basic argument that immediately follows, Aristotle fixes on a class of items, Platonic Forms, that do count as primary, that enjoy an essence in the primary sense, and that are duly identical with their essences. He suggests that on this last point, arguably, Aristotle is motivated by the thought that for any set of entities that are fundamental in a given ontology, to the question "what is the essence of this item?" the only possible answer must be: itself. Lewis argues that the resort to Platonism in the elaboration of the basic argument does not undercut Aristotle's arguments. Lewis explains that in a fresh round of arguments, Aristotle connects a principle from the theory of "Izzing and Having" to show that if the identity of a Platonic Form with its essence fails, then impossibly, no Forms will be known and no essences will exist. The second application of uniformity on which this latter argument depends has been criticized, but Lewis concludes that Aristotle and Plato are allies against the charge of fallacy.

Cass Weller, in "*Metaphysics* Z.11 and Functionalism," discusses the closely related notion of function, in terms of which Aristotle defines the essences of substances or primary existents. Weller suggests that Aristotle's dialectical flirtation with compositional plasticity regarding humans in *Metaphysics* Z.11

would appear to lend support to the claim that he subscribes to the idea that humans are functional kinds that supervene on their material constituents and more specifically that he subscribes to the idea that psychological states are functional states that supervene on physiological states. Weller argues that this only appears to be the case.

Fred D. Miller, Jr., in "Aristotle on Belief and Knowledge," examines Aristotle's epistemology, arguing that reason is exercised in belief as well as knowledge throughout Aristotle's philosophical system. Miller notes that while Aristotle maintains that "he who has beliefs is, in comparison with the one who knows, not in a healthy state," in Aristotle's works on natural science as well as on ethics and politics he evidently places great importance on certain beliefs, especially those called "reputable." This raises the issue, for Miller, of how belief is related to knowledge in Aristotle's epistemology and generates four questions: If belief differs from knowledge in that it can be false, how is false belief possible? If belief can be false, how is knowledge possible? How is it possible to believe and know the same objects? And how can belief be of use to philosophy? In discussing Aristotle's answer to the latter question, Miller examines Aristotle's account of dialectic and its relation to science in the strict sense. He also offers an interpretation of the Aristotelian doxastic method relying on "reputable beliefs" and contrasting it with the Cartesian method. The two methods, Miller maintains, seem to be concerned primarily about two different sorts of doxastic failure: Descartes is most worried about accepting false opinions, whereas Aristotle is more worried about failing to grasp true opinions. These correspond to two different sorts of doxastic vice: the propensity to believe the false and the failure to believe the truth. This prompts the question as to which of his methods better approximates doxastic virtue. Miller contends that the Aristotelian approach is in keeping with Aristotle's general teleological approximism: One should strive for the best, but, if that is unattainable, one will be better off insofar as one reaches a state nearer to the best. Reputable belief is often the closest we can come to strict knowledge. Moreover, Miller adds, it is reasonable in view of Aristotle's contextualist epistemology that a science should be content with a level of certainty appropriate for its subject matter.

Finally, Charles M. Young, in "Aristotelian Grace," concludes with a gracious and edifying essay on an unjustly neglected Aristotelian virtue. Young describes Aristotelian grace (*Nicomachean Ethics* V.5 1133a3-5) as the natural force that takes the good that we do to and for one another and returns, magnifies, and ramifies it. He argues that as a response to goodness, Aristotelian grace should be distinguished both from the grace of God and from grace under pressure (what Hemingway called guts), each of which responds, in its own way, to evil. Young illustrates and explains why grace is both natural and a force, and illustrates and explains a few of its returns, magnifications, and ramifications.

In keeping with Young's account of grace, this collection of essays is a fitting tribute to David Keyt and his valuable contribution to the study of ancient Greek philosophy.

Bibliography

Keyt, David. 1963. The fallacies in *Phaedo* 102A-107B. *Phronesis* 8: 167–172.
Keyt, David. 1969. Plato's paradox that the immutable is unknowable. *The Philosophical Quarterly* 19: 1–14.
Keyt, David. 1971. The mad craftsman of the *Timaeus*. *Philosophical Review* 80: 230–235.
Keyt, David. 1973. Plato on falsity: *Sophist* 263B. In *Exegesis and argument: Studies in Greek philosophy presented to Gregory Vlastos*, ed. Edward N. Lee, Alexander P.D. Mourelatos, and Richard Rorty, 285–305. Assen: Van Gorcum.
Keyt, David. 1978. Intellectualism in Aristotle. In the special Aristotle issue of *Paideia*, 138–157.
Keyt, David. 1983. Intellectualism in Aristotle. In *Essays in ancient Greek philosophy*, vol. II, ed. John P. Anton and Anthony Preus, 364–387. Albany: SUNY Press. (Revision of 1978.)
Keyt, David. 1985. Distributive justice in Aristotle's *Ethics* and *Politics*. *Topoi* 4: 23–45.
Keyt, David. 1987. Three fundamental theorems in Aristotle's *Politics*. *Phronesis* 32: 54–79.
Keyt, David. 1989. The meaning of *Bios* in Aristotle's *Ethics* and *Politics*. *Ancient Philosophy* 9: 15–21.
Keyt, David. 1991a. *A companion to Aristotle's Politics*, co-ed. Fred D. Miller, Jr. Oxford: Blackwell Publishing.
Keyt, David. 1991b. Aristotle's theory of distributive justice. In *A companion to Aristotle's Politics*, ed. David Keyt and Fred D. Miller, Jr., 238–278. (Substantial revision of 1985.)
Keyt, David. 1991c. Three basic theorems in Aristotle's *Politics*. In *A companion to Aristotle's Politics*, ed. David Keyt and Fred D. Miller, Jr., 118–141. Oxford: Blackwell. (Revision of 1987.)
Keyt, David. 1993. Aristotle and anarchism. *Reason Papers* 18: 137–157.
Keyt, David. 1995. The four causes in Aristotle's *Politics*. In *Aristotelian political philosophy*, vol. 1, ed. K.I. Boudouris, 101–107. Athens: International Center for Greek Philosophy and Culture.
Keyt, David. 1996. Aristotle and the ancient roots of anarchism. *Topoi* 15: 129–142. (Abridged version of 1993.)
Keyt, David. 1999. *Aristotle politics books V and VI*. Translation with introduction and commentary. Oxford: Clarendon Press.
Keyt, David. 2007. *Freedom, reason, and the polis: Essays in ancient Greek political philosophy*, co-ed. Fred D. Miller, Jr. Cambridge: Cambridge University Press, 2007. Published simultaneously as *Social Philosophy & Policy: Ancient Greek Political Philosophy*, 24.

A Life in the Academy

David Keyt

1 Arsenal Technical High School

The first serious book that came into my hands, a book I still possess, was Ralph Waldo Emerson's *Essays* in a slender four-by-six-inch volume on onionskin paper with soft leather covers. I remember entering into a new world filled with many unfamiliar words, though all of its details are now forgotten. This new world was my own discovery and had no connection with the courses in physics, chemistry, and mathematics I was taking at Arsenal Technical High School in Indianapolis, a large and wonderful school spread over many buildings on a spacious college-size campus. Emerson's essays led quickly to those of Henry David Thoreau and then somehow to Schopenhauer's, which in turn led inevitably to *The World as Will and Idea* (in the Modern Library edition). Schopenhauer darkened my youth. His idea that everything in the universe, even inanimate matter, is the result of, and is driven by, the blind striving of the will, with its corollary of the senselessness of existence, seemed to describe, externally, the titanic clash of wills of the World War that had just ended and, internally, the sense, not uncommon among adolescent males, of being, as Sophocles puts it, enslaved to "a raging and savage master" (Plato, *Rep.* I 329c3-4). But Schopenhauer also set me on the path I was to follow in life: I now knew that I wanted to read more philosophy, and his remark somewhere in one of his essays that every educated man knows Greek led me to sign up for that language my first week in college.

For my high school graduation, my parents gave me a copy of Spinoza's *Ethics*, which I read avidly that summer. I remember that I was particularly eager to discover whether Spinoza allowed for personal immortality. On the flyleaf of their gift, they had hopefully (but regrettably not presciently) written "We predict David will also become a great philosopher in his day."

D. Keyt (✉)
Department of Philosophy, University of Washington,
Savery Hall, Seattle, WA 98155, USA
e-mail: keyt@uw.edu

2 Kenyon College

On an afternoon in late summer of 1947, I boarded a train for Columbus, Ohio, carrying a large suitcase and, to read on the train, a copy of Freud's *Introductory Lectures on Psychoanalysis* for aid in my project of psychoanalyzing myself. The following morning I continued on to Gambier and to Kenyon College—the town and the college are virtually identical—on a train consisting of a locomotive pulling a single passenger car. Kenyon at that time was a men's college with a small faculty and about six hundred students, most of whom were recently discharged veterans attending college on the GI bill. Though I may have been the youngest student at Kenyon that year, I had no trouble mixing with the older men. I had held a man's job at adult wages every summer since turning fifteen, an opportunity afforded by the scarcity of men outside the armed forces as the Second War reached its climax. I was attending Kenyon on a tuition scholarship supplemented by a small grant from a foundation in Indianapolis.

When I first heard about Kenyon and that I might have an opportunity to go there, my only question was whether it had courses in philosophy. Not only did it have such courses, but they were taught by two first-rate philosophers, Philip Blair Rice and Virgil Aldrich, each of whom was to be a future president of the western (later renamed "central") division of the American Philosophical Association, Rice in 1952–1953 and Aldrich in 1957–1958. Rice was a dedicated philosopher with a comprehensive well-thought-out philosophy deriving from Kant and George Santayana. While I was at Kenyon, he was working on the material that would go into his book *On the Knowledge of Good and Evil* (Rice 1955), a book that gives a good picture of the state of metaethics at midcentury, when normative ethics was on the backburner. Aldrich, the author of *Philosophy of Art* (Aldrich 1963) and *The Body of a Person* (Aldrich 1988), among other works, left Kenyon for the University of North Carolina at Chapel Hill in 1965 and then upon retirement from there in 1972 became an adjunct professor at the University of Utah.

Immediately upon arriving at Kenyon, I had a fateful meeting with my advisor, a French mathematician. I had a mathematician as an advisor because it was assumed that I would be majoring in mathematics. It was primarily my score on the mathematics portion of the college entrance examination that had won me my scholarship. I had taken every mathematics course offered at Tech including analytic geometry and had received one of the two medals in mathematics awarded at graduation. Though I was eager to jump immediately into calculus, my advisor was skeptical of my own estimate of my ability and preparation and insisted that I take the introductory course, which was mostly devoted to analytic geometry with only a smidgen of calculus. That gave me one easy course my first year but also allowed a love of mathematics to begin its transmutation into a love of logic. That was the first result of this fateful meeting. The second concerned the foreign language needed to satisfy Kenyon's graduation requirements. With Schopenhauer's remark in mind, I raised the possibility of taking Greek. Perhaps because my advisor was multilingual himself, he remarked rather casually that one foreign language was about as difficult to learn as another. So I signed up for Greek and, though I did not know it at the time, began laying the foundation of an academic career in Greek philosophy. The third of my four academic courses that semester was, of course, philosophy. These three courses set the trajectory of my four years at Kenyon and, indeed, of my whole career in teaching and scholarship.

The primary text of the introductory philosophy course, which was taught by Aldrich, was Plato's *Republic*. I remember reading the simile of the cave for the first time—I can't remember whether we had to draw a picture of the cave or not—and being struck by Plato's tripartition of the soul, seeing it as a forerunner of Freud's similar tripartition. I look back on this class every time I teach my own course on the *Republic* and read the dialogue one more time. The *Republic* seems as fresh, as enchanting, and as enigmatic to me today as it did on first reading. I never tire of introducing it to a fresh crop of students. I find it an ideal philosophical text for a variety of reasons. First of all, there is Plato's literary power: I do have favorite passages that I like to read aloud in class just for their fineness. Then there is the wide range of the work. Every part of philosophy is represented: theory of meaning, epistemology, metaphysics, philosophy of mind, ethics, political philosophy, philosophy of education, philosophy of religion, and aesthetics. Next, there is the point of view itself. The Platonism of the *Republic*, in one area after another, is the default position in philosophy, the position one is initially and naturally drawn to upon being introduced to a philosophical issue, a position one must either accept or find a clever way of evading. Finally, there is the remarkable fact that the *Republic* displays the full toolkit of philosophical techniques and strategies that have been used over the last 2,400 years including, but not limited to, argument, counterexample, thought experiment, analogy, and conceptual analysis.

The postwar years were the glory years for Kenyon. Among my classmates were the actor Paul Newman, who appeared in all of the stage productions, the comedian Jonathan Winters, the poet James Wright, the writer Edgar ("E. L.") Doctorow, and the future prime minister of Sweden Olaf Palme, tragically assassinated in 1986. Wright was a personal friend; the others more distant. All of the students and most of the unmarried faculty dined together in a large Gothic dining hall three times a day in the manner of an Oxford college, which meant that, though not everyone was a personal acquaintance, no one was a total stranger either. The most renowned person on the faculty was the poet and critic John Crowe Ransom, who had been brought to Kenyon to launch *The Kenyon Review*. (Rice was a coeditor.) His well-attended course on modern poetry, which I audited my senior year, was my most memorable course at Kenyon.

Recently my roommate at Kenyon, Roger Whiteman, sent me a copy of a long-forgotten essay torn from an issue of the student literary magazine HIKA along with a note that said simply and solely "You published in good company" referring to two of the other contributors, Wright and Doctorow. The essay, entitled "The Problem of Immortality from an Atheistic Point of View," (Keyt 1951) had been inspired by Diotima's speech in Plato's *Symposium*. Reading it for the first time in sixty years was an unsettling experience, like reading a long-forgotten diary, but not as embarrassing as I feared. Though personally the problem is more pressing now than it was sixty years ago, the passage of time had given me no new ideas about it. (The last sentence was written before I had read Mark Johnston's *Surviving Death* [Johnston 2010].)

Early Sunday morning February 27, 1949, Old Kenyon dormitory (where I had lived originally) burned to the ground when a small fire that had been started in one of the fireplaces after a Saturday night party spread through cracks in the chimney to the whole building. Nine students perished including a close friend. Except for this tragedy, my four years at Kenyon were a happy time during which my intellectual horizons were vastly extended. However, when years later I was invited to return as a faculty member, I turned the opportunity down, not wishing to move from a cultured metropolis on the Pacific Coast with a world-class opera and an international airport to a small isolated town in rural Ohio.

The outside examiner for my senior honors thesis was the young philosopher and future postmodern novelist William Gass, whose early life I was oddly destined to track. Four years earlier Gass had graduated from Kenyon magna cum laude with high honors in philosophy and had continued on in philosophy at Cornell as a Susan Linn Sage fellow. Now, by the grace of his evaluation, I was graduating from Kenyon with the same honors, and, having inherited the Susan Linn Sage fellowship from him, was on my way to Cornell. In correspondence with him recently I discovered that, a decade or so after leaving Cornell, we had coincidentally both reviewed Paul Engelmann's memoir of the young Wittgenstein (Keyt 1969b; Gass 1970). Thus, for an instant I was even tracking Gass's writing career. Alas, at that moment the thread of destiny snapped.

I wrote my honors thesis on the problem of free will from a Freudian perspective, thus leaving Kenyon on the same note with which I arrived.

After I graduated from Kenyon, I didn't see Virgil Aldrich again until I presented a paper at Utah in 1990. I stayed with him for two nights, and we had the opportunity to reminisce about Kenyon and about Rice, who was killed in an auto accident soon after the publication of his book. To my astonishment Aldrich remembered a crack I had made forty years before at Kenyon, which had evidently struck home, about the pretentiousness of a large and stately (used) car he had just bought.

3 Cornell University

I entered the Sage School of Philosophy in 1951, two years after Wittgenstein made his legendary trip to Ithaca to visit Norman Malcolm. Those were heady days in philosophy at Cornell, which was then, as it remains to this day, a bastion of analytic philosophy. The "new" philosophy of Wittgenstein was spread, not only by the dominating personalities of Malcolm and Max Black, but by the surreptitiously circulating typescripts of *The Blue Book* and of remarks on the philosophy of mathematics. We studied the *Tractatus Logico-Philosophicus* in a seminar given by Black when he must have been collecting material for his commentary on that work (Black 1964). Under Black's guidance the *Tractatus* seemed to be a beacon of light rather than a pool of darkness. Hearkening to the light, I wrote some of my first articles about it (Keyt 1963b, 1964, 1965). I also remember being among a select few with whom Malcolm discussed the recently published *Philosophical Investigations*. His influential early review of that work appeared in the *Philosophical Review* in 1954 (Malcolm 1954).

Gregory Vlastos was a third major figure at Cornell, and my total exposure to Greek philosophy at Cornell consisted of two seminars of his: one on Plato and one on Aristotle. The Plato seminar highlighted the Third Man Argument of the *Parmenides*, on which Vlastos was then writing his seminal paper and which also appeared in the *Philosophical Review* in 1954 (Vlastos 1954). (My first wife, Mary, typed the final drafts.) Vlastos was the unenviable speaker at the Cornell Philosophy Club on the notable occasion, still talked about in my day, when during the discussion following his lecture, an old oddly dressed stranger, who had listened quietly and unobtrusively, began a fierce inner struggle to say something and, by token of grimaces and tortured gestures well known to the club members because long mimicked by Malcolm and his students, revealed his identity—"It's Wittgenstein!" Gass vividly describes the occasion (Gass 1970).

John Rawls joined the Cornell faculty in 1953. Though I wasn't particularly interested in ethics at that time, I sat in on several sessions of his seminar on justice. One thing I remember about the seminar is that it began with Aristotle's complex treatment of justice in the fifth book of the *Nicomachean Ethics*. After I left Cornell I had no further contact with Rawls until the early 1970s when, along with virtually everyone else in philosophy, I was writing a paper on *A Theory of Justice* (Rawls 1971). Being interested in the structure of ethical theory, I was intrigued by Rawls' pursuit of a moral geometry where principles of justice are deduced with all the rigor of deductive logic from a description of a contractual situation. But as I studied his book further, I became concerned, among other things, about the legitimacy of his polemical use of the social contract, his notion that the faults in the premise set associated with a given conception of justice are inherited by the principles expressing the conception—for example, that the difficulties faced by the interpretation of the initial contractual situation that he postulates for the principle of average utility transfer to the principle itself. This seems uncomfortably close to the fallacy of inferring that the conclusion of a valid argument is false because one or more of its premises are false. I sent him a draft of my paper and promptly received a reply in which he developed his ideas further. I revised my paper on the basis of his response, received his comments on my second draft, and was given permission to quote from his letters in the published version of the paper (Keyt 1974). Shortly thereafter I was in the audience when he delivered the presidential address at the eastern division of the American Philosophical Association in 1974 in Washington D.C. When I ran into him by chance after the address, he invited me back to his suite for a drink. Though one might have expected a celebratory crowd after such a notable event, the only other person there in addition to Rawls and myself was Tom Nagel. I never saw Jack again. My next and last correspondence with him was in the mid-1980s when I sent him an offprint of an article of mine on Aristotle's theory of distributive justice, which contained a footnote tracing his distinction between the *concept* of justice and various *conceptions* of justice back to *Nicomachean Ethics* V. He wrote me a note expressing his pleasure with the lineage of his distinction. It may be difficult for those who were not around at the time to appreciate the impact of Rawls and of *A Theory of Justice*. The range, depth, and originality of the work restored normative ethics to its proper place in philosophy, and the civility of the man helped transform philosophical discourse from the blood sport it had become into something more collegial.

So much for the faculty. Among the graduate students the philosophically most lively was Edmund Gettier, who was destined to realize the Walter Mitty fantasy of every assistant professor of philosophy facing a tenure review with an embarrassingly short list of publications—namely, to come up with an idea like Russell's paradox that (1) overturns a received doctrine in philosophy and (2) can be written on a postcard (Gettier 1963). The classmate with whom I began a lifelong association, Jerry Santas, was two years behind me. Though we had different interests at Cornell, we wound up working on the same topics in the same ancient philosophers using the same techniques of analysis and reaching much the same conclusions.

I never considered writing a dissertation in Greek philosophy. Since I continued with Greek at the graduate level at Cornell with Friedrich Solmsen among others, it would have been an obvious choice. But I wanted to work with either Black or Malcolm in the theory of meaning. (I started with Black but finished with Malcolm, Black being on leave my final year.) I chose to write on C. I. Lewis because his large work, *An Analysis of Knowledge and Valuation* (Lewis 1946), had been out for only a few years, because it was written with great clarity, and because it defended a kind of realism and I was then an antirealist. Its three parts are on meaning and analytic truth, empirical knowledge, and valuation, respectively. I had been introduced to the third part by Rice at Kenyon. (Value theory, almost forgotten now, was much discussed in the first half of the twentieth century.) For my dissertation I now turned to the first part (Keyt 1955). It wasn't until I was given the opportunity a decade or so later to write a discussion article on the collection of papers in the Schilpp volume on Lewis (Schilpp 1968) that I turned my attention to the second part and to his work late in life on ethics that was intended to complete and to crown his elaborate philosophical system. My conclusion after all this study and analysis is that little of this grand system survives scrutiny (Keyt 1973b).

4 The U.S. Army

The Korean War having begun in June of 1950 while I was still at Kenyon, my four years at Cornell were all by the grace of a student deferment. The war with its hundreds of thousands of casualties was over when I received my Ph.D. in 1955. The draft, however, had not yet ended; and I was immediately called up. After the trauma of induction, I found the rest of my two-year tour of duty not a heavy burden. I quickly discovered two facts about the army: first, in peace time it is primarily an educational institution, and second, it is organized bureaucratically. It was a familiar environment, not so different from a large university. Before basic training was over, I was familiar enough with the bureaucracy to secure a posting to a small research unit at Fort Benning in Georgia charged with field-testing new infantry equipment prior to adoption. My job was to copyedit the reports that field-grade infantry officers were writing. It was a soft job in all but one respect: due to the dearth of enlisted men in my unit, I probably "pulled K.P." (i.e., worked in the mess hall) more often than any other private in the army. Since I never had night duty and since, being married, I was permitted to live off base, I was able during my second year to teach, in civilian clothes, an evening class in philosophy at the extension of the University of Georgia in Columbus. The armed forces were completely integrated by this time, and on base blacks and whites associated comfortably with each other. Off base strict racial segregation with its thinly veiled threat of violence still prevailed. The local newspaper marked the anniversary of every battle of the Civil War that took place in Georgia.

5 The University of Washington

As my tour of duty wound down, I went on the job market and secured an instructorship at the University of Washington in Seattle where they were searching for someone in ancient philosophy. My knowledge of ancient Greek had given me an edge, since it was rare in those days for those teaching ancient philosophy in this country to know Greek. I had been hired on the basis of a letter from Cornell without presenting a paper, visiting the campus, or even being interviewed. (There were no funds to bring candidates for nontenured positions to campus, and there would be none for many years.) The university, which was slowly transforming itself from a teaching institution into a teaching and research institution, was less than half its current size. The philosophy department consisted of three full professors—Arthur Smullyan, Abraham Melden, and Melvin Rader—and an equal number of men on their first contract. Among the latter was a man who had been in the Resistance in occupied Norway, Paul Dietrichson. (A short time later I was to have a colleague, Laurent Stern, who had survived the Holocaust.) Both Smullyan and Melden left the department for greener pastures in the 1960s, Smullyan moving to Rutgers, where he eventually became chairman, and Melden to a nascent, though not yet existing, Irvine, where he founded the philosophy department. (He invited me to accompany him, but where he saw a great university, I saw only a desert.) Rader, who entered the University of Washington as a freshman and never left it for very long, was a prolific writer, authoring introductory philosophy texts, books on social philosophy and aesthetics, and even a book on Wordsworth. The defining moment of his life came during the McCarthy era in the late 1940s when he was falsely accused before the infamous Washington State Un-American Activities Committee of being a member of the Communist Party (Rader 1969). If the accusation could have been made to stick, Rader would have been fired with little prospect of finding an academic post elsewhere. Indeed, one member of the department at that time, Herbert

Phillips, a self-admitted Communist, was fired and worked the rest of his life as a skilled laborer.

The university was, and remains, on the quarter system. When I arrived, the course load was six courses over three quarters. Most courses met five days a week. Course preparation, grading, and a considerable expenditure of time on the graduate program left little, if any, time for research during the nine months of the academic year. Research had to be done in the summer. But there was always the problem of subsisting for twelve months on nine-months' pay. One could often secure a small summer grant. When that was unavailable, I would, in the early years, teach evening courses for extra money during the academic year to free up the summers for research. Even so, for many years there was the feeling (and the actuality) of returning every summer to the poverty of student days, particularly with a growing family to support. Large projects are difficult to sustain and to complete when one can work on them only three months a year. That was a prime reason that I and many others in the same situation wrote articles instead of monographs. In order to better balance teaching and research, the philosophy department lightened the teaching load of its faculty first to five courses over three quarters and then years later, when no one was watching, to four. It was expected, of course, that time freed up for research would be spent on research, and along with the lighter teaching load came the demand that the bibliography of a candidate for promotion to associate or full professor list a book or two. I was safely a full professor long before that came about.

I don't recall what courses I taught my first year aside from an introduction to logic and a survey course on ancient philosophy, but from early on my teaching schedule consisted of a mix of logic courses at various levels, contemporary philosophy, and Greek philosophy. (Many years later I had the opportunity and the pleasure of teaching several courses in the Classics department on Aristotle directly from the original Greek.) Like most beginners I worked long hours seven days a week and was often only one class ahead of my students. My education, especially in Greek philosophy, only now really began. The works from which I learned the most were Francis Cornford's translations and commentaries on Plato's later dialogues (Cornford 1935, 1937, 1939), W. D. Ross's commentaries on Aristotle (Ross 1924, 1936, 1949), Harold Cherniss's *Aristotle's Criticism of Plato and the Academy* (Cherniss 1944), and H. Bonitz's *Index Aristotelicus*, which is much more than an index (Bonitz 1955).

My first publication (Keyt 1961) came from the study of these books rather than from anything I learned in graduate school. It would surely have been sufficient for a novice to hazard a first article on either Plato or Aristotle, but for some reason now lost to me, I decided to write on Aristotle's criticism of Plato, which involved not only interpreting each philosopher but also confidently judging the accuracy of the one's reading of the other. A second paper on Greek philosophy followed two years later (Keyt 1963a). Restricting myself this time to the logical analysis of a single climactic argument in the *Phaedo*, I argued that Plato had fallen into a brace of logical fallacies. To accuse a classical philosopher of committing a logical fallacy is like throwing raw meat to wolves. Responses were quick in coming and continued sporadically for over thirty years. One of the latest is by one of my own colleagues at the University of Washington, Cass Weller (1995).

6   The 1960s

Even though the University of Washington has been my permanent home, I've never felt isolated in the northwest corner of the country. I've taken advantage of the University's liberal leave policy to go on sabbaticals whenever I was eligible and to accept almost every visiting appointment that came my way. In the 1960s I was away for three of the ten years at UCLA, Wisconsin, and Cornell. I arrived at UCLA in 1962 two months before the Cuban Missile Crisis. (I knew the crisis was serious when I discovered that the residents of our West Los Angeles neighborhood had cleared the shelves of the local supermarket.) Richard Montague, whose murder in 1971 is still unsolved, was the star of the philosophy department, though Rudolph Carnap was still around as an emeritus professor. I saw Montague in action only once—when the wondrously strange Austrian logician Georg Kreisel came down from Stanford to read a paper to the departmental colloquium. Montague broke in while Kreisel, whose appearance was as striking as his personality, was delivering his paper and accused him of confusing mathematical induction and inductive definition. Kreisel calmly waved his hand in a circular motion and said, "All questions at the end." Montague objected, insisting that Kreisel follow the local custom, which permitted such interjections. Kreisel repeated what he had just said, waved his hand calmly again, and continued.

My one encounter with Carnap was at a cocktail party. I chanced to be standing alone with him and used the occasion to ask about his personal impression of Wittgenstein. He had begun to say something about Wittgenstein being more an artist than a scientist when Hans Meyerhoff, the translator of Paul Friedländer's three-volume work on Plato (Friedländer 1958–), walked up and with a crack about Wittgenstein put an end to our conversation. The Schilpp volume on Carnap (Schilpp 1963) appeared not long after. From his intellectual autobiography in that volume, I discovered how the conversation might have continued if it had not been interrupted: "[Wittgenstein's] point of view and his attitude toward people and problems, even theoretical problems, were much more similar to those of a creative artist than to those of a scientist; one might almost say, similar to those of a religious prophet or a seer.... [T]he impression he made on us [i.e., the members of the Vienna Circle] was as if insight came to him as through a divine inspiration, so that we could not help feeling that any sober rational comment or analysis of it would be a profanation" (Schilpp 1963, pp. 25–26). (Meyerhoff was tragically killed in 1965 in an auto accident involving one of his own students.)

In 1962 the Pacific Division of the American Philosophical Association met shortly after Christmas on the Berkeley campus of the University of California. The chancellor, Edward Strong, who had once been chairman of the Berkeley philosophy department, invited the entire division to the chancellor's residence for hosted cocktails, an event that, due to the growth of the division, would be unimaginable today.

Some time after I returned to Seattle, the department got a word that Gilbert Ryle would be giving a lecture at the University of British Columbia. Since none of us had ever met him, an eager contingent drove north to hear him. After his lecture, of which I remember nothing, we were invited to join the local philosophers at the Faculty Club for a chat with the great man. We conversed for a while in a desultory fashion. Ryle looked bored and tired. I seized the opportunity to ask if, as rumor had it, he was writing a book on Plato. It was as if a flare had been ignited. His tiredness dropped away, and he proceeded to tell us his idea that Plato's *Dialogues* were written for oral presentation at literary contests in such venues as the Athenian and Olympic Games. The various interlocutors in a dialogue would be assigned to different speakers, as in a play, and—this was an important point—Plato always reserved the role of Socrates for himself. I asked him about the *Sophist* and the *Politicus* where Socrates does not appear. He responded that Plato lost his teeth and was ashamed to perform in public. Continuing to play the straight man in what I was beginning to suspect was a set piece, I plowed on. "Ah," I said, "how do you account for the appearance of Socrates in the *Philebus*, which was supposedly written after the *Sophist* and *Politicus*?" He drew himself up in his chair and after a long pause replied, "He got false teeth." When *Plato's Progress* (Ryle 1966) was published, I was eager to see if the story about false teeth was in it. It isn't. Socrates' disappearance is attributed to illness on Plato's part rather than a loss of teeth (p. 28), and the problem of his reappearance in the *Philebus* is obviated by dating the composition of the dialogue before the composition of the *Sophist* and *Politicus*, contrary to the consensus of the stylometricians (pp. 251–56).

The next time I was away was in 1966–1967 when I was a junior fellow at the recently established Institute for Research in the Humanities at the University of Wisconsin in Madison. Friedrich Solmsen, with whom I had read Thucydides at Cornell, had been one of the Institute's first appointments. Solmsen was part of the grand tradition in German philology. He had written his dissertation under Werner Jaegar on the relative chronology of the two parts of Aristotle's *Analytics* (Solmsen 1929) and after receiving his degree had been invited to join the select reading group hosted by the great German philologist Ulrich von Wilamowitz-Moellendorff. In a memoir about Wilamowitz, he writes that "the gap between Wilamowitz and us 'Anfänger' [neophytes] was discouraging. Fortunately he was invariably patient and polite, so that the consciousness of what we gained consoled us for the disappointment with our performance" (Solmsen 1979, p. 92). The gap between Wilamowitz and Solmsen in dealing with a Greek text was as nothing compared to the gulf between Solmsen and me. (With respect to philosophy it was a different story.) I was trying at that time to understand Plato's conception of a Form. I was interested in particular if Plato conceived of a Form as an entity with properties or attributes. If he did, it seemed to me that, to avoid paradox, he would need to sort these attributes along Aristotelian lines. This led naturally to a study of Aristotle's description of Platonic Forms. Two papers emerged from this study (Keyt 1969a, 1971), though only the first was completed at the Institute. While working on it, I discovered a first principle of scholarship: in studying a passage from a classical philosopher, begin by listing every possible way the passage can be interpreted and then search the secondary literature for a defense of each of these ways by a reputable scholar—there will be one (or, if not, soon will be).

I returned to Seattle and served one year as the acting chairman of the philosophy department before assuming a visiting appointment at Cornell. In September of 1968, after settling my wife and my two children, Sarah and Aaron, in Ithaca and before the semester began, I flew from New York to Vienna to take part in the XIVth International Congress of Philosophy, my first trip overseas and a high point of my career. I was reading a paper on Wittgenstein and the Vienna Circle in Vienna, and on the dais there was even an original member of the Circle, an ancient Victor Kraft. In my paper (Keyt 1968), which was to be my last on Wittgenstein, I discussed the idea that the vagueness or indeterminacy of ordinary language is an illusion—that everyday language is in reality absolutely precise and clear—an incredible idea that Wittgenstein embraces in the *Tractatus* but totally rejects in the *Philosophical Investigations*. I argued that Moritz Schlick, the center of the Vienna Circle, had adopted this idea, along with much else, from the *Tractatus* in a series of lectures he had given in London in 1932 entitled "Form and Content" (Schlick 1938). (Schlick was murdered by an insane student in 1936.) When the session was over and I was leaving the room, a man came up to me and asked rather aggressively if I had read Schlick's early writings. After I confessed that I had not, he told me that I was then in no position to criticize Schlick and marched off. I asked the person standing next to me who that person was, and he replied, "Oh, that's A. J. Ayer."

I was not going to be so deep into Europe without seeing Greece, so when the conference ended, I flew to Athens for my first sight of the ruins of classical Greece and my first visit to the Archeological Museum in Athens.

I returned to Cornell for what was to be the most turbulent year in its history, as the student protests that had ricocheted from Berkeley to Columbia reached Ithaca. Though the student unrest at Cornell involved all three of the great issues of the 1960s—authority, the Vietnam War, and race—race became the predominant issue due to the forceful agitation of a group of black students inspired more by Malcolm X than by Martin Luther King, Jr. Events came to a climax on April 19, 1969. To increase the pressure on the administration to meet their demands, a large number of black students took possession of Willard Straight Hall, the student union. Rifles were passed to them by friendly supporters, ostensibly for self-defense. In this incendiary, testosterone-fueled situation, the administration panicked, perhaps justifiably—the blacks weren't the only ones in upstate New York with guns—and acceded to all the demands of the black students in order to end the takeover quickly. ([Downs 1999] gives a full account.) As a visitor I followed these events with the detachment of Lucretius gazing from shore at a foundering ship (*De Rerum Natura* II.1-4), not realizing that the ship to which I would be returning would find itself in rough waters.

The turmoil at Cornell was not only about race, and the agitators were whites as well as blacks. Four of the white agitators moved to the Pacific Northwest and joined the Seattle Liberation Front, a radical group founded by a recently hired faculty member in my department—hired fortunately for just one year. In February 1970, the SLF organized a demonstration at the Federal Courthouse, which turned violent, and in March it led a demonstration on campus. For the events at the Federal Courthouse, eight members of the group, the Seattle Seven (so-called because one had disappeared), were indicted on charges of inciting a riot, damaging federal property, and conspiracy. Their trial in November and December ended in a mistrial. The judge cited the defendants for contempt of court, however, and sent them immediately to prison, though the contempt citation was overturned eleven months later (Crowley 1995). The fact that the founder of the SLF was a member of the philosophy department gave rise to the notion that the department was fostering the demonstrations, and at one point the idea was floated in the state legislature of removing the malignancy by simply deleting funding for the philosophy department from the state budget. The social and political turmoil of this period, along with its callous and juvenile slogan about the need to break eggs in order to make omelets, stimulated a desire in me to teach a course on some of the classical works in political philosophy, and that course led in turn to a shift in my research interests from metaphysics and theory of meaning to moral and political philosophy.

Years later, those who were witness to this turmoil were astonished to read in the news that the former leader of the SLF was providing spiritual counsel in the Clinton White House.

7 The 1970s

I was department chairman for most of the 1970s and had to handle the fallout from the turmoil of the 1960s and early 1970s. One of the problems I had to deal with at that time was an associate professor who decided that everyone who enrolled in his courses, whether or not he or she came to class—there were of course no examinations to draw invidious distinctions among students—would be given a grade of 4.0 (on a 4-point scale). His courses had enormous enrollment and minimal attendance. That even those interested in the ostensive subject of the course—*The Aquarian Gospel of Jesus* in one instance—did not attend may have been due to the fact that he would sometimes walk into class, assume a lotus posture, and play a flute or stare at the ceiling in silence. As department chairman, I was concerned that any state legislator who got wind of this would likely revive the idea of defunding the philosophy department. However, firing a tenured professor, though possible, is not easy. In the event, the fellow died unexpectedly and by so doing spared the department a great deal of unpleasantness—though not the unpleasantness of feeling relief at the death of a colleague and onetime friend. A second problem I faced as chairman was a lawsuit against the university brought by a faculty member of the department whose contract had not been extended. When the suit went to trial, I found myself on the witness stand describing the faculty meeting where the reappointment had been discussed and voted on. One of the questions I was asked was whether anyone at the meeting had been inhibited from speaking. When I described the raucous debate and mentioned my difficulty in bringing it to a conclusion, I thought I got a sympathetic glance from the judge. Ruling from the bench, he dismissed the suit with prejudice.

In 1970 I attended the six-week Summer Institute in Greek Philosophy and Science at Colorado College in Colorado Springs. About fifty scholars—all male, as I recall—took part, including such prominent philosophers and scholars as Gregory Vlastos, John Ackrill, G. E. L. Owen, David Furley, Bernard Williams, and Richard Rorty. This was where a generation of scholars got to know each other and where many friendships were forged. One young scholar whom I met for the first time and who was to become a good friend was Frank Lewis. When those who were young in 1970 reminisce, the first thing they recall is the group of young women who were in residence to study dance and with whom we shared the dining facilities at the college. Thus, both minds and bodies were being exercised that summer— whether there was any melding of mind and body I cannot say. Plans were laid during the Institute for a Festschrift for Vlastos. My contribution, on Plato's analysis of falsity in the *Sophist* (Keyt 1973a), was an attempt to understand a Platonic text by matching interpretative possibilities with diverse philosophical theories of the early twentieth century.

The next summer I made a second trip to Greece for a longer visit. My transatlantic ticket on Scandinavian Airlines was for a polar flight from Chicago to Copenhagen followed by a flight from Copenhagen to Athens. These were what some regard as the good old days when airfares were regulated and airlines could compete only in the services they provided. Thus, when my flight to Chicago landed and I descended the stairs from the door of the plane to the tarmac, a car was waiting at the foot of the stairs to drive me to the departure gate for SAS; when I landed in Copenhagen, another car took me to a first-rate hotel in the city where the airline put me up for the night, providing both dinner and breakfast, before whisking me back to the airport the next morning for the flight to Athens. The service was similar on the return flight.

I can't remember exactly where I visited on the mainland, though I certainly went to Delphi. From Athens I flew to Iraklion on Crete to visit the archeological museum in that city and to see the Minoan ruins at Knossos. While I was searching for a room in Iraklion I fell into conversation with an older English-speaking Cretan, who compared mainland Greeks unfavorably with his fellow islanders. Looking first to the ground and then to the sky as he progressed from one end of his sentence to the other, he intoned in a rich baritone, "They have gotten gold and forgotten God." Returning to Athens, I flew to London to see the city and, being partly of Scottish descent, to travel north to see a bit of Scotland. When I arrived in Edinburgh, I discovered a summer cultural festival in full swing. In spite of the festival, I had no difficulty getting a reasonably priced room and reasonably priced tickets for the musical events I was interested in—more of the good old days. Returning to London, I took a train to Oxford for lunch at Brasenose College with Ackrill to scout the possibility of doing a volume of the Clarendon Aristotle Series on *Politics* V and VI. When I broached the subject, Ackrill remarked that the Clarendon volume on *Politics* III and IV by Richard Robinson (Robinson 1962) had not sold well, and went on to say that he took that fact to signify that there was insufficient interest to justify further volumes on the *Politics*. This, however, was not to be the end of the matter.

In the summer after that—the summer of 1972—Vlastos came to the University of Washington to deliver the Jessie and John Danz lectures, for which I had nominated him several years before. A Danz lecturer, during a single week, gives three public lectures, a version of which is then published by the University of Washington Press. Anyone familiar with the revision of these lectures, *Plato's Universe* (Vlastos 1975), will recognize immediately that the material, though of great interest to historians and philosophers of science, is not suitable for oral presentation to the general public, most of whom will not have read the *Timaeus*, the subject of most of the slender volume. The three lectures were given in a large auditorium, which was full for the first lecture, sparsely occupied for the second, and empty except for a few loyal philosophers and classicists for the third. (His public lecture on Plato's feminism [Vlastos 1989], given years later at many places, was a much greater success.) Whatever his public reception, his visit afforded me the opportunity of several lengthy and valuable conversations. Vlastos was of great help to me throughout my career. His letters of recommendation carried great authority, and he continued to write them for me for years.

One such letter helped me receive a fellowship in 1974–1975 to the Center for Hellenic Studies, located on Embassy Row in Washington D.C. across the street from the house of the man who had endowed the Center, Paul Mellon. The director at the time was the renowned classics scholar Bernard Knox, and there were eight annual fellows. The Center provided lodging in outlying buildings on its campus, individual offices in the main building, and for the fellows who were there alone, three meals a day. Except on weekends all eight fellows lunched together around a large table in the dining room with Knox at its head. It was bad form to skip lunch even when one's writing was going well. Knox, who was born in England and had gone to Cambridge, would often regale us with stories of his adventures in the Spanish Civil War and as an officer in the United States Army during the Second War. In the fighting in Spain, he had been shot in the throat and left for dead by his comrades. In the Second War he had parachuted behind the Allied Lines to arm and organize French Resistance forces and after that had worked with the partisans in North Italy. Sitting silently at the table with this swashbuckler was a mild and timid German scholar, Paul Siegfried Jäkel, who had, at the end of the war, served reluctantly, as a youth of fifteen, in Hitler's Wehrmacht. Jäkel and I became close friends during our time at the Center, being the same age and having similar interests. (Among his other works, he coedited the three volumes of *Laughter Down the Centuries* [Jäkel 1994].)

I was at the Center to work on Aristotle's *Politics*. I was drawn to the treatise for several reasons. First of all, it was a largely unread treatise; I seldom met anyone working in Greek philosophy who had even skimmed through it. From a philosophical point of view, it was virgin territory waiting to be explored. Secondly, it seemed to me that the widely read and closely studied *Nicomachean Ethics* could not properly be understood without understanding the political philosophy that Aristotle intended to go with it. Thirdly, I was curious to see if the sort of logical analysis that was proving so fruitful in understanding Plato's *Dialogues* and other parts of Aristotle might shed light on some of the opaque passages in the *Politics*. And, finally, I wanted to see if the disparate ideas expressed in the treatise could be brought together into a coherent system. I eventually got some interesting results, though they were slow in coming.

While I was in residence at the Center, my second wife, Christine, was in India doing research for a dissertation on the seventh-century Indian Buddhist philosopher and logician Dharmakirti (Christine Keyt 1980). Knox allowed me to use two months of my fellowship in travel with Christine around India and Nepal, travel that was partly for sightseeing and partly for her research. Christine had introductions to leading Hindu scholars in Delhi, Jaipur, Ahmadabad, Mysore City, Bangalore, Madras, and Benares, some of whom even invited us into their homes. Twice I was invited to give a talk on contemporary American philosophy, which had to be given off-the-cuff as I had no books or notes with me. Both times the discussion after the talks drifted toward religion.

Soon after I returned to Seattle from Washington D.C., John Cooper's book on the *Nicomachean Ethics, Reason and Human Good in Aristotle* (Cooper 1975) came into my hands. Studying it stimulated a desire to turn for a while to one of its subjects—the human good. Aristotle frames his discussion of the subject in terms of the claims of two conflicting lives, the political and the philosophical, and ranks the former below the latter. But what are these lives? On one interpretation each of the lives that Aristotle describes is but one aspect of a total human life, and the best life for a man includes both aspects—both a political life and a philosophical life. By a second line of interpretation, each life is a total human life, and the best life is a life focused exclusively on philosophical activity. In his book Cooper adopts the exclusive interpretation and claims that *bios*, the Greek word for "life," is never used anywhere to refer to just one aspect of a total human life. From my study of the *Politics*, I was convinced that Cooper must be wrong about the word, and I wrote a paper defending an inclusive interpretation of the ideal life (Keyt 1978, 1983). To my great surprise—since scholars so seldom change their minds—Cooper then wrote a paper (in which mine comes in for a great deal of critical attention) recanting his earlier position and coming part way around to my interpretation (Cooper 1987). I say "part way around" because in his paper Cooper, though now embracing an inclusive interpretation of the best life, stands firm on his understanding of the Greek word *bios* and attempts, in a two-page footnote, to rebut my understanding of the word. Such an opportunity for further debate on a matter of Greek usage was not to be missed. With great eagerness I began searching for other passages in Greek literature to buttress my reading and published a retort (Keyt 1989).

Aristotle's abstraction of various lives from a person's total life is relevant to this very memoir. For what I am describing is an academic life in abstraction from a total life with personal and familial, as well as professional, dimensions. It would be uncharitable for the reader to suppose that the author had no life apart from his academic life. (On the principle of charity see below.)

In the summer of 1979, a year after stepping down from the chairmanship of the department, I conducted an NEH Summer Seminar for College Teachers on Aristotle's ethical and political philosophy. This seminar gave me the opportunity to discuss some of my ideas on the *Politics* with a group of postdocs, some of whom were destined for distinguished careers in Greek philosophy. Three with whom I've maintained contact are Allan Gotthelf, known for his original work on Aristotle's biology (Gotthelf 2012); Nicholas Smith, who wrote a much cited article on Aristotle's account of natural slavery (Smith 1991) before becoming an authority on the Socrates of the early dialogues; and David J. Depew, whose main work has been in the philosophy of evolutionary biology, but who wrote several articles bearing on Aristotle's political philosophy, most notably (Depew 1995).

As my chairmanship was winding down, I suggested to Paul Grice on one of his occasional visits to the northwest that he should consider giving some graduate seminars in our department upon his retirement from Berkeley. The succeeding department chairman pursued the idea, and in the autumn of 1981 Grice drove his Volkswagen Beetle north from Berkeley to offer a weekly seminar for one quarter in our department. For the next two years, he made the same autumn drive for the same purpose. His seminar, as heavily attended by faculty members as by graduate students, was the intellectual and social highlight of the week. The social aspect of the occasion began with the good-humored discussions in the seminar itself and continued on in the conversation at the local tavern to which we all repaired when the class was over. His favorite philosophers were Aristotle and Kant—his copy of the *Grundlegung* had long ceased being a pamphlet and become a sheaf of detached leaves. He explained to me once the Gricean method of interpreting an Aristotelian text. He would read a difficult and obscure passage and determine the problem Aristotle was addressing. He would then set the text aside, think about the problem, and try to arrive at a reasonable solution. When he would reread the passage, he claimed that he could now usually understand Aristotle's words: they could now be seen to express the very solution that he, Grice, had worked out himself! His philosophical intensity, his sociability, his appearance, and the central role of human rationality in his philosophy always made him for me a Socratic figure.

8 Princeton and Hong Kong

During my next sabbatical, in 1983–1984, I was a member of the Institute for Advanced Studies in Princeton in the history of philosophy section of the School of Historical Studies, a section that ceased to exist when its head, Morton White, retired. Vlastos once again lent me his support, which, according to White, had carried the weight in the selection process. Since so many things flowed from my year at the Institute, my debt to Vlastos is substantial. For several years I had been focusing on two principal concepts in Aristotle's *Politics*: nature and justice—the main concepts of the treatise, aside from such strictly political concepts as city, citizen, constitution, and the like. An invitation to deliver a paper at a conference at Irvine in January 1984 provided the spur to organize my work on the latter concept, and I set to work assembling a paper on Aristotle's theory of distributive justice. The basic idea was a formulation of Aristotle's principle of distributive justice as an equation of ratios in a notation that was adequate to capture all facets of the principle, an equation as central to Aristotle's theory of distributive justice as $E = mc^2$ is to Einstein's special theory of relativity (Keyt 1985, 1987).

The mention of Einstein reminds me of a startling experience I had one morning at the Institute. As I walked up to the main building, I noticed a well-polished vintage car of the 1930s parked in front and upon entering the building was taken aback to encounter Einstein risen from the dead—or at any rate his very spit and image. The man turned out to be an actor waiting around to star as Einstein in a scene being shot for a film about Einstein, a film for which I've been waiting in vain for over a quarter of a century.

After preparing the paper on justice for publication, I turned to the concept of nature in the *Politics* and set about analyzing the complex passage at the beginning of the *Politics* where Aristotle argues for three central ideas: that the polis is a natural entity, that man is by nature a political animal, and that the polis is prior in nature to the individual (Keyt 1987, 1991c). I delivered the first version of this paper before the Classical Philosophy Colloquium at Princeton in December 1984. I was justifiably nervous the night before the event and unsurprisingly had an anxiety dream. I dreamt I was outside the lecture hall in a vestibule and was about to enter the hall, walk to the podium, and deliver my paper. A friend came bounding out of the hall and whispered to me, "Aristotle is in the audience!" Leaving me alone to collect my wits and buck up my courage, he then returned to the lecture hall. I was rattled and had almost decided to flee when he reemerged and whispered to me again, "Don't worry, it's only Wittgenstein." The anxiety that gave rise to this dream turned out to be justifiable. My paper drew heavy fire, though I emerged with many fruitful suggestions for use in preparing a revision.

A third paper on the *Politics* (Keyt 1993, 1996) followed shortly thereafter. Robert Nozick's *Anarchy, State, and Utopia* (Nozick 1974) had sparked an interest in me in philosophical anarchism, especially its aversion to compulsion and coercion. I set out to study the role of coercion in Aristotle's political philosophy, where I expected to find that Aristotle, like most modern political philosophers, regarded coercion as a normal and necessary part of government. I found the very opposite to be the case: Aristotle regarded coercion to be a necessary feature only of constitutions that are "deviant," not of those that are "correct." Thomas Hobbes, the father of modern political philosophy, seems to have understood this when he criticized Aristotle for distinguishing correct from incorrect constitutions. In claiming that coercion is a necessary feature of all constitutions, Hobbes in effect made Aristotle's theory of deviant constitutions the whole of constitutional theory.

For years a term paper that contrasted my "anarchic" reading of the *Politics* with the "totalitarian" reading of Jonathan Barnes (1990) was offered for sale on the web. Until it eventually vanished I followed its fluctuating price with the curiosity of a visual artist following the price of a work of his at auction as it changed hands.

Harold Cherniss was a professor emeritus at the Institute when I arrived, though he still had an office and came to it every day. (What is retirement like at a research institution? Cherniss remarked once that all it amounted to was having one's pay cut in half.) He spent most of his time maintaining his elaborate bibliography of Plato, carefully entering the information on each new book and article on an index card.

He was still sharp, and I was pleased to be able to discuss Plato with him and to bring my wife to his house for afternoon tea with him and his wife. On one of those afternoons, we somehow got around to talking about Wilamowitz, and he mentioned that he had attended some of his lectures in Berlin in the 1920s. He said that Wilamowitz would pepper his lectures with remarks about the political situation in Germany and that his students would applaud by loudly stamping their feet on the floor. The remarks were of such a nature that they caused Cherniss to develop an intense dislike for the man. I don't recall how he characterized the remarks, but Solmsen's description of the antidemocratic, anti-Catholic, anti-Semitic Prussian lens through which Wilamowitz viewed Weimar Germany (Solmsen 1979) would explain Cherniss's antipathy.

It was at the Institute that I was first able to use that great gift of modern technology to classical scholarship, the digital library of ancient Greek literature known as the *Thesaurus Linguae Graecae*. To access this database in the early 1980s required a mainframe computer. Time on such a computer was a scarce commodity and unavailable at the University of Washington. Thus, it was a great privilege to be allowed to use the Institute's mainframe. Once I was shown how, I used it regularly. Before arriving at the Institute I had spent odd moments over an entire quarter assembling, with paper and pen, a list of every occurrence of every word in the *Politics* on the root *phusi-* (i.e., the Greek words for "nature" and "natural"). Using the mainframe it took me about ten minutes to check the accuracy of the list. (I had missed one occurrence.) Within a year of returning from my sabbatical, I acquired my first desktop computer. I began wanting one after hearing that some early-adopting philosophers found writing easier on a computer. This turned out to be the case for me too—as long as I had something to say. When ideas were lacking, a blank computer screen turned out, alas, to be just as hard to fill as a blank sheet of paper. (My first computer was a Radio Shack TRS-80, Model III, with two floppy disk drives, one for the software and the other for the output. The keyboard, monitor, and hardware were united in a single unit; there was no mouse; the monitor did not display a desktop with icons; and the printer to which the computer was attached was an elaborate and expensive mechanical device.) I still marvel at how quickly the academy became computerized.

In the autumn of 1987, I found myself in Hong Kong, a place where I would not have been except for a friendship forged at the Institute with a fellow member, the linguistic philosopher Jay Atlas. The year before my trip to East Asia, Jay was on an exchange appointment at the University of Hong Kong; and when a second philosopher in the Hong Kong department, Laurence Goldstein, expressed a desire to arrange a similar exchange with someone in the United States, Jay mentioned my name. So Laurence and I changed places, and for one semester I wound up teaching Chinese students at a British university. I taught two courses: one on Plato's *Republic* and the other in logic. My best student, as so often happens, was in logic. In lecturing on the *Republic*, I emphasized the criticism of Athenian democracy throughout the dialogue—the implicit criticism early in the dialogue as well as the explicit criticism in book VIII—and suggested that the political debate in the dialogue is primarily between those who advocate rule by an enlightened elite and those who champion democracy. I thought that my students might have some strong ideas on one side or the other of this debate given their political situation. They knew something of democracy from living in a colony belonging to a democracy (even though democracy within Hong Kong itself was limited), and they knew something of rule by an (allegedly) enlightened elite due to the city's proximity to the People's Republic of China. But being extremely shy, they were reluctant to speak up in class, so I was never able to gauge their response to Plato. Outside of class some of the students became more talkative when, in October, the Hong Kong stock market crashed, in tandem with markets throughout the world. Those who had been playing the market—there were quite a few—couldn't conceal their distress.

In 1987 the transfer of Hong Kong to the People's Republic of China lay in the future, so the colonial status of the city was still much in evidence (as was the United States Navy). One could have lunch in an English pub where the beer, the food, the patrons, the bar maids, and the ambience were straight from Britain. To me and, I believe, to most of my English and Irish colleagues, Hong Kong seemed like Disneyland, a magical, unreal place where one visits for a short span but does not reside permanently. The spectacular nighttime cityscape from the ferry plying the waters between the island and Kowloon was certainly magical. For one who could not read a single character of Chinese, the neon signs on the buildings lost their linguistic (and commercial) function and became works of pure art.

No sooner had I had returned to Seattle than I received an invitation to visit at Princeton for one semester the following autumn, while Michael Frede (sadly now deceased) went on leave. Christine and I were happy to return to Princeton. I was given two courses: a graduate seminar on Aristotle's *Politics* and Vlastos's old course, Plato and His Predecessors. John Cooper attended the seminar, and he and I sat at the opposite ends of a long rectangular table with the graduate students on either side. When I would say something the least bit provocative, their heads would all turn to the opposite end of the table to see if John had a response. It was an active class, and I had a great time. My seminar stood in stark contrast with the one given that semester by Mark Johnston, which was more like a departmental colloquium than a graduate seminar. It was attended by three or four prominent Princeton philosophers and a gaggle of mature philosophers from other institutions. It took a brave student indeed to hazard a question in such an environment.

At one of the departmental social events, I asked Saul Kripke if he remembered the affair of the phantom job candidate that happened during one of Saul's brief visits to Seattle in the early 1970s while I was department chairman. He had indeed remembered and proceeded to remind me that the man's name was "Theodore McGonigle" and to recount the details of his dossier. The affair took place during that unique period in human history when, due to the rapid and enormous expansion of higher education, the number of open entry positions in philosophy far exceeded the supply of new Ph.D.s and when, as a consequence, at the meetings of the American Philosophical Association, department chairmen had to wait in line in order to interview job applicants. During Saul's visit to my department, some of my younger colleagues reported to me that Saul had mentioned to them an outstanding new Ph.D. who was eager for personal reasons to move to the northwest. This was exciting news. I was shown the candidate's impressive and unusual dossier and was eager to schedule a department meeting to move quickly on this unusual opportunity. But before I could do so, the wind was pulled from the sails. It was all a hoax. The jokesters lost their nerve and confessed, to my great disappointment, that the candidate was a creation of Saul's imagination and that his name, as I should have recognized, belonged to The Great McGonigle, the vaudevillian juggler played by W. C. Fields in his 1934 movie *The Old Fashioned Way*. I was disappointed, not only that the candidate was fictitious but that the conspirators had not allowed the affair to play itself out. Their timidity seemed to suggest doubts about their chairman's sense of humor.

9 The Road Not Taken

In the autumn of 1990, I flew to John Wayne Airport to fill in for one quarter at Irvine, while Jerry Santas went on leave (without leaving town). As at Princeton I taught a graduate seminar on Aristotle's *Politics* and an undergraduate course on Greek philosophy, though the latter course this time was Jerry's course on the *Republic* and the *Nicomachean Ethics*. The primary challenge of a course devoted to these two works is to manage the jolt when the students move from the accessible and inviting literary style of a Platonic dialogue to the terse abstractions of an Aristotelian treatise—to replenish the oxygen that drains from the air of the lecture hall when one turns from the Myth of Er to the first book of the *Ethics*. Aside from the teaching, I enjoyed the opportunity to talk at leisure with Jerry and to renew a long-standing friendship with Abe Melden, then an emeritus professor. As I indicated earlier, Jerry and I have a similar approach to Plato and Aristotle and generally agree in our interpretations. Jerry also told me something of his life on the island of Lefkas under the Italian and then the German occupation during the Second War—the Italians were not as frightening as the Germans—and of the civil war on the island following the war. Jerry's account of the viciousness of civil war among a small population that had been intermarrying for generations bore out the comment of Herodotus that civil war is worse than foreign war in the same proportion as foreign war is worse than peace (8.3.1). When I asked Jerry if he ever mentioned his experiences during these troubled times in his classes, he said he had not. (My teachers were similarly reticent. Those who were veterans of the First or Second War or had fled Nazi Germany never uttered a word in class about their experiences, though one of my teachers at Cornell continued to wear his combat boots.)

Visiting Irvine for a quarter allowed me to return to the place in the yellow wood where two roads diverged and, thirty years before, I took the one more traveled by. It was impossible not to reflect on that ancient decision when, during my visit, the departmental library was dedicated to, and renamed in honor of, Abe Melden, the founder of the department. If, instead of remaining in Seattle, I had accepted Abe's offer to aid in the foundation, would there have been a Keyt Alcove in the Melden Library? My academic career would undoubtedly have been different, to say nothing of the lives of those in my family. Jerry's life and the lives of those in his family would probably have been different too; for if I had gone to Irvine, the department might well have decided that one appointment in Greek philosophy was enough. Taking the one road rather than the other made all the difference.

10 Working with Others

In March of 1988 I participated in a conference on "Methodological Approaches to Plato and his *Dialogues*" organized by the philosophy department of Virginia Polytechnic Institute. My contribution was a paper on a question that sometimes arises when a reader notices a gap in a Platonic argument. Such a gap can often be filled by an idea from elsewhere in the *Dialogues* or from cultural knowledge that Plato can reasonably be assumed to possess. But sometimes it cannot be. What then? That was the question I addressed in my paper. When I was invited to revise the paper for publication, I enlisted the help of my colleague Marc Cohen, and we spent a pleasant summer rethinking, reworking, and rewriting it. We reviewed the secondary literature on the Third Man Argument of the *Parmenides*, an argument with the problematic sort of gap, and noted that the increasingly refined interpretations of the argument made liberal use of the principle of charity. We wrote up our results, and while I was teaching at Princeton, I took a bus to New Brunswick and presented them to a philosophy colloquium at Rutgers. Having just hosted a conference on the use of the principle of charity in the philosophy of Donald Davidson, the Rutgers department was primed for our line of argument. I was pelted from all directions but came away with a raft of ideas that Marc and I used in revising our paper. In March of 1989 we appeared together at a session of the Pacific Division of the American Philosophical Association. I read our revised paper and let Marc brave the objections from the audience and from the two commentators: Jerry Santas and Martin Tweedale. Returning to Seattle, we revised the paper yet again, added a principle of parsimony to answer the most serious challenge to our views, and prepared the paper for publication (Keyt 1992).

Work on this paper was for us a voyage of self-discovery. We were trying to understand and to articulate what we had been doing all of our professional lives. In particular we wanted to bring to light the tacit assumptions we ourselves had been making in our work on Greek philosophy. In searching for these assumptions, we found that we were using, whether we were fully aware of it or not, the very principles we were seeking to articulate—the principles of charity and parsimony—though it would be safe to say that we used the former more than the latter.

The person with whom I've had the most extensive collaboration is Fred Miller. Fred and I go back a long way. He was a graduate student in philosophy at the University of Washington for five years beginning in 1966. During that time he attended a couple of my seminars and under my direction wrote a dissertation on truth and being in Aristotle (Miller 1971). After that he spent a year at Harvard working with Gwil Owen, and then while settling in at Bowling Green State

University founded the Social Philosophy and Policy Center. Within a short time after that I was surprised to discover that Fred had turned his attention, just as I had, from Aristotle's *Metaphysics* to his *Ethics* and *Politics*. It would be easy to infer that one of us was following the other's lead. But this was not the case. That we both ended up concentrating on Aristotle's *Politics* was an accident in the Aristotelian sense of the word, coming at the end of distinct causal chains. My interest in the *Politics*, as I mentioned earlier, was sparked by the political turmoil of the 1960s. Fred, on the other hand, began working on Aristotle's *Ethics* and *Politics* out of interest in Aristotle's *Metaphysics*! He hoped to better understand the abstract theory of the *Metaphysics* by seeing how Aristotle applied it in the practical sciences. (My future colleague Jean Roberts was to take yet a third route to the long-neglected treatise. The work of hers that would culminate in *Aristotle and the Politics* [Roberts 2009] sprang from an interest in the social dimensions of Aristotle's putatively egocentric ethical theory [Roberts 1989].)

In October of 1986 Fred and I both read papers on the *Politics* at a conference in New York sponsored by the Society for Ancient Greek Philosophy and hosted by Baruch College. What do we remember of the conference? That the World Series was being played and that we just happened to see on a TV monitor the most memorable incident in the series as it was taking place—the infamous error of the Red Sox first baseman Bill Buckner at the end of game six that allowed the Mets to stay alive and ultimately win the series. Neither of us was interested in the World Series that year, but memory works in strange ways. Two years later we joined forces and began soliciting the articles for *A Companion to Aristotle's Politics* (Keyt 1991a).

The next time we worked together was in the autumn of 2001, when I was a visiting scholar at the Social Philosophy and Policy Center. Our project was to write the chapter on ancient Greek political thought for the *Handbook of Political Theory* being assembled by Gerald Gaus and Chandran Kukathas (2004). One major problem was to devise an original way of traversing such well-trod ground. Our solution was to organize the chapter, not by philosopher, but by theory: relativism, contractualism, Platonism, naturalism, and anarchism. The facilities and the support at the Center were outstanding. Fred and I each had a research assistant, and the four of us met together for a seminar one afternoon each week. In preparation for the seminar, I would write up several pages and distribute them ahead of time to the others, who would then bring their suggestions and criticisms to the seminar. I would revise the pages in the light of our discussion, distribute the revision along with several fresh pages, and go through the same process the next week. By the time the semester was over, the chapter was finished (Keyt 2004). Once a month during the semester, Fred and I drove together to Ohio State to participate in a group that was reading and studying the Greek text of Aristotle's *Metaphysics*, an event that provided a welcome opportunity to renew and strengthen ties with Alan Silverman. It would have been a delightful semester if the terrorist attack on the Twin Towers on September 11 had not thrown a pall over everything.

Five years later Fred and I collaborated on a third project, coediting a volume of essays on ancient Greek political philosophy (Keyt 2007a). As the contributors to the many volumes of *Social Philosophy & Policy* know, the Social Philosophy and

Policy Center has a pleasant and effective way of producing its journal. For this particular issue the Center arranged a three-day, all-expenses-paid conference of the contributors in La Jolla. Following the usual procedure, the Center had distributed the papers beforehand, and each contributor arrived at the conference with written comments on all the other papers. We discussed each paper in turn. The contributors then had the opportunity to revise their papers in the light of the discussion before returning them to the editors for copyediting and publication. One bonus of the conference was the opportunity it afforded, during some of the breaks between sessions, to discuss Aristotle with Christopher Shields, Fred's intellectual son, my intellectual grandson, and Vlastos's intellectual great grandson—the Apostolic succession, as Vlastos once quipped to Fred (before the procession had gotten as far as the fourth generation).

Early in 1992 I received a letter from John Ackrill reopening our discussion from two decades before about my doing *Politics* V-VI in the Clarendon Aristotle Series. Doubts about finding an audience for the *Politics* having eased, Oxford University Press was seeking to supplement Richard Robinson's volume on *Politics* III-IV with three other volumes on the remaining six books of the treatise. Having lined up Trevor Saunders and Richard Kraut for the volumes on *Politics* I-II and VII-VIII, respectively (Saunders 1995; Kraut 1997), Ackrill now invited me to translate and write a commentary on the two remaining books. Thus began my third collaboration.

Ackrill's invitation came at a good time for me since I was scheduled for a sabbatical the following academic year. I did not realize at the time that the project would require 6 years of steady work to complete. During that time I carried on an active correspondence with Ackrill. Most of it was devoted to problems of translation, but British and American politics were mentioned from time to time, as well as the tragic death of Princess Diana. He quoted John Milton to me once, and in reply I asked him about his classmate at Oxford, Philip Larkin. He said that to his contemporaries Larkin was likeable but shy and that he had a quite embarrassing stammer. When I indicated a personal preference for Larkin over Milton, Ackrill responded in his gentle way—"I suggest," he wrote, "we don't attempt to grade him as against Milton: different as chalk and cheese." With respect to these two poets, the phrase is perhaps more than a cliché, the anxiety and existential terror evoked by Larkin's dark poems (Larkin 1988) being as distant from the bright spiritual promise of *Paradise Lost* as the taste of chalk from the taste of cheese.

In translating Aristotle's Greek Ackrill thought it good policy to follow the Greek word order. Given that Greek is an inflected language, one might find such a policy surprising; but Ackrill claimed that following the Greek order almost always clarifies the logic or intended emphasis or connection. Ackrill was particularly good in his suggestions about Greek particles, which are so important in Aristotle's prose. To give one example, he thought that *dio* is better rendered as "that is why" than as "hence" or "therefore," and that *dio kai* can often be neatly rendered as "that is precisely why." I found his ideas about translation congenial. I wanted to create a modern translation that was more readable and more accurate than any on offer. Following Ackrill's suggestion, I took preservation of the word order to be one mark among others of accuracy. This restriction encouraged a nimble engagement with language in much the way that the form of a haiku or a sonnet does. Like others who have done volumes in the Clarendon Aristotle Series, I found that I quite enjoyed the search for an accurate and readable rendition of Aristotle's Greek.

Ackrill had fewer suggestions about the commentary than the translation. One issue between us concerned the historical examples with which book V is laden. Ackrill thought the commentary should ignore them completely and focus entirely on philosophy. I objected strenuously (and successfully) on the ground that the commentary should provide the knowledge that Aristotle took for granted in his original audience but that would be lacking in his twenty-first-century readers. The historical examples also reveal just how rough Greek politics could be. Without the historical and geographical notes, it would not have been the book I wanted to write. To my surprise I discovered I enjoyed every phase of bookmaking including the preparation of the general index and the index locorum, which turned out to be much easier than I had expected, given a computer, an electronic copy of the typescript, and a little imagination.

Before I was very far along on this project Ackrill and his coeditor Lindsay Judson asked if I would be interested in providing a supplementary essay to a reissue of Richard Robinson's Clarendon volume on *Politics* III and IV. This I was happy to do (Keyt 1995), and in so doing I found myself following along in Robinson's tracks just as years before I had followed along in Bill Gass's. Though I never met Robinson, he had taught at Cornell before I arrived, and I picked up his track there when Gregory Vlastos recommended I read his book *Plato's Earlier Dialectic* (Robinson 1941) as a good introduction to the logical analysis of ancient texts. He preceded me at the Institute for Advanced Study, and while there he worked on his Clarendon volume (Robinson 1962), the book that first ignited my interest in the *Politics*. When I arrived at the Institute, I discovered his signature on a great many of the checkout cards for the library books I was borrowing. Now an essay of mine was to be attached (with his consent) to his Clarendon volume, and my Clarendon volume was to immediately follow his in the series. It was as if I had been asked to write an epilogue to *The Tunnel* (Gass 1995) with Gass's blessing and a follow-up novel to boot.

Under the head of "working with others," I must also mention my dissertation students. I've had seven, with all of whom I've maintained contact. Two wrote dissertations on Aristotle, two on Plato's *Republic*, and three on topics outside Greek philosophy. I've already mentioned Fred Miller's dissertation on Aristotle. The other person to write on Aristotle was Ronald Milo (1962), who had a long career at the University of Arizona and wrote a well-received book on the typology of immorality (Milo 1984). The first person to write a dissertation with me on the *Republic* was Peter Vernezze (1989), who taught at Weber State before dashing off to teach English in China as a Peace Corp volunteer. He gives an account of his experience in China in *Socrates in Sichuan* (Vernezze 2011). The other person to write on the *Republic* was Nils Rauhut (1997), currently chair of the department of philosophy and religious studies at Coastal Carolina University and author of an introductory text in philosophy, now in its third edition (Rauhut 2010), and coeditor of a book of readings to go along with it (Rauhut and Bass 2009). The three others who did dissertations with me are all linked by their interest in logic. Bangs Tapscott, whose dissertation was in the philosophy of language (Tapscott 1968), spent his career at the University of Utah and authored an elementary logic text (Tapscott 1976). Richard Parker, whose career was spent at California State University, Chico, wrote his dissertation on metaphysics (Parker 1973) before realizing the Walter Mitty dream of everyone who has ever taught a course on practical logic, namely, to author a text on the subject that smothers its competition and earns its author a million dollars. The text is now in its tenth edition (Parker and Moore 2011). (Who says there's no money in philosophy?) Gwynne Taraska, a pure logician, wrote a highly original dissertation on nonclassical mathematical logic (Taraska 2009), with codirectors, Arthur Fine and myself, looking over her shoulder.

11 August in Greece

In 1994 Christine and I spent a sunny August in Greece. We traveled first to the island of Corfu to join a group of scholars that had been assembled to discuss the launching of Project Archelogos, the brainchild of Theodore Scaltsas. From there we proceeded to the city of Ierissos at the root of the Athos peninsula in northern Greece to participate in an international conference on Aristotle's political philosophy. Since I was then fully engaged in writing my commentary on *Politics* V, the conference could not have come at a better time for me, and I took full advantage of the opportunity to hear and to discuss a wide variety of papers on Aristotle's political philosophy. The conference arranged excursions to the archeological sites in the vicinity, giving the conferees the opportunity to visit the ruins of Stagira, where Aristotle was born, and of Aegeae, where Philip II was buried. At the archeological museum in Thessaloniki, we saw a skeleton that was reconstructed from bones found in a royal tomb excavated at Aegeae and labeled as Philip's, which certainly made tangible Aristotle's account of Philip's assassination in *Politics* V. When we visited the ruins of Stagira, we were surprised at how well their location and layout satisfied the physical requirements of the ideal city sketched in *Politics* VII. The circuit of the walls at Stagira was a vivid reminder of the insecurity of life in a small ancient Greek polis.

Another of the excursions arranged by the conference was a visit to Mount Athos to see the monasteries, to view an early Aristotelian manuscript, and to have lunch with the monks at one of the Greek Orthodox monasteries. (This trip was open of course only to the males at the conference.) The buildings and the art within their walls were well worth seeing. However, the librarian in charge of the manuscript couldn't be found, and the lunch at the monastery turned out to be a disappointment, at least for me, in spite of the excellent food and wine we were served. Since many of the monks spoke decent enough English, I was looking forward to hearing something about a monk's life, but as soon as we were seated, the abbot offered grace and then remarked that the custom of the monastery was to eat in silence. So we ate together, smiled at each other, and then went our own ways without a word being spoken, aside from our expression of gratitude for the hospitality as we rose from the table.

I had one other experience relating to the Greek Orthodox Church when the metropolitan for the area dined with us at the hotel on the final night of the conference. Being one of the older conferees, I was given a seat beside him when we went in for dinner. The metropolitan spoke decent, though not perfect, English. So here was my opportunity to converse with a primate of the Orthodox Church. Searching for a topic of mutual interest and without realizing how sensitive a topic I was broaching, I asked him about the ecumenism that was then in the air. I was unprepared for the heat and passion of his response. He saw ecumenism as an attempt by the Roman Catholic Church to extend its tentacles and was certain that the Greek Orthodox clergy who supported it were secret agents planted by Rome.

When the conference at Ierissos ended, Christine and I spent several weeks traveling around central and southern Greece. I particularly wanted to see Sparta, though I knew that the ruins there gave little hint of the power of the ancient city, just as Thucydides had foreseen (I.10.2). Visiting the meager ruins on a summer evening, I was enchanted by the beauty of the surrounding mountains.

12 The New Century

My translation of and commentary on *Politics* V and VI was published in 1999 (Keyt 1999). I was pleased that the book appeared at the end of the old century rather than the start of the new, since the commentary was written with the wars, the political turmoil, and the political systems of the twentieth century in the background. The political unrest in the United States during the Vietnam War was a spur to writing the book.

With the book finished I found myself, like many other scholars, contributing single chapters to multiauthored books rather than articles to professional refereed journals. The focus of the academy seemed to have shifted from journals to "*Companions*." I've already mentioned the chapter on ancient Greek political thought Fred Miller and I coauthored in 2001 and the *Companion* we coedited a decade earlier. Having taught courses on Plato's *Republic* for years, I thought I was ready at last to hazard a couple of papers on the dialogue. In one I tried to encapsulate Plato's political philosophy by analyzing his use of the analogy of the ship of state (Keyt 2006b), and in another I tried to give a coherent account of the concept to which the *Republic* is devoted—justice (Keyt 2006c).

When I read the paper on the ship of state at a meeting of the Pacific Division of the American Philosophical Association, David Reeve was one of the commentators. (Rachana Kamtekar was the other.) A few years earlier he had read the penultimate version of my translation of *Politics* V and VI while he himself was translating the entire treatise, and had given me several helpful suggestions. His comments on my translation and on my paper were the culmination of a long association going back to his early days at Reed, where he had landed after graduate school at Cornell. Due to the proximity of Seattle and Portland, our connections with Cornell, and our shared interests, I considered David, until his flight to North Carolina, virtually a colleague. That we should both end up working on Plato's *Republic* and Aristotle's *Politics* is another Aristotelian coincidence similar to the ones noted earlier.

In addition to the two papers on Plato, I wrote three on Aristotle. The first was a synoptic account of Aristotle's political philosophy (Keyt 2006a); the second addressed a subject that straddles his moral and political philosophy (Keyt 2007b); and the third, for a change of pace, was a paper on the *Prior Analytics* (Keyt 2009).

The return to Aristotle was inevitable. Aristotle has for me and many other philosophers and Aristotelian scholars the magnetic attraction of truth. One must, of course, separate basic Aristotelian principles and ideas from the odd or outdated or morally unacceptable ideas that, in Aristotle's treatises, often tag along. What is so surprising is that the general principles to which Aristotle subscribes usually survive the separation. Sometimes, indeed, the general principles are incompatible with the problematic bits. Aristotle's principle that actuality temporally precedes potentiality—that "the actual member of a species is prior to the potential member of the same species" (*Met* IX.8 1049b18-19)—is incompatible with (supposedly empirically confirmed) spontaneous generation; his natural teleology has no need of, and his hylomorphism is incompatible with, substances beyond the realm of nature (i.e., prime movers); his psychological theory does not easily accommodate a psychic element that survives death; and his conception of what it is to be human rules out the idea that any human beings are slaves by nature. (For this last claim see [Keyt 2006a, pp. 406–7].)

As I mentioned earlier, Plato's *Republic* expresses in my view the default position in the various areas of philosophy, the position that has a natural initial plausibility. A great deal of subsequent philosophy can be understood as an attempt to avoid the default position, and in attempting to avoid it, philosophers are forever coming back to Aristotle. What philosophers find compelling is Aristotle's struggle to avoid Platonism without falling into materialism, nominalism, or Protagorean relativism. Think of those toilers in the philosophy of mind who have used an Aristotelian conception of the psyche to avoid physicalism on the one hand and a Platonic mind-body dualism on the other, or of those philosophers of mathematics who adopt an Aristotelian theory of mathematical objects in order to avoid Platonic realism without reverting to nominalism.

The invitation from Georgios Anagnostopoulos to write the chapter on the *Prior Analytics* for the *Blackwell Companion to Aristotle* was particularly welcome. My own Walter Mitty dream was to make some immortal technical contribution, however small, to logic—perhaps a Keyt's Corollary. As it turned out, my sole contribution to logic was this chapter on deductive logic. When the volume was published and began to be reviewed, Marc Cohen called my attention to this astounding sentence in one review: "It is exhilarating to witness David Keyt … lay into Aristotle's *Prior Analytics* with a ferocity that makes his allotted 20 pages a dense, exhausting, but ultimately satisfying read" (Kukkonen 2011, p. 84). "Exhilarating," "ferocity"! Nowadays such high-octane words are not easily associated with the *Prior Analytics* or anything written about it; they recall rather the musing of Doctor Faustus in the sixteenth-century play of Christopher Marlowe—"Sweet Analytics, 'tis thou hast ravish'd me!" In my long academic career, words like these had never before been associated with a work of mine. But, like wisdom, they are not to be despised simply because they come late.

My love of logic, as I noted earlier, was rooted in a youthful love of mathematics. My formal training in logic was as limited as my formal training in Greek philosophy, consisting as it did of just two courses: an undergraduate course based on Cohen and Nagel's *An Introduction to Logic and Scientific Method* (Cohen and Nagel 1934) and a graduate course based on Strawson's *Introduction to Logical Theory* (Strawson 1952) and Quine's *Methods of Logic* (Quine 1950). The material covered in these two courses was not much more extensive than that covered in the introductory logic course that became a regular part of my teaching schedule. I picked up set theory and the metatheory of logic from studying them on my own. I was one of those odd fellows who would take a logic book along when camping in the Rockies or visiting Paris and Munich. When I was assigned a more advanced logic course my second year at the University of Washington, the text I selected was Barkley Rosser's *Logic for Mathematicians* (Rosser 1953), a one-volume condensation of the three large volumes of *Principia Mathematica*. As I plowed through the text a week ahead of my students, I often regretted that I had not availed myself of the opportunity of taking Rosser's logic course at Cornell. For metatheory, I studied Steven Kleene's classic *Introduction to Metamathematics* (Kleene 1952), though I never used it as a text in a course.

One of my regular courses throughout my teaching career was on the soundness and completeness of first-order logic. I was eager to go beyond this. When the department lost the last of its formally trained logicians, I audaciously volunteered to lead a cohort of interested students through the proofs of Gödel's two incompleteness theorems, using *Computability and Logic* (Boolos and Jeffrey 1974; later Boolos et al. 2002) and the new software program *Turing's World* (Barwise and Etchemendy 1993). Once again I was just a week ahead of the class. I pulled it off by typing out and distributing a detailed proof of every preliminary theorem leading up to the main prizes. I realize now, having repeated the course many times, how inadequate that first course was: there were some holes in the series of proofs that were only subsequently plugged. To my surprise the best graduate student in it told me that it was the best course he had had in college. A teacher needs to be skeptical of such praise, since it is all too easy for a student to sense the academic's hunger for recognition and his susceptibility to flattery, but I think in this case the comment was sincere. The course required a larger contribution than usual from the students, so he was more fully engaged than he had ever been in his other courses.

In teaching logic one is teaching a skill, and a budding logician can no more pick up this skill by attending lectures than a budding pianist can learn to play the piano from attending recitals. That's why the students in logic classes need to be constantly doing problem sets. It slowly dawned on me that in courses on Plato and Aristotle, the teacher is cultivating a skill just as he is in his logic courses. Reading a Platonic or Aristotelian text with understanding is not all that different from unraveling a proof in set theory or a metaproof in logic, and writing clearly about Plato and Aristotle bears an analogy to proof construction in set theory or metalogic. I reluctantly came to the conclusion that courses on Plato and Aristotle should, therefore, be conducted much like courses in logic, with regular exercises to cultivate reading and writing skills. Ideally a student should come to each class clutching at least a paragraph of his or her own words discussing some assigned topic relating to the reading assignment. I say I came to this conclusion "reluctantly" because it means that an instructor has a stack of papers to read after every one of his classes. But the rewards of this technique in terms of student performance are many. Require that the exercise be typed; allow it to be revised (in pencil) during class on the basis of what is learned then and there; don't accept late papers; and most of the common problems of the classroom—poor attendance, lack of preparation, inability to follow a lecture or a discussion, classroom apathy and disengagement, and inability to write—are addressed, if not eliminated. The instructor gets to know his students better, and classes are more lively. Moreover, when students catch on and become more skillful, they begin writing at greater length without any encouragement and even in the face of admonitions about prolixity. They learn that writers write every day, and the instructor learns to read fast. (I should report that, to my loss, regret, and chagrin, I avoided an English teacher at Kenyon, Denham Sutcliffe, who followed a similar teaching regimen, because, as a student, I found his regimen too demanding. Probably some of my students feel the same way, though none has had the courage to say so to me directly.)

One other thing I learned about teaching is that no style or technique works well forever. Once a method becomes routinized, it is liable to turn stale, and that is exactly what is beginning to happen in my classes with the technique described above.

By the spring of 2007, the earth was revolving around the sun for its fiftieth time since I first set foot on the campus of the University of Washington. To mark the occasion, Fred Miller proposed that the philosophy department of his alma mater host a two-day conference on Greek philosophy, ending with a banquet. The chairman of the department, Kenneth Clatterbaugh, readily agreed, and with seed money from Fred, plans for a Keytfest went forward. The event found further generous financial support in Daniel Fisher, a student and auditor of many of my courses. The conference began on a lovely Friday afternoon in May. Jerry Santas read the opening paper, and his paper was followed on Saturday by others from Nils Rauhut, Mark McPherran, Fred Miller, and Charles Young. These five papers became the nucleus of the current Festschrift. The banquet that evening was attended by the speakers, most of my departmental colleagues, a sprinkling of past graduate students, the spouses of the foregoing, and the three members of my family—Christine, Sarah, and Aaron. Richard Parker, decked out in a tuxedo and patent leather shoes, was the master of ceremony and wit. For me the celebration was an emotional affair, a wonderful opportunity, not granted to many, to reflect on a long professional life in the company of many of those who participated in it at different points along the way.

In writing about the Keytfest, I find it impossible not to notice how novelistic an ending it provides for this memoir. Indeed, in writing a memoir one inevitably imposes on one's life an order more characteristic of a work of fiction than of the life as it was actually lived always moving forward into an indeterminate future (see Aristotle, *De Interpretatione* 9). I've always believed in the higher truth of fiction—that nothing is really true until it is authenticated by fiction (see Aristotle, *Poetics* 9 1451a36-b11). To my eyes, then, this novelistic rendering adds authenticity to my professional life rather than taking it away. It lends this life more reality than ragged memory alone bestows upon it.

After the above was written, the windup of my career became even more novelistic. Almost immediately upon notifying my department of my desire to retire on the last day of 2012, I received an invitation from Kenyon to deliver a Larwill lecture in the spring of 2013—to return for a swan song to where it all began. When I mentioned the invitation to Bill Gass in an email about something else, he replied that he had himself returned to Kenyon to speak (and on another occasion to receive an honorary degree "just in case the value of the original one had run out"). Thus, to add yet a further degree of symmetry to my academic life—as if the swan song at Kenyon were not enough—at its end, as at its beginning, I find myself following in Gass's track. The thread of destiny was apparently not entirely severed.

Since the visit to Kenyon lies in the future, its story must await (an unlikely) second edition of this Festschrift.

13 Last Things

No one could have guessed that the generation I was born into four months after the Crash of 1929 was to be known as the "lucky" generation. We were lucky to be too young to serve in the Second War and too old for the Vietnam War. Not all of us were lucky enough to miss (or, indeed, to survive) the Korean War, but many, like me, enjoyed student deferments and went into the military later during a time of profound peace. Ours was the first generation in American history to be smaller than the preceding one, which meant that jobs were easy to find. Then, to cap it all off, federal law eliminated mandatory retirement in the United States, even for academics, just as the leading wave of my generation was about to be ushered out. (See Carlson 2008.) In this memoir I've mentioned the many lucky opportunities that have come my way. I must add my luck in having congenial colleagues and forbearing students at the University of Washington and the other institutions with which I have been associated and in having so many friends among the small community of Platonic and Aristotelian scholars.

But the best luck of all was finding philosophy early and being allowed to spend my professional life in the academy doing philosophy. We who are privileged to lead such a life are fortunate indeed. First of all, we have an incredible amount of autonomy. In conducting our research and doing our teaching, there is barely a glance over our shoulder. Secondly, we have the opportunity to forge true friendships untainted by commerce (see *Nicomachean Ethics* VIII and IX). Thirdly, we spend our time among the young. If we don't look in the mirror, we can almost forget that time has been inexorably advancing. And, finally, there is the intellectual activity itself. Aristotle believes that when we are engaged in theoretical activity, we are akin to gods: "If God is always in that good state in which we sometimes are," he says, "this is wonderful; and if in a better state, yet more wonderful" (*Metaphysics* XII.7 1072b24-26). Those of us who have had the good fortune to spend our lives studying and discussing works of genius—the *Dialogues* of Plato, the treatises of Aristotle, the writings of Wittgenstein, and the ideas of Gödel—can only agree. We have been engaged in something divine. We have been blessed.

Acknowledgments I'm much indebted for the encouragement and suggestions that I received on various aspects of this memoir from Larry Bonjour, Kenneth Clatterbaugh, Robert Coburn, Marc Cohen, Charles Marks, Fred Miller, Jerry Santas, and Bangs Tapscott. I'm especially grateful for the trenchant criticism of my son Aaron and my wife Christine, who were undaunted by the frowns, sighs, and protests their comments invariably elicited.

Works Cited

Aldrich, Virgil. 1963. *Philosophy of art*. Englewood Cliffs: Prentice-Hall.
Aldrich, Virgil. 1988. *The body of a person*. Lanham: University Press of America.
Barnes, Jonathan. 1990. Aristotle and political liberty. In *Aristoteles' "Politik": Akten des XI. Symposium Aristotelicum*, ed. Günther Patzig, 249–263. Göttingen: Vandenhoeck and Ruprecht.
Barwise, Jon, and John Etchemendy. 1993. *Turing's world*. Stanford: CSLI Publications.
Black, Max. 1964. *A commentary to Wittgenstein's Tractatus*. Ithaca: Cornell University Press.
Boolos, George, and Richard Jeffrey. 1974. *Computability and logic*. Cambridge: Cambridge University Press.
Boolos, George, John Burgess, and Richard Jeffrey. 2002. *Computability and logic*, 4th ed. Cambridge: Cambridge University Press.
Bonitz, H. 1955. *Index Aristotelicus*. Graz: Akademische Druck- u. Verlagsanstalt. (Reprint of 1870 original.)
Carlson, Elwood. 2008. *The lucky few: Between the greatest generation and the baby boom*. Dordrecht/London: Springer.
Cherniss, Harold. 1944. *Aristotle's criticism of Plato and the Academy*. New York: Russell and Russell.
Cohen, Morris, and Ernest Nagel. 1934. *An introduction to logic and scientific method*. New York: Harcourt, Brace, and World Inc.
Cooper, John. 1975. *Reason and human good in Aristotle*. Cambridge, MA: Harvard University Press.
Cooper, John. 1987. Contemplation and happiness: A reconsideration. *Synthese* 72: 187–216.
Cornford, Francis. 1935. *Plato's theory of knowledge*. London: Routledge and Kegan Paul.
Cornford, Francis. 1937. *Plato's cosmology*. London: Routledge and Kegan Paul.
Cornford, Francis. 1939. *Plato and Parmenides*. London: Routledge and Kegan Paul.
Crowley, Walt. 1995. *Rites of passage: A memoir of the sixties in Seattle*. Seattle: University of Washington Press.
Depew, David J. 1995. Humans and other political animals in Aristotle's *History of Animals*. *Phronesis* 40: 156–181.
Downs, Donald Alexander. 1999. *Cornell '69: Liberalism and the crisis of the American university*. Ithaca: Cornell University Press.
Friedländer, Paul. 1958. *Plato*. Trans. Hans Meyerhoff. Vol. 1, New York: Pantheon. 1964. Vol. 2, New York: Pantheon. Vol. 3, Princeton: Princeton University Press.

Gass, William. 1970. A memory of a master. In *Fiction and the figures of life*, 247–252. New York: Knopf. Originally published in *The New Republic*.

Gass, William. 1995. *The tunnel*. New York: Knopf.

Gaus, Gerald, and Chandran Kukathas (eds.). 2004. *Handbook of political theory*. London: Sage Publications.

Gettier, Edmund. 1963. Is justified true belief knowledge? *Analysis* 23: 121–123.

Gotthelf, Allan. 2012. *Teleology, first principles, and scientific method in Aristotle's biology*. Oxford: Oxford University Press.

Hobbes, Thomas. 1651. *Leviathan*. London: Andrew Crooke.

Jäkel, Paul Siegfried, (co-ed.). 1994. *Laughter down the centuries*. 3 vols. Turku: Turun Yliopisto.

Johnston, Mark. 2010. *Surviving death*. Princeton: Princeton University Press.

Keyt, Christine Mullikin. 1980. Dharmakirti's concept of the *Svalaksana*. Dissertation. University of Washington.

Keyt, David. 1951. The problem of immortality from an atheistic point of view. *Hika* 16: 3–6.

Keyt, David. 1955. *C.I. Lewis's theory of meaning*. Dissertation. Cornell University.

Keyt, David. 1961. Aristotle on Plato's receptacle. *American Journal of Philology* 82: 291–300.

Keyt, David. 1963a. The fallacies in *Phaedo* 102A-107B. *Phronesis* 8: 167–172.

Keyt, David. 1963b. Wittgenstein's notion of an object. *The Philosophical Quarterly* 13: 13–25.

Keyt, David. 1964. Wittgenstein's picture theory of language. *Philosophical Review* 73: 493–511.

Keyt, David. 1965. A new interpretation of the *Tractatus* examined. *Philosophical Review* 74: 229–239.

Keyt, David. 1968. Wittgenstein, the Vienna Circle, and precise concepts. In *Proceedings of the XIVth International Congress of Philosophy,* vol. 2, 237–246, Vienna.

Keyt, David. 1969a. Plato's paradox that the immutable is unknowable. *The Philosophical Quarterly* 19: 1–14.

Keyt, David. 1969b. Review of *Letters from Ludwig Wittgenstein with a memoir* by Paul Englemann. *Dialogue* 8: 128–131.

Keyt, David. 1971. The mad craftsman of the *Timaeus*. *Philosophical Review* 80: 230–235.

Keyt, David. 1973a. Plato on falsity: *Sophist* 263B. In *Exegesis and argument*, Studies in Greek Philosophy Presented to Gregory Vlastos, ed. Edward N. Lee, Alexander P.D. Mourelatos, and Richard Rorty, 285–305. Assen: Van Gorcum.

Keyt, David. 1973b. The philosophy of C. I. Lewis. *Philosophical Review* 82: 491–516.

Keyt, David. 1974. The social contract as an analytic, justificatory, and polemic device. *Canadian Journal of Philosophy* 4: 241–252.

Keyt, David. 1978. Intellectualism in Aristotle. In the Special Aristotle Issue of *Paideia*: 138–157.

Keyt, David. 1983. Intellectualism in Aristotle. In *Essays in ancient Greek philosophy*, vol. II, ed. John P. Anton and Preus Anthony, 364–387. Albany: SUNY Press. (Revision of 1978.)

Keyt, David. 1985. Distributive justice in Aristotle's *Ethics* and *Politics*. *Topoi* 4: 23–45.

Keyt, David. 1987. Three fundamental theorems in Aristotle's *Politics*. *Phronesis* 32: 54–79.

Keyt, David. 1989. The meaning of *BIOS* in Aristotle's *Ethics* and *Politics*. *Ancient Philosophy* 9: 15–21.

Keyt, David. 1991a. *A companion to Aristotle's Politics*, co-ed. Fred D. Miller, Jr. Oxford: Blackwell Publishing.

Keyt, David. 1991b. Aristotle's theory of distributive justice. In *A companion to Aristotle's politics*, ed. David Keyt and Fred D. Miller, Jr., 238–278. (Substantial revision of 1985.)

Keyt, David. 1991c. Three basic theorems in Aristotle's *Politics*. In *A companion to Aristotle's politics*, ed. David Keyt and Fred D. Miller, Jr., 118–141. (Revision of 1987a.)

Keyt, David. 1992. Analyzing Plato's arguments: Plato and Platonism. With S. Marc Cohen. In *Methods of interpreting Plato and his Dialogues*, ed. James C. Klagge and Nicholas D. Smith, 173–200. Supplementary volume of *Oxford Studies in Ancient Philosophy*. Oxford: Clarendon Press.

Keyt, David. 1993. Aristotle and anarchism. *Reason Papers* 18: 137–157. (Abridged version of 1996.)
Keyt, David. 1995. Supplementary essay. To the reissue of *Aristotle's Politics, Books III and IV*. Trans. with commentary by Richard Robinson, 125–152. Oxford: Clarendon Press.
Keyt, David. 1996. Aristotle and the ancient roots of anarchism. *Topoi* 15: 129–142.
Keyt, David. 1999, *Aristotle's politics, books V and VI*, translation and commentary. Oxford: Clarendon Press.
Keyt, David. 2004. Ancient Greek political thought. With Fred D. Miller, Jr. In *Handbook of Political Theory*, ed. G.F. Gaus and C. Kukathas, 303–319. London: Sage Publications.
Keyt, David. 2006a. Aristotle's political philosophy. In *A companion to ancient philosophy*, ed. Mary Louise Gill and Pierre Pellegrin, 393–412. Oxford: Blackwell Publishing.
Keyt, David. 2006b. Plato and the ship of state. In *The Blackwell guide to Plato's Republic*, ed. Gerasimos Santas, 189–213. Oxford: Blackwell Publishing.
Keyt, David. 2006c. Plato on justice. In *The Blackwell companion to the philosophy of Plato*, ed. Hugh H. Benson, 341–355. Oxford: Blackwell Publishing.
Keyt, David. 2007a. *Freedom, reason, and the polis: Essays in ancient Greek political philosophy*, co-ed. Fred D. Miller, Jr., Cambridge: Cambridge University Press. Published simultaneously as *Social Philosophy & Policy: Ancient Greek Political Philosophy*, 24.
Keyt, David. 2007b. The good man and the upright citizen in Aristotle's *Ethics* and *Politics*. In *Freedom, reason, and the polis: Essays in ancient Greek political philosophy*, ed. David Keyt and Fred D. Miller, Jr., 220–240. Cambridge: Cambridge University Press.
Keyt, David. 2009. Deductive logic. In *A companion to Aristotle*, ed. Georgios Anagnostopoulos, 31–50. Oxford: Wiley-Blackwell.
Kleene, Steven. 1952. *Introduction to metamathematics*. Amsterdam: North-Holland.
Kraut, Richard. 1997. *Aristotle politics books VII and VIII*. Oxford: Clarendon Press.
Kukkonen, Taneli. 2011. Review of *A Companion to Aristotle*, ed. Georgios Anagnostopoulos. *Philosophy in Review* 31: 84–88.
Larkin, Philip. 1988. *Collected poems*. London: Marvell.
Lee, Edward N., Alexander P.D. Mourelatos, and Richard Rorty (eds.). 1973. *Exegesis and argument, studies in Greek philosophy presented to Gregory Vlastos*. Assen: Van Gorcum.
Lewis, C.I. 1946. *An analysis of knowledge and valuation*. La Salle: Open Court Publishing.
Malcolm, Norman. 1954. Wittgenstein's *Philosophical investigations*. *Philosophical Review* 63: 530–559.
Miller, Fred D. 1971. *Aristotle's account of being and truth*. Dissertation. University of Washington.
Miller, Fred D. 1995. *Nature, justice, and rights in Aristotle's politics*. Oxford: Clarendon Press.
Milo, Ronald. 1962. *Aristotle on practical knowledge and weakness of will*. Dissertation. University of Washington.
Milo, Ronald. 1966. *Aristotle on practical knowledge and weakness of will*. The Hague: Mouton.
Milo, Ronald. 1984. *Immorality*. Princeton: Princeton University Press.
Nozick, Robert. 1974. *Anarchy, state, and utopia*. New York: Basic Books.
Parker, Richard. 1973. *The theory of relations in Russell's metaphysics*. Dissertation. University of Washington.
Parker, Richard, and Brooke Noel Moore. 2011. *Critical thinking*, 10th ed. New York: McGraw-Hill.
Quine, Willard Van Orman. 1950. *Methods of logic*. New York: Henry Holt.
Rader, Melvin. 1969. *False witness*. Seattle: University of Washington Press.
Rauhut, Nils. 1997. *In search of Thrasymachus: The role of Thrasymachus in the ethical argument of Plato's 'Republic'*. Dissertation. University of Washington.
Rauhut, Nils. 2010. *Ultimate questions: Thinking about philosophy*, 3rd ed. Upper Saddle River: Prentice Hall.
Rauhut, Nils, and Robert Bass (eds.). 2009. *Readings on the ultimate questions: An introduction to philosophy*, 3rd ed. Upper Saddle River: Prentice Hall.
Rawls, John. 1971. *A theory of justice*. Cambridge, MA: Belknap Press.
Rice, Philip Blair. 1955. *On the knowledge of good and evil*. New York: Random House.

Roberts, Jean. 1989. Political animals in the *Nicomachean Ethics*. *Phronesis* 34: 185–204.
Roberts, Jean. 2009. *Aristotle and the Politics*. Oxford: Routledge.
Robinson, Richard. 1941. *Plato's earlier dialectic*. Ithaca: Cornell University Press.
Robinson, Richard. 1962. *Aristotle Politics books III and IV*. Oxford: Clarendon Press.
Ross, W.D. 1924. *Aristotle's metaphysics*. 2 vols. Oxford: Clarendon Press.
Ross, W.D. 1936. *Aristotle's physics*. Oxford: Clarendon Press.
Ross, W.D. 1949. *Aristotle's prior and posterior analytics*. Oxford: Clarendon Press.
Rosser, Barkley. 1953. *Logic for mathematicians*. New York: McGraw-Hill.
Ryle, Gilbert. 1966. *Plato's progress*. Cambridge: Cambridge University Press.
Saunders, Trevor. 1995. *Aristotle Politics books I and II*. Oxford: Clarendon Press.
Schilpp, P.S. (ed.). 1963. *The philosophy of Rudolf Carnap*. La Salle: Open Court Publishing.
Schilpp, P.S. (ed.). 1968. *The philosophy of C.I. Lewis*. La Salle: Open Court Publishing.
Schlick, Moritz. 1938. Form and content, an introduction to philosophical thinking. In *Gesammelte Aufsätze 1926–1936*, 151–249. Wien: Gerold.
Smith, Nicholas. 1991. Aristotle's theory of natural slavery. In *A companion to Aristotle's Politics*, ed. David Keyt and Fred D. Miller, Jr., 142–155. Oxford: Blackwell Publishing
Solmsen, Friedrich. 1929. *Die Entwicklung der Aristotelischen Logik und Rhetorik*. Berlin: Weidmann.
Solmsen, Friedrich. 1979. Wilamowitz in his last ten years. *Greek, Roman, and Byzantine Studies* 20: 89–122.
Strawson, Peter. 1952. *Introduction to logical theory*. London: Methuen.
Tapscott, Bangs. 1968. *Proper names: How they are and what they mean*. Dissertation. University of Washington.
Tapscott, Bangs. 1976. *Elementary applied symbolic logic*. Englewood Cliffs: Prentice-Hall.
Taraska, Gwynne. 2009. *A logic for disorderly domains*. Dissertation. University of Washington.
Thurber, James. 1939. The secret life of Walter Mitty. *The New Yorker*. March 18: 19–20.
Vernezze, Peter. 1989. *The happiness of Plato's philosopher-kings*. Dissertation. University of Washington.
Vernezze, Peter. 2011. *Socrates in Sichuan: Chinese students search for truth, justice, and the (Chinese) way*. Washington, DC: Potomac Books.
Vlastos, Gregory. 1954. The third man argument in the *Parmenides*. *Philosophical Review* 63: 319–349.
Vlastos, Gregory. 1975. *Plato's universe*. Seattle: University of Washington Press.
Vlastos, Gregory. 1989. Was Plato a feminist? *Times Literary Supplement* 485(4): 276, 288–289.
Weller, Cass. 1995. Fallacies in the *Phaedo* again. *Archiv für die Geschichte der Philosophie* 77: 124–134.
Whitehead, Alfred North, and Russell Bertrand. 1910. *Principia mathematica*, vol. 1. Cambridge: Cambridge University Press. 1912, vol. 2. 1913, vol. 3.
Wittgenstein, Ludwig. 1922. *Tractatus logico-philosophicus*. New York: Harcourt, Brace, and World Inc.
Wittgenstein, Ludwig. 1953. *Philosophical investigations*. Trans. G.E.M. Anscombe. Oxford: Blackwell Publishing.
Wittgenstein, Ludwig. 1958. *The blue and brown books*. Oxford: Blackwell Publishing.

Moral Psychology in Plato's *Apology*

Thomas C. Brickhouse and Nicholas D. Smith

1 Introduction

Ever since the time of Aristotle, philosophers have understood the Socratic[1] account of motivation to be a very strong version of intellectualism.[2] Here is how Aristotle understood the Socratic theory:

> Some say that if he has knowledge of how to act rightly, he cannot be akratic; for, as Socrates thought, it would be strange for a man to have knowledge and yet allow something else to rule him and drag him about like a slave. For Socrates was entirely opposed to this view and held that there is no such thing as *akrasia*; for he thought that no one with the right belief does what is contrary to the best, but if a man does so, it is through ignorance. Now this argument obviously disagrees with what appears to be the case; and if a man acting by passion does so through ignorance, we should look into the manner in which this ignorance arises. For it is evident that an akratic man, before getting into a state of passion, does not think that he should do what he does when in passion. (*NE* VII.3 1145b22-31)[3]

A theory of motivation is an "intellectualist" one if it holds that all voluntary human behavior follows from an intellectual (which, in this case, is to say, a cognitive) state or feature of the agent. That Socrates was an intellectualist, there can be no doubt. In both the *Gorgias* (467c5-468d5) and the *Meno* (77d7-e2),[4] Socrates

---

We began reading the works of David Keyt early in our academic careers, and each of us feels deeply indebted to him and his work for our own engagement in the field—particularly in our thinking and teaching on the topic of Aristotle's *Politics*. Smith also had the wonderful opportunity to take an NEH Summer Seminar on Aristotle with Keyt in the summer of 1979 and has from that time onward regarded Keyt as a special mentor and friend.

T.C. Brickhouse (✉)
Department of Philosophy, Lynchburg College, Lynchburg, VA 24502, USA
e-mail: brickhouse@lynchburg.edu

N.D. Smith
Department of Philosophy, Lewis and Clark College, Portland, OR 47219, USA
e-mail: ndsmith@lclark.edu

argues that people always act in such a way as to pursue what they think is best for them, among the options they perceive as presently available to them. Accordingly, when people pursue what is actually bad for them, it is because of a false belief: They wrongly suppose that what they are pursuing is actually something good for them.

As far as we know, no one doubts that Socrates' conception of motivation was intellectualist in this sense. But scholars have generally concluded that precisely because Socrates supposed that all human action followed cognition, he must afford no place in the explanation of human action for psychological potentials other than purely cognitive ones; in other words, they assume he must hold that such things as appetites and passions play no direct role of any kind in leading people to behave as they do. Those who characterize Socrates' view in this way do not commit him to the absurd position that people do not even experience appetites or passions, of course. Instead, they characterize the appetites and passions simply as events internal to the agent.[5] In this view, hunger, for example, is simply a pang one feels when one's stomach is empty; fear is a discomfort one feels when one believes one is in danger; and so on. The appetites and passions, conceived in this way, may be pleasurable or painful, but they contribute to motivation *only* insofar as the one experiencing them has some belief about whether having such experiences is good or bad for them. And whatever beliefs the agent may have about this subject are themselves, again, not to be explained by the agency of the appetites and passions, but instead on the basis of some cognitive activity performed by the agent: Perhaps the beliefs came as a result of (proper or improper) education, or perhaps the beliefs came as a result of (correct or incorrect) reasoning performed by the agent. In the traditional view of Socratic intellectualism, then, it would never make sense for Socrates to say or to concede that people ever do anything *because they are hungry* or *because they are angry* or *because they are fearful*—for people do not ever do what they do *because* of such things. Instead, they do what they do because of what they *believe* they should do. If they behave badly, accordingly, it is only because they have followed some false belief. In order to modify bad behavior, then, all that needs to be done is to persuade the wrongdoer to modify the beliefs that have led him or her to do wrong.[6]

In our recent work, we have been disputing this view of Socrates' conception of motivation.[7] Much of the evidence for the view we have lately argued finds Socrates granting some role to appetites and passions in the explanation of human action, as well as a variety of roles for activities intended to effect the appetites and passions—for example, corporal punishment—and ultimately intended to modify human behavior. We have contended that no adequate sense can be made of many of the things we find Socrates saying in Plato's early dialogues unless his motivational theory is understood differently from what is given in the traditional accounts. Specifically, we have argued that the appetites and passions play a significant causal role in how agents generate beliefs about what is best for them in given circumstances, and that some intervention aimed at curbing or "disciplining" the appetites or passions may be needed for some wrongdoers to be able to change their ways.

Some of the most striking evidence for our view can be found in Plato's *Gorgias*, especially in the last part of that dialogue, where Socrates goes to work on Callicles. But precisely because that discussion seems so clearly to require a moral psychology that is inconsistent with the traditional account of Socratic moral psychology, many scholars have argued that evidence from the *Gorgias* shows less about the Socratic view than it does about Plato's own emerging views. In this essay, we consider what we find in one dialogue that all scholars recognize as belonging to the group relevant to the study of Socrates: the *Apology*.[8] Socrates does not have much to say about the influence of appetites in the *Apology*, it is true. But the text is rich in references to the potentially dangerous effects of passions on the way people act. We will survey the evidence of Socratic moral psychology in this work and will show that it quite plainly indicates a significant and causally potent role at least for the passions in explaining human behavior, a role of precisely the kind our own account of Socrates' intellectualism provides.

2 Text #1: *Apology* 21b1-23e3

At 21b1, Socrates begins his explanation to the jury of how he has come to have a reputation as a dangerous sophist. The gist of the story is that having heard about the Delphic Oracle to Chaerephon, Socrates set out to discern the meaning of the puzzling oracle, by seeking out those reputed to be most wise and comparing himself to them. In subjecting these others to elenctic scrutiny, Socrates repeatedly discovers that even—indeed, especially—those who were the most respected for their putative wisdom actually wholly lacked wisdom and, worse, failed to realize how much they lacked it. His first encounter set the tone for many others:

> After conversing with him, I thought that this fellow seems to be wise to many other people and most of all to himself, yet he isn't. And then I tried to show him that he thought he is wise but he isn't. And so, as a result, I became hated by him and by many of those who were there. So, as I went away from him, I concluded to myself that I am, indeed, wiser than this person. I'm afraid that neither of us knows anything admirable and good, but this fellow thinks he knows something when he doesn't, whereas I, just as I don't know, don't even think I know. At least, then, I seem to be wiser in this small way than this one, because I don't even think I know what I don't know. From him, I went to someone else, one of those reputed to be wiser than the first person, and the very same thing seemed to me to be true, and at that point I became hated by that guy and by many others too.
>
> After that I went from one person to the next, and although I was troubled and fearful when I saw that I had become hated, nevertheless I thought I had to make the god's business the most important thing. In searching for the meaning of the oracle, I had to proceed on to all who had a reputation for knowing something. And, by the Dog, Athenians – for I must tell you the truth – the fact is that I experienced something of this sort: Those who enjoyed the greatest reputation seemed to me, as I searched in accordance with the god, to be pretty much the most lacking, whereas those who were reputed to be less worthy of consideration were better men when it came to having good sense. (*Ap.* 21c5-22a6)[9]

After interrogating politicians, poets, and artisans, Socrates came to understand that he was, indeed, the wisest of human beings but only because he alone recognized how ignorant he really was. But there was a terrible cost to Socrates' inquiry—the growing anger and resentment against him that was building among those whose ignorance had been exposed:

> This very investigation, Athenians, has generated for me a great deal of hatred, which is most difficult to handle and hard to bear, and the result has been a lot of slandering, and the claim made that I'm "wise." (*Ap.* 22e7-23a3)

The growing anger among his "victims" is also augmented by another factor:

> But in addition to this, the young who follow me around, doing so of their free will, who have complete leisure—the sons of the richest people— enjoy hearing people examined, and they often imitate me, and then try to examine others. And then, I imagine, they find an abundance of people who think they know something but know virtually nothing. That's why those who are examined by them get angry with me and not with them, and say that a certain Socrates completely pollutes the land and corrupts the youth. And when anyone asks them what I do and what I teach, they have nothing to say and draw a blank, but so they don't appear to be confused, they say what's commonly said against all philosophers—"what's in the heavens and below the earth," "doesn't believe in gods," and "makes the weaker argument the stronger." But I think they wouldn't want to say what's true, that they're plainly pretending to know, and they don't know anything. Insofar, then, as they are, I think, concerned about their honor, and are zealous, and numerous, and speak earnestly and persuasively about me, they have filled your ears for a long time by vehemently slandering me. It was on this account that Meletus, Anytus, and Lycon came after me: Meletus angry on behalf of the poets, Anytus on behalf of the craftsmen and politicians, and Lycon on behalf of the orators. The result is that, as I was saying when I began, I'd be amazed if I were able to refute in such a little time this slander you accept and that has gotten out of hand. There you have the truth, men of Athens, and in what I'm saying I'm neither hiding nor even shading anything large or small. And yet I know pretty well that in saying these things I'm making myself hated, which is evidence that I'm telling the truth and that such is the slander against me and that these are its causes. (23c2-24b1)

Socrates' explanation of how he came to be brought to trial is well known among scholars. We have quoted at length from the passage, however, in order to make clear just how poorly this passage fits with what the traditional view has to say about Socratic intellectualism. Socrates' explanation of how he came to be on trial, it seems to us, makes it abundantly clear that he believes that the experience of a passion—those mentioned in this case are pride, humiliation, and anger—can lead people to do things they would not otherwise have done, things they also *should not do*. The sequence of events is this:

1. Socrates interrogates someone, revealing that person's ignorance.
2. The person's pride is injured; the person feels publicly humiliated and becomes angry.
3. The person's anger leads him to want to slander Socrates.
4. But the humiliation of those interrogated and their pride are such that they cannot bring themselves to reveal the truth: that it is their own ignorance that led to their humiliation.
5. So instead, they concoct the convenient story—"what's commonly said against all philosophers"—and accuse Socrates of being a word-twisting, atheistic sophist.

6. These "first accusers" (see 18d7-e2) and the nasty slanders they have bruited about are what led to Meletus making the formal accusation and to Anytus' and Lycon's giving support to that accusation.

In the traditional account of Socratic motivational intellectualism, passions such as pride, humiliation, and anger explain nothing about how human beings behave. In this passage, it seems to us perfectly obvious that these passions play a major role in explaining how people have actually behaved toward Socrates. Socrates also cautions his jurors at the end of this passage not to allow the anger they may feel to cloud their ability to see that Socrates is doing nothing but telling the truth.

3 Text #2: *Apology* 29e3-30a3

In this text, Socrates explains that even the threat of death will not deter him from his "mission" in Athens:

> I won't stop philosophizing and exhorting you and pointing out to any of you I ever happen upon, saying just what I usually do, "Best of men, since you're an Athenian, from the greatest city with the strongest reputation for wisdom and strength, aren't you ashamed that you care about having as much money, fame, and honor as you can, and don't care about, or even consider wisdom, truth, and making your soul as good as possible?" And if any of you disputes me on this and says he does care, I won't immediately stop talking to him and go away, but I'll question, examine, and try to refute him. And if he doesn't appear to me to have acquired virtue but says he has, I'll shame him because he attaches greater value to what's of less value and takes what's inferior to be more important.

On the face of it, Socrates seems to be cautioning his jurors that they cannot hope that he will be frightened into behaving himself in ways that will keep him out of further trouble. But a traditionalist could always object that Socrates does not actually explicitly here make the claim that fear *can* lead people to act in certain ways. We will see, in the next text we discuss, that he actually does make this claim elsewhere. In the present text, however, Socrates characterizes himself as *exhorting* others and also talks about how he *shames* his fellow countrymen.

Now, perhaps those inclined to the traditional view of Socratic motivational intellectualism could explain what Socrates means when he says he "exhorts" his fellow Athenians in a way that makes no reference at all to an emotional appeal. But we find it simply implausible to suppose that a traditionally intellectualist account can be given for what Socrates has in mind when he claims to shame others. In a fascinating recent study, Paul Woodruff describes shame in the following way: "Shame is a painful emotion one feels at the thought of being exposed in weakness, foolishness, nakedness, or perhaps even wickedness, to the view of a community whose laughter would scald. Shame is closely related to fear of exclusion from one's group, since derision generally marks the exposed person as an outsider" (2000, p. 133). Socrates' claim in this passage from the *Apology* to shame some of those he talks with will come as no surprise to those of us who have read Plato's dialogues. We often find Socrates engaging in the very activity to which he refers here in the *Apology*: He bullies some of his interlocutors, cajoles some, and exhorts some. And some he belittles and mocks.[10] In the light of the abundance of evidence that Socrates often used shame in his conversations, Woodruff draws a conclusion (though he does not signal it precisely as such) that cuts directly against what traditionalists have said about Socratic motivational intellectualism: "I believe that Socrates could defend elenchus, but to do so he would have to move outside the limits of what he or his contemporaries would consider rational" (p. 140). Indeed, the uses of, and appeals to, shame cannot be explained in neutrally epistemic terms. When people respond to feelings of shame, at least part of what explains their behavior is the fact that they have an unpleasant emotional experience. Socrates makes no secret of the fact that he often seeks to create this experience in others and to use it in such a way as to lead them to change their ways.

4 Text #3: *Apology* 32b1-32d4

A little later in his defense speech, Socrates reminds his jurors of two times in the past where, despite great danger to himself, he refused to act in any way he regarded as unjust:

> My district, Antiochis, was in charge of the Council, when you wanted to judge as a group the ten generals who failed to pick up those who died in the sea-battle. What you wanted though was against the law, as you all realized some time later on. At that time, I was the only one of the Councilors in charge who opposed you, urging you to do nothing against the law, and I voted in opposition. And though the orators were ready to denounce me and arrest me, and though you urged them to do so by your shouting, with the law and justice on my side I thought that, though I feared (*phobêthenta*, 32c2) imprisonment or death, I should run the risk rather than to join with you, since you wanted what's not just. These things happened when the city was still a democracy.
>
> But when the oligarchy came to power, the Thirty summoned me and four others to the Rotunda and ordered us to bring Leon from Salamis to be put to death. They often ordered many others to do such things, since they wanted to implicate as many as possible in their causes. At that time I made it clear once again, not by talk but by action, that I didn't care at all about death—if I'm not being too blunt to say it—but it mattered everything that I do nothing unjust or impious, which matters very much to me. For though it had plenty of power, that government didn't frighten (*exeplêxen*, 32d4) me into doing anything that's wrong.

The relevance of these passages to our thesis is also plain: Although fear can make some people do things they might later regret, in at least these two cases, those in power had not been able to use fear to induce unjust behavior from Socrates. If fear could never play any role in explaining why people behave the way they do, as the traditional account of Socratic motivational intellectualism would have it, Socrates' claims about his own resistance to fear in this passage would be incomprehensible and otiose.

5 Text #4: *Apology* 34b6-34d1

In this text, Socrates cautions his jurors about how anger might lead them to violate their jurors' oath "to judge according to the laws" (see *Ap*. 35c2-5) and instead cast their vote in anger:

> Well then, men, this and perhaps other things like it are about all I can say in my defense. Perhaps some one of you may be angry when he thinks about himself if he went to trial on a less serious matter than this and he begged and pleaded with lots of tears with the members of the jury, and brought in his children, as well as many other relatives and friends in order to be shown as much pity as possible. But I'll do none of these things, and although in doing this, I appear to him to be running the ultimate risk. Then perhaps when some of you consider this, you'll become more closed-minded about me and, having become angry, will cast your vote in anger.

As we found in the first text we discussed, it is here again quite clear that Socrates is concerned that some jurors might feel that Socrates' own behavior humiliates them for the bad behavior they have displayed in the past. This humiliation will then lead them to feel anger toward Socrates, and this anger could lead them to vote against Socrates, despite their better judgment—that is, despite the fact that they would *not* vote against Socrates, but would vote instead for his innocence, if only they could maintain a sober and unemotional perspective. The risk to Socrates, then, is that the feelings of humiliation and anger some jurors may feel toward him will induce them to act in a way they would not otherwise act. As we have now seen for several other passages in the *Apology*, if—as the traditional view of Socratic motivational intellectualism would have it—emotions play no role in the way we come to do what we do, Socrates' admonition to the jurors in this passage would be senseless.

6 Conclusion

In fact, these are not the only passages in the *Apology* in which Socrates notes the potential effects of shame, humiliation, fear, anger, hatred, or many other emotions on people. Nor is the *Apology* an unusual dialogue in its references to emotions and/or appetites. But our review of these passages should be enough to establish that Socrates was no stranger to the power appetites and passions could wield in a human life. Because we do not deny that Socrates is an intellectualist, however, we have argued that the ways in which the emotions work on people are by effecting what beliefs people bring to bear on the decisions facing them at any given time. Strong emotions can dislodge and lead to the displacement even of beliefs that one had held steadfastly in one's life. As a result, in the view we have explored in this essay, Socrates held that good moral agents must be especially vigilant not to allow their emotions to lead them to change those beliefs about how to live and how to act that they would hold in cooler, more reflective moments. Even the best of moral agents will experience some emotions, of course. As Socrates argues in the *Protagoras*, those with moral knowledge—those whose possession of virtue is complete—will never make the wrong choices, for knowledge cannot be "dragged about like a slave" (*Prt.* 352b8-c2). But for Socrates himself and all those whom he exhorted to the pursuit of virtue, lacking such secure moral knowledge, the best possible way is always to lead "the examined life," for which the full measure of one's cognitive capacities—not intoxicated by the distorting influences of strong appetites or passions— is required. Good decisions, according to Socrates, will almost certainly never flow from beliefs whose causal origins may be found in strong appetites or emotions.

Notes

1. By "Socrates" and "Socratic" in this essay, we mean only to refer to the character of that name and views given to that character in Plato's early or Socratic dialogues. We include the following dialogues in this category in alphabetical order: *Apology, Charmides, Crito, Euthydemus, Euthyphro, Gorgias, Hippias Major, Hippias Minor, Ion, Laches, Lysis, Protagoras,* and *Republic* I. Some scholars argue against including some of these (especially *Gorgias* and *Republic* I), but we are not persuaded by the arguments for excluding them. (See Brickhouse and Smith 2003 for full discussion.)
2. The term "intellectualism" is given both to accounts of human motivation and to accounts of human virtue. Scholars have generally agreed that Socrates is an intellectualist of both sorts. Although we agree with this general view and find many connections between the two sorts of intellectualism in Socrates, we focus only on his motivational intellectualism in this essay.
3. Taken from Apostle and Gerson (1991), translation modified.
4. Santas (1979, ch. 6) does not regard these two passages as arguing for the same view. Penner and Rowe (1994) argue for the view that the two passages do argue for the same view. We agree with Penner's and Rowe's arguments on this issue.
5. This line was suggested in Penner (2001).
6. Examples of scholarly accounts we shall call the "traditional view" include Cooper (1999), Irwin (1977, 1995), Nehamas (1999), Penner (1990, 1991, 1996, 1997, 2000, 2001), Penner and Rowe (1994), and Reshotko (1992). We also argued for a version of this view in Brickhouse and Smith (1994, ch. 3). Indeed, with the sole exception of Devereux (1995), to whom we owe a significant debt in our own arguments in this paper, every scholar we know who has written on Socratic moral psychology has endorsed the traditional view.
7. See Brickhouse and Smith (2000, pp. 179–181, 216–226, 2002a, b).
8. Even Charles Kahn, whose skepticism about "Socratic philosophy" is well known, says that the *Apology* "can properly be regarded as a quasi-historical document, like Thucydides' version of Pericles' funeral oration," and that "there are external constraints that make his *Apology* the most reliable of all of our testimonies concerning Socrates" (Kahn 1996, pp. 88–89).
9. All translations are the authors' own, from Brickhouse and Smith (2002b).
10. We are indebted to Daniel Sanderman for calling our attention to this aspect of Socratic philosophizing and to the fact that it provided support for the view of Socratic motivational intellectualism we were developing.

Bibliography

Apostle, H.G., and L.P. Gerson (trans.). 1991. *Aristotle: Selected works.* 3rd ed. Grinnell: Peripatetic Press.
Brickhouse, Thomas C., and Nicholas D. Smith. 1994. *Plato's Socrates.* New York: Oxford University Press.
Brickhouse, Thomas C., and Nicholas D. Smith. 2000. *The philosophy of Socrates.* Boulder: Westview Press.
Brickhouse, Thomas C., and Nicholas D. Smith. 2002a. Incurable souls in Socratic psychology. *Ancient Philosophy* 22: 1–16.
Brickhouse, Thomas C., and Nicholas D. Smith. 2002b. *The trial and execution of Socrates: Sources and controversies.* New York: Oxford University Press.
Brickhouse, Thomas C., and Nicholas D. Smith. 2003. Apology of Socratic studies. *Polis* 20: 108–127.
Cooper, John M. 1999. Socrates and Plato in Plato's *Gorgias*. In *Reason and emotion: Essays in ancient moral psychology and ethics theory*, ed. John M. Cooper, 29–75. Princeton: Princeton University Press.
Devereux, Daniel T. 1995. Socrates' Kantian conception of virtue. *Journal of the History of Philosophy* 33: 381–408.
Irwin, Terence. 1977. *Plato's moral theory.* Oxford: Oxford University Press.
Irwin, Terence. 1995. *Plato's ethics.* Oxford: Oxford University Press.
Kahn, Charles. 1996. *Plato and the Socratic dialogue: The philosophical use of literary form.* Cambridge: Cambridge University Press.
Nehamas, Alexander. 1999. Socratic intellectualism. In *Virtues of authenticity: Essays on Plato and Socrates*, ed. Alexander Nehamas, 27–58. Princeton: Princeton University Press.
Penner, Terrence. 1990. Plato and Davidson: Parts of the soul and weakness of will. In *Canadian philosophers: Celebrating twenty years of the Canadian Journal of Philosophy*, ed. David Copp. *Canadian Journal of Philosophy* 16: 35–72.
Penner, Terrence. 1991. Desire and power in Socrates: The argument of *Gorgias* 466A-468E that orators and tyrants have no power in the city. *Apeiron* 24: 147–202.
Penner, Terrence. 1996. Knowledge versus true belief in the Socratic psychology of action. *Apeiron* 29: 199–229.
Penner, Terrence. 1997. Socrates on the strength of knowledge: *Protagoras* 351B-357E. *Archiv für Geschichte der Philosophie* 79: 117–149.
Penner, Terrence. 2000. Socrates. In *Cambridge history of Greek and Roman political thought*, ed. C.J. Rowe and Malcolm Schofield, 164–189. Cambridge: Cambridge University Press.
Penner, Terrence. 2001. Desire, action and self-interest in Socratic philosophy. Symposium paper given at the American Philosophical Association, Pacific Division, San Francisco.
Penner, Terrence, and Christopher Rowe. 1994. The desire for the Good: Is the *Meno* inconsistent with the *Gorgias*? *Phronesis* 39: 1–25.
Roshotko, Naomi. 1992. The Socratic theory of motivation. *Apeiron* 25: 145–170.
Sanderman, Daniel R. Forthcoming. Why does Socrates mock his interlocutors? *Skepsis* 15: 431–441.
Santas, Gerasimos. 1979. *Socrates: Philosophy in Plato's early dialogues.* London/Boston: Routledge and Kegal Paul.
Woodruff, Paul B. 2000. Socrates and the irrational. In *Reason and religion in Socratic philosophy*, ed. N.D. Smith and P.B. Woodruff, 130–150. New York: Oxford University Press.

Socrates, the Athenian

Jean Roberts

> This is justice: never yield, never retreat, never abandon your station, in war and in court and everywhere, do what your city and fatherland orders, or persuade it about the nature of justice. It is impious to use force against your mother and father, and even more so to use it against your fatherland. (*Crito* 51b7-c3)[1]

This is a familiarly difficult passage, difficult because although these words are uttered by Socrates in the *Crito*, they do not seem to articulate an attitude toward Athens and its laws that fits with what we otherwise see of Socrates in Plato's dialogues. I will argue in what follows that when the dialectical context in which Socrates makes these claims is properly understood, he turns out not to be advocating unqualified and absolute allegiance to law, despite what the above passage taken out of context seems to propose. The troubling claim, nevertheless, turns out to be part of a perfectly genuine and sincere statement from Socrates of his own understanding of his relation to Athens. Socrates is not saying anything he does not believe, even for what might seem to be the noble aim of getting Crito to accept his decision to remain in jail.

First, why does it seem so unlikely that Socrates believed that he was simply and straightforwardly obliged to do anything whatsoever Athens ordered him to do? The *Apology* is regularly and reasonably cited here. At his trial Socrates proudly reports two cases of his refusal to do what he believed wrong even when he was in mortal danger for refusing because it was in violation of a civic order (32a4-d8). The first case, in which he refused to take part in trying ten generals together, can arguably be understood as a defense of, rather than as disobedience to, Athenian law, since, as Socrates describes it, he refused precisely because such a trial was unlawful. The second case, in which he refused to go along with bringing Leon from Salamis

---

This was written in honor of my colleague David Keyt and to congratulate him on outlasting even Socrates as a teacher of philosophy.

J. Roberts (✉)
Department of Philosophy, University of Washington, Seattle, WA 98195-3350, USA
e-mail: jroberts@u.washington.edu; jroberts@uw.edu

during the reign of the Thirty, might also be read as a matter of defending rather than failing to respect (democratic) Athenian law; this reading is perhaps somewhat more contentious, however, since it would require getting straight about Plato's or Socrates' views about governmental legitimacy and authority. Nevertheless, the moral of both stories is supposed to be that Socrates has gone through his life steadfastly applying an independent standard of justice to all his actions. More straightforward and more directly relevant to the case at hand is Socrates' threat to disobey should the jury tell him to quit practicing philosophy.[2] Someone who can say to the jury—whose order he is explaining and to whom he is defending his obedience in the *Crito*—that "I will obey the god rather than you" (29d3-4) is not a person who takes the laws of Athens as the highest moral authority.

With enough interpretive care or imagination, discrepancies between dialogues can usually be explained or explained away. The opening exchanges of the *Crito*, however, seem to mirror the *Apology* rather than the later *Crito* passage quoted above. Well-worn Socratic themes are rehearsed in response to Crito's appeal to Socrates to escape. Only living well, or justly, matters, not merely living, and hence the only consideration of relevance in his present circumstances is whether or not escaping is just (48b3-c1). The question about the justice of the proposed action is to be answered in the expected way, by deliberation in keeping with principles held by Socrates throughout his life. At a sufficiently abstract level, following this procedure of doing only what is just as determined by the elenctic method may be consistent with a requirement of absolute obedience to the laws of Athens, but surely only by crediting those laws with moral infallibility. Even the Laws themselves, when they become a speaking character of sorts later in the dialogue, do not claim moral expertise of that kind.

Thus, the content of the passage with which I began is sufficiently at odds with what is said elsewhere by Socrates, even in the *Crito* itself, that it seems natural to try to read it as something other than an expression of Socrates' own beliefs. Indeed, the context and the form of the *Crito* itself can seem to lend support to this line of interpretation. The difficult part, the apparently conflicting passage quoted above, although it is uttered by Socrates, is uttered by Socrates speaking as, or for, the personified Laws of Athens who make the bulk of the argument against escaping. Surely this dramatic ploy has some philosophical significance, and surely it is some kind of distancing maneuver. Perhaps then we are meant to understand that Socrates does not himself endorse anything in the speech of the Laws, any more than he should be seen as endorsing the thoughts expressed by other characters in any of the other dialogues.

Yet, even if the speech of the Laws is to be taken as coming from a completely independent character, one might still wonder why the Laws of Athens are given the dialogue's main argument for its conclusion. Here one might appeal to the dramatic setting to explain why Plato might have wanted someone other than Socrates to provide the argument. Socrates is faced with Crito, who is represented as an intimate friend but one who has apparently failed to absorb Socratic teaching about what matters in life. Socrates seems genuinely concerned to calm Crito down and make him feel content with Socrates' decision to stay in Athens and die. He might then have thought that giving his own real reasons for not leaving Athens, since Crito had failed to understand in the past, would not satisfy the immediate need to reassure Crito. Time is short and Crito needs to be given an argument that he can understand and be persuaded by, and surely allegiance to law is a more familiar notion than allegiance to one's own reason. Moreover, the fact that Socrates has already publicly declared and explained on recognizably Socratic grounds that, given the unjust conviction, he prefers death in Athens to going elsewhere also seems to point to his not giving his real reasons to Crito for refusing to escape.[3] The real reason, one might think, is, as he said in court, that there just isn't any life worth living available to him once he has been convicted, since no other city would tolerate him as Athens has, and life is only of value if he can live in the way he has been living. Further support for the thought that Socrates and the Laws are functioning as quite separate characters with distinct views about justice might be taken from the fact that some of Crito's early arguments about the effects of Socrates' decision on his reputation and on his friends and family and their reputations are first dismissed out of hand by Socrates early in the *Crito* when he sounds most like the regular Socrates but are then responded to in kind by the Laws. This is easily taken as demonstrating that the Laws, not perhaps surprisingly, and unlike Socrates, take appeals to the consequences of actions as serious moral argument. Along the same lines, Socrates when speaking directly as himself argues that injustice never justifies retaliatory wrongdoing, but when speaking as the Laws says, more weakly, only that inferiors cannot retaliate against superiors.[4]

On the other hand, at the end of the day, there remains something very seriously disturbing about having to conclude that words come out of Socrates' mouth that, even though uttered in impersonation and thus attributed to that extent to another, he did not believe. It is, after all, Socrates himself who does the impersonating, and the considerations presented by the Laws are offered by Socrates speaking for himself as ones to be taken seriously. He also in his own voice quite directly and explicitly endorses what the Laws say at various crucial points along the way (51c3-5, 52a6-8, d6). Moreover, early on in the conversation, before the Laws step on the stage, Socrates emphasizes the desirability of investigating in common with Crito whether or not his former beliefs hold true (46d-e); he follows this by remarking that he is particularly intent upon persuading Crito of the rightness of his decision (48e3-4). His subsequent insistence that Crito be sure that he agrees with him that injustice is never right, even if done to those at whose hands one has suffered injustice—because no genuine joint deliberation (*koinê boulê*) is possible for those who do not share this belief (49d2-9)—surely also implies that he intends the entire conversation to be one whose conclusion is to be reached on grounds understood and believed by both of them. It thus seems impossible to avoid the inference that if Socrates does not endorse what the Laws say, he is simply lying to Crito. The dramatic setting is not one that allows for irony, and the dissembling can hardly then seem benign.

Of course, everything I have been suggesting is motivated by the assumption that an explanation is needed for an inconsistency between what Socrates believed and what he, or he when speaking as the Laws of Athens, says in the *Crito*. Further consideration of the argument in the *Crito* itself may show, however, that no such explanation is needed.

Crito first argues that Socrates should escape because allowing him to die will be a cause of shame for his friends, and moreover because it is wrong for him not to save himself and wrong of him to abandon his children (44b5-46a8). Socrates' response is the expected one. Just as it is not worth living with a severely damaged body, it is even less worth living with a severely damaged soul. Mere life is of no particular value; only living well, or justly, matters, and hence the only consideration of relevance in Socrates' present circumstances is whether or not escaping is just (48b3-c1). One ought never do wrong. More substantively and radically, and marked as such by Socrates (49d2-5), is the claim that the fact that a wrong has been done to one does not matter. That is, retaliation for wrongdoing or injury in the form of further wrongdoing or injury is still wrongdoing or injury and therefore is not to be done.[5] One should never do wrong to, harm, or injure anyone, period. (Doing injustice or wrong (*adikein*) is said to be no different from doing injury or harm (*kakôs poiein*) (49c7-8).) The unjust conviction is thus implicitly taken off the table as a consideration relevant to what Socrates can now be justified in doing. This removal is, however, only implicit at this point. Crito has not actually introduced the injustice of the verdict in any straightforward way as grounds for the rightness of fleeing, even if it is floating about in the back of his mind as a source of embarrassment and shame for Socrates and his friends. Crito is happy enough to agree with the principle of non-retaliation here, where he apparently sees no implications for the case at hand and is eager to side with Socrates. When the issue does later become explicit (at 50c1-3), he is, at least initially, quick to approve of counting the unjust verdict as a reason for Socrates to do injury to Athens.

For the moment, however, Crito is content to go along with Socrates' absolute ban on wrongdoing. Socrates then asks whether one ought to do those just things one has agreed to do (49e5-7). This introduces a particular kind of wrongdoing or injustice; one way of doing injustice or injuring another is to fail to do those just things that have been agreed to. But what is the point of the qualification on the keeping of agreements? That is, what is Socrates ruling out in saying that the failure to do what one agreed to when it is just is wrong rather than saying that the failure to do what one agreed to do is always wrong? First, it is important to note that it is not the agreement itself which Socrates says must be just, but the action to be undertaken to keep the agreement. So it would be quite unnatural to read the question as phrased as concerned with the conditions under which agreements might be made. Socrates seems unconcerned here with whether or not the agreement was coerced or whether a party to the agreement was deceived; presumably these sorts of requirement are obvious and can go without saying. Does he then simply mean that there is no obligation to do the unjust things one has agreed to do, but only an obligation to do the just ones? Agreements to murder and steal should, one would have thought, not have been made to begin with, rather than made and not kept. It is hard not to see the relevance of the passage in *Republic* I (331c1-9) about the arms borrowed from the friend who then becomes insane. The example figures there as a counterexample specifically to the claim that justice is returning what one owes, but since that is really just a version of doing what one has committed oneself to do, it fits nicely enough with the *Crito*, despite the fact that the language of agreement is not used in the *Republic*. The moral complication with agreements, of course, is that the keeping of even justly made agreements to do what is just might require that injustice be done when the time comes to act in fulfillment of the commitment. Plato wants to make room for the case in which what was knowingly and decently agreed to, because the conditions under which the agreement was made were fair and open and the action promised was not of a kind in any way morally suspect, turns out to be unjust in the particular circumstances in which the agreed upon action is to be performed. There was nothing wrong with borrowing weapons from the then-sane friend, and nothing wrong with promising to return them on demand or at some particular time, but there is something wrong with doing what was promised when the friend has become insane. The point about the keeping of agreements here in the *Crito* is introduced as a very general and abstract principle, the broader point being that actions that would not otherwise be obligatory can become so by agents somehow committing themselves to do them; there seems then nothing particularly technical in Socrates' use of the vocabulary of agreement. Since it is behavior or actions of a certain *kind* that are committed to, the qualification about the justice of those actions needs to be added simply because, as any good student of Socrates knows, any instance of a kind of action may turn out to be unjust in particular circumstances. It would be an unparalleled description of virtue in terms of behavior alone were Socrates to assert here that any action that constitutes the keeping of a justly made agreement is necessarily just. The principle being stated then is that it is just to do what has been agreed to, unless what is done thereby is something that is, in the circumstances in which action is to be taken, independently identifiable as unjust.

Crito agrees quickly to the general principle but is then puzzled when Socrates, applying it to the case at hand, asks: "See what follows then. If we leave here without the permission of the city do we do injury where we least ought, or not? Do we abide by those things we have agreed to, they being just, or not?" (49e9-50a3).[6] Crito is presumably puzzled in part simply because the argument has fairly quickly moved from dismissing his argument in favor of escape to introducing positive arguments against escape. Crito's arguments were all about why Socrates' escaping was good for Socrates and his family and friends; no consideration was given to any possibility of Socrates being positively obliged to stay, and certainly no particular consideration of the possibility of Socrates being obliged to Athens and its laws to stay. The moral principles Socrates has been running through were probably accepted by Crito due to their familiarity and without seeing ahead to how Socrates was meaning to use them in the case at hand. No doubt the fact that the particular sort of wrong Socrates is suggesting as a possibility here is the failure to keep an agreement that ought to be kept further obscured matters for Crito. The suggestion that Socrates' failure to obey here would not only be wrong but that the wrongness would consist in the failure to keep an agreement certainly begs for an account of the agreement in question.

The Laws of Athens are introduced as a character at this point to explain the question about an agreement that Crito cannot understand or consequently answer. They explain the question by describing in some detail an agreement between Socrates and Athens and thereby articulating a conception of citizenship and its attendant duties. Given the way in which they are introduced, it seems quite forced and unnatural to understand the Laws of Athens as a character alien to Socrates. After Socrates has hinted, by raising the question about agreements, that escaping might be a failure to keep an agreement of the kind that ought to be kept, and after Crito expresses his inability to see the point of the question, Socrates says, in effect, "Well, here, this is what the laws of Athens can say to me." Surely this is to be understood as Socrates putting the Laws' case for them, letting them explain Socrates' suggestion that he would be doing wrong to them in escaping. The speech the Laws give aims generally to make the case against Socrates' escaping but aims specifically to establish that Socrates has an agreement with Athens that escaping would break. Almost all of what they say is a spelling out of the roots and terms of that agreement.[7]

The Laws (and the city taken as a political community, *to koinon tês poleôs* (50a8)) begin by pointing out that the failure to respect the authority of legal judgments is destructive of those laws. Disobedience, in this case failing to duly recognize the lawful verdict of a court, is an injury to the city. This, again, is a narrowing of the question in a way unanticipated by Crito. From the beginning Socrates makes it all a question about justice and rightness, but immediately before and as he introduces the Laws as a speaker, the issue is narrowed further to become one about justice to Athens. Once this is set as the question and then once the question about the justice of escaping is made by the Laws into a question about whether Socrates should do injury to Athens, then the only possible rejoinder available to him is, as he himself suggests (at 50c1-2), that he is justified in ignoring the verdict because the verdict was unjust. The Laws respond by saying that the agreement Socrates has made with them does not allow for this exception to his obligation to obey them (50a8-c6) and proceed to argue for that claim. It is important to see here that there are not two independent considerations advanced by the Laws at the outset, as an overly quick reading might suggest, one about the destructiveness of thwarting the verdict and one about agreements; rather, ignoring the verdict would be an injury because he has agreed not to disobey.

Socrates' commitment to Athens, the Laws argue, does not allow for returning a wrong in kind because it is not a commitment to an equal. Athens and its laws have functioned as a sort of super-parent in Socrates' life. He can have no complaint against them insofar as they have managed his birth and education and development. The city is said to be "more worthy of honor, more sacred ... than your father or mother or all your other ancestors" (51a7-9). The argument is put in terms that Crito, who has shown himself to be attracted to fairly traditional and conservative moral views, can particularly appreciate, by assimilating the relation to the laws to exactly those kinship relations that Crito finds most compelling. But there is no reason to think that this is just for Crito, that Socrates is saying either only what Crito already believes or anything that he himself does not believe. The promotion of the laws to a position of moral authority superior to that of parents is, one can plausibly presume, a Platonic twist on traditional kinship ties. The Laws use the notion of obligation arising from personal ties that Crito relied on in his opening plea to Socrates while reversing the order of allegiance that Crito, in his holding of traditional views, had in mind. I take it that Socrates means to endorse the analogy with parents expressed by the Laws here. The point is that there are some basic brute facts of one's existence that bring with them moral obligations. The analogy is of course only partial since the citizen-city relation is a sui generis one. The citizen-city relation is, on the one hand, more important and more obligating than the child-parent one; on the other hand, at least in the case of Athens, the relation is different from that of children and parents insofar as it can, in theory—albeit no doubt with difficulty in most cases in practice—be dissolved. The citizen-city relation so-described introduces a duty of respectful allegiance that does not depend on anything like moral infallibility. This is, of course, Socrates' main point here.

The Laws then proceed to bring this point to bear directly on the case at hand, by saying that Socrates' disobeying by escaping would be an injustice, given what they have done for him and his acknowledgment of what they have done for him. His staying in Athens his whole life is taken as an acknowledgment of the good done to him, and of the obligation thereby incurred. The Laws take his remaining as agreeing (by deed, *ergô* (51e3)) to do what they say. Hence they conclude: "and he who does not obey we say commits a threefold injustice, because we gave birth to him and he does not obey, and because we nourished him, and because having agreed to obey he neither obeys nor persuades us" (51e4-7).[8] This is more or less the conclusion of the Laws' argument; what is added is a matter of hammering home the ways in which Socrates in particular seemed devoted to Athens and hence to have agreed to live as a citizen of Athens (to 52d7). But what does this all come to? The "threefold" injustice does not represent three distinct and individually sufficient reasons for thinking that escaping would be wrong, as it is usually taken to.[9] The temptation to read it this way is no doubt encouraged by the diffused organization of the argument it comes in; the counting seems blessedly clear and analytic. But in fact consideration of what precedes it suggests that this way of reading it really does not make sense of what has been said. The Laws do not ever come close to saying that simply being born in Athens imposes a duty of obedience, nor do they suggest that being educated in Athens by itself does so, and although the "agreement" is cited several times as the source of the obligation, it is always described by reference to the other two conditions. It is not the bare fact of consent, but the admitting to the benefit of Athenian birth and upbringing by continuing residence that is said to ground the obligation to obey. It seems then more in keeping with the context here to understand the three conditions referred to as three parts or aspects of the committed citizenship that ground the Laws' claim to Socrates' allegiance. Socrates is a citizen with a citizen's attendant obligation to obey because he was born in Athens of citizen parents, was raised and educated there, and then signaled his recognition and acknowledgment of this relation by staying in Athens throughout his adult life. Socrates' commitment to obey is not then so much like a promise or a public act of consent that in one fell swoop obliges the agent as it is an acknowledgment of the rules of a practice or institution in which he has found himself happily, or at least satisfactorily, embedded. The point is put quite negatively in fact. That is, it is Socrates' failure to leave that secures his obligation; in light of his birth and education, the presumption is that he is a citizen of Athens with a citizen's duties to Athens. We thus find here the acceptance and recognition of good done, and not just any good, but conferring of identity and indeed life, couched as an agreement made with the good-bestowing political entity.

On the reading just suggested, the Laws offer a subtle and relatively unfamiliar sort of argument for obedience to law. The description of the moral relation of a citizen to his city as an agreement between two parties is easy to misunderstand. The first, and easiest, temptation to set aside is that of assuming any similarity to modern "social contracts." Socrates' agreement is clearly not an agreement between citizens to regulate themselves. We do get something like this from Plato (Glaucon) in the *Republic* (358e3-359b5), although even there the point is not to legitimate the authority of law but to explain the genesis of morality and law in general through a self-interested protective deal to cooperate. It is of course the view to be rejected there. Nor does Socrates' agreement, although it is clearly taken as binding Socrates to obey the laws of Athens, bestow authority on those laws; the question here is not about the legitimacy of Athenian law but about the obligation of Athenians to that law. The legitimacy is assumed; it is presumably taken to be as obvious as parental authority over minor children. It is also tempting though, since both Socrates in setting the stage for the Laws and then the Laws themselves make the alleged agreement of Socrates to obey the basis of his obligation, to simply read in later and more familiar assumptions about consent and promises, with all the attendant worries about the magic of words or actions that oblige.[10] But difficulties aside, the model does not fit well here. There is not any isolated act of Socrates that counts as signaling his agreement to live as a citizen; only his continuing to live in Athens signals the acknowledgment of the obligation, so the consent has to be taken as tacit. Even so, and more importantly, as we have seen, it is not the consent in and of itself that binds here; the circumstances of that tacit consent, including most importantly its background, are crucial to its power to bind. This kind of implicit consent is more complicated because it is essentially part of an ongoing relation. It is thus much more like the implicit consent to follow household rules that might be thought to be given by an adult child by continuing to live in his parents' home. Here the obligation can be seen to be assumed just by stepping into an established institution with familiar practices, just as anyone entering any household would be expected to respect the practices of that household.[11] In the case where there is a history of the kind parents and children have, however, the obligation can also easily be seen as depending in various ways on that history. It is partly a matter of intimate familiarity with the practices that raises the expectations for respecting them (and consequently, there are things nonfamily members cannot perhaps be expected to know) and partly a matter of particularly owing respect to the heads of that particular household. Hence, although the entering into the house can be described reasonably enough as agreeing to abide by its rules and practices, the ground for the obligation is far more complicated than a simple act of consent, whether tacit or not.[12]

After the Laws conclude that Socrates would be breaking his agreement to live as a citizen of Athens (53a5-6) if he were to flee, they turn back to some of the concerns originally raised by Crito and initially dismissed by Socrates (53a8-54b1). Coming at this point in the argument, after the wrongness of escape has been established, the reintroduction of these questions need not be seen as a retraction on Socrates' part of his earlier dismissal or as an indication that Socrates does not endorse in his own person what the Laws say here in the dialogue. This would all be better seen as on a par with reintroducing the good consequences of living justly in Book IX of the *Republic*. The consequences do not settle the matter, but there is no obligation to ignore them as long as the more central considerations have been looked at. Socrates, even in the early part of the discussion where he is turning the whole debate away from Crito's concerns, admits that he cares about the money his friends would have to spend (45a4-5). There is then nothing inconsistent in pointing out that, in addition to being wrong, Socrates' escaping would not help his friends or family or generally have the beneficial and welcome consequences that Crito had hoped for.

The upshot of the speech of the Laws then is that it would be wrong and injurious for Socrates to disobey the law of Athens by escaping because he is committed to obey as a citizen of Athens, a status he enjoys because of accidents of birth and upbringing and which he has acknowledged and embraced by remaining in Athens throughout his long life. Now, granting that Socrates in speaking as the Laws of Athens means to acknowledge what they say as an accurate description of his political obligation, does this commit him to doing anything Athens tells him to? Escaping was determined by the Laws' argument to be a breaking of an agreement with Athens and hence an injury and an injustice. This is a straightforward application of the principle Socrates put on the table right before the Laws appear on the scene. That principle, however, stipulated that what has been agreed to should be done only if it is just. The Laws' speech establishes that there is an agreement always to obey the law and that this agreement would be broken if Socrates were to escape. As I have been reading this, Socrates does himself admit to the agreement described by the Laws. He does not thereby, however, commit himself as a moral matter to doing just anything ordered by Athens because that agreement falls under the more general principle that introduces the Laws' speech. That principle requires the keeping of agreements not absolutely, but only as long as doing so does not require doing injustice. Socrates describes himself as having agreed to do whatever Athenian law demands, but like any agreement, that agreement is to be kept only so long as keeping it does not mean doing injustice. The claim made by the Laws of Athens about Socrates' obligation to obey them is a description of the content of a particular agreement or commitment, not a general principle about the justice of keeping agreements; as such it does not conflict with the general statement about the justice of keeping agreements with which Socrates leads into the speech of the Laws. Socrates is, nevertheless, obliged in this case to keep his commitment because he is not being ordered to do anything unjust; he is being forced to suffer injustice, which for Socrates, at least, is a very different matter.[13]

Thus, the speech of the Laws is embedded in a broader argument about moral obligation. Socrates should never do wrong, even when wronged. One kind of wrong is failing to do what one has agreed to do as long as it is just. Socrates has agreed to obey the laws of Athens. Keeping that agreement in this case does not require doing injustice. Hence it would be wrong for Socrates not to keep the agreement. The speech of the Laws describes, accurately to Socrates' mind, his obligations to Athens from Athens' point of view, but not from his own point of view. This explains the otherwise curious dramatic ploy of Socrates speaking as the Laws instead of as himself when describing his obligations to Athens. From Socrates' own point of view, however, he is not bound absolutely to obey Athenian law, since from the broader moral perspective, his moral obligations are not exhausted by that law.

This switch in point of view can also account for the different tone taken about retaliation by Socrates and by the Laws. Since it is the inequality in their positions that is argued by the Laws to make retaliation from Socrates inappropriate, the argument at least leaves open and probably implies that retaliation toward an equal is different and acceptable. The question is what bearing this has on the broader interpretation of the dialogue. Does it, to return to the earlier question, show that once the Laws appear on the stage, we no longer have Socrates' own opinions being given? The first thing to be noted is that although the contrary implication is there, nothing in the Laws' argument actually hangs on any belief in the justifiability of retaliation in some circumstances; the only premise about retaliation in play is the one saying that inferiors ought not retaliate against superiors, and that is perfectly compatible with Socrates' earlier more general prohibition on retaliation. The possibly discrepant implication in the Laws' speech is perhaps then a bit too dialectically subtle to be doing any important signaling. It is more likely, it seems to me, that Socrates is resisting making the Laws of Athens implausibly Socratic. He can resist in this way while perfectly well making the effective parts of the Laws' argument rely on considerations that he himself can endorse as a correct statement about Athenian citizens' obligations to Athens. Indeed, he explicitly agrees in his own voice with these parts of the argument and secures Crito's agreement as well.

Socrates describes himself as having agreed to obey and as bound by that agreement as long as it does not require him to do injustice. There may be a lingering worry that making such an agreement, albeit tacitly, is irrational or duplicitous, since it appears that he is not really committed to obeying always, as the terms of the agreement as seen by Athens stipulate, but only to obeying as long as doing so requires no injustice. Here again the switch in point of view matters. Athens does not, of course, see its citizens' obligation to obey as qualified in the way Socrates does. No law can say that individuals under its jurisdiction are obliged to obey only when it seems to them right to do so. Socrates can perfectly well agree that citizens as citizens are obliged to obey always, and that this is what bestowing all the benefits of citizenship justifies the city in expecting of citizens.

This way of reading Socrates' arguments here has the advantage of giving him a coherent position consistent with the sorts of things he says elsewhere. It allows him to mean everything that he utters in the *Crito* while still making philosophical sense of the switch in voice. The speech of the Laws does describe Socrates' own conception of his relation and obligation to Athens. In recognizing and embracing his citizenship, he has agreed to obey, but despite the fact that agreements of this kind can, as in the case at hand, require almost anything of the committed, they cannot require what can never be required—the doing of injustice. The absolute legal obligation is nested in, and qualified by, the broader moral obligation to avoid injustice, which is defined independently of the law—as indeed is obvious from the description of the obligation to obey as based in consent to, rather than in the inherent justice of, that law.

Although Socrates does not argue that he has an absolute unqualified obligation to obey, he does have a very strong notion of his obligation, and this should not be surprising. It is Socrates after all who turns the question about escape into a question about his obligations to Athens rather than simply a question about his own good. The strength of Socrates' notion of his obligation should not be surprising given the nature of the political discussion as outlined above, nor should it be surprising coming from the man who described himself at his trial as having devoted his entire life to the good of his city.

Notes

1. Translation is by the author.
2. Strictly speaking what Socrates says is that if acquitted on the condition that he be quiet, with the threat of death for disobedience, he would still disobey. The fact that the case is hypothetical does not change the principle being stated, that sometimes a jury's order is to be disobeyed. The Brickhouse and Smith (1989, pp. 143–47) suggestion that the case is really like the trial of the generals insofar as such a verdict would have been illegal and Socrates thereby justified in disobeying it, even if accurate as a point about Athenian law, is simply not reflected in what Socrates says. What he says rather is that since it would be wrong for him to disobey the god and cease practicing philosophy, he will not do so even if ordered on pain of death to do so. This is to be understood neither as a statement that any order may be disobeyed as long as the legally determined punishment is accepted nor as a statement that orders to do wrong should be disobeyed but that nevertheless punishment is to be accepted. Socrates is simply saying that if ordered to do wrong, he would disobey, even on pain of death.
3. This general line of interpretation, although in far more subtle and carefully worked out forms than I am capturing here, can be found in Congleton (1974) and Harte (1999).
4. See, for a recent articulation of this point, Harte (1999, pp. 120–25).
5. I take it that the principle here, more specifically, is that being the victim of injustice, suffering injustice, does not, in and of itself, change what one is allowed to do to the perpetrator of that injustice. It should not be understood to mean that no response is allowed to the doing of injustice. The wicked ought to be punished; punishment is not properly construed as retaliation on the part of, or for the sake of, the victim. Nor would this principle rule out the demanding of restitution for injury or harm done. Nor would it rule out defending against unjust (or, of course, just) attack. The point is simply that those who do injustice must nevertheless be treated justly.
6. The Greek is ambiguous, saying literally that one ought to stick with those just things one has agreed to, but since this is certainly meant to repeat the question asked two lines earlier that does clearly refer to the actions to be done rather than the agreements to be made, it seems reasonable to resolve the ambiguity of this sentence in that direction.

7. For a different construal of the dialectical movement here, see Lane (1998).
8. I take the "persuade" clause not as offering any interesting qualification of the general obligation but as a description of Athenian legal and political practices. I do not see that it matters, for my purposes here, which of those practices in particular the Laws are supposed to be pointing to.
9. See, for example, Kraut (1984, pp. 51–3).
10. Most famously on the negative side, of course, is David Hume in "Of the Original Contract," but now also see Brown (2006).
11. See Vlastos (1974) for the claim that actions can constitute binding tacit agreement and can even do so when agents have no genuine options in the circumstances.
12. There may, of course, be all kinds of intelligent disagreement about how strong children's obligations to parents are. My only point here is that Socrates' analogy is perfectly coherent and not morally insane.
13. Cf. remarks about not being harmed in the *Apology* (30c6-d1, 41c8-d2).

Bibliography

Allen, R.E. 1980. *Socrates and legal obligation*. Minneapolis: University of Minnesota Press.
Brickhouse, Thomas C., and Nicholas D. Smith. 1989. *Socrates on trial*. Princeton: Princeton University Press.
Brown, Lesley. 2006. Did Socrates agree to obey the laws of Athens? In *Remembering Socrates: Philosophical essays*, ed. Lindsay Judson and Vassilis Karasmanis, 72–87. New York: Oxford University Press.
Congleton, Ann. 1974. Two kinds of lawlessness. *Political Theory* 2: 432–446.
Harte, Verity. 1999. Conflicting values in Plato's Crito. *Archiv für Geschichte der Philosophie* 81: 117–147.
Hume, David. 1994. Of the original contract. In *Political essays*, ed. Knud Haakonssen. Cambridge: Cambridge University Press.
Kraut, Richard. 1984. *Socrates and the state*. Princeton: Princeton University Press.
Lane, Melissa. 1998. Argument and agreement in Plato's Crito. *History of Political Thought* 19: 313–330.
Reeve, C.D.C. 1989. *Socrates in the apology*. Indianapolis: Hackett Publishing.
Vlastos, Gregory. 1974. Socrates on political obedience and disobedience. *The Yale Review* 63: 517–534. New Haven.
Weiss, Rosalyn. 1998. *Socrates dissatisfied: An analysis of Plato's Crito*. New York/Oxford: Oxford University Press.

Socrates on the Impossibility of a Reasonable Politics

Stephen M. Gardiner

> I think it is better to have my lyre or a chorus that I might lead out of tune and dissonant, and have the vast majority of men disagree with me and contradict me, than to be out of harmony with myself, to contradict myself, though I'm only one person.
>
> (*Grg.* 482b-c)[1]
>
> Throughout my life, in any public activity I may have engaged in, I am the same man as I am in private life....
>
> (*Ap.* 32e-33a)

How could such a good guy be so wrong? How could Socrates the man[2] be so impressive in his main political acts and yet so misguided (even naïve) as a political theorist? This is one central paradox facing contemporary readers of Plato's Socratic dialogues. To resolve it, many try to isolate Socrates' political philosophy from his practice. He was, we are told, simply concerned with a different set of political questions than those that interest us; and when we see this, the paradox dissolves, his views are largely rehabilitated, and any appearance of a contradiction is removed.

In this essay, I take on three tasks. First, I explore three versions of the isolationist strategy, those offered by Karl Popper, Richard Kraut, and Rachana Kamtekar. Second, I argue that although these accounts make progress, they do not ultimately resolve the paradox. Third, I suggest a rival ("accommodationist") view that aims to reconcile Socrates' personal behavior with his theoretical commitments by embracing a strongly pessimistic account of Socratic politics. On this interpretation, Socrates' fundamental political concern is with the very possibility of a good, well-functioning society that is responsive to both reasons and the well-being of its citizens. His worry is that the demands of a reasonable politics are high, unlikely to be met, and perhaps necessarily so. This pessimism explains the apparent disconnect

---

This essay was written in honor of David Keyt, for a lifetime of inspiration, in print and otherwise.

S.M. Gardiner (✉)
Department of Philosophy, University of Washington, Seattle, WA 98195, USA
e-mail: smgard@u.washington.edu

between Socrates' theory and his practice, and also why Socratic politics initially seems to have an unusual (and "isolated") focus. It also casts light on why Socrates is sometimes thought to be a founder of political thought and why his views are of enduring interest.

1 Three Paradoxes

The main paradox that will concern us involves the apparent disconnect between Socrates' personal conduct and his theoretical claims. (Hence, I shall call it "the Disconnect Paradox.") On the one hand, some of Socrates' political behavior seems extremely admirable, even heroic. First, he has a track record of defending those who were about to be victims of injustice against the excesses of his own state and people. Plato tells us of two, apparently well-known, acts. When serving on the Council, Socrates stood alone against an attempt by the majority to try ten generals as a body for their failure to rescue the survivors of the battle of Arginusae during a violent storm—an attempt that was both illegal and unjust, as the majority later recognized (*Ap.* 32b-c); and when Athens was briefly under the control of a severe oligarchy (the Thirty Tyrants), he ignored their command to bring another citizen for execution (*Ap.* 32c-e).[3] Second, much of Socrates' political action is done openly, in public, and at great personal risk. For example, in the two cases just mentioned, he faced a strong likelihood of suffering imprisonment or death for his actions. More generally, he frequently expresses his willingness to die for his beliefs and ultimately, of course, does die for them. Indeed, when it comes to it, Socrates faces his death despite having many opportunities to avoid it—either by giving up his philosophical mission or through flight to another city—and he does so in large part because of his commitment to his fellow citizens and to the state itself. Given all of this, there seems no doubting Socrates' personal political courage, his integrity, his commitment to his principles, or even his loyalty to his fellow citizens.

On the other hand, Socrates' political theory can seem extreme, myopic, and dangerously naïve. Consider three charges put forward by Rachana Kamtekar in a recent paper. First, Socrates' political reasoning "fails to recognize a citizen's need for protection from the city" (Kamtekar 2006, p. 214); second, Socrates "misguidedly focuses on the question of sovereignty or 'who should rule the state?' to the neglect of the question of how to design the political institutions to check the abuses of political power" (ibid., p. 226)[4]; and third, Socrates is unreasonably pessimistic about the possibility of a reasonable politics, having "an implausibly low estimate of most people's capacity for political judgment" and "an implausibly high estimate of the specialized knowledge required for politics" (ibid., p. 214). Such complaints are serious. The first makes Socrates appear hopelessly politically naïve, the second suggests that his approach to political thought is bizarrely myopic, and the third implies that Socrates had both a strangely jaundiced view of human abilities and an even stranger (because exalted) view of what politics is all about.[5] In short, how could such a good guy be so wrong?

While the Disconnect Paradox is the main problem to be considered in this essay, two related paradoxes are also worth mentioning. To begin with, Socrates seems to have conflicting instincts about the importance of political engagement. (Call this "the Engagement Paradox.") On the one hand, he is very demanding in his views of the character, scope, and centrality of social and political activity. For example, he believes that the aim of politics is to benefit one's fellow citizens by making them happy, and that this consists in making them morally virtuous and wise (*Euthd.* 292d-e); he says that the true politics (*Grg.* 521d), which he practices, therefore involves devoting oneself to examining virtue and exhorting one's fellow citizens to it, as this confers the greatest benefit on them, that of caring about goodness and wisdom before other possessions (*Ap.* 36c-e); and he adds that engaging in these activities constitutes the greatest good for a human being (*Ap.* 38a). All of this suggests a radical reconception of both the depth and breadth of political commitment.

On the other hand, Socrates seems bizarrely complacent about some major aspects of political life. First, as a matter of theory, his apparent reason for failing to recognize the need of citizens to be protected from the power of the city is extreme. He claims that he should respect the city's decision to execute him because "not doing so would constitute an attempt to destroy the law, that the laws are like a citizen's parents, that by staying and not expressing dissatisfaction with the laws the citizen agrees to obey them" (Kamtekar 2006).[6] Second, as a matter of political practice, Gregory Vlastos complains that Socrates is insensitive to the importance of contributing to standard forms of political debate and action. In the *Apology*, Socrates somewhat proudly confesses to the jury that he has never been involved in normal political discourse. As Vlastos points out, this runs against Athenian tradition. Pericles infamously declared "we alone regard someone who takes no part in politics not as one who sticks to his own business but as a man who is good for nothing" (Thucydides, 2.40.2; cited by Vlastos 1971, p. 128). In addition, Vlastos claims that Socrates' attitude is "incomprehensible" in light of the historical circumstances. He mentions just two momentous decisions made in the Assembly during Socrates' adulthood: one strategic and one moral (ibid., p. 128–30). In the first case, the decision to aid the Segestans which led to war with Sparta resulted in a huge military disaster for Athens, including military deaths of around forty thousand and the loss of another seven thousand to an extreme form of slavery. In the second case—the decision to punish Mytilene for its defection to Sparta by executing all the men and selling the women and children into slavery—a moral catastrophe was only barely averted by the narrow reversal of the original decision on the next day and the last-minute arrival of this news in Mytilene. Vlastos insists that a man like Socrates would surely have had something positive to contribute to such important political discussions; and in any case, given the stakes, he should at least have tried (ibid., p. 128). Third, Socrates' apparent responses to such worries—that he is the only true politician because he engages in the kind of one-on-one dialogues that he does, and that a genuine philosopher would not last long in the political realm—seem too quick, even glib, especially in the face of major political tragedies such as those Vlastos mentions.

The third paradox emerges from this last point. Kamtekar (ibid., p. 215) worries that too strong an emphasis on Socrates' claim to practice what she calls "politics in some extraordinary sense" makes it hard to understand why he has been traditionally understood, in courses in political theory and philosophy, as at least a major voice in the development of political thought, and sometimes even as "the founder of political philosophy" (Strauss 1989, pp. 68–69; cited by Kamtekar 2006, p. 215). If Socrates is really so blind or indifferent to many major political concerns, how can he play such a role? (Call this "the Foundational Role Paradox.")

The three paradoxes are serious and interconnected. In this essay, I will focus on the first: How are we to account for the apparent disconnect between Socrates' theories and his practice?[7] This is a challenging question. But our need to ask it should also give us pause. What makes us moderns so sure that Socrates is misguided in theory, given that we are so inclined to approve of his practice? This sense of misgiving increases when we consider the most obvious explanations for the paradox: ignorance and (admirable) hypocrisy. Are we really to say that Socrates does not *understand* the political import of some of his own actions? Or that he consistently abandons his theoretical commitments for the sake of doing the right thing? Neither of these alternatives seems attractive. On the one hand, the apparent extent of disconnect between theory and practice is just too great for us to think that a person as reflective as Socrates—and one so concerned with the importance of acting on one's principles—could be ignorant of it (cf. *Grg* 482b-c, quoted above). On the other hand, it is even less appealing to say that Socrates is an admirable hypocrite (cf. Bennett 1974). After all, Socrates himself infamously regards true weakness of will—acting against what one knows to be right—as impossible (cf. *Meno* 77b-78b; Irwin 1977, p. 79).

There are reasons, then, to seek an alternative, more charitable explanation of Socrates' positions. Two strategies suggest themselves. The first is to argue that the troublesome parts of Socratic political theory can be suitably *isolated* from his practice (and perhaps also from their apparently damning implications), so that in the end there is nothing to be explained. The thought here is that once we understand what concerns Socrates in each domain, we will see that his political theory and his practice deal with very different subject matters. (Call this "the Isolation Strategy.") Most theorists sympathetic to Socrates favor such a strategy, including Karl Popper, Richard Kraut, and, more recently, Rachana Kamtekar. In this essay, I will be primarily concerned with these arguments and in particular with Kamtekar's position. Still, toward the end of the essay, I suggest a more ambitious strategy for arguing that contrary to initial appearances, Socrates' admirable political practice does indeed flow from his political theory. (Call this "the Accommodation Strategy.") Such a strategy would obviously appeal to fans of Socrates; the question is how to make it work. My suggestion will be based on the idea that Socrates' attractive values are coupled with a deep but not at all implausible pessimism about the prospects for a reasonable politics. It is this combination that raises serious challenges for political philosophy and helps to justify Socrates' foundational role in the history of political thought.

2 A Grand Isolationism

Let us begin with the charge that "Socrates fails to recognize a citizen's need for protection from the city" (Kamtekar 2006, p. 214). It should be acknowledged from the outset that there is something perplexing about this complaint. For one thing, it seems unlikely that Socrates could have *failed to notice* these issues, given his social setting. As Kamtekar notes, the Athenians already thought that checking political power was an important practical and theoretical issue. So, Socrates would simply not have been paying attention if he were oblivious to such concerns. For another, Socrates' heroic political actions (*Ap*. 32b-e, mentioned above) seem precisely to involve attempts to protect individuals against unjust exercises of political power. Hence, there appears to be a tight connection between what makes Socrates' actions laudable and his theory repulsive, such that it strains credibility to believe that he could be blind to the centrality of this problem for political philosophy. Given these observations, it seems highly implausible that Socrates did not consider the possibility that citizens might need protection from the state. If possible, we must seek some alternative explanation for his apparent silence about this issue in his political thought.

One approach to the Disconnect Paradox is to try to deflect it. This is the main thought behind the Isolation Strategy, whose principal proponent is Karl Popper. Popper is (infamously) extremely critical of Plato's political thought, regarding it as shamefully elitist and ultimately totalitarian. Indeed, he accuses Plato of "enlist[ing] the humanitarian sentiments ... in the cause of the totalitarian class rule of a naturally superior master race" (Popper 1966, p. 119). However, when it comes to Socrates, Popper is sympathetic to the point of indulgence, acquitting him of both Plato's general and particular errors.

In general, Popper claims that Socrates is not a totalitarian or indeed any kind of enemy of democracy. On the contrary, Popper calls him not merely "a friend of democracy" (ibid., p. 191) but also "a good democrat" himself (ibid., p. 128). Moreover, Popper credits Socrates with being "the champion of the open society" (ibid., p. 191) and with making "the greatest contribution" to the "new faith of the open society, the faith in man, in equalitarian justice, and in human reason" (ibid., p. 189). On Popper's reading, to the extent that Socrates is critical of democracy, the criticism is internal—"a democratic one, and indeed of the kind that is the very life of democracy"—so that he bears only a "superficial resemblance" to the genuine critics of the open society, such as Plato (ibid., p. 189).

With respect to Plato's particular errors, Popper claims that Socrates is not focused on the question of who should rule and, indeed, that his concerns are not truly political. We are told that Socrates' "emphasis" is "on the human side of the political problem," "the personal aspect of the open society" (ibid., p. 191), and what Socrates is concerned to criticize about his contemporary "democracy and democratic statesmen" is their "lack of intellectual honesty, and ... obsession with power politics" (ibid., p. 191). Their mistake, according to Popper's Socrates, is to miss the "things that matter" in human life (ibid., p. 191).

Popper's core idea seems to be that Socrates' focus is on an individualist moral doctrine dedicated to intellectual perfection (ibid., p. 191). This moral doctrine does have some important political implications, most directly for what it suggests about both the personal characteristics of individual political leaders and their appropriate aims. According to Popper, Socrates' focus on our intellectual limitations yields an unusual account of the central methods and subject matter of politics (more on this later). However, though Popper tentatively concedes[8] that Socrates probably did give an answer to the "Who should rule?" question, and that this answer bears some similarity to Plato's, he also argues that the resemblance is only superficial. Socrates may have agreed with Plato that the best should rule, and that this meant the wisest. But for Socrates this wisdom was "simply the realization: how little do I know!" (ibid., p. 128). Hence, for him, the wise were just those who had this kind of intellectual honesty.

According to Popper then, the kind of wisdom that concerns Socrates is neither unduly demanding nor prone to worries about political elitism. Indeed, Popper goes on to claim that Socrates was ultimately a radical individualist and "equalitarian" who believed that everyone, even the slave, could be taught (ibid., p. 129). Given this, the only authority that the "wise" could command was that of "waking up" the uneducated and encouraging them to be self-critical (ibid., p. 131), and, according to Popper's interpretation, even this mission could be carried out only through example, by the teacher's proving himself to have that authority by exhibiting the necessary self-criticism (ibid., p. 130). The implication of all this, on Popper's reading, is that Socrates' approach to politics is primarily educational:

> [Socrates] felt that the way to improve the political life of the city was to educate the citizens to self-criticism. In this sense he claimed to be "the only politician of his day," in opposition to those others who flatter the people instead of furthering their true interests. (Ibid., p. 130; citing *Grg.* 251d-e)

For this reason Popper believed that Socrates was wrong to call himself a "politician" and should instead be described as a "teacher."

In summary, on Popper's account, though Socrates offers an answer to the "Who should rule?" question, the answer is a disarming one. It appears to threaten neither elitism nor oppressive regimes but rather to be minimal in scope, noninvasive, and very respectful of autonomy and individuality in its means. The picture is strikingly different to that offered by Popper's vision of Platonic totalitarianism. Most notably, not only does it seem compatible with liberal values, it also appears to have a natural affinity to, and be headed in the direction of, some form of democracy.

Popper's account underwrites a strong isolationist strategy in defending Socrates against the charge that he "fails to recognize a citizen's need for protection from the city." On the one hand, Socrates' silence on matters of limiting state sovereignty and protecting the individual can be explained. Popper himself excuses Socrates by saying "with his emphasis on the human side of the political problem, he could not take much interest in institutional reform. It was the immediate, the personal aspect of the open society in which he was interested" (ibid., p. 191). Popper does not explain this inference. But presumably the idea is that Socrates is just confronting a very different kind of question than those dominant in modern political philosophy, and we should not simply assume that one concern must imply the other. On the other hand, Popper's account suggests that the crucial concerns are nonetheless latent in Socrates' philosophy; for, among the "greatest generation" of thinkers who helped to establish the idea of the open society, Popper credits Socrates with the idea that "there is nothing more important in our life than other individual men, the appeal to men to respect one another and themselves" (ibid., p. 191). Indeed, Popper calls Socrates "perhaps the greatest apostle of an individualist ethics of all time" (ibid., p. 128).[9]

If we accept all of this, then we can push aside any claim that Socrates' philosophy is somehow unaware of or indifferent to the plight of the individual. Instead, Popper will presumably say that he is simply addressing a different aspect of that same concern. In addition, he can claim that his characterization of Socrates' moral commitments fits well with his political practice. Now we can understand why Socrates the man strives to protect the individual against political injustice, even though he does not focus on institutional reform in his political theory. The concern for the individual is central to Socrates' whole approach.

In conclusion, combining Popper's basic account with a strong principle of charity, there is a robust prima facie case for an isolation strategy. Popper's reading implies that there is no direct reason to implicate Socrates in Plato's authoritarianism, and there is strong circumstantial evidence that Socrates could not be committed to such views.

3 A Reluctant Isolationism

Popper's view holds strong attractions for anyone interested in rehabilitating Socrates as a philosophical hero. Still, some concerns remain. To see some of them, we can turn to a related isolationist view put forward by Richard Kraut.

Kraut questions the key move of attributing to Socrates a radically self-effacing approach to political leadership. First, he disputes the Socratic credentials of the view that the only wisdom relevant to politics is knowledge of one's own ignorance (Kraut 1984, pp. 207–15). Though he knows that he is ignorant, Socrates does not see himself as a moral expert. Hence, since he thinks that moral expertise is worth seeking, he seems to believe that more advanced knowledge is possible.[10]

Second, Kraut casts doubt on the claim that waking up the deluded is the only political role that Socrates sees for the wise. He (ibid., p. 233) points out that in both the *Gorgias* and *Republic* book I, Socrates speaks of a political craft concerned with human well-being that those entitled to rule must have mastered. Whether these dialogues represent Socratic or Platonic views is, of course, disputed. But Kraut (ibid., p. 235) also suggests that both the *Apology* and the *Crito* contain related claims: " … To do an injustice and disobey a superior [*beltion*], whether divine or human: that, I know, is bad and shameful" (*Ap.* 29b6-7); and "What if someone has knowledge of justice, the good, and other such matters? Shouldn't we follow him, and feel shame and fear before him?" (*Cri*, 47c9-d2). On Kraut's reading, in these passages Socrates is asserting the "highly authoritarian" (ibid., p. 194) thesis that human superiors ought to be obeyed.

Kraut's own interpretation is less indulgent than Popper's but still tends to rehabilitate Socrates to modern readers. In his view, Socrates was an authoritarian in theory but "a democrat of sorts" in practice (ibid., p. 217). On the one hand, he saw "no theoretical justification" for democracy (ibid., p. 232) and believed that "if there ever are moral experts, then they will be entitled to obedience from the rest of us" (ibid., p. 233). However, on the other hand, Kraut claims that Socrates believed that this kind of expertise is extremely difficult to attain. Hence, in practice he favored democracy because it allows for the limited form of moral progress that is possible (ibid., pp. 228 and 232), so that "there was no feasible alternative that he preferred" (ibid., p. 232).

In the end, then, Kraut's justification of Socrates is very similar in style to Popper's. Again, Socrates takes the legitimate scope of politics to be narrow and nontraditional—focused on the moral and intellectual improvement of the citizens—and yet remains some kind of friend to democracy. Kraut addresses a significant limitation of Popper's account by conceding that Socrates was an authoritarian in principle. Still, he insists that Socrates had views about reality that made him skeptical that this ideal could ever be realized, so that in practice he preferred democracy.

Kraut's case is impressive. Still, the interpretation leaves some major questions unanswered. First, it does not consider why Socrates fails to address the challenge of protecting the individual in his accounts of either ideal or nonideal (democratic) politics. Of course, in the ideal case—where the wise rule—Socrates may have thought that such protections were unnecessary, putting his faith instead in the virtuous not to err.[11] Still, this tends to resurrect the charges of myopia and naïveté, especially since Plato—despite his apparent authoritarianism in the *Republic*—does consider the need to limit the temptations of the wise. More importantly, the neglect of the nonideal case seems even more surprising. If Socrates really believes that the ideal cannot be achieved, then why is he not more concerned about the place of the individual in the best kind of nonideal (i.e., democratic) politics or indeed with any other features of that politics? If he has even a limited enthusiasm for democracy, then why isn't he concerned to describe the best form of democracy that is possible? Second, on Kraut's view, Socrates' politics is still politics in some extraordinary sense. Like other isolationists, Kraut does not really explain Socrates' contribution to political thought.

In addition to these unanswered questions, there are worries about Kraut's unabashed authoritarianism: "I take Socrates to believe that if there ever are moral experts, then they alone should have political power; they should give commands to the other citizens, and these commands ought to be obeyed" (ibid., p. 233). The main worry is that Socrates becomes unappealing in the face of modern liberal sensibilities. This is, of course, far from a decisive reason to dismiss Kraut's interpretation. Nevertheless, it does sit uneasily with the fact that Socrates usually does seem appealing to us moderns, for the kinds of reasons pressed by Popper. Perhaps Popper himself goes too far, but that does not mean that there is nothing to what he says.

Consider, for example, Socrates' style in interacting with others (e.g., *Ap.* 21-22). There, the concern with bowing to superiors hardly seems evident. On the one hand, he does not take up the mantle of a superior. Though the oracle has said that he is the wisest of men, Socrates is humble about this, largely keeping his thoughts to himself and hoping to lead others to realize their folly through their own thinking. Moreover, he approaches his discussions with intellectual openness and generally treats his interlocutors as equals, even when they are clearly less ready for such work than he is.[12]

On the other hand, he is not subservient in his basic approach. When he seeks out other allegedly wise men, he does not begin by submitting himself to their instruction, to see what he can learn, but rather subjects them to rigorous examination. Nor does he encourage his interlocutors simply to yield to (apparently) superior views, but rather to resist and reexamine them until they are sure in their own minds that they agree. He never suggests that people should treat authority as its own warrant, as a self-justifying deliverer of commands. Instead, his true allegiance seems to be not to superior individuals, but rather to superior reasons: to going where the best arguments lead.[13]

In short, Socrates is very anti-authoritarian in his approach to others and to the project of moral improvement. Hence, Popper seems right to regard him as individualistic and "equalitarian" in important respects, especially given his concern not just for the well-being of others but also for the need for their "superiors" to answer to them and to offer good arguments. Given this, we should be reluctant to attribute even utopian authoritarianism to Socrates. If there are other ways of understanding his views, they would fit better into our overall understanding of him.

4 A New Isolationism

Given this, I now turn to Kamtekar's alternative isolationist account. This account is best understood by focusing on her second charge against Socrates' politics, that he mistakenly identifies the fundamental question of politics as the "Who should rule?" question. According to Kamtekar, this charge embodies a misunderstanding of Socrates' project. She argues that the "Who should rule?" question is not, in fact, Socrates' own, but rather one supplied by the tradition that precedes him. On her reading, Socrates' predecessors saw the main question in political philosophy as being whether democracy, oligarchy, or tyranny was the best form of government and defined themselves politically in terms of their allegiance to one of these forms. Socrates' innovation, according to Kamtekar, was to reformulate the "Who should rule?" question so that people could step back from such allegiances and ask prior questions about the purposes of political rule. Moreover, she claims, this innovation rules out some kinds of answer and so makes a certain kind of political progress possible. In essence, Kamtekar's view is that Socrates' seminal contribution to political theory is to provide a "conceptual breakthrough" (2006, p. 224) that "inaugurates nonpartisan evaluation of political regimes" (ibid., p. 216) and invalidates some forms of political elitism (ibid., p. 224). This is done through "spelling out the normative implications of ruling being a profession" (ibid., p. 226).

The main virtue of Kamtekar's account is that it appears to redeem Socratic political theory in the eyes of a modern audience. First, since Socrates' transformation of the "Who should rule?" question makes room for nonpartisan politics and rules out the worst kinds of political elitism, Kamtekar implies that the political effects of Socrates' fundamental political concerns are laudable by contemporary standards. Socrates turns out to be a good guy in theory as well as in practice, and the central paradox of Socrates' politics is extinguished.

Second, Kamtekar's account also appears to defuse the worry about Socrates' neglect of the issue of preventing abuses of power. Like other isolationists, she maintains that the issues that motivate Socrates are elsewhere in political theory, so that the neglect is understandable.

Third, although it is less clear how Kamtekar's account addresses the worry about Socrates' pessimism about politics, she does stress that Socrates' concerns about ignorance apply not only to democracy but, more broadly, to other kinds of political regime as well. It is not clear exactly how far Kamtekar wants to press this observation. She seems to argue at least that Socrates' pessimism does not *necessarily* lead to authoritarianism, and so that there is nothing *essentially* partisan about his concerns (cf. Brickhouse and Smith 1994). She may also want to go further and say that pessimism is not essential to Socrates' wider project, and so that our tendency to reject it need not undermine interest in his political theory. Finally, perhaps more ambitiously, she sees the beginnings of an argument for democracy in Socrates' pessimism cast in a more moderate form.

In summary, Kamtekar addresses each of the three charges put forward in the Disconnect Paradox—the neglect of potential abuses, the focus on the "Who should rule?" question, and the pessimism—and in a way that restores Socrates' foundational role in political theory. Her approach is broadly similar to Popper's, but also in some ways more radical. It is similar in that it defends Socrates by distinguishing between different questions and acknowledges that his discussion is both separate from, but also relevant to, the "Who should rule?" question. However, it offers an alternative account of the rival question and one that is more straightforwardly political and embedded in the tradition of pre-Socratic political thought. Moreover, it suggests that Socrates has a more direct and transformative approach to the "Who should rule?" question than Popper and Kraut imply.

Kamtekar's strategy has some advantages over the previous isolationist strategies. For one thing, she makes clear a specifically political dimension to Socrates' approach. For another, she emphasizes a side of that approach—the connection of questions of sovereignty with the issue of the purpose of political rule—that does need emphasis. Still, I do not think that her account is satisfactory overall. In the remainder of this section, I will raise three central challenges to it; in Sect. 5, I will sketch an alternative understanding of Socrates' political thought.

4.1 A Conceptual Breakthrough

My first challenge is to the claim that Socrates offers a crucial conceptual breakthrough. I do not wish to say that there is nothing innovative about his approach. The real questions concern what kind of innovation he provides and whether it is a necessary one. According to Kamtekar, the crucial moves involve the notions of a craft (or "profession") and nonpartisanship. So, what are Socrates' contributions here?

We should begin by noticing that the idea that there is a political craft, and that it aims at benefiting the citizens, is not new. As Kamtekar notes, Protagoras and the other sophists already employ this notion (*Prt.* 321c-22d). Given this, the critical innovation must be in Socrates' use of the idea. Kamtekar's focus is on nonpartisan evaluation. Drawing on the *Theaetetus*, she characterizes the relevant distinction as follows: partisan political speech is "speech in the service of personal and political interests," whereas nonpartisan speech "seeks the truth about justice and injustice" (ibid., p. 224, citing *Tht.*173a-e, 175c-d). For Kamtekar, the key issue is one of allegiance. As she puts it:

> The consequence of defining ruling as a profession aimed at the improvement of citizens and using this definition to answer the question "who should rule?" is that *it becomes possible* to criticize existing regimes *without becoming an ally of any of the parties vying for power*—in the particular case of Socrates' criticism of the Athenian democracy, of the oligarchs. (Ibid., p. 224; emphasis added)

In other words, nonpartisan arguments "*can in principle be detached* from the partisan point of view advancing them—oligarchic or democratic or monarchic"— and are "instances of a *neutral investigation* of the question from some agreed-upon starting point" (ibid., p. 224; emphases added).

Unfortunately, Kamtekar's claim that Socrates is the one who makes such evaluation possible seems overblown. In particular, as she acknowledges, Socrates' predecessors recognize at least two considerations on which answers to the "Who should rule?" question can be grounded, namely, service to the citizens and the intrinsic superiority of the ruler.[14] Yet, it seems to me that each of these can be (and indeed, usually is) given a nonpartisan reading. If this is correct, the alleged innovation put forward by Kamtekar's Socrates appears unnecessary. The possibility of nonpartisan political discussion is already present.

Is it correct? One reason to think so comes from Herodotus. There, three advocates of democracy, oligarchy, and monarchy offer reasons for the superiority of their chosen view. The democrat states two main objections to monarchy, one procedural and one substantive. The procedural objection is that the monarch is not accountable for his actions and so becomes arrogant: "How indeed is it possible that monarchy should be a well-adjusted thing, when it allows a man to do as he likes without being answerable?" (Herodotus, from Robinson 2004, p. 153). The substantive objection is that the monarch commits atrocities, especially against individuals: "The worst of all is that he sets aside the laws of the land, puts men to death without trial, and subjects women to violence." Democracy, by contrast, is said to incorporate accountability and (presumably because of this) to be "free from all those outrages which a king is wont to commit." Similarly, the proponent of oligarchy objects to the ignorance, insolence, and chaotic behavior of the many, while the monarchist argues that oligarchy is prone to faction, feud, and bloodshed.

On one natural reading of this exchange,[15] the various advocates are putting forward reasons that they think ought to be taken seriously by both those in rival camps and those with no prior allegiance. This reading is plausible because there is nothing essentially partisan about concerns about unbridled power, atrocities committed against individuals, and the undesirability of violent civil strife. However, if this reading is correct, the possibility of nonpartisan political discussion is already present.

Kamtekar considers this kind of objection and concedes that nonpartisan discussion is possible before Socrates.[16] Still, she responds:

> But possibility is not history, and we do not see nonpartisan evaluations of forms of rule prior to Socrates.... Prior to Socrates, debates about who should rule are partisan: although the parties offer arguments which can in principle be detached from the partisan point of view advancing them—oligarchic or democratic or monarchic—*in practice they are never so detached*, and there are no instances of a neutral investigation of the question from some agreed-upon starting point. (ibid., 224; emphasis added)

In Kamtekar's view, then, the crucial point concerns not whether nonpartisan debate *might have* occurred before Socrates, but whether it actually did so; and she claims in no uncertain terms that it did not.

A number of things might be said about this response. First, several of Kamtekar's claims about Socrates' innovation are initially stated in more uncompromising terms than the above passage suggests. As we have seen (ibid., p. 224, quoted above), not only does she initially define nonpartisan argument using the phrase "can in principle be detached," but she claims that Socrates is responsible for a "conceptual breakthrough" (ibid., p. 224) through which nonpartisan evaluation "becomes possible" (ibid., p. 223). Given the current passage, it seems that we must now interpret these claims in a nuanced way, as referring to some kind of historical possibility and historical breakthrough. But what this means needs to be made clear. Hence, more must be said.

Second, and more importantly, though not as strong as a straightforwardly modal claim, Kamtekar's historical assertion still amounts to a substantial (and bold) empirical conjecture: that before Socrates political arguments were offered that in principle could have been detached from the partisan point of view of those putting them forward, but in fact never were. Moreover, this conjecture is made in a context where there is scant textual evidence of any kind. Our sources for explicitly political philosophy in the Greek tradition prior to Socrates are remarkably thin. Under such circumstances, inferences about what it was not historically possible to say, or even what was in fact not ever said, made on the basis of the *absence* of explicit evidence must be treated with extreme caution. Otherwise we are in danger of concluding that the early thinkers said, or were capable of saying, very little at all, and in my view, this seems to show too little respect for the intellectual life and abilities of Socrates' predecessors and contemporaries (which, after all, included the likes of Homer, Solon, Pericles, Herodotus, and Thucydides).

Third, Kamtekar's conjecture is not clearly correct. As we have seen from Herodotus, even in the limited textual evidence that there is, reasons are offered which are not obviously partisan in any strong sense. For one thing, they do not appear to beg the question against rival political positions: that is, they do not assume background beliefs shared only by fellow partisans. For another, they appeal to a set of considerations (e.g., atrocities, civil strife) that can be assumed to be held in common, as at least part of the correct currency of political debate.

There are then serious obstacles to Kamtekar's interpretation. Still, perhaps these would be softened if a more specific understanding of what it is to be "nonpartisan" were at hand.[17] I am not sure what understanding Kamtekar would favor. However, one possibility would be the claim that prior to Socrates, political arguments, whatever their merits, are partisan in the sense that they are (1) always put in the mouths of partisans and (2) always taken by the audience to be self-serving, rather than to appeal to neutral considerations.

Unfortunately, I do not think that this interpretation of partisanship helps. Even if true, the first claim—political arguments are always put in the mouths of partisans—would hardly be decisive. What matters here is not who says what, but what they say and why they say it. Even if only partisans speak, if what they are doing is putting forward their real reasons for advocating their position—explaining why they are partisans of a particular sort and hoping to persuade others on that basis—then there is nothing problematic about this kind of debate.

Given this, the crucial claim appears to be the second—that political speech before Socrates is always self-serving and understood to be so. There is some hint of this at the beginning of the Herodotus passage, where Herodotus says, "At the meeting speeches were made, to which many of the Greeks gave no credence, but they were made nonetheless" (Robinson 2004, p. 153). This suggests that much of the original audience was skeptical about the motives and honesty of the speakers.

Still, we should not be too quick to be cynical about the kind of political speech possible at this time. First, Herodotus says only that "many" of the Greeks gave no credence to the speeches. He does not say that no one did or that no one understood what it would be like for such speeches to be offered in good faith. Indeed, it is hard to understand what is going on—including even what the most skeptical among the Greeks thought was going on—if no one had any idea what it would be to offer nonpartisan arguments. If all that *anyone* thought was possible was for people to offer purely self-serving arguments, then the purpose of a debate seems unclear.

Second, even in our limited set of sources, we do have at least one example of a partisan for one form of rule arguing that in a particular context, another form of rule is appropriate or defensible because it is more responsive to an independent consideration. Pseudo-Xenophon, an advocate of oligarchy, acknowledges that democracy can be justified because of the role played by the people in defending the city. Hence, he appears to accept that oligarchy and democracy can be assessed against an independent criterion in such a way that his favored conception can (indeed, ought to) lose.[18]

Third, Kamtekar's innovation is not one Socrates appears to claim for himself. Though he claims to be the only true politician *of his day*, he acknowledges that others have come before him (*Grg.* 521b, 526b). Hence, if true politics requires nonpartisan political speech, then we can conclude that Socrates at least thought that such speech was possible before his time. Moreover, the specific example Socrates gives of a just politician is that of Aristides, and we have reason to think that he did practice nonpartisan political speech and was appreciated by the Athenians for doing so. Writing much later, Plutarch says:

> Themistocles telling the people in assembly that he had some advice for them, which could not be given in public, but was most important for the advantage and security of the city, they appointed Aristides alone to hear and consider it with him. And on his acquainting Aristides that his intent was to set fire to the arsenal of the Greeks, for by that means should the Athenians become supreme masters of all Greece, Aristides, returning to the assembly, told them, that nothing was more advantageous than what Themistocles designed, and nothing more unjust. The Athenians, hearing this, gave Themistocles order to desist; such was the love of justice felt by the people, and such the credit and confidence they reposed in Aristides. (Plutarch 2008, p. 103)

Given all this, I conclude then that it seems unlikely that Socrates' critical innovation was to introduce the possibility of nonpartisan political evaluation.

4.2 Socrates as Partisan

My next two challenges to Kamtekar's interpretation are tightly connected. One claims that the alleged innovation itself appears to be grounded in the consideration of service to the citizens. It is only because Socrates insists that the ruling craft must benefit the ruled that his argument goes through. But this is to invoke the service consideration. The other claims that because of this, on Kamtekar's interpretation, Socrates' own employment of the alleged innovation is itself highly partisan.

I'll begin with the charge of partisanship. Kamtekar claims that one advantage of Socrates' approach is that it makes certain elitist arguments illegitimate. Specifically, Socrates is supposed to rule out arguments that rely on a stark interpretation of the superiority consideration: that the intellectually superior deserve power simply as a reward for their superiority and may therefore use it to their own advantage. Against such arguments, Kamtekar tells us that Socrates concedes that the superior deserve power but insists that they use this power to benefit the citizens.

Unfortunately, the success of this argument depends on the legitimacy of Socrates foisting the second of the pre-Socratic considerations—that the citizens be benefited—onto his opponents. Notice that against the stark interpretation of the superiority position, this move is question-begging: since the very refusal to countenance the service consideration distinguishes the stark interpretation as such, one cannot dismiss that interpretation merely by pointing out that it does not accept the claim that the citizens must be benefited.

Now, I want to be clear about my point here. I am emphatically not questioning the importance of Socrates' actual argument. On the contrary, I regard that argument as critical, for three basic reasons. First, I believe that Socrates' reasoning is basically correct, since it emphasizes one of the central themes of Socratic and later political philosophy that political arrangements must be justified to those subject to them in terms that in some sense they can accept. Second, the argument successfully accommodates some intuitions behind political elitism but in a way that is ultimately subversive. Hence, it makes a major contribution to the evolution of the subject. Most obviously, it disarms the elitist position by revealing that there is a significant burden of proof against it for those who are sympathetic to the service consideration. Less obviously, in denying the superiority claim, Socrates is separating out moral claims about natural superiority from political claims about ruling. Therefore, he may be making a basic move that differentiates between moral and political philosophy and so prefiguring the idea that the two areas might raise distinct questions.

My point, then, is not that there is something especially wrong with Socrates' argument, but that Kamtekar's account of his aims is suspect. If Socrates really is trying to transform the terms of the debate and render some forms of argument thereby illegitimate, he is clearly not doing this in a nonpartisan way. For ruling out substantive positions merely by assertion is a highly partisan maneuver—Socrates is left simply begging the question against his opponents.[19]

4.3 Lobbying as a Profession

There is an obvious response to the objection I have just made. Socrates argues that the idea that citizens must be benefited by those ruling them is derived from the very notion of ruling as a craft (or "profession" as Kamtekar calls it). Hence, it may be said that Socrates' argument is appropriately neutral. This, of course, would be a natural response for Kamtekar, since it is the mediation of the dispute through the notion of a craft that she believes is the vehicle for Socrates' innovation.

Still, I do not find this response persuasive. For one thing, Socrates' account of a craft is controversial, as Kamtekar recognizes; for another, and perhaps more importantly, Socrates is not very charitable in his characterization of the sophistic craft. In both cases he appears to beg the question in the strictest sense: his descriptions of both craft in general and the sophistic craft in particular are such that no one who did not already accept a rival position would agree to them.

Let us begin with the characterization of the sophistic craft. Socrates' argument, according to Kamtekar, requires that we accept the notion that ruling is a profession that the sophists are claiming to teach. However, it is not clear that all sophists should accept this characterization. Instead, some might claim merely to teach people how to get their way within the assembly on particular issues that matter to them. That is, they might claim to be teaching citizens the craft of being effective lobbyists for their favorite causes.

This makes a difference because being a professional lobbyist does not have the same norms as being a professional ruler in Socrates' sense. First, some might argue that being a lobbyist does not require regulating one's actions based on their effects on the whole city. Indeed, they would claim that the norms of lobbying explicitly rule that out. It might be said that just as (presumably) it would be inappropriate for a defense attorney to regulate his actions according to how they might benefit the prosecution, so it might be inappropriate for a lobbyist to regulate her behavior according to its benefits to society at large, rather than to her particular client. Second, someone might argue that lobbying for some particular interest group does not require subordinating the ends of that group to any prior, internal ends of lobbying itself. Instead, the argument will probably be that the ends of any particular lobbying activity are given externally, by the interest group by whom the lobbyist is engaged.

The claim that sophists teach the profession of lobbyist—rather than the profession of politician as Socrates understands it—seems to fit well with some aspects of the sophists' wider characterizations of themselves. For example, as Kamtekar notes, the sophists disavow any position on who should rule the state, and they advertise themselves as trying to impart purely instrumental knowledge to activists of all political persuasions (democrats, oligarchs, and prospective tyrants).

Now, none of this implies that society at large might not have reasons for restricting the kind of activity in which the sophists are engaged. (Presumably it does, and on my interpretation, part of Socrates' point is to bring this out.) But that is not the same as saying that it must be *internal to the goals of the profession of rhetoric* to be thinking of what is best for society. That only comes if one argues that a concern for benefiting the citizens at large is internal to the goals of the profession of lobbying, which is a characterization the sophists resist.

Of course, Socrates is arguably right to point out the conflict between the sophists and their rhetoric, on the one hand, and the legitimate ends of society on the other. The sophists claim to be either (a) socially neutral—and merely private individuals—or (b) actually socially beneficial. But Socrates' questions reveal that (b) is unfounded and (a) is dubious. Therefore, there are real questions about whether society should welcome this new profession.

Given all of this, I conclude that although Socrates uses the notion of profession to make his points and raise questions about sophistry, he does not do so in a nonpartisan way. If he were genuinely nonpartisan, he would focus the discussion on the question of which "profession" to allow or encourage and what its scope should be. But Socrates simply asserts his answers to these questions.

So far, I have claimed that Socrates is more conventional in his approach to political questions than Kamtekar's account suggests. However, I also think that her way of setting up the debate tends to obscure an important respect in which Socrates' political theory is genuinely radical. Kamtekar labels the first consideration by which regimes are judged—that which I have called "service to the citizens"—"protection." However, this term seems to me misleading because it suggests that the notion of protection must now cover a lot of ground.

First, one possible concern is protection from external threats. This seems to be what Homer's Sarpedon and Pseudo-Xenophon have in mind in the passages Kamtekar mentions:

> Why is it you and I are honored before others ... it is our duty in the forefront of the Lykians to take our stand and bear our part of the blazing of battle. (Homer, *Illiad* XII 310-16, p. 37)

[In Athens] the poor and the people generally are right to have more than the highborn and wealthy for the reason that it is the people who man the ships and impart strength to the city; the steersmen, the boatswains, the sub-boatswains, the look-out officers, and the shipwrights —these are the ones who impart strength to the city far more than the hoplites, the high-born, and the good men. This being the case, it seems right for everyone to have a share in the magistracies, both allotted and elective, for anyone to be able to speak his mind if he wants to. (Pseudo-Xenophon, I.2; from Marchant 1984)[20]

Second, citizens might believe that politics is concerned with protection from internal forces as well. For example, as Kamtekar states, in Thucydides' account of the debate at Syracuse (6.39), "the oligarchs contend that the wealthy are best able to rule because they are the least tempted to take the city's money for themselves." Moreover, she characterizes the protection consideration in terms of preserving the citizens from "the violence of faction and feud." Similarly, in the same passage, the democratic leader Athenagoras responds to the oligarch's argument by saying: "While an oligarchy allows the many their shares of dangers; it takes more than its share of the profits—not only that, it runs off with everything" (Thucydides, 6.39).

Third, citizens might judge constitutions based on their effects on well-being. Hence, Kamtekar characterizes Pseudo-Xenophon as disapproving of the Athenian constitution "because the Athenians prefer the well-being of the inferior at the expense of the superior (I.1)" and refers to the "the standard characterization of the ruler as a shepherd" in Homer and Xenophon.

This spectrum of views suggests two things. First, the label "protection" is misleading. As I have suggested, it is better to think of the consideration as one of the services the ruler says he will provide to the ruled, where these include, but are not limited to, protection. Second, the distinctions that are internal to the category may be at least as important as those external to it. By this I mean that much in political theory rests on how one understands the scope of politics, that is, the things with which it is legitimately concerned. Freedom from external threats, for example, seems like a very minimal security concern. Freedom from internal strife moves further than this but would still be compatible with a minimal night watchman state favored by some contemporary libertarians. But well-being is a more robust concern, suggesting the purview of a welfare state or liberal democracy. Finally, and most importantly, Socrates' own characterization of the interests of the citizens with which politics is legitimately concerned seems wider than any of these (cf. *Grg.* 522b-e). Socrates thinks that the ruler should be most concerned with *making* the citizens good. But this apparently perfectionist concern goes far beyond what many people in the "protection" camp would consider society's legitimate role. Indeed, it is a substantial enough revision that it may imply that Socrates is, after all, trying to effect a radical transformation in how the traditional "Who should rule?" question is to be understood. However, this is not a transformation that would necessarily endear him to contemporary audiences. Many modern liberals insist on either the complete or at least a partial neutrality of the state with respect to the personal values of the citizens and their visions of how they should live their lives. In this respect, then, many would find Socrates markedly illiberal.

In summary, I agree with Kamtekar that part of what is important about Socrates' political thought is his claim that rulers must have specific credentials and so be answerable to the citizenry in some ways. Still, I doubt that this implies that he was responsible for a conceptual revolution. In my view, the basic idea that political institutions might be assessed in a nonpartisan way—from the point of view of the people as such—was already at least implicit in Greek political writing, and it is implausible to assert that it was not explicit in actual discussion, given that the historical record is so thin. Moreover, to the extent to which Socrates' arguments about the profession of politics are revolutionary, they are not nonpartisan in any interesting sense. For one thing, Socrates aims to dismiss some views through arguments that—irrespective of how persuasive they are to his own side, and indeed to most of us—would be regarded as deeply question-begging by his opponents. For another, Socrates expands the notion of answerability and the scope of politics in a radical, and even potentially unwelcome, way.

5 Pessimism

Kamtekar's third objection to Socrates' political thought is that he is implausibly pessimistic about the prospects for a reasonable politics.[21] This charge might look less threatening if we paid more attention to its context.

First, there is the matter of our reaction to Socrates. As we have seen, there is no textual evidence (in Plato's writings or anywhere else) that Socrates was a partisan of democracy. But there is evidence of an opposition to authoritarianism. For one thing, as Popper observes, Socrates does appear in some ways to be a radical individualist, and this individualism is in tension with authoritarian regimes. For another, his emphasis on the need to justify political institutions to those affected by them is radical in his time and also closely related to the central tenet of many modern liberal theories. In short, Socrates has the kinds of sympathies that are characteristic of modern liberal theorists, particularly those with a central concern for autonomy, such as Mill, Kant, and Rawls. So, we have the feeling that Socrates ought to be a liberal, and since most modern liberals are democrats, this makes us think that he ought to be sympathetic to democracy.[22]

Second, we must recognize that there is some distance between what we think of as democracy and Socrates' own vision and experience of it. In the contemporary United States and Europe, the main political institutions are not democracies in Socrates' sense, but rather elected aristocracies or oligarchies. Moreover, at least in theory, these institutions are responsible for, and intervene in, only a limited sphere of their citizens' lives and do incorporate individual protections.

Nevertheless, third, Socrates' concerns about democracy are not completely foreign to contemporary audiences. On the one hand, consider Kamtekar's complaint that Socrates has a "low estimate of most people's capacity for political judgment." The basic reason for this low estimation is his concern about the average person's ability to discern truth and good arguments from rhetoric and manipulation. But this concern is alive and well in the contemporary polis. Citizens of all political persuasions worry about a political environment dominated by big media, spin doctors, political parties, special interest politics, and money. Moreover, they have specific concerns about the role of sound bites, attack ads, and simplistic cultural imagery in influencing elections. People often say that "we get the government that we deserve," and they do not mean this as a compliment.

On the other hand, consider Kamtekar's charge that Socrates has a "high estimate of the specialized knowledge required for politics." One aspect of this is the concern that political leaders should have the kind of knowledge required to engage in sensible political leadership: knowledge of the world, human nature, and the social and political context. However, this too is a prevalent demand in the modern context.[23] Indeed, many complain that modern elections and political parties tend to undervalue real expertise and instead favor mediocrity. Another aspect of the concern is Socrates' belief that political leaders should have moral virtue and so an understanding of and deep commitment to the common good. In particular, he worries that the politics of rhetoric encourages the development of character traits that are good for neither political leaders nor their citizens. Again, these worries are not unusual in contemporary democracies. Moreover, they are, if anything, more pronounced in the modern state, where so much of what political leaders do is hidden from view or obscured by spin.

Socrates' concerns thus seem highly relevant and widely shared in the contemporary context. Moreover, they are deep enough that many people agree with Sir Winston Churchill's famous statement that "democracy is the very worst of political systems, except for all the others that have been tried."[24] If Socrates' attitudes are implausible—as Kamtekar claims—then it is not because he is pessimistic but because he is much more pessimistic than contemporary Churchillians.

In my view, Socrates is much more pessimistic, and this is part of what is so interesting, challenging, and important about his politics. Unlike Churchill, Socrates appears not to take much comfort in the "except for all the others" observation, regarding it as a tragic, rather than slightly regrettable, state of affairs. Popper may be right that Socrates' ideal would be an open society of well-educated and liberal-minded individuals. But Socrates himself seems to be skeptical that merely "waking people up" will be enough to achieve this. Why is this?

Socrates believes that it is training in wisdom directed toward the common good that constitutes the real profession of politics. For such a politics to be possible, citizens would have to be largely immune to rhetorical manipulation and pandering. This implies, Socrates seems to think, that they would need to be highly educated for the purpose by people who knew how to educate them. However, this, of course, poses a number of problems: Where are we to find such educators? How can we prevent their being corrupted and guard against abuses of power if they are corrupted? How are we to convince people to put all this in place to begin with? Is trying to do so even compatible with the liberal values that Socrates apparently holds?

In the end, Socrates seems skeptical about all of this. First, he believes that the existing political education—that provided by the sophists—has the wrong target. It focuses on mastering rhetoric, rather than overcoming it, and it does not investigate the human good, but rather treats naked ambition and existing desires as their own warrant.

Second, Socrates' views about knowledge imply that suitably educating people to be effective citizens would be a very demanding business. As Plato makes apparent, this makes it tempting to think that centralized and systematic mass education is needed; but this seems to require giving over to authorities a huge amount of power over a large range of public life, a prospect which is worrying given Socrates' concerns about existing institutions. Conspicuously, Socrates does not begin by advocating a massive social engineering project. Instead, he is more concerned with the prior question of whether it is even possible to teach the most central knowledge required—that of virtue. In addition, in the absence of a compelling answer to that question, it is hard to believe that he would be comfortable with a top-down approach and quite reasonable to think that he would fear that the cure might be worse than the disease.[25]

Third, in any case, Socrates seems to believe that people as they are would never accept the kind of leadership required to bring about a reasonable politics. Getting the assent of the people requires addressing them where they are, more susceptible to rhetoric than truth. But, in Socrates' view, reasonable political leaders would never stoop to rhetoric, and moreover, if they did so, this would be self-defeating, blinding the citizens to truth, and damaging the leaders themselves (e.g., *Ap.* 31d). Given this concern, Socrates believes that the only course open to him is to stay out of regular political discourse and pursue his solo educational mission, trying to benefit his fellow citizens on an individual basis, and in doing so lay the foundations for real political reform. Moreover, he believes that even this more limited kind of activity is ultimately doomed, as the forces of blind and acquisitive political power will not tolerate his presence for long.

Socrates, then, is a severe pessimist about politics. Still, his reasons for pessimism are not glib; they are not even unfamiliar to us, but rather fall at the extreme end of what many citizens and writers have believed about politics throughout the ages. At the heart of these worries are two basic challenges to the possibility of a reasonable politics: first, that it demands a vision of citizens that seems impossible to put into place—and perhaps also to maintain once in place— without violating the very values it seeks to honor, and, second, that a society with unreasonable politics will probably not tolerate any substantial exercise of the relevant values for long (at least when they seem likely to lead to change).

6 Resolving the Paradoxes

One advantage of this sketch of Socrates' pessimism is that it can resolve the first paradox: Socrates' political thought can explain his personal behavior. In the normal political realm, Socrates believes that it is impossible for one to bring about the kind of transformation needed for reasonable politics without using rhetoric and thereby damaging oneself and those whom one seeks to transform and without creating institutions which, in the absence of a reasonable politics to run them, are even more dangerous. Given all of this, Socrates shies away from traditional politics, fearing that he would do neither himself nor others any good in the effort, and engages in his own nontraditional politics, although he is fully aware of its limited prospects for success and the ultimate likelihood that he himself will perish.

Thus, Socrates' political theory is consistent with his acts of heroism. First, when he thinks that he can or must act, he does so. Hence, he refuses to cooperate in political vendettas and so protects individuals against great harms. On such occasions, the action is necessarily individual and does not require an appeal to the ways of rhetoric or the faulty values of the polis. However, second, on other occasions, where he believes that his action would either be futile or incur further harms, Socrates does not act. These are the situations—including those mentioned by Vlastos—in which he would need to appeal to rhetoric and the erroneous values of the assembly in order to have a real chance of success. Third, most of the time he avoids direct political action but devotes himself to pursuing his core liberal values in the only way he thinks is possible, even when he believes that he cannot ultimately succeed, and that his own destruction is more or less inevitable. Socrates is not, then, inconsistent in his public and personal attitudes.

He is also not inconsistent in his views about political engagement—the second paradox. His neglect of protections for the individual, major political crises, and politics in the traditional sense are not borne of complacency. He stands by his claims about the seriousness of social and political demands on the individual and seeks to live them out in the only way he sees as possible, even given the severe costs and low probability of success. It is just that he is a radical pessimist about public life under democratic systems, and this pessimism colors his attitude to traditional political action.[26]

Finally, this account of Socrates' politics can help us with the third paradox, of understanding his role as a founder of political thought. For one thing, his is a useful pessimism. In our time, as in his, some citizens of democracies are too prone to believe that the mere granting of a vote, or the power to speak in an assembly, is enough to justify political institutions. But Socrates points out the serious difficulties facing this view. In addition, Socrates raises deep questions about the purpose of politics, including what freedoms are desirable, whether they are secure under particular institutions, and whether our social structures actually contribute to our good, as individuals or as a people. In short, Socrates poses central challenges that later political philosophy then struggles to answer: What features would a decent political society have? How would it be justified, especially to its own citizens? Is a genuinely good society even possible?

More generally, much of the debate about Socrates' politics concerns whether he prefers democracy or authoritarianism. To my mind, this misses the central thrust of his contribution. Though I agree with most other recent writers in believing that he prefers open, liberal, and even democratic society to some extent over the available alternatives, I do not think that specific forms of government are his main concern. (This helps to explain his relative silence about how to design and defend specific institutions.) In my view, Socrates is most worried about the characteristic defects of political systems *considered as such*. Moreover, he asks the right questions about this, and he is not at all out of date in his concerns. His focus is on the very possibility of a good, well-functioning society, and in particular one that is responsive to reasons and to the (true) well-being of its citizens. In the face of the complacent and cynical musings of some of his predecessors and contemporaries, and the fanciful utopian thinking of some of his successors, this is a useful and vital contribution. Socrates' challenges are ones we should continue to take seriously today.[27]

Notes

1. For these and other translations of Plato in this essay, see Cooper (1997).
2. In this essay, I assume (for the sake of argument) that this is the person described by Plato in the so-called early dialogues and perhaps in the *Gorgias*, *Meno*, and *Republic* as well. I do not consider whether a more unitary (e.g., nondevelopmental) account of Plato's works is possible or plausible and hope not to beg any questions on that issue here.
3. Both examples are cited by Kamtekar (2006, pp. 214–15), who sets up a similar statement of the paradox; Popper (1966, p. 128) also cites the latter example.
4. Kamtekar calls this the "Popperian complaint." Still, as she recognizes, though Popper does make such a criticism of Plato, his attitude to Socrates is very different (as we shall see below).
5. It seems especially difficult to reconcile this extremism with the fact that Socrates has shown by his own actions that he is ready to defy that authority in some cases and when these cases seem to be precisely ones in which he can protect others by doing so.
6. This concern is, of course, the subject of much scholarly debate (see, e.g., Kraut 1984 and Brickhouse and Smith 1994). But since addressing it would take us far beyond the bounds of one short essay, I shall leave it aside here.
7. It is worth noting that there is some disconnect between the theoretical charges as well. Why is Socrates so complacent about the authority of the state when he recognizes the epistemic problems? Why, given them, is he so focused on the question of who should rule, rather than on establishing the limits of authority?
8. Popper's hesitation is evident from the way he discusses the possibility. For example, he introduces it with the phrase "*It is not unlikely* that he [Socrates] demanded (like Plato) that the best should rule" (p. 128, emphasis added). Similarly, he likes to qualify future mention of Socrates' answer to the question. For example, on p. 129, he says, "the Socratic demand (*if he ever raised this demand*) that the best, i.e., the intellectually honest, should rule ..." (emphasis added).
9. Popper defines individualism as opposed to collectivism (Popper 1966, pp. 100–102). When it is coupled with altruism, he claims that it is "the basis of our Western civilization" and "there has been no other thought which has been so powerful in the moral development of man" (ibid., p. 102).
10. Kraut (1984, p. 205, note 31, citing Guthrie) adds that if knowledge of one's own ignorance alone counted as wisdom, then Socrates would have said that the slave is already wise when, realizing that he cannot double the area of a given square, he becomes eager to learn (*Meno* 84a3-c2). But even when the slave finally sees the solution, Socrates says that he still lacks mathematical knowledge (*Meno* 85b8-e7).
11. Kraut (ibid., p. 208) suggests that Socrates doubts that human beings even have the capacity to attain the knowledge necessary to rule well. This suggests that the problem arises even for ideal theory, if we include in that idea such capacities (as, e.g., Rawls does in his concept of "realistic utopia"). It also makes the Socrates neglect even more surprising.
12. This claim is, of course, controversial. In it, I follow Kraut (1984) and Irwin (1977, 1996).
13. This, presumably, is the best way for an accommodation strategy to address the passages that Kraut cites. The strength of Kraut's view is that this is hardly the most obvious reading of these passages. But it is worth remembering that our overall understanding of Socrates also matters and Kraut's interpretation has significant difficulties here that our accommodation strategy does not face.

14. Kamtekar, 217. Kamtekar calls the first consideration one of "protection," rather than service. But I prefer the original label, since it captures the concern for well-being that I mention later.
15. Kamtekar herself cites the passage in support of her own view, so this reading is not the only possible one.
16. This response is in the published version of Kamtekar's paper but not in the original presentation version, suggesting that it is intended specifically as a response to my objection.
17. In the passage above, Kamtekar claims that although there are arguments before Socrates that are (a) in principle nonpartisan, (b) "in practice they are never detached from the partisan point of view advancing them." So, she is assuming a contrast between (a) and (b) which rests on a sense of "detached" that is contrasted with and separable from the possibility of nonpartisan argument. It is not clear to me what this sense of "detached" is.
18. Marchant (1984).
19. One might object to my use of the term "partisan" here. It is true that in this argument Socrates is neither speaking as an advocate of democracy, oligarchy, or monarchy nor explicitly ruling out one of these approaches. Hence, if we restrict the notion of "partisan argument" to such contexts, then we cannot call Socrates a partisan here. Still, such a restriction seems unwarranted. Clearly, the stark version of the superiority argument is influential in both oligarchic and monarchistic camps, and one of the major considerations at stake in the political debate as Socrates finds it. To simply rule it out in the way that Socrates does—by assuming things that a proponent of the stark view has no need to concede—therefore does seem partisan at a deeper level.
20. Note that Pseudo-Xenophon appears to take this to be a sufficient reason for democracy. This becomes important when we come to my claim about Socrates' expansion of the usual understanding of the service consideration.
21. As we have seen, Kamtekar herself does not have much to say about this problem; she merely stresses that Socrates' concerns about ignorance apply not only to democracy but to other kinds of political regime as well.
22. On the other hand, of course, we must contrast Socrates' apparent sympathy for liberalism with his clear endorsement of perfectionism. Some believe that perfectionism and liberalism are incompatible. And Plato's views at least appear to have strong antiliberal elements.
23. For example, in the 2008 presidential election campaign, Barack Obama was publicly criticized for lacking executive experience and John McCain for confusion about the basics of the political situation in Iraq.
24. Hansard Society, November 11, 1947.
25. Remember here that Socrates is thinking of mass education in the virtues.
26. For one criticism of his pessimism, see Vlastos (1971, pp. 15–17).
27. I thank Roger Crisp, Norman Dahl, David Keyt, and Jean Roberts for their comments on an earlier draft of this chapter. Several sections were originally written and presented as comments on Rachana Kamtekar's "The Politics of Plato's Socrates" at the *Arizona Colloquium in Ancient Philosophy* in Spring 2005. A revised version of Kamtekar's paper later appeared as Kamtekar (2006). I am grateful to Mark McPherran for the invitation to Arizona and to Eric Hutton, Paul Woodruff, and Rachana herself for helpful discussion. It should be clear from what follows that I have been heavily influenced by her approach. Even though I do not, in the end, endorse it, I appreciate the scholarship of it, the questions it raises, and the inspiration provided for further study.

Bibliography

Bennett, Jonathan. 1974. The conscience of Huckleberry Finn. *Philosophy* 49: 123–134.
Brickhouse, Thomas C., and Nicholas D. Smith. 1994. Socratic politics, chapter 5. In *Plato's Socrates*, ed. Thomas C. Brickhouse and Nicholas D. Smith. Oxford: Oxford University Press.
Cooper, John. 1997. *Plato: Complete works*. Indianapolis: Hackett Publishing Company.

Irwin, T.H. 1977. *Plato's moral theory*. Oxford: Oxford University Press.
Irwin, T.H. 1996. *Plato's ethics*. Oxford: Oxford University Press.
Kamtekar, Rachana. 2006. The politics of Plato's Socrates. In *A companion to Socrates*, ed. Sara Ahbel-Rappe and Rachana Kamtekar, 214–227. Oxford: Blackwell Publishing.
Kraut, R. 1984. *Socrates and the state*. Princeton: Princeton University Press.
Marchant, E.C. (ed. and trans.). 1984. *Pseudo-Xenophon: The Athenian constitution*. Perseus project. Available at: http://www.perseus.tufts.edu/hopper/text?doc=Perseus%3Atext%3A1999.01.0158&redirect=true
Plutarch. 2008. *Plutarch's lives, vol. 12*. Charleston: Bibliolife.
Popper, Karl. 1966. *The open society and its enemies. vol. 1, The spell of Plato*. Princeton: Princeton University Press.
Robinson, Eric (ed.). 2004. *Ancient Greek democracy*. Oxford: Blackwell Publishing.
Strauss, L. 1989. On classical political philosophy. In *An introduction to political philosophy*, ed. Hilail Gildin. Detroit: Wayne State University Press.
Vlastos, Gregory. 1971. The paradox of Socrates. In *The philosophy of Socrates*, ed. Gregory Vlastos. New York: Anchor.

Retaliation in the *Crito*

Merrill Ring

1 Setting the Stage

R. E. Allen (1980, p. 66) rightly locates the *Crito* in one major fifth-century intellectual context. "But the dialogue stands as comment on a great fifth-century debate, conducted not only by sophists and dramatists but by plain men and politicians, on the nature of law and legal obligation." I am guessing that Allen is misled by contemporary problems to overlook the fact that another intellectual current of the fifth century involved a debate, perhaps not as powerful, about the acceptability of retaliation, of vengeance. While the major dramatic work in that regard was Aeschylus' *Oresteia*, the *Crito* must be seen as playing as significant a role in the aftermath of that debate as it did in the one which Allen mentions.

It shall be my aim here to subject what Socrates has to say about retaliation in the *Crito* to close scrutiny, both descriptive and critical. The outcome of this investigation will not be favorable to Socrates' case for refusing to escape.

After hearing and rejecting Crito's case that Socrates should escape, Socrates produces an extended argument by which he attempts to establish that it would be wrong for him to escape. His case has the following form: he secures Crito's acquiescence in two principles—that retaliation is wrong and that one ought to keep one's agreements. He then argues, speaking as a personification of the laws which constitute Athens as the *polis* it is, that to escape would be to act contrary to each of those two principles. Hence, it would be wrong for him to escape.

While David Keyt was not able to render me more than an amateur in Greek philosophy, he has shaped my philosophical practice so deeply that, no matter what topic I write about, his footprints are all over the result.

M. Ring (✉)
Department of Philosophy, California State University-Fullerton,
Fullerton, CA 92834-6868, USA
e-mail: m36ring@earthlink.net

There are some preliminary points to be made concerning the above description of the outline of Socrates' argument.

(1) Regarding Socrates' conclusion that "it would be wrong for him to escape," the best translation of *adikein* in the *Crito* is as "wrong," not as "unjust." The issue of those competing translations is, of course, a staple of Platonic commentary. Commentators agree that in general either is possible. There are some arguments that, in the text of the *Crito*, *adikein* must be, or should be, understood in terms of justice. None of those arguments succeeds in establishing the point.[1] What Socrates brings to bear on his proposed escape is the question of whether it would be right or wrong to do so.

(2) Concerning Crito's "acquiescence in two principles," something must be said both about my counting and, the easier of the matters, the declaration that there are principles involved. Nobody disagrees that Socrates attempts to defend his refusal to escape on principled grounds. What commentators overlook, however, is that, even though Socrates lacks the relevant modern terminology, he explicitly contrasts the proper way of proceeding, namely, via principles, with Crito's procedure which looks to consequences. His entire speech from 48b-d says, in effect, "We must not consider consequences—namely, matters of money and the effects on my reputation, on my children, and especially on my life—but rather what can be determined to be right, i.e., what follows from adherence to moral principles." There is more than a little flavor of Kant in the *Crito*'s Socrates.

While there certainly are a number of principles enunciated in the relevant portion of the text, 49a-e, only two are immediately employed by Socrates to establish that it would be wrong for him to escape. The others occur in various lemmata aimed at establishing one of that pair of principles. All of that will become clear in the body of this essay.

I shall not work through the standard writings on the *Crito* to show that my description of Socrates' positive arguments differs significantly from what is currently available: that would take me too far out of my way. What I contend here should be compared not only with the text but also with other commentators.[2]

(3) With respect to my claim that as part of the case Socrates makes against escape, he "argues, speaking as a personification of the laws," I should note that this characterization implies that I am not adhering to the recent thesis of Roslyn Weiss (1998) that the speech of the Laws does not contain Socrates' own views and so cannot be used, as I do, for his argumentation as to what he ought to do. The present account is offered within the interpretive tradition which finds that the long speech of the Laws of Athens contains theses importantly employed in the construction of Socrates' case that his escaping would be wrong. I shall make no attempt here to present and criticize Weiss' views: that is an entirely different project. The way to see my contribution to the discussion is to understand it as presenting the best critical representation of Socrates' arguments against escape within the orthodox tradition of reading the *Crito*.

I shall, then, working in that non-Weissian tradition, take it that Socrates, having told Crito to ignore consequences and stick to matters of principle (48b-d), leads up to his case against escape from 48d to 49a: "Let us examine this question [whether it is right or wrong for me to try to get out of here without the approval of Athens (48b-c)] my good friend, and if you have any objections to the argument, make them and I will listen...."[3] From 49a to 49e, he produces the (two) principles which he shall rely upon. At 49e-50a he asks what follows from those principles: "Consider now what follows. If we leave here without the city's permission, will we be causing undeserved harm? And shall we be breaking a legitimately established agreement?"[4] Since Crito cannot say what follows from Socrates' principles and cannot answer those questions, Socrates produces the speech of the Laws which spells out the answers and thereby provides the remainder of the case against escape.

2 The Project

The second of the two principles upon which Socrates hangs his case concerns the propriety of fulfilling agreements. Having obtained Crito's acceptance of that principle, without any argument being necessary, he then holds that he has an agreement with Athens concerning his obedience to her laws and lawful decisions. From those facts and that principle, the conclusion is derived that escaping would be wrongly violating that agreement.

Overwhelmingly, scholarly writing on the *Crito* and the issue of Socrates' case against escape has been concerned with the manner of, and the legitimacy of, Socrates' application of the principle "One ought to keep one's agreements" to questions of (his) obeying the law. That attention is deserved, for the issues are important both for understanding Socrates and for understanding our own obligations to the state. I shall not, however, be further adding to that discussion.

My topic is rather the first of those principles and the use to which Socrates puts it. The principle in question is "Retaliation is wrong." Socrates, holding that retaliation is wrong, then argues, again in the speech of the Laws, that escaping would be retaliating against Athens for the verdict at his trial and hence would be wrong in light of the principle.

There has been very little consideration of this material in discussions of the *Crito*. That is due, in part, to the fact that translations have soft-pedaled that way of putting the principle, thereby helping to obscure the fact that retaliation is one of Socrates' chief concerns in the dialogue. The preference for translating *antadikein* has been for some soft equivalent, such as "in return," "repay," "hitting back," and "giving back." Socrates, however, investigates whether or not it is right to injure, to harm, someone because they have harmed you—and that is what retaliation is. The matter could legitimately be put, and terms thus translated, even more strongly: one of Socrates' major concerns in the *Crito* is with the rightness or wrongness of revenge, vengeance. However, I shall opt for the more moderate "retaliation."

The absence of discussion of the issue in the critical philosophical literature is not only produced by the weak rendering of *antadikein*. Inquiry into the *Crito* has also been shaped by our own political concerns: the issues of obligation to the state and of civil disobedience are clearly relevant to our life and times, while the theme of retaliation strikes us as less central to our moral and political concerns.

It will be helpful to be more specific here at the outset about both the nature of Socrates' argument and my intentions with respect to it. His argument concerning retaliation can be schematized as follows:

(P1-a) Retaliation is wrong.
(P2-a) Escaping would be retaliating.
(C-a) Hence, escaping would be wrong.

It should be noticed that Socrates realizes that something more than those two premises is required to show conclusively that escape would be wrong. In particular cases, principles may be "overridden"; that is, action contrary to a principle may be justified by the facts of the case. Socrates (not being Kantian at this point) realizes that merely to establish the fact that escaping would be retaliating is not sufficient, even in light of the principle, to establish the wrongness of his escape: for there may be features of the particular case which would justify escape. That is, he is aware that he also must show that this particular piece of retaliation would not be justified. The recognition comes out at 50a where he asks "Will we be causing undeserved harm?" While the issue of causing harm concerns whether escape would be retaliating, the reference to "undeserved" concerns whether the act might be a case of justified retaliation. The proof that his retaliation would not be justified comes later in the speech of the Athenian Laws when it is contended that the polis stands in a quasi-parental relation to its citizens and that, in his case, it has fulfilled (admirably) its quasi-parental responsibilities. (That same contention plays a role in the argument concerning fulfilling agreements.)

With that addition, the basic schema is complete. What I shall henceforth be concerned with are Socrates' attempts in the *Crito* to establish each of the premises (P1-a) and (P2-a) of that basic argument. It is these lemmata to the main argument that I shall find to fail. In the next section, I shall examine his attempts to show that retaliation is wrong, and in the section following, the object of interest will be his argument that for him to escape would be to retaliate.

3 Proving the Major Premise

While Socrates does not argue for the principle that one ought to keep one's agreements—that is stated and Crito immediately accepts it (49e)—he does argue at some length that retaliation is wrong. There has been no critical examination of that argument. This is due, I believe, to the thought that, in condemning retaliation, Socrates was taking a higher moral position than that of his contemporaries. But even if his view is a moral advance, it is of moral, as well as scholarly, interest to see whether his defense of that position is acceptable.

Socrates' strategy is to establish the principle that retaliation is wrong by showing that it follows from other principles. He does not, that is, object to retaliation by pointing to undesirable consequences. The actual conduct of the strategy (49a-e) involves two independent maneuvers: he attempts to derive the wrongness of retaliation from two different first principles. Let us take these up one at a time. The first derivation (49a-c) is as follows:

> S: Do we say that one must never do wrong willingly? Or is it a matter of circumstances? ... Is that our view or not?
> C: That is our view.
> S: So one must never do wrong.
> C: No.
> S: Then one must not do wrong even when one has been wronged, which is contrary to what most people believe.
> C: Evidently not.

That argument has the following schema:

(P1-b) One must never willingly do wrong (no matter what the circumstances.)
(C1-b) Therefore, one must not do wrong even when (the circumstance is that) one has been wronged.
(C2-b) Therefore, retaliation is wrong.

Before assessing the argument, there are four comments to be made. The first two of these comments concern the relationship of my representation of the argument to what is found in the text. (1) What I have as the first premise is a conflation of two separate lines in the text, namely, "(Do we say that) one must never do wrong willingly? Or is it a matter of circumstances?" and "So one must never do wrong." I believe this conflation does no violence to the original. (2) Much more importantly, the ultimate conclusion in the representation, (C2-b), is not given in the text. I am treating what is given as an enthymeme with the obvious conclusion omitted. More will be said of that later.

The other two comments concern matters that are found in the text, matters which are not strictly part of the argument yet which are very important for understanding the context of Socrates' attempted proof. (3) The two occurrences in the text of the above premise are separated by some moral exhortation by Socrates. This exhortation, marked in the quotation above by the ellipsis, runs:

> Is doing wrong never good or honorable, which is what we have concluded in the past? Or have our conclusions been abandoned in our recent circumstances? After all these years, Crito, should we think that our talk has been nothing more than a children's game? Surely the truth is what we used to say that it was—no matter whether most people agree with us or not, no matter whether believing it makes life easier or harder. Wrongdoing is completely harmful and shameful for the one who does it. (49a-b)

Socrates is attempting to secure agreement from Crito with what he wants to use as the premise in the argument. What should be noticed about that exhortation are the following points: it is said that Crito and Socrates have, in the past, accepted as a matter of rational conviction that one must never willingly do wrong, that there is a danger of surrendering their conviction in the present, emotion-laden, circumstances; it is implied that in adhering to this principle, they are in opposition to the many (*hoi polloi*). The nature of the popular view is not made clear however. There are two equally plausible interpretations: that the many simply reject the principle that one must never do wrong willingly, perhaps reject it in favor of a contrary principle, or that the many accept the principle in an attenuated form, "One must not do wrong willingly," dropping the "never" because it is thought that in some circumstances (e.g., where one has been wronged), wrongdoing is either justifiable or excusable. It is not necessary to decide between them. It is enough to recognize that Socrates presents his argument in the context of a claim that the many do not accept the principle which constitutes his first premise.

(4) Lastly, Socrates twice claims that his (and Crito's) views are contrary to those of the many, once in the exhortation and once as appended to the textual occurrence of the conclusion (C1-b). That remark concerning what most people believe in connection with (C1-b) should be specially noticed. Since this conclusion will turn out to be equivalent to a denial of the propriety of retaliation, Socrates is in effect saying that most people would defend the propriety of retaliation. (The *Oresteia* obviously was not successful in changing the view of the majority.) Similar interpretive options as above are open here; the popular view may be either that retaliation is right or that retaliation is justifiable or excusable in certain circumstances. Again, whatever the detailed reading of what most people hold, the conclusion of this argument on Socrates' part is explicitly located in a context of claimed opposition to the view of the many.

The preliminaries now completed, it is time to examine the derivation critically. Start with the premise (P1-b). Let us henceforth drop the clause "no matter what the circumstances" since that is but a reinforcement of the word "never" occurring in the body of the premise. Further, for immediate purposes only, let us read the premise as "One must never do wrong," that is, omitting for now the word "willingly."

What remains certainly has the look of a moral principle. That is, it has the right shape and the words seem appropriate to its being a principle. However, it is not and cannot be a principle, moral, or otherwise. I do not mean that it is an unacceptable principle, as, for example, "One must try to hit children in crosswalks." Rather it is not a principle at all. A genuine principle is such because it has the function of guiding conduct, because it has a role to play in determining what a person shall do and in justifying actions. Notice that very little is imposed by this condition: factual propositions also have a role to play in guiding and justifying conduct. A principle, however, functions to specify that some type of act is right or wrong, required or forbidden (or permitted). Principles come in a wide variety of linguistic shapes. Nonetheless, it is correct to say that they have the canonical form "Such-and-such kind of things are right/wrong."

Consider now "One must never do wrong." That is a linguistic form exhibited by genuine principles, for example, "One must never steal." Putting that last in canonical form, we obtain "Stealing is wrong." Now if we attempt to put Socrates' premise in that same canonical form, we obtain "Wrongdoing is wrong." So unmasked, Socrates' premise does not pick out any type of act and add the information that this sort of act is wrong and so to be avoided.[5] What Socrates has done is to employ a disguised tautology rather than a substantial principle as a premise from which to derive his principle about retaliation.

At this point, it will be recalled that I have been temporarily working with a reduced version of the "principle." The original version in the *Crito* reads "One must never do wrong willingly." It might be objected to my argument above that the word "willingly" makes all the difference. What is otherwise an empty tautology becomes a genuine principle with the addition of "willingly." To respond to that objection properly will require going a long way round.

It is reasonable to suppose that the presence of the qualification "willingly" has led commentators to overlook the peculiarity of Socrates' premise. For with that word, this premise can be heard to be another assertion of the familiar Socratic claim "No one does wrong willingly."

While it is obvious that there is some connection between the *Crito* and that familiar claim, it is not the case that the "principle" in question is another instance of Socrates' denial of *akrasia* (of weakness). What Socrates has to say in those places in the *Meno*, *Gorgias*, and *Protagoras* where he is shown arguing that no one does wrong willingly is quite incompatible with the advocacy and acceptance of a moral principle specifiable as "One must never do wrong willingly."

He argues in those other dialogues that people always conceive what they are doing as good or right. That, he claims, is a fact of human nature. Now what would be the connection between those views and the principled premise of the *Crito*? Suppose we attempt to say that the principle somehow lies behind the fact or produces the fact. That will not work. Saying that the fact is derived from the principle distorts Socrates' intention in speaking of a fact of human nature. Facts about how people are by nature are not contingent upon people adopting a principle of behavior. Moreover, if the (purported) fact that no one willingly does wrong were dependent upon "One must never willingly do wrong," then, to achieve the required universality of the fact ("No one willingly ..."), Socrates would be committed to holding that everyone has adopted that principle. In his exhortation of Crito, however, contrary to holding that everyone accepts the principle, he clearly implies that most people do not share that principle with him.

The principle that no one willingly does wrong, then, is not primitive for Socrates; it does not produce the fact about people's behavior. But any other purported connection between fact and principle will not do logically. It would follow from any other combination that "One must never do wrong willingly" is not an operable principle. If it is a matter of human nature that no one willingly does wrong, then no one can willingly do wrong. It would then be pointless to recommend and defend as a principle of conduct that one must never willingly do wrong. For such a recommendation and employment presupposes that it is possible for someone to do wrong willingly. If one urges the fact, logical consistency precludes advocating the principle.

If we compare the views of the *Meno*, *Gorgias*, and *Protagoras* with those of the *Crito*, we find Socrates in a difficulty analogous to that of Bentham: Socrates urges, on the one hand, that people should conduct themselves in a certain way, namely, that they should not do wrong willingly (as Bentham urges that people should seek pleasure and avoid pain); on the other hand, Socrates claims that people, being what they are, could not act otherwise, that is, could not do wrong willingly (as Bentham claims people could not fail to seek pleasure and avoid pain).

That particular inconsistency is just one feature of a larger problem. What must be recognized is that the implications of the *Crito* with respect to the possibility of weakness are not compatible with the view expressed in those other dialogues. Consider: as we have seen, Socrates exhorts Crito to retain his rational conviction in "One must never do wrong willingly," and it is clearly implied that Crito needs that support in order to maintain his conviction in the face of Socrates' impending death and consequently to be willing to connive at doing what is wrong. (That escaping would be wrong is already assumed at this point in the dialogue. That shows only that Socrates has thought his argument through. There are no questions begged.) It sounds as if Socrates were counseling Crito not to allow what he rationally holds to be overcome by fear. It must be remembered that "being overcome by fear" is mentioned in the *Protagoras* as an explanation offered by the many to account for some instances of weakness: knowingly doing wrong because one is afraid. Further, the fear of death and its effects on rational behavior is one of the major themes of both the *Crito* and the *Apology*. These considerations which bear on the question of whether the possibility of weakness is contemplated in the *Crito* are seconded by the very fact that the pronouncement "One must never do wrong willingly" is introduced there. In order for this pronouncement to be a guide to conduct, it must be possible for people willingly to do wrong. Given the previous considerations which form the context of its introduction, there is every reason to think that the Socrates of the *Crito* did realize that the offering of that "principle" presupposes that people (Crito even) might willingly do wrong.

The doctrine of the *Crito* is not, then, the typical Socratic view expressed in those other dialogues. The possibility of weakness is allowed there and the circumstance of "being overcome by fear" is offered to account for it.[6]

This excursus into weakness was undertaken in light of an objection that, while "One must never do wrong" is tautological, it becomes a substantial principle with the addition of the word "willingly." A remark of Woozley's constitutes a suggestion regarding the sorts of case in which such a principle would be applicable. In the *Apology*, Socrates tells of the time he and four others were summoned before the Thirty Tyrants and told to fetch Leon of Salamis for execution. The others complied; Socrates went home. Socrates comments "I should probably have been put to death for this, if the government had not fallen soon afterwards" (32d). About that situation, Woozley (1971, p. 306) says "This is in line with one theme in the *Crito*, viz. that...there are no circumstances in which one should willingly do wrong; if that is so, a man should not willingly do wrong, even when he receives an order from his government to do something which is in fact wrong." Woozley writes as if the situation were as follows: Socrates was ordered by the government to do something which he knew to be wrong; he might have given in to the fear of death or punishment and so willingly done wrong; instead, he acted upon the principle "One must never willingly do wrong" and so did not do what was wrong.

Will that work? Could "One must never willingly do wrong" function as a principle in such cases?

If we look at Socrates' own words in the *Apology*, we find that he did not see his action as depending on such a principle. He says "On this occasion, however, I again made it clear not by my words but by my actions that death did not matter to me ...; but that it mattered all the world to me that I should do nothing wrong or wicked. Powerful as it was, the government did not terrify me into doing a wrong action" (33d). What he was ordered to do was wrong. Why, in the circumstances, did he not do what was wrong? It was not because he followed a principle saying that one should not knowingly or willingly do wrong. What he cites as having a bearing on his behavior, over and above the wrongness of what he was ordered to do, is first having been serious about the nature and requirements of morality (its mattering a great deal that he should not do something wrong). Being serious about an act which is known to be wrong is not the same thing as bringing a further principle to bear on the situation. Second, he cites as affecting his behavior the fact that death did not matter to him, that he had established a proper attitude toward death (especially relative to doing what is wrong.) In short, Socrates' own explanation of why he did not give in to fear and so do what was wrong is that he was serious about what it is for something to be wrong and that he had come to see death as not fearful.

The trouble with thinking that any further principle could prevent a potential weak act is that the agent is already saying "I know it is wrong—but (e.g.,) I'm afraid." That is, the principles having a bearing upon the situation have already been invoked and yet the moral understanding of what is to be done has been overcome by fear, by something, as it were, unprincipled. What the agent needs is a diminution of the fear or a review of the moral situation, not another principle. What is wrong with the specific "principle" in question ("It is not right to willingly do wrong") is that it tells the agent absolutely nothing new. He or she already knows that by doing the weak act, he or she would be willingly doing something wrong.

I would not wish to imply that the words "One must never willingly do wrong" could have no effect on someone in such a situation. So might a hug or a tear or a drink—and these probably have a better chance of shoring up one's convictions than those words. But whatever works, works. If those words do succeed here, however, it would not be qua principle.

Woozley seems to have seen the situation in the *Crito* this way: recognizing implicitly that the "principle" was introduced in a context in which weakness is being allowed and that its introduction is a sign of that admission, he took it that the principle was introduced as a defense against weakness, as something that could be invoked against an incipient weak act. On the contrary, no principle could function that way. Moreover, it is clear from the *Crito* that Socrates realized that. What he exhorts Crito to do is not to lose his conviction in just that principle. If "One must never willingly do wrong" is introduced as a principle, it too can be the sort of thing that one can fail to live up to because one is weak.

If the kind of case Woozley cites cannot support the idea that "One must never do wrong willingly" is a genuine principle, what kind of case could? None. The addition of the word "willingly" makes no difference. The added word is unable to convert the tautology "One must never do wrong" into a substantial principle. For what we have with the additional word is something whose canonical form is "Doing wrong willingly is wrong." That too does not specify some kind of act and add the information that this kind of act is wrong. Rather it repeats itself and so the "principle" remains a tautology.

So much for criticism of the premise (P1-b) of Socrates' first derivation. The logic of the step from that premise to the first conclusion ("Therefore, one must not do wrong even when one has been wronged") is impeccable. If one must never do wrong, and if wrong is wrong no matter what the circumstances, then when the circumstance is that one has been wronged, wrong is still (of course) wrong and so must not be done.

The ultimate conclusion "Retaliation is wrong," however, does not follow from "One must not do wrong even when one has been wronged" unless an additional tacit premise is inserted. What is required for it to follow is:

(P2-b): Retaliation is doing wrong when one has been wronged.

That required premise is a definition of retaliation. Moreover, given that particular definition, all of Socrates' preceding explicit discussion is irrelevant—for the ultimate conclusion follows directly from the definition. If retaliation is doing wrong when one is wronged, it immediately follows that retaliation is wrong. If the text did not have the argument as an enthymeme with the final conclusion omitted, it would have been too apparent that the derivation hinges on a definition of retaliation—and upon nothing else.

Recall that Socrates presents his views as being in opposition to the views of the many (*hoi polloi*). He holds that retaliation is wrong, while most people regard retaliation as right. But that interesting disagreement is further explained, given the definition of retaliation that Socrates must adopt to get the conclusion, as a dispute between those who hold that it is wrong to do wrong no matter what the circumstances and those who hold that it is right to do wrong under certain conditions. Of course, technically Socrates wins that dispute—tautologies are wonderful that way. On the other hand, his opponents will not be interested in the terms of the disagreement as he proposes them. They will cheerfully agree with the tautology "It is never right to do wrong" and still insist that retaliation is right. For they will not concede his definition of retaliation. And they will be correct in not conceding it. In short, Socrates' first argument establishes exactly nothing about the rightness or wrongness of retaliation.

Given the complete failure of that argument—neither premise, that is, neither the supposed principle nor the definition, is remotely acceptable—it is very necessary, then, that Socrates has, as he does, a second argument against those who accept retaliation. He launches into this second derivation from a quite different first principle immediately upon finishing the first derivation (49c).

S: Consider also the following. Ought one to injure others Crito? Yes or no?
C: No, one shouldn't, Socrates.

S: Well then, if one must not injure others, is it right to injure others in retaliation for injuries you have suffered, which is what most people hold?
C: No, it isn't right.
S: And it isn't right precisely because injuring people is no different from wronging them?
C: Yes.
S: Therefore, it is wrong to retaliate or to injure anyone, no matter what they have done to you.

Let me schematize the argumentative core of that passage as follows, leaving the remainder to be accounted for later.

(P1-c) Injuring others is wrong.
(P2-c) Retaliation is injuring others because they have injured you.
(C-c) Therefore, retaliation is wrong.

The second premise here, a definition of retaliation, is not in the text, but it is obviously relied upon and so can be supplied. Further, in this argument, Socrates does not fasten on a definition of retaliation which would be rejected by those who accept it as right, by most people. In fact, the definition here is not problematic at all.

Since the premises are unobjectionable and since the logic looks good, it might seem that he has produced a satisfactory argument against retaliation. But it will not work —and Socrates knows that it will not.

A retaliationist might respond "Your premises are acceptable, but your grasp of how principles are employed in moral reasoning is weak. Principles can be 'overridden.' To take an example (anachronistically) from book I of the *Republic:* one ought to return what one is holding for others. But if the item is a weapon and the owner goes mad? Obviously do not return it. In this case too, one ought not to cause injuries. But it is reasonable to recognize a class of cases in which the principle is not decisive. When one has been injured, it is right to injure in return. That is, retaliation is the right course in those circumstances."

Socrates knows that this will be the response. For instead of resting content with the argument as given, he inserts into the text an additional claim, something which falls outside what is so far schematized. This additional material is "And it isn't right precisely because injuring people is no different from wronging them." (That translation, while normal, will have to be considered very soon.) Having asserted that, and with Crito's concurrence, Socrates then finishes the argument by restating the conclusion that retaliation is wrong.

What Socrates inserts is an explanation of why the conclusion just drawn is true: returning injury for injury received is wrong because injuring and wronging are the same thing. Why does Socrates need to say that given what he has already said in premise (P1-c)? Doesn't the original premise, in conjunction with the definition of retaliation, show the wrongness of retaliation? Why appeal to something further? It is because Socrates realizes that the defender of retaliation will claim that those are cases of justified infliction of injury on another. He is attempting to block that maneuver.

The manner of stopping up the hole, however, is drastic. What he offers amounts to the following additional premise:

(P3-c) "Injuring" means "doing wrong."

What Socrates attempts to do with that addition is to define "injury" in such a way as to preclude the possibility of justified injury and so evade the objection that injuries caused by retaliating are justifiable. In doing that, Socrates rules out much more than retaliation. If "injuring" means "doing wrong," then neither self-defense nor punishment, as well as retaliation, can be justified. Now it may be that none of those things can be justified. But such matters are issues of substance, requiring much moral sense and argument. None of them can be settled by appealing to a definition of "injury," whether it be the one Socrates gives or any other.

At this point, it becomes necessary to attend to Kraut's (1984, p. 26) complaints concerning the translation which produces the idea that Socrates is committed to treating the infliction of injury as the same as the commission of wrongdoing. He must be quoted at some length.

> *Kakourgein* is frequently translated "to injure," "do injury," "work injury", etc. (thus Grube, Tredennick, and Allen), and in certain contexts this is preferable.... But I am convinced that in this part of the *Crito* a great deal of damage has been done by using "to injure" for *kakourgein*. ... [If we do so], then Socrates will be taken by many readers to be opposed to any act of damage or harm to a person or city. But it is quite clear that Socrates has no such view.... He knows as well as we do that wars do physical damage and harm to human beings and cities, but he is not unconditionally opposed to war.[7]

Presumably the "great deal of damage" that Kraut has in mind which results from employing the standard translation of *kakourgein* as "to injure" is damage to our understanding of the *Crito*. He does not spell out what that damage is. However, it is clear in my reading above precisely what the effect is of taking it that Socrates identifies injuring or doing harm to people with wrongdoing. Socrates makes that claim in an attempt to block a reasonable objection to the manner in which he employs the moral principle "Injuring people is wrong" in order to conclude that retaliation (appropriately defined) is wrong. If that translation is accepted, Socrates' reply to the objection fails and so too does his current argument against retaliation.

There, then, is damage wrought if the normal translation of *kakourgein* is employed here, though one might say that it is not so much damage to our understanding of the text as it is to Socrates' argument.

However, Kraut will reply that understanding Socrates' claim to be that there is no difference between injury and wrongdoing is to commit him to a thesis that he does not hold. Recall Kraut's argument above that since Socrates does not unconditionally oppose war even though it causes injury both to cities and to those who inhabit them, Socrates must not view harm as invariably wrong. Thus, the harm occurs to our grasp of the text.

One could just as easily say that Socrates does hold the thesis that injury and wrongdoing are identical: there it is in the midst of the *Crito*! The crucial thought, however, is not that claim of Kraut's but the evidence he adduces for saying that

Socrates does not hold that thesis: he "knows as well as we do" that wars, legally sanctioned punishment, self-defense, and so on cause harm to people but he nowhere objects to those activities.

But if there is anything we know about philosophers, especially those in the midst of defending some substantial claim, it is that they are quite capable of uttering remarks which do not square with what they otherwise know. G. E. Moore made a career of pointing this out. For example, the idealist knows perfectly well that he had breakfast before he went to lecture but in lecture asserts that time is unreal.

It is a perfectly legitimate interpretative move to hold that in arguing for an important thesis, Socrates makes an identification which commits him to the denial of what he otherwise knows. The legitimacy would be seriously in doubt if he elsewhere explicitly rejected the identification. He does not.

Moreover, one can even see why Socrates, without acting in bad faith in the argumentative process, could be led to remark "But injuring people is no different from wronging them." The principle "Injuring people is wrong" is employed by Socrates in the argument at hand. Someone who had already treated "Wrongdoing is wrong" as a principle might easily be led to say, in the heat of battle as it were, that there is no difference between the description of the deed proscribed in any correct principle and the assertion of the deed's wrongness since wrongness is built into the very description of a prohibited line of action. That is, there is no difference between harming someone and wronging him.

In short, Kraut's desire not to translate *kakourgein* normally at this place can appear to be a case of special pleading designed to save Socrates from an embarrassment. Translating it as "injuring" or "harming," on the other hand, gives the remark, even if misguided, an important logical role in Socrates' reasoning. He is trying to set aside a likely objection to his argument. Unfortunately, the move he makes to do so, identifying injury and wrongdoing, is highly objectionable.

Clearly, the retaliationist rightly will not accept the specification or definition of harm or injury, offered by Socrates. Consequently, this second attempt to derive the wrongness of retaliation from first principles joins the first as wholly unsuccessful.

4 Proving the Minor Premise

Socrates, however, takes it that he has successfully established the principle that retaliation is wrong. He was out to establish that principle in order to employ it as the first premise of one of his two arguments against escape, an argument schematized earlier as

(P1-a) Retaliation is wrong.
(P2-a) Escaping would be retaliating.
(C1-a) Escaping would be wrong.

In support of this case against his escaping, Socrates also attempts to establish the factual premise above that escaping would be retaliating. In this section, I shall consider his argument to show that escaping would be retaliation, that is, causing injury to those who have harmed him because they have harmed him.

There are some important assumptions employed in this lemma. First, Socrates and Crito take it that the judgment passed on Socrates at his trial was wrong and so constitutes an injury to him. Thus, a condition for an act to be retaliatory is satisfied. Second, it is held that Socrates' reason for escaping would be that he was wronged at the trial. All of the other reasons for escape have been presented by Crito earlier and have already been rejected. This one alone remains. Finally, it is assumed that the *polis* is responsible for the wrong judgment and so would be the object of retaliation. Later in the dialogue, the Athenian Laws hold that the jury is responsible for the injury. At the beginning, however, it is assumed that the *polis* and its legal system are at fault.

We are now in a position to see how Socrates argues for the factual premise of the retaliation objection to a possible escape. (P1-d) is the result of the three assumptions above.

(P1-d) Socrates would be escaping because he was wronged by the *polis*.
(P2-d) Escaping would be causing harm to the *polis*.
(C1-d) He would be causing harm to the *polis* because he was wronged by the *polis*.
(P3-d) Causing harm because one is wronged is retaliation.
(C2-d) He would be retaliating by escaping.

What gets set out in the text is (P2-d). "Or perhaps you imagine it possible for a *polis* not to collapse if the judgments of its courts are ignored by its citizens?" (50b). His escape would be the rejection of a legal judgment by a citizen acting as a private person. The consequences of such nullification would be the destruction of the *polis* conceived of as a system of relations embodied in laws and authoritative judgments.

Clearly, he is not saying that the consequences of his escaping would be the collapse of Athens, either immediately or soon after his escape. That comes out in his earlier remark "at least as far as you can" (50b). His escape would not be sufficient to destroy Athens; at best he would be a contributor to that destruction. At most, then, he would be causing harm or injury to the *polis*, the amount of which is not (and could not be) specified.

With premise (P2-d) and a definition of retaliation (P3-d) clearly relied upon, the conclusion of this lemma (C2-d=P2-a), along with what Socrates takes to have been previously established, namely, that retaliation is wrong, enables him to say to Crito "Thus it would be wrong to escape."

To see what goes wrong with that solid-looking argument, consider a theme immediately sounded when the retaliation argument is broached. The first thing the Laws say to Socrates is "Tell us Socrates, what is it that you have in mind to do? Do you intend to do anything else by this exploit to which you are putting your hand than to destroy both ourselves the Laws and the entire city—at least as far as you can?" (50a-b). Crito enthusiastically agrees for both of them (50c) that that aim cannot be denied, that such destruction or harm would be what is intended. (Clearly Crito has not been talked out of his retaliatory views by the preceding arguments.)

That is, the relevant parts of the discussion of a possible escape by Socrates are carried on under the assumption that an escape would have a retaliatory aim, that the intention would be to cause harm to Athens because the *polis* had wronged him.

I shall argue that Socrates had no such retaliatory intention. Some might find my own intentions peculiar. Surely a person knows what he intends. How can I challenge Socrates' statement of his own intentions? Even worse, I am not a part of Socrates' world—if Crito did not challenge that claim, how can I presume to do so? We shall see.

Notice first that all the evidence other than those two questions posed by the Laws and the answer given to the questions indicates that a desire to retaliate is not appropriate to Socrates' character. He nowhere appears as a vengeful, vindictive person. Even here in the *Crito,* he does not say "I'm going to get even with them"; the claim that Socrates intends the destruction of Athens is politely, if enthusiastically, phrased by Crito, not even by Socrates. Nor does he here give the slightest expression of feelings of bitterness and revenge. It is surely remarkable that one who is contemplating the destruction of a state through a retaliatory act should appear so free of the desire to retaliate.

Further, the earlier argument concerning the wrongness of retaliation fits most peculiarly with a continued desire (even if there was one originally) on Socrates' part to secure a return for the wrong he has suffered. That is, someone who wanted to retaliate and who then became convinced that retaliation is wrong would no longer have the same motives as before. Yet, even after arguing so strenuously that retaliation is wrong and that wrong is wrong and not to be done, in this later passage, Socrates goes on talking calmly as if he were motivated by revenge, by a desire to retaliate.

There is one further point which is decisive against such an account of his intentions. Let us suppose that Socrates does have the desire to strike back at the state. And also suppose that the consequences of his escaping would be what he says they would be: injury or harm to the state. Suppose finally that he knows, as he says he does, that those consequences would ensue. All other things either being equal or being as they are represented in the *Crito*, what would Socrates do, given that he wants to retaliate? He would escape. That is, given the intention, the knowledge of harmful consequences to the requisite object would be a decisive reason for escaping. Yet look at what happens. Knowledge of the consequences is a reason for not escaping! The only reasonable conclusion is that Socrates had no intention of retaliating.

The appropriate question is "Why did Socrates accept Crito's account of his motivation, that his intention was to retaliate, when he so patently did not have any such aim?" To answer that we must turn to the lemma which concludes "Escaping would be retaliating." The key to that argument is (C1-d), the conclusion that he would be causing harm because he was wronged. This is derived from the premises "He would be escaping because he was wronged" and "Escaping would be causing harm." The rule employed in the derivation is a substitution rule for equivalents.

In the context, however, the substitution is not legitimate. The error is a variation of substituting into an intensional context. That is, the move here is analogous to substituting from the identity "Scott is the author of *Waverley*" into "He knows that the author of *Waverley* wrote *Ivanhoe*" to obtain "He knows that Scott wrote *Ivanhoe*."

In the present case, even though "escaping" may be descriptively equivalent to "causing harm," it does not follow that one who intends to escape also intends to cause harm. The person who is putting arsenic in the water may not know that the water is the city's supply and so not intend to poison the inhabitants. So someone in Socrates' position may intend to escape and not intend to cause harm even though it is true that to escape is to cause harm.

The proper objection here is "Ah, but the person putting the arsenic into the water does not know that putting the poison in the water is equivalent to poisoning the people because she does not know that the water is the city's reservoir. But Socrates knows that escaping would be causing harm."

While true, that still will not entitle Socrates to the derivation. Even if Socrates were to escape knowing that harm would come to Athens, it would not follow that he intended the harm. I walk across the lawn knowing that some blades of grass will be broken and some insects squashed, but I do not intend those things. The doctor gives you a shot knowing that it will cause you pain, but he does not intend that the pain be inflicted upon you. The broken grass, the dead insects, and the soreness of the arm are unintended consequences of what is being done. So too, Socrates' escape may be known by him to cause harm, yet he need not intend the harm.

Of course, that unintended harm may come from a proposed act should be taken into account in deciding what to do. In fact, the amount of unintended harm may be sufficient to deter one from doing whatever it is that is known to produce such harm. But that is not Socrates' argument. He allows that he intends to cause the harm, that he intends to retaliate. He does not claim that the knowledge that harm will result as an unintended byproduct of his escape is what is deterring him from escaping.

It should now be clear why Socrates strains to get us to believe that he intends to destroy or harm the state. It is only with that intention that he is justified in employing the substitution rule in his derivation and so justified in inferring that he would be causing harm because he was wronged. And only with that established can he further conclude that escaping would be retaliating.

One can retaliate only if one intends to. Accidental injury to a possible object of retaliation is not retaliation. To make the argument work, to show that escape would be wrong because it would be retaliation, he must intend to cause injury. But, as I have argued, he had no such intention. The derivation will not work. His escape would not be retaliation and hence, on the grounds that he cites, would not be wrong.

A problem remains for which I have no answer. Why was Socrates so determined to describe his escape as retaliation when to do so he had to falsify his motives? It is not that he failed to notice that the substitution rule, to have a legitimate use in this context, requires the intention to cause injury—for he does enter the claim that that is his intention. He could have argued that escaping would harm the state and that the harm would be undeserved. All of the elements for that argument are present in the text. Yet he does not so argue. Rather, something seems to have convinced him that escaping would have to be retaliating, and that therefore he must have the intention to cause harm. I have no plausible suggestions as to what might have produced such a striking conviction.

Notes

1. Woozley (1979, pp. 18–21) argues that in the *Crito*, beginning at 48c, the text must be understood in terms of justice. His argument for that contention is very bad. He points out, correctly, that "Wrongdoing need not have a victim, but injustice must." However, he concludes from this that, because Athens is conceived of as being victimized if Socrates were to escape, the *Crito* must be treated as concerned with injustice. But that conclusion concerning the proper translation of *adikein* requires not the asserted premise that wrongdoing need not have a victim but that wrongdoing cannot have a victim. That premise is surely not so. If I punch you in the nose, that is a piece of wrongdoing which victimizes you but certainly is not a matter of being unfair (unless of course a long story about passing over alternative noses and more appropriate victims is told). There are items in the speech of the Laws which are a protest in terms of fairness, but it must not be forgotten that being unjust in some specific way is a form of wrongdoing.

   Kraut (1984, p. 25) also argues that the best translation of *adikein* in the *Crito* is "unjust." He has two reasons. The first is the claim that since all translators agree that *dikaia* at 49e6 must be understood as "just," that should be mirrored in the translation of *adikein* at 49b8. That simply is not so: *dikaia* is being used for a special purpose at 49e6 and need not be mirrored anywhere else. See note 4. His second reason is much more complicated: see note 7 and the associated text for a discussion.
2. The chief commentaries which form the background to my discussion are: Woozley (1979), Kraut (1984), Santas (1979), and Allen (1980).
3. My versions of the text throughout are somewhat freewheeling by ordinary standards of exactness. The aim has been to make the passages more readable. I think nowhere, unless otherwise noted, does anything I say depend upon the details of the translation.
4. At 49e6 Socrates states the principle concerning agreements and also adds a qualification—both the principle and its qualification are repeated in the question Crito cannot answer at 50a3. The qualification concerns whether the agreement is *dikaia*. Socrates could have stated the principle baldly: "One ought to fulfill one's agreements" or "Breaking agreements is wrong." The reminder that there are defeating conditions (e.g., coercion, misinformation) for agreements could have been postponed until later in the discussion. Socrates, however, builds that reminder into the initial statement of the principle as an immediately given qualification. Kraut uses the fact that the qualification requires an obligating agreement to be *dikaia* to argue that the best translation of that word throughout the *Crito* is in terms of justice. That *dikaia* is used in stating a necessary condition for an agreement to obligate seems to me to have no bearing whatsoever on how it ought to be understood in other places in the dialogue. In fact, I have, above, translated the term as "legitimate" without doing any harm to Plato's intention: "And shall we be breaking a legitimately established agreement?"
5. I have an excellent one-panel *Non Sequitur* cartoon (by Wiley) from 1999. The caption is "Moses and the First Draft." In front of Moses, there is a stone tablet saying "Don't Do Bad Things." Moses is calling up to Jehovah "It might leave a little too much room for rationalization. Maybe you should try breaking it down to a few specifics." Socrates' move is a version of Jehovah's.
6. Woozley (1979, p. 21) notices the conflict between the *Crito* and the other relevant dialogues: "Incidentally, the claim here that a man should not act unjustly, if he can help it, might seem inconsistent with the more familiar Socratic paradox that nobody does what is unjust, if he can help it." Woozley wants to save Socrates from inconsistency: hence the "seem" above.

The rescue is made by drawing a distinction between knowing something to be wrong and only believing it to be: weakness is possible if only the latter condition holds. I, on the other hand, am not here interested in that salvation project and so I go ahead and say that there is an inconsistency, no matter how things might eventually be worked out.

7. Kraut solves the problem by translating *kakourgein* here as "treating wrongly." In order, then, to not have Socrates' thesis end up as the tautology "Treating someone wrongly is no different from wronging them," he then urges that *adikein* be translated as "unjust" so that the thesis becomes "Treating someone wrongly is the same as acting unjustly." In advising that solution, we find Kraut's second reason for holding that *adikein* should be translated as "unjust" in these sections of the *Crito*. See note 1.

Bibliography

Allen, R.E. 1980. *Socrates and legal obligation*. Minneapolis: University of Minnesota Press.
Kraut, Richard. 1984. *Socrates and the state*. Princeton: Princeton University Press.
Santas, Gerasimos. 1979. *Socrates: Philosophy in Plato's early dialogues*. London: Routledge and Kegan Paul.
Weiss, Roslyn. 1998. *Socrates dissatisfied: An analysis of Plato's Crito*. New York: Oxford University Press.
Woozley, A.D. 1971. Socrates on disobeying the law. In *The philosophy of Socrates: A collection of critical essays*, ed. Gregory Vlastos, 299–318. Notre Dame: University of Notre Dame Press.
Woozley, A.D. 1979. *Law and obedience: The arguments of Plato's Crito*. Chapel Hill: University of North Carolina Press.

How Virtuous Was Socrates?

Nils Ch. Rauhut

1 Introduction

It has become common to think of Socrates as a literary creation of Plato rather than as a historical flesh and blood Athenian citizen. The following essay is a reminder that what we think about the moral character of the historical Socrates matters. I begin by arguing that the moral character of the historical Socrates plays a role in our understanding of Socrates' philosophy in Plato's dialogues. In the second part of the essay, I reevaluate what Alcibiades' speech in Plato's *Symposium* tells us about the moral character of the historical Socrates. I examine three different approaches to Alcibiades' speech and argue that all three of them fail to explain the humor in the speech. Based on this result, I develop and defend a new interpretation. I argue that the key to understanding the speech is Alcibiades' use of irony that reveals that Socrates has not advanced to the top of the ladder of love but is still struggling to integrate eros within his life. Socrates emerges not as an otherworldly saint who has acquired all the cardinal virtues but rather as a human who tries to come to terms with his erotic desires.

2 The Philosophical Significance of Socrates' Moral Character

It seems appropriate to evaluate famous philosophers exclusively in the light of their ideas and arguments and to ignore in this evaluation the details of their personal lives. When we study Bertrand Russell, for instance, we want to know what he had

---

This essay is dedicated to David Keyt who taught me the art of love.

N.C. Rauhut (✉)
Department of Philosophy, Coastal Carolina University, Conway, SC 29528, USA
e-mail: nrauhut@coastal.edu

to say about denoting or about sense data, but we do not care much about the fact that he was fired from Trinity College or that he was married several times. When we study John Rawls, we are interested in the original position or the difference principle, but we do not really need to know that two of his younger brothers died after contracting diseases from him. We might note these personal anecdotes about famous philosophers, but we should not let them influence or cloud our judgments about the value of the respective philosophies.

Although this practice of separating the personal life from the analysis and evaluation of philosophical theories is quite reasonable, we should not follow it in the case of the historical Socrates. Socrates' philosophy cannot be clearly separated from our understanding of his moral character. Eduard Zeller writes in this context:

> There is no instance on record of a philosopher whose importance as a thinker is so closely bound up with his personal character as a man as it was in the case of Socrates .... [I]n the case of others it is easier to separate the fruits of their intellectual life from the stock on which they grew; doctrines can generally be received and handed down quite unchanged by men of different characters. In the case of Socrates this is not nearly so easy. His teaching aimed far less at definite doctrines ... than at a special tone of life and thought, at a philosophical character and an art of intellectual inquiry. (1881, p. 53)

I think that Zeller is right on this point. In the case of Socrates, there indeed exists an essential link between his philosophy and his personal life. I am inclined to think that most scholars would agree with this assessment as well. But even if this claim is not very controversial, it seems worthwhile to reflect more on this striking feature of Socrates' philosophy. Why should it be the case that the historical Socrates differs from all other great philosophers in that his philosophy is necessarily linked to his personal life? In this section, I will clarify in more detail why Socrates' character and personality have philosophical significance and why any attempt to come to terms with his philosophical thought presupposes an understanding of his character and personal life as well.

Socrates' philosophical methodology—the *elenchus*—is more than a test of whether various moral claims are logically consistent with each other. During a Socratic conversation, Socrates insists that his interlocutors tell him what they really believe. The *elenchus* is thus not simply a test of philosophical claims and beliefs but also—and perhaps foremost— a test and examination of human beings and the way in which they live.[1] By conducting an elenctic examination, Socrates shows his interlocutors more than that they hold contradictory moral beliefs. He also shows them that they harbor within their psyches conflicting and incompatible dispositions. These conflicts in their psyches contribute to the fact that the interlocutors are unable to develop successful definitions of the virtues. Their intellectual deficiencies are closely tied to their moral deficiencies. Once we appreciate this feature of the *elenchus,* it becomes clear that Socrates evidently believes that philosophical arguments and positions are closely related to the moral character of the person who advances them. From a Socratic perspective, specific philosophical arguments can then also be seen as expressions of a certain state of character. This might be one of the reasons why Plato, when he chose to write about Socrates, found the dialogue form such a natural way of writing.

In order to illustrate how the interplay between philosophy and moral character influences our understanding of the historical Socrates, it is useful to consider a specific example. At the end of the *Apology* (40b-41c), Plato describes Socrates as presenting a well-known argument for the thesis that death is a "good thing" (40b). Socrates argues for this thesis by claiming that death is one of two things: it is either like a dreamless sleep or else a relocation of the soul to a better place. Since death is something good in both cases, Socrates concludes that no matter what death turns out to be, we can be confident that it is a blessing. Scholars have been divided on how to interpret this argument. On the one hand are those critical of Socrates like Roochnik who concludes that, in this argument, Socrates "unintentionally committed errors that college sophomores can readily identify" (1985, p. 216). On the other hand are those who are more amenable to Socrates' argument like Rudebusch who holds that "the argument is seriously defensible" (1999, p. 66). Both interpretations have merit. The critics of Socrates' argument are correct to point out that it seems to overlook the possibility that death might be a relocation to a terrible and frightening place. The defenders are right to remind us that there might be perfectly good reasons in Socrates' overall ethical and religious philosophy that justify his omission of hell as a reasonable possibility. However, if we take the idea seriously that Socrates' philosophy and his moral character are closely connected, a third and, in my view, superior interpretation of the argument becomes available. In order to understand this interpretation, one needs to grasp that, according to Plato, courage is linked to our beliefs about the afterlife. In the third book of the *Republic*, Plato writes, "… do you think that anyone ever becomes courageous if he is possessed by this fear [of Hades]? … [C]an somebody be unafraid of death … if he believes in Hades full of terrors?" (III 386b). This passage illustrates that, according to Plato, a truly courageous person will not take the traditional and frightening stories about Hades seriously. Not believing in Hades is a necessary condition for being fully courageous. This insight gives us a clue of how we ought to interpret the argument about death at the end of the *Apology*. The main goal of that argument is not to establish from a detached and neutral point of view what reasonable people ought to think about death. The argument is essentially linked to Socrates' moral character, and the cogency of the argument is linked to Socrates' character as well. The critics are correct to point out that the argument overlooks the possibility that death is a relocation to Hades, but this argumentative shortcoming is meant to highlight the courageous character of the historical Socrates. Socrates' failure to consider all logical possibilities—which at first blush might look like an embarrassing logical blunder—can now be seen as an expression of an admirable character trait. A person who, when it comes to thinking about death, does not dwell on frightening logical possibilities is a person who is truly courageous, and this is what Plato wants us to see at the end of the *Apology*.

This specific example illustrates and supports a more general point. When we try to understand and access the philosophy of the historical Socrates, it matters what we think about his personality and character. When we look at particular passages and arguments of Plato's dialogues, it is useful to evaluate these passages in the light of what we know about Socrates' personality. These character considerations will rarely be decisive, but it seems to me that they ought to play a useful role in shaping our understanding of Socrates' philosophy. Before we attribute a certain type of hedonism, or moral psychology, or ethical theory to the historical Socrates we should ask ourselves whether these philosophical positions are compatible with what we know about the character and personality of this remarkable philosopher.

3 The Socratic Problem and the Character of Socrates

I hope that I have established so far that what we think about Socrates' personality and character has philosophical significance. Socrates' character is deeply intertwined with his philosophy. Let me now turn to a more central topic of my essay. What do we know about the character and personality of the historical Socrates? It is at this point that we encounter the Socratic problem. Do we have any reliable evidence that tells us what historical Socrates was really like? One might be tempted to sidestep this question by focusing on Plato's Socrates rather than the historical Socrates. But this method of avoiding the Socratic problem works best if we restrict our focus on the content of Socrates' philosophy. It makes sense to distinguish the philosophy of Plato's Socrates from the philosophy of the historical Socrates. However, such a distinction does not seem to work when we deal with the character and personality of Socrates. In terms of character, Plato's Socrates is identical to the historical Socrates. The character traits which Plato attributes to Socrates are not the character traits of an imaginary character in an artistic play but the character traits of a particular flesh and blood Greek Athenian. This is supported by the fact that the person who is called "Socrates" in Plato's dialogues remains—with respect to his character—the same throughout, even if the philosophical position he advocates undergoes radical change. It follows therefore that those who take the search for the moral character of Socrates seriously cannot avoid dealing with the Socratic problem. Does this mean that any attempt to discover the character and personality of the historical Socrates is doomed to failure? I would like to suggest that it is not.

It seems to me that the Socratic problem is much less daunting if we focus on the character of the historical Socrates rather than on his philosophy. We have already seen that the personal traits of Socrates remain constant throughout Plato's dialogues. This means that for the purpose of understanding his character, we do not need to make any assumptions about the chronological order of the dialogues. When it comes to clarifying Socrates' personality, passages from the *Symposium*, *Phaedo*, and *Theaetetus* offer just as much insight as the so-called early dialogues like the *Charmides* or *Laches*. Moreover, not only can we consider all of Plato's dialogues—with the exception of the *Laws*—as legitimate sources of evidence, but we can also make use of Xenophon and Aristophanes. Although the testimony of Xenophon and Aristophanes is not very trustworthy as a source of understanding concerning the content of Socrates' philosophy, it is entirely reasonable to use their writings to gain insights into the character and personality of the historical Socrates. The task of saying something reliable and reasonable about the character and personality of the historical Socrates is much more manageable than the task of saying something reliable about the philosophy of the historical Socrates. The Socratic problem, thus, does not pose an insurmountable barrier to the exploration of the character and personality of the historical Socrates.

4 The Speech of Alcibiades and Socrates' Attitude toward Eros in the *Symposium*

Although an exploration and account of the moral character of the historical Socrates is possible and worthwhile, it is clear that it cannot be done within the limits of this essay. I, therefore, would like to narrow my focus here to one particular passage in Plato and one particular character trait of Socrates. The passage in question is the speech of Alcibiades at the end of Plato's *Symposium*, and the character trait in question is Socrates' attitude toward eros. There can be little doubt that our understanding of Socrates' sexuality has been shaped to an extraordinary degree by this passage. My overall goal in this essay is to show that there are good reasons for thinking that Alcibiades' speech in the *Symposium* has been misunderstood. If interpreted correctly, it supports a very different view of Socrates' attitude toward sexuality than is normally presented in the secondary literature. In order to present my reasons for this view, it is useful to begin with a brief summary of Alcibiades' speech in Plato's *Symposium*.

After Socrates finishes his magnificent speech about eros, Alcibiades—all of a sudden—enters the house of Agathon. He is drunk and surprised to find Socrates, whom he initially does not notice, on the couch next to Agathon. The party decides that drinking in silence would be uncivilized and that Alcibiades therefore should speak in praise of Socrates. Alcibiades starts his speech by comparing Socrates to a satyr. He says, "Nobody, not even you, Socrates, can deny that you look like them" (*Smp.* 215b). However, in spite of Socrates' appearance, Alcibiades claims that his words have a profound impact on him: "The moment he starts to speak, I am beside myself, my heart starts leaping in my chest, the tears come streaming down my face…" (215e). According to Alcibiades, Socrates is the only person in the world who is able to make him feel ashamed. Alcibiades continues his speech by describing his attempts to seduce Socrates. He arranges to be alone with Socrates on several occasions but is surprised to find that Socrates shows no sexual interest and "has his usual conversations with him" (217b). These rejections only increase Alcibiades' desire, and on one particular occasion, after he has tricked Socrates to sleep in his house, Alcibiades "slips under Socrates' coat, and puts his arms around this man … and spends the whole night next to him" (219 b-c). Alas, in spite of all his efforts, Socrates turns him down—it was, Alcibiades claims, "as if I had spent the night with my own father or older brother!" (219d). Alcibiades then continues to praise Socrates' civic virtues. He describes his bravery at the battle of Potidaea and at Delium. He finishes his speech by stressing the uniqueness of Socrates. He says:

> There is a parallel for everyone—everyone else, that is. But this man here is so bizarre, his ways and his ideas are so unusual that search as you might you will never find anyone else, alive or dead, who's even remotely like him. The best you can do is not to compare him to anything human, but to liken him, as I do, to Silenius and the satyrs.... (221d)

Alcibiades' speech in praise of Socrates has produced a wide variety of colorful and conflicting interpretations which contain, as Kenneth Dover observed astutely, "so much unjustified and implausible assertion and so little rigorous argument" (1980, p. 6). However, I would like to show that most, if not all, of these interpretations—in spite of their glaring differences—paint a very similar picture of Socrates' attitude toward sexuality. I will then proceed to show that there are reasons to reject this description of Socrates' character, and that consequently all interpretations of Alcibiades' speech share a common weakness. This observation creates some necessary space for an alternative interpretation of Alcibiades' speech. I will develop and defend such an alternative reading at the end of my essay.

5 Interpretations of Alcibiades' Speech

In the light of the wide variety of interpretations of Alcibiades' speech, my argumentative task is not easy. It is clear that I cannot explore and describe all the different interpretations that have been advanced in the past. I will, therefore, explore the following argumentative strategy. I will describe three very different interpretations of Alcibiades' speech, and I will try to show that they share a common view of Socrates' attitude toward sexuality. My hope is that we can reasonably generalize from this observation and claim with some degree of plausibility that if these three very different interpretations share a common view of Socrates' attitude toward sexuality, then most others share this view as well, since I am aware of no important interpretation that departs from this view.

Let us begin with a somewhat older interpretation of Alcibiades' speech. Friedrich Schleiermacher describes the purpose and message of the speech as follows:

> [The speech of Alcibiades] exhibits Socrates to us in the unwearied enthusiasm of contemplation, and in joyous communication of the results, in the contempt of danger and exaltation above eternal things, in the purity of his relations, and in his inward divinity under that light and cheerful exterior; in short, in that perfect soundness of body and mind, and consequently, of existence generally. (1836, p. 210)

For Schleiermacher, the main purpose of Alcibiades' speech is to show us the true nature of the historical Socrates. After reading the speech, we are supposed to see and understand that Socrates possesses all of the cardinal virtues. Socrates is courageous, wise, and has perfect self-control. If we follow Schleiermacher, the speech of Alcibiades is about Socrates the person, but it does not offer us any crucial insights about the nature of eros.

Martha Nussbaum, on the other hand, advocates a very different reading of Alcibiades' speech (1979 and 1986). She argues that the speech contains one of the most central theories of love in the *Symposium*. According to Nussbaum, Alcibiades' description of his love for Socrates offers us a particular and individualistic account of love that has one unique individual as its object and which stands in sharp opposition to the objective, impersonal account of love that is developed in the speech of Diotima. Alcibiades' speech shows us that "there are some truths about love that can be learned only through the experience of a particular passion of one's own" (1986, p. 185). And these particular idiosyncratic truths are not accessible to the distant, objective gaze of pure philosophical reflection that wants to transform our love into the love of the eternal Forms. Nussbaum thus sees the speech of Alcibiades as a defense of the role of literature in moral learning, and she claims that the speech "contains the most serious objection raised in the *Symposium* against Socrates' program for the ascent of love" (1979, p. 139). If we follow Nussbaum, we need to see the last two speeches in Plato's *Symposium* as offering us a momentous and life-altering choice: either we follow the path of philosophy and give up on love for individual human beings or else we follow the call of literature and open ourselves to the unpredictable fragilities of a life shaped by personal eros. Alas, the choice is a tragic one since we cannot have it both ways.

A third type of interpretation of Alcibiades' speech is offered by Frisbee Sheffield. Although Sheffield, like Nussbaum, holds that the speech of Alcibiades contains a theory of love, she disagrees with Nussbaum that Alcibiades' theory of love stands in opposition to Socrates' prior speech. According to Sheffield, Alcibiades' speech "works closely together with Socrates" (2006, p. 185) and aims to complete the Socratic theory of eros "by showing us the philosopher as a complex mixture of the human and the divine" (p. 195). If we follow Sheffield's interpretation, we can learn from the speech of Alcibiades "that we need not choose between the pursuit of divine wisdom and engagements with others" (p. 206). The Socrates who emerges from Alcibiades' speech shows us how we can pursue intellectual wisdom in a distinctly human life that takes the relationship with other individual humans seriously.

At first glance, the interpretations of Schleiermacher, Nussbaum, and Sheffield appear to be very different. However, it seems to me that in spite of their pronounced differences, all three interpretations share a common element. All three seem to entail that the Socrates who is presented to us by Alcibiades is a person who has mastered the forces of eros by integrating it successfully into his philosophical life. It is true that Schleiermacher, Nussbaum, and Sheffield offer different accounts of how this integration and education of eros takes place. Schleiermacher seems to believe that Socrates is able to tame eros because Socrates is blessed by nature with a "perfect soundness of body and mind" (1836, p. 210). I take this to mean that Schleiermacher pictures Socrates as a type of moral saint whose sexual urges are by nature easier to control than they are for most normal human beings. Nussbaum, on the other hand, seems to believe that Socrates is able to control eros by giving up on loving individuals, whereas Sheffield seems to think that Socrates is able to educate his attraction to individuals by his pursuit of philosophy in a distinctly human life. In spite of these differences, we can see one common theme in all three interpretations: Socrates emerges in the speech of Alcibiades as a person who has tamed and mastered eros. It seems to me that this view is misguided. It is, at the very least, not compatible with the picture of Socrates that emerges from the speech of Alcibiades. I will examine this incompatibility below.

6 Alcibiades' Speech and the Problem of Humor

One key difficulty I see in the view of Socrates as a master of eros is that it fails to make sense of the response Alcibiades' speech receives from the audience. Plato tells us that Alcibiades' speech "provoked a lot of laughter" (222c). This is significant and it deserves an explanation. Why is Alcibiades' speech so funny? It seems to me that all three above interpretations have a hard time accounting for the comic character of Alcibiades' speech. This is most obvious with respect to Nussbaum's interpretation. If Nussbaum is correct and Alcibiades' speech is indeed "a story of intense passion for a unique individual as eloquent as any in literature" (1971, pp.133–34), then it is hard to see why the audience would consider it funny. Personal stories about passionate love affairs can be tragic, arousing, or happy, but they tend not to be funny. Imagine for a moment that I were to tell you about the most important love affair in my life. I hope that my personal story of love might move you or that it might inspire you, but I surely would be surprised if everyone in the audience were to start laughing. It seems inappropriate, if not bizarre, to laugh about personal love stories even if one is drunk. Something very similar is true for Schleiermacher's interpretation. If the main purpose of the speech is to show us that Socrates has all the cardinal virtues, then there is again nothing humorous in Alcibiades' speech. Sheffield perhaps has the best chances of explaining the comic nature of Alcibiades' speech. According to her, the speech has the elements of a satyr drama. By this she means that Alcibiades' speech revisits themes of the prior serious speech of Socrates just like a satyr play revisits the serious themes of a prior tragedy. Alcibiades' speech therefore inverts and distorts some of the serious elements of the prior speech on love, but ultimately serves as a translation of the otherworldly account of Platonic love into human terms. According to Sheffield, we are therefore "invited to laugh at the man who wanders around in a state of ignorance talking of pack-asses and cobblers and the man who pursues the beauty of the young" (2006, p. 194). However, Sheffield is also clear that these humorous elements in Alcibiades' speech "do not serve to undermine Socrates' character and life. Rather, they return always to the philosopher's virtue. And this is what we might expect from the satiric genre" (p. 194). It seems then that Sheffield's interpretation succeeds in explaining why there are humorous elements in Alcibiades' speech, but the interpretation still cannot explain why everybody at the very end of the speech bursts out into loud laughter. If Sheffield is right, the audience ought to laugh in the middle of the speech at the very time when Alcibiades makes humorous remarks, but they ought not to laugh at the very end because the overall message of the speech is a serious one and adds important elements to a successful understanding of eros.

7 The Irony and Humor of Alcibiades

Given that these three interpretations fail to explain the humor of Alcibiades' speech adequately, we have reasons to look for a different approach. I think we should take the irony in Alcibiades' speech very seriously and should make it one of the central elements in our interpretation. That Alcibiades is in an ironic mood is obvious from the start. When he first becomes aware of Eryximachus, he says, "O Eryximachus, best possible son to the best possible, the most temperate father: Hi" (214b). It is obvious that this hyperbolic praise of Eryximachus, who throughout the entire *Symposium* is portrayed as an arrogant, self-important buffoon, is extremely ironic. However, Alcibiades' greeting of Eryximachus is also extremely funny. The humor is based on the fact that Alcibiades says ironically what Eryximachus really seems to believe about himself. Eryximachus is indeed very pleased with his life and his accomplishments as a doctor. He truly seems to believe what Alcibiades says ironically about him, namely, that he is indeed "the best possible son of the best possible father." Alcibiades shows himself as a master of a certain kind of irony. He is able to express ironically what Eryximachus truly believes about himself. Such irony not only requires a tremendous amount of psychological insight into another person but it also reveals publicly the true psychological makeup of the person. Alcibiades' ironic style of speaking is clearly closely related to the Socratic *elenchus*. I would like to suggest that his subsequent speech about Socrates should be read as an expression of the same kind of irony. His praise of Socrates is indeed mock praise—his speech is, as he himself points out, a "punishment [of Socrates] in front of everybody" (214e). However, Alcibiades does not simply say just any outrageous thing about Socrates. He says only what Alcibiades thinks Socrates truly believes about himself. This is the reason why Alcibiades stresses so often in his speech that he is only speaking the truth (214e and 217b) and why he gives Socrates the right to interrupt him if he "says anything that is not true" (215a and 217b). Alcibiades indeed presents us with the truth, but it is the truth of how Socrates thinks of himself. Since he presents this truth ironically, he thereby suggests playfully that Socrates suffers from a form of self-deception. What is more hilarious than ironically telling Socrates, the master of irony, that the image he has of himself is out of touch with reality?

In order to more clearly understand my reading of Alcibiades' speech as ironic, consider the following example. At 216d Alcibiades says:

> Believe me, it couldn't matter less to him [Socrates] whether a boy is beautiful. You can't imagine how little he cares whether a person is beautiful, or rich, or famous in any other way that most people admire. He considers all these possessions beneath contempt, and that is exactly how he considers all of us as well. (216d-e)

It strikes me that this passage expresses what Socrates truly believes about himself. Socrates genuinely believes that he is indifferent to the physical appearance and the social standing of his interlocutors. All he cares about is the moral character of the people he meets. But Alcibiades' speech is also ironic in that it suggests that Socrates could be mistaken about himself in this respect. Could it be pure coincidence that the person who professes that he does not care about the physical appearance and social standing of his interlocutors spends his whole life in the company of beautiful, gifted, and rich young men like Agathon, Phaedrus, Pausanias, and Aristophanes? It is this ironic tension between Socrates' self-image and his actual life that makes Alcibiades' speech so funny.

In my view, it is this interplay between truth and irony that provides the key to a correct understanding of Alcibiades' speech. Alcibiades tells us the truth about how Socrates sees himself, but he also ironically suggests that Socrates is a bit of a narcissist. The image Socrates has of himself and his mission in life is out of touch with reality.

In order to buttress my interpretation, let us look at Alcibiades' description of the effect Socrates' arguments supposedly have on his listeners. Alcibiades says:

> You know, people hardly ever take a speaker seriously, even if he's the greatest orator; but let anyone—man, woman, or child—listen to you [Socrates] or even to a poor account of what you say—and we are all transported, completely possessed. (215d)

Is it plausible to read this description as the literal truth? It seems to me that Alcibiades' again presents us with the truth of how Socrates sees himself. Socrates is convinced that his words and his conversations are more important than the speeches of Pericles and Protagoras, but Alcibiades' suggest ironically that this perspective is out of touch with reality.

Let us also consider Alcibiades' description of Socrates at the battle of Delium:

> I had an opportunity to watch Socrates [during the battle] ... well, it was easy to see that he was remarkably more collected than Laches. But when I looked again I couldn't get the words of Aristophanes out of my mind: in the midst of battle he was making his way exactly as he does around town ... with swaggering gait and roving eye.... Even from a distance it was obvious that this was a very brave man who would put up a terrific fight if anyone approached him. (221b)

It seems to me that this description truly captures how Socrates saw his own performance on the battlefield. He sees himself as a ferocious and courageous soldier, even if he might walk a bit funny. However, there is reason to doubt whether Socrates truly was as effective a soldier as he believes himself to be. The historical facts seem to suggest that Alcibiades was the courageous soldier who saved Socrates,[2] and that Socrates' image of himself is somewhat problematic in the light of what really happened on the field of battle. The guests at the Symposium are of course well aware of what happened at Delium and Potidea, and this is the reason why they burst into loud laughter.

I hope that my analysis of these passages in Alcibiades' speech has made it tempting and plausible to read the whole speech of Alcibiades as a unique mixture of irony and truth and to conclude that the main purpose of the speech is an ironic deconstruction of Socrates' self-image. If this is correct, we should also reevaluate what Alcibiades says about the intimate details of his relationship with Socrates. We have seen that Alcibiades describes his relationship with Socrates as a one-sided affair. It is Alcibiades who tries to seduce Socrates, while Socrates is indifferent to Alcibiades' physical advances. If we read Alcibiades' claims in this context as expressing a combination of irony and truth in the manner I have detailed above, we cannot take his description of his relationship with Socrates at face value. It is true that Socrates understands his relationship with Alcibiades only as a moral and educational bond. He is interested in educating and shaping Alcibiades' character. However, if irony is also part Alcibiades' speech, we are driven to the conclusion that the relationship between Socrates and Alcibiades was probably at one point also physical and sexual in nature. This would have been well known to all the participants in the *Symposium,* and it is this background knowledge which makes this part of the speech so hilarious.

It is clear that this conclusion is rather controversial. There are, however, some puzzling features of the speech that make perfect sense if we adopt my interpretation. First, Alcibiades compares Socrates to a satyr throughout his speech. Many commentators have developed sophisticated explanations of what Socrates could possibly have in common with satyrs. On my interpretation of Alcibiades' speech, the parallels between satyrs and Socrates are obvious. Just like satyrs, Socrates has a ferocious sexual appetite and is driven by his sexual desires. In Greek art, satyrs are often depicted as having large erections and it seems to me that Alcibiades is hoping that we have this picture of satyrs in mind when we hear him say that Socrates is just like them. My interpretation offers a smooth explanation of what Socrates and satyrs have in common.

Second, my interpretation is supported by what we know about Greek homosexuality. In Greek culture, respected forms of homosexuality were assumed to be an asymmetrical relationship between an older lover, the *erastes*, and a much younger boy, the *eromenos*. It was expected that only the *erastes* had sexual interests and that the *eromenos* would neither initiate nor enjoy sexual activities. This supports an ironic reading of Alcibiades' account of his intimate relationship with Socrates. If we deny the ironic nature of Alcibiades' speech and take it as literal truth, then we are left with the conclusion that Alcibiades—the *eromenos*—was actively interested in having sex with an older man. This would be a shameful admission. It might be objected here that Alcibiades, who was shameless in so many other ways, might have also transgressed traditional Greek norms for homosexual relations. However, if we take this position, we are again at a complete loss at how to explain the laughter at the end of Alcibiades' speech. If we assume that the speech captures the literal truth about the intimate details of the relationship between Socrates and Alcibiades, then we must conclude that Alcibiades was publicly admitting to having shameful sexual desires. Such a public admission might be daring or shameless, but it certainly is not funny. My interpretation, on the other hand, is much more plausible. If the relationship between Socrates and Alcibiades followed the traditional and respected form of Greek homosexuality, then it is obvious why Alcibiades' speech is funny.

Third, if we interpret Alcibiades' speech literally, then Alcibiades emerges as a flawed and vain person who is stuck in a vicious cycle of repetition and unable to benefit from Socrates' advice. Although this is a well-established image of Alcibiades, it is—in my view—an unsatisfactory picture. If Alcibiades is such a flawed person, why then is Socrates attracted to him? We know that Socrates loved Alcibiades (see, e.g., *Protagoras* 309b), but the standard interpretation of Alcibiades' speech in the *Symposium* leaves it mysterious why Socrates was interested in establishing a relationship with such a flawed young man. If, on the other hand, we adopt an ironic reading of Alcibiades' speech, Alcibiades emerges as a brilliant mind whose mastery of irony is equal to that of Socrates. Not only does Alcibiades understand what Socrates is trying to do, but he is also able to question and test Socrates' deepest aspirations. If we adopt an ironic interpretation, then Alcibiades does to Socrates what Socrates did to Agathon: he exposes the narcissistic elements in his character. It is therefore not surprising that Socrates is so attracted to Alcibiades. He is the only one who measures up to him. This is not to say that Alcibiades has no flaws. He is clearly a problematic person, but whatever his character flaws are, they are not as obvious and boring as a literal reading of Alcibiades' speech would suggest. An ironic reading explains the unique and seductive brilliance of Alcibiades' mind, and I take that as an additional advantage of this interpretation.

Suppose for a moment that we accept my ironic interpretation of Alcibiades' speech. What implications does this have for our picture of Socrates' attitude toward sexuality? If my reading of Alcibiades' speech is correct, we have reasons to reject the view that Socrates is only a Platonic lover of young boys. Socrates' attempts to seduce Alcibiades are also physical in nature. Socrates is therefore—to use a distinction from Pausanias' speech in the *Symposium*—not only engaged in heavenly love but also in common physical love. Socrates himself is struggling with the physical attraction he feels for young men. Although he is sometimes able to resist these impulses and manages to redirect them entirely toward philosophical activity, he succumbs in other situations—as, for example, in his relationship with Alcibiades—to the physical temptation of eros. The picture of Socrates' sexuality that emerges from my reading of Alcibiades' speech is similar to Ruby Blondell's view of Socrates' sexuality. Blondell (2006) argues that Socrates should be viewed as occupying all steps on the "ladder of love." According to her, we should see Socrates as embodying a variety of different kinds of love relationships. I believe that this interpretation of Socrates is essentially correct, and that my own reading of Alcibiades' speech is compatible with her interpretation. Alcibiades' speech shows us that Socrates was not only a refined Platonic lover but also—at certain times in his life—an active lover of particular male bodies.

8 Concluding Considerations

Let me conclude by considering two objections to my reading of Alcibiades' speech. First, after the end of the speech, Plato writes, "Alcibiades' frankness provoked a lot of laughter, especially since it was obvious that he was still in love with Socrates"

(222c). It might be objected that I have tried to get a lot of mileage out of the first part of that quotation but that I have completely overlooked the fact that the second part of the quotation contradicts the gist of what I say about Alcibiades' speech. At first glance, the objection appears very powerful. Since this passage is not part of Alcibiades' speech, it is clear that one cannot argue that the quotation is ironic. It is indeed true that Alcibiades is in love with Socrates. And while this may seem incompatible with my conclusion that Socrates was the one pursuing and seducing Alcibiades, I do not think it is. According to a more contemporary understanding of love, a person who is in love with somebody is presumed to be *doing* something. If Bill is in love with Sue, we assume that Bill is calling Sue, or sending her flowers, or asking her for a date. Being in love seems to entail some form of activity. However, I do not think that this is true for traditional Greek homosexual love. The *eromenos* takes pleasure in being pursued by the *erastes*. He enjoys being the center of attention, but he himself remains passive. If we understand the relationship between Socrates and Alcibiades in a more traditional way—and we have already seen above that a more traditional way of understanding the relationship between Socrates and Alcibiades is nicely compatible with my interpretation—then it is clear what Alcibiades' love for Socrates entails. As the former *eromenos,* Alcibiades still desires to be pursued by Socrates. Alcibiades is still in love with Socrates because he desires that Socrates pursue nobody but him. This is the reason why he is bothered by Socrates' obvious interest in Agathon and why he presents a speech that does not portray Socrates in a very flattering light. Alcibiades' love for Socrates is fully compatible with my interpretation of Alcibiades' speech.

Let us consider a second objection. It is clear that Plato's *Symposium* is a masterfully written dialogue. Every artistic detail seems to have philosophical significance. We thus should expect that the speech of Alcibiades has philosophical significance as well. However, it seems that on my interpretation of the speech of Alcibiades as ironic, the speech is funny but bare of any philosophical weight. We thus should prefer an interpretation like that of Nussbaum or Sheffield which can explain why the speech is philosophically important. I think this objection is not successful. Even if we adopt an interpretation of Alcibiades' speech as thoroughly ironic, it does not follow that the speech has no important role to play in the overall setting of speeches in the *Symposium*. If my interpretation is correct, then Socrates emerges as a person who struggles with integrating erotic desires within a philosophical life. This offers an important insight into the nature of eros. The speech of Alcibiades is a general warning to all philosophers that eros can never be tamed by philosophy. Even the greatest philosopher of all struggles with erotic temptations. What Plato wants us to see through the speech of Alcibiades is that eros has a very dangerous aspect. As Plato later says in Book IX of the *Republic*:

> There is a dangerous, wild, and lawless kind of desire in everyone, even in the few of us who appear moderate. (IX 772b)

This lawless erotic desire is present in everyone, but it is especially dangerous to philosophical souls. If Plato's *Symposium* were to end without Alcibiades' speech, we would walk away from it with the impression that erotic impulses are naturally conducive to leading good and virtuous lives. It would seem in this case that with a bit of philosophy and education, we can all climb the ladder of love and reap the benefits of the higher forms of eros. Alcibiades' speech is a reminder that even those like Socrates who have reached the higher levels of love are always at risk. Eros is never safe for the philosophical soul. There is always the chance that it leads to tyranny and slavery. And this fate cannot safely be avoided even in the presence of the greatest philosopher of all time.

I have argued in this essay that it matters what we think about the moral character of the historical Socrates. If my interpretation of Alcibiades' speech in Plato's *Symposium* is correct, Socrates does not emerge as a completely virtuous role model who has completely integrated all of his desires with the help of a comprehensive vision of the good. We should see him instead as a person who is in between virtue and vice. At times Socrates is a follower of Diotima who reaches for the higher stages of love, but at other times Socrates remains erotically attached to his great love Alcibiades. Socrates is active on all stages of the ladder of love, but he is unable to integrate these various love relationships into a harmonious whole.

Notes

1. I agree here with Jonathan Lear who stresses the similarities between the Socratic elenchus and psychoanalysis. For a more detailed discussion, see Lear (1998b), especially pages 162–165.
2. The battle of Delium in 424 BCE ended in a chaotic retreat of the Athenian forces. Alcibiades, who fought on horseback and saved Socrates, was later decorated for his bravery during the retreat.

Bibliography

Blondell, Ruby. 2006. Where is Socrates on the 'ladder of love'? In *Plato's Symposium: Issues in interpretation and reception*, ed. J.H. Lesher, Debra Nails, and Frisbee C.C. Sheffield, 147–178. Washington, DC: Center for Hellenic Studies.
Brickhouse, Thomas, and Nicholas Smith. 2002. *The trial and execution of Socrates: Sources and controversies*. Oxford: Oxford University Press.
Dover, Kenneth. 1978. *Greek homosexuality*. Cambridge, MA: Harvard University Press.
Dover, Kenneth. 1980. *Symposium*. Cambridge: Cambridge University Press.
Lear, Jonathan (ed.). 1998a. *Open minded: Working out the logic of the soul*. Cambridge, MA: Harvard University Press.
Lear, Jonathan. 1998b. Eros and unknowing: The psychoanalytic significance of Plato's *Symposium*. In *Open minded: Working out the logic of the soul*, 148–166. Cambridge, MA: Harvard University Press.
Lesher, J.H., Debra Nails, and Frisbee C.C. Sheffield. 2006. *Plato's Symposium: Issues in interpretation and reception*. Washington, DC: Center for Hellenic Studies.
Moravcsik, J.M.E. 1972. Reason and eros in the ascent passage of the *Symposium*. In *Essays in ancient Greek philosophy*, vol. I, ed. John P. Anton and G.L. Kustas, 285–302. Albany: State University of New York Press.
Nussbaum, Martha Craven. 1979. The speech of Alcibiades: A reading of Plato's *Symposium*. *Philosophy and Literature* 3: 131–172.

Nussbaum, Martha Craven. 1986. *The fragility of goodness: Luck and ethics in Greek tragedy and philosophy*. Cambridge: Cambridge University Press.

Reeve, C.D.C. 1992. Telling the truth about love: Plato's *Symposium*. *The Boston Area Colloquium in Ancient Philosophy* 8: 89–114.

Reeve, C.D.C. 2006. Plato on eros and friendship. In *A companion to Plato*, ed. Hugh H. Benson, 204–307. Malden: Blackwell Publishing.

Roochnik, David. 1985. *Apology* 40c4-41e7: Is death really a gain? *The Classical Journal* 80(3): 212–220.

Rudebusch, George. 1999. *Socrates, pleasure, and value*. Oxford: Oxford University Press.

Santas, Gerasimos. 1988. *Plato and Freud: Two theories of love*. Oxford: Basil Blackwell.

Schleiermacher, Friedrich, and William Dobson. 1836. *Schleiermacher's introduction to the dialogues of Plato*. Cambridge: J. & J. J. Deighton.

Sheffield, Frisbee C.C. 2006. *Plato's Symposium: The ethics of desire*. Oxford: Oxford University Press.

Zeller, Eduard, and Sarah Frances Alleyne. 1881. *A history of Greek philosophy from the earliest period to the time of Socrates*. London: Longmans, Green, and Co.

Plato's *Republic* as a Vocation

Allan Silverman

> The final result of political action often, no, even regularly, stands in completely inadequate and often even paradoxical relation to its original meaning... However, some kind of faith must always exist. (Weber 1946, p. 117)

> The possibility that the factual world is the outcome of a systematically disordered whole produces still another major difference between the epic political theorist and the scientific theorist. Although each attempts to change men's views of the world, only the former attempts to change the world itself. (Wolin 1969, p. 1080)

The title of the paper and the quotations above direct us to two essays: the first is the great sociologist Max Weber's 1918 speech at Munich University, *Politics als Beruf*, which we translate "Politics as a Vocation," and the second is eminent political theorist Sheldon Wolin's address to a Conference for the Study of Political Thought fifty years later, "Political Theory as a Vocation," published later in the *American Political Science Review*. I pass over what little I know about the circumstances and interests of Weber and Wolin that prompted their powerful critiques.[1] My aims in this essay are twofold. First, with the help of Weber and Wolin, I want to consider in which ways the notion of a vocation, and its role in understanding political theory, might help us to appreciate the political theory of Plato's *Republic*. In particular, I want to use Weber and Wolin as a launch point for reconsidering how we are to regard Plato's principle of specialization,

---

David Keyt and his work have been models to which I have aspired and fallen short since I first read his essay on the Mad Craftsman as an undergraduate. His essays are gems: clean, taut, inspired, and often revisionist arguments on some of the most critical passages and topics across every aspect of ancient philosophy. I hope that my contribution imitates his work at least in one of these dimensions.

A. Silverman (✉)
Department of Philosophy, The Ohio State University, 230 North Oval Mall,
350 University Hall, Columbus, OH 43210n-1365, USA
e-mail: silverman.3@osu.edu

one person-one job, to which one might add—a job he or she is born to do. Insofar as the principle admits of an explanation in terms of antecedent natures—each is born to do one specific job—I think that Plato, if he accepts the principle at all, accepts a very weak reading of antecedent nature. Instead, I think it is better to view the principle in the light of a person's single-minded focus when he or she thinks she is called to something. Second, I want to explore how Plato's account of education in the *Republic* comports with the principle of specialization to shed light on the purpose of the educational institutions of the *Kallipolis* and thus on Plato's account of the nature and aims of the state. Among other theses, I think that the earliest stages of education are designed for all the citizenry; that while the educational cursus specified for the would-be philosopher is perhaps the best training Plato can imagine, it is not a necessary condition for becoming a philosopher; and, lastly, that the design of educational institutions suggests that the aim and nature of the state is neither the stability of the state nor the (re)creation of a limited number of philosopher-rulers, but rather the moral betterment of the greatest number of citizens, that is, the happiness of all the citizenry. In brief, I think that the state and its educational institutions reflect Plato's belief that the appetitive, spiritive, and rational elements of the soul are plastic and thus shaped by education and environment.

1 Weber and Wolin

I am not sure that I know what a vocation is. Its root is the Latin *voco, vocare, vocavi, vocatum*, and thus we think of it as, and often translate it as, "a calling," though we need to keep in mind its primarily passive aspect, namely, being called or summoned, as in being called or summoned by God. In this vein, however, it is appropriate to note that the idea of being called need not imply any unwillingness, and indeed there is often a strong desire to pursue one's calling. Hence, the first entry for the term in my handy *Webster's Ninth* is: "a summons or a strong inclination to a particular state or course of action; especially a divine call to the religious life." Insofar as pursuit of what one strongly desires is part and parcel of all accounts of deliberative action, those who think that citing one's vocation as the reason for action is different from citing one's strong or strongest desire must say what is special about a vocation, that is, what distinguishes it from a strong desire. In this respect, one might think, correctly, that those concerned with this sense of vocation find their interests aligned with ethicists who focus on accounts of singular ethical judgments, as opposed both to accounts that rely on universalizable judgments and to accounts that take one's personal projects to have value distinct from the values of traditional consequentialist or nonconsequentialist ethical theories. One might appeal to the first sense of vocation in describing the life project of the philosopher-ruler, especially his appreciation of the circumstances facing him when called upon to descend back into the cave.

The juxtaposition of "summons or strong inclination" seems a fit way to express the ambiguity of the compulsion that sends him down.[2]

There is, however, another sense to "vocation," aptly cited as the second entry in *Webster's*: "the work in which one is regularly engaged: occupation."[3] One might think that the second sense, especially if given a negative nuance, captures Plato's sentiments about the banausic activities of the laboring or working class in the *Kallipolis*. (Sometimes we academics think of vocational training or vocational schools when we reflect upon those who practice a vocation.) One might equally raise the question of how we, twenty-first-century academic philosophers who engage in the interpretation and teaching of Plato's *Republic*, practice our vocation—in other words, what views have we of our enterprise as philosophical interpreters of it, that is, as those engaged in political theory, as well as in the training of others, students in general, and those among them who will go on to be academic theorists or called to politics. Is it an occupation, or maybe even a banausic occupation, or are we in some manner summoned to the task in virtue of a strong inclination? Indeed, is it a personal project to which we are called?

These two concerns may be united in a fashion, first through consideration of the question: What is Plato's aim in writing the *Republic*? I mean not only the question of who is his audience but also the question: How does he think his different audiences can each benefit from reading the *Republic*? So, for instance, if one takes a pessimistic view of the argument within the dialogue, to the effect that it is all about the creation of philosopher-rulers, and that only a very few folks indeed can ever hope to become philosophers owing to nature's exceedingly niggardly allotment of the requisite intellectual gifts to the citizens, one might then think that Plato's target audience is just a few special readers down through the centuries—whether one thinks that the targeting is done through irony or secret doctrines, or whether one thinks that the target itself is a few especially smart folks who have the requisite linguistic, mathematical, and philosophical chops to appreciate the philosophical subtleties. Conversely, if one thinks that every reader is the target audience, then one must equally think that there is some good that each of us can gain from reading the dialogue and being nurtured in understanding it by those of us who are teaching it. Accordingly, one might also think that within the *Republic* there must be some good that each of the citizens, regardless of their class, can derive from the rule of the philosophers, and that the design of the argument is to secure the best outcome for all. The extent to which one is an optimist about the *Republic* will be a function of what good(s) is (are) possible and for how many. My hunch is that one's position on the question of what it takes to become a philosopher, and who or how many are born endowed with the requisite skills, influences and maybe even determines how one thinks of the ethical and political theory presented within the *Republic*, Plato's aim in writing the *Republic*, and one's attitude as a teacher and philosopher interested in the *Republic*. And here is where Weber and Wolin come in.

Weber's task is "to understand by politics only the leadership, or the influencing of leadership, of a political association, hence today, of a state" (Weber 1946, p. 77). He rejects the definitions of a state in terms of ends, contending that sociologically the state can be defined only in terms of the specific means peculiar to it, namely, the use of physical force. This turns quickly to the questions of domination, obedience, and authority. Leadership comes from custom or mores, from legality, or from an extraordinary and personal gift of grace, and this latter gives rise to the notion of a calling (p. 79). In organizing the necessary means to achieving and maintaining domination, the material goods, and the bureaucratic offices and functionaries, the modern state has isolated these material means in the hands of its leaders. During this process, starting with service to the prince, there has arisen, according to Weber, a whole class of professional politicians different from those who are charismatic or called rulers, who serve the prince/ruler. At this juncture, Weber introduces the second sense of vocation. He distinguishes those for whom politics is an avocation, the occasional politician who acts politically when called upon, for example, to vote, or those who, "as a rule, are politically active only in the case of need and for whom politics is, neither materially nor ideally, 'their life' in the first place" (p. 83).[4] (Think of the nonphilosophers in the *Kallipolis*.) In contrast, there are those who make politics their vocation, either in that they live for politics or they live off of politics. For these individuals, politics is a profession, requiring those prescribed skills needed to maintain control of the material goods and political or administrative institutions for the purposes for which the institutions are designed or, sometimes, as the charismatic leader directs.[5]

In Wolin's essay, the circumstances are the discipline of political science in the 1950s and 1960s, where the behavioral revolution is well under way and the work of Kuhn on scientific revolutions is permeating the academy. The emphasis of the "new science" on the value-free nature of politics stands in contrast to the traditional approach to political theory of which Wolin is a champion. The need for vision, the need for the special insight into what is possible, a "skill" which allows the great theorist to transcend the actual and to offer a different perspective on what political authority, obedience, and goods amount to, is threatened by the routinization being promulgated by behavioralist luminaries in the profession of political science. Weber's two senses of "called to politics" are echoed in Wolin's appeal to keep separate the empirical, professional aspects of political science, or, better, the training of political scientists, from the need to train those who might be called to politics as political leaders.[6] The problem with the discipline of political theory is that some of its practitioners think specific skill sets are required of all students in the discipline and that all areas of political science, including political theory, should be focused on politics as it is found or practiced in actual states.[7] Political science, or political theory, is becoming a profession that eschews imagination and vision in favor of description, analysis, and prediction. For most theorists, however, and for all the great theorists "… the imaginative reordering of political life that takes place in theorizing is not confined to helping us understand politics" (Wolin 1960, p. 20). "Fancy neither proves nor disproves; it seeks, instead, to illuminate, to help us become wiser about political things" (ibid., p. 19).

In both Wolin and Weber, then, we find the dichotomy of routinization or a special skill set contrasted with the special gifts of the epic theorist or those called to politics. While many have remarked upon the difference between Weber's state and

Plato's or Aristotle's conception of the polis, there has been little attention paid to the notion of vocation, especially the vocation of the professional politician with his special set of learned skills. In one respect this is unremarkable. In the *Republic*, Plato devotes almost no space to the political establishment, the bureaucratic administration that will undoubtedly be required to implement the policies of the philosopher-rulers. There is the statement (*Rep.* VII 540a) about the fifteen years each philosopher will have to spend administering the state before he (re?)turns to philosophy. Insofar as the philosopher-ruler is best equipped to manage the state, it seems likely that his abilities derive less from his vision of the Forms than from his experience in the fifteen years of city management that he alone will have endured. To the extent that educational, judicial, economic, and political decisions will have to be made to ensure that faction, envy, and jealousy do not overwhelm the state, they will be made by these city managers, albeit under some guidance from the rulers themselves.

But if Plato ignores the skills required by professional politicians in this sense, that is, people who know how to *run* the state as opposed to *rule* the state, we can get quite a different impression about the rulers from the rigorous educational training that each philosopher must go through. Here, if anywhere in Plato, it is easy to think that there is indeed a very special set of skills that enables one to be a philosopher. But I want to suggest that not only is there reason to doubt that these skills or disciplines are needed in order to address political or administrative problems, it is not even clear what role they play as prerequisites for philosophical investigation.

The issue of professional training manifests itself in and is reinforced by one's understanding of and interpretation of the principle of specialization, the doctrine that each person should do one job.[8] In its perhaps most specific form, the idea is that each job or craft has not only its own definitive end, for example, the production of shoes or houses or knowledge of the Good but also a skill set that is deemed requisite for becoming and being proficient at the job (see *infra* pp. 139–142). While this may be true of certain crafts, it is uncertain whether it is true of philosophy. When, after his discussion of the propaedeutic sciences, Plato turns at last to dialectic, he speaks opaquely about seeing affinities and the ability to give and exact an account of the nature of things, returning ultimately to the metaphors of book VI of the *Republic* and the need to dissociate from the material, visible realm and turn the soul in a different direction. Pressed by Glaucon to say what is the nature of this dialectic and what are its divisions and ways, Socrates begs off, telling Glaucon that he will not be able to follow (*Rep.* VII 532e-533a). Socrates seems to have believed that he can do philosophy with every citizen who is a Greek speaker, and he is skeptical that there is a routine (other than elenctic question and answer) the teaching and learning of which makes one virtuous or a true politician. Plato also concedes (*Rep.* VII 520b; *Leg.* I 642d, XII 951b) the possibility that one can be a spontaneous or natural philosopher. The problem seems to me to be similar to the complaint voiced by Wolin against the behavioralist. The idea is that there are teachable skills that are uniquely necessary such that a would-be philosopher must learn them in order to gain the synoptic vision that qualifies one as a philosopher. Should one infer from the cursus of disciplines in book VII of the *Republic* that, for instance, one who cannot pass through solid geometry lacks the ability to become a philosopher? No doubt the skills developed in the ten years of advanced education are thought by Plato to be particularly germane to the problems facing the would-be philosopher, whether this would-be philosopher is engaged in dialectical inquiry into the Forms and whatever else is a suitable object of dialectical inquiry or is immersed in his fifteen-year term of public administration. But the urge to follow to the letter what Socrates says in the course of the argument and adopt the idea that these skills are *required* is fed by, and feeds into, lines of interpretation of the dialogue prevalent in *our* community.[9]

One line of interpretation, associated with Burnyeat's wonderful essay "Utopia as Fantasy,"[10] concerns how we are to treat the fantasy that is Plato's *Republic*. Burnyeat urges us to take seriously the recommendations, voiced through Socrates, as Plato's blueprint for the creation of the *Kallipolis*, for instance, banishing from a community everyone older than ten years of age. The idea that the reader is being directed to think that if we follow the procedures and recommendations then we will find a *Kallipolis* being born seems to others to get wrong the purpose of fantasy and to lay Plato, and Burnyeat, open to the charge that the *Republic* is inconsistent. Indeed, I think that any reader who maps out all of Socrates' recommendations and proclamations quickly becomes aware that there, at least, are tensions in the program. Some find the problem of genesis to be insurmountable, if we follow the fantasy as blueprint.[11]

Ober, approaching the historical context from the vantage point of the debate between the fifth- and fourth-century defenders and critics of the democracy, draws attention to the clash between those who think that the traditional educators, the laws, the demos, and so on are well suited to the task of training citizens in virtue and, on his account, those like Plato who think that the relatively informal democratic Athenian approach to civic education is inadequate. "Athenian critics of democracy devised theoretical models of formal educational institutions designed to teach each resident of the polis to act in ways that were appropriate to his or her station." [12] Following Ober we should expect the studies prescribed in book VII, since they would constitute professional training, to be *a theoretical model of formal education*, which the philosopher uniquely enjoys and which permits him to manage the affairs of the *Kallipolis*. And, accordingly, we might expect to find in the *Republic* a commitment to the notion, embraced by many of democracy's elite critics, that there is a station assigned by nature to each individual, and thus expect a series of tests throughout the educational process that assign individuals to their appropriate station—the principle of specialization with its accompanying idea of antecedent natures.

Whether one thinks that Plato intends the *Republic* to be a blueprint for the creation of the *Kallipolis* or intends it to be a theoretical model of formal education turns in no small measure on what one takes Plato's aims in writing the dialogue to be and what means he deploys in helping the reader understand those aims (see above pp. 127–131). We the readers and teachers are asked to think and imagine, to reflect on what to take at face value in the argument and what to regard as rhetorical flourish, to recognize gaps and to fill them in, and to decide on areas of emphasis in reconciling conflicting demands imposed by the argument. Ober and Burnyeat are right that at times Plato offers rather detailed recommendations. This is especially true, I think, not of his commitment to the sciences as a necessary propaedeutic to philosophy, but of the ideas guiding his attempt to create an ideal culture, what Burnyeat (1999a) refers to as the total culture: material, moral, and musical, founded on principles vastly different from those prevalent in Athens and elsewhere. But balancing the attention to detail prevalent in Socrates' remarks (throughout books II, III especially 400e ff., and X,) about musical modes, material culture, and the ways in which the total culture seeps unawares into every inhabitant's soul, there is noticeably little time spent discussing how the new total culture will be imposed or promulgated by the management of the state, and distressingly few specifics on the crucial early stages of education, to include who receives this education. If it is a blueprint, key elements are not filled in. Indeed, it is not entirely clear whether the principal goal of the design is to educate a small cadre of enlightened philosophers so that they might ensure, to the extent nature permits, a stable state (in part through the monopolization of the use of force) or whether the goal is to secure a state in which each citizen is educated to the highest level to which he can attain.[13]

Whatever Plato's goal, the *Republic* is a revolutionary treatise and in many ways antidemocratic. But, I think, the core of its criticism is not that most lack the formal education needed to rule (themselves or the state) effectively or that most, due simply to inadequate intelligence (*their appropriate station*), cannot be educated. Rather, the core of its attack is on the idea that individual political autonomy is intrinsically valuable, that political power is a per se good such that each should pursue it. The purpose of the fantasy is not then to develop a detailed blueprint of a series of steps by which we are to create a state or to develop a set of courses or tests, to include the courses and tests that a would-be philosopher must pass through, and to determine the station of each individual. It is, rather, to allow and encourage every reader/citizen to break free of the mindset that accords value to political power, to break free of what one experiences in the everyday affairs of the polis, and to reconceive the nature of ethical and political values. The studies described in book VII are perhaps best suited to turning the soul from this world to the world of Being, but they are not sine quibus non for such a turn. With Wolin, the sine qua non is vision or imagination, not a devotion to specific skills.

2 Education in the *Republic*

Whether or not philosophy requires the special training depicted in the *Republic* and whether Plato thinks that only a very limited number of individuals are by birth capable of succeeding at that training requires an assessment of Plato's remarks about education, Plato's political goals in designing this educational system (see the next section), and of Plato's principle of specialization (to which I turn in the final section).

Education enters the discussion with the second, fevered or luxurious city that is to be purged. Having abandoned itself to the unlimited acquisition of wealth, disregarding the limit set by our necessary wants (*Rep.* II 373d-e), this city will go to war with its neighbor(s) in order to obtain the land to provide for its wants. War requires a military, and, given the one person-one job principle borrowed from the establishment of the first city (369c-370d), there needs to be a group of "guardians," whose development will require the greatest science and training, equivalent to the seriousness of their occupation (374e). Their task will be to defend the city from both external and internal threats. The character or nature of those suited to be guardians is then likened to the watchdog: keenly perceptive, quick and strong, brave and spirited, and gentle toward friends and harsh toward enemies. And then almost as an afterthought, in addition to these traits of spirit (*thumoeides*), guardian candidates must be philosophical in nature, *philosophos ten phusin*. Having settled on these traits as the necessary features of guardians (376c), Socrates creates an education based on the traditional model of *mousike* and *gumnastike* to mold the very malleable character of youths in order to isolate students with the appropriate physical, emotional, and cognitive dispositions to become guardian-soldiers. In large measure, the discussion of poetry and song emphasizes the perfectly good and beneficent nature of the gods and seeks to instill admiration for moderation and the other moral virtues. The key to advancement for the student is that he or she comes to identify his or her own good with that of the polis (III 413c9-e3).

Let us, then, consider the stages of one's training, from birth to the age of fifty, when the education of the lucky few is finally complete. While it is not easy to identify each of these stages in great detail,[14] we seem to have a major division between two stages, separated by two or three years of military training roughly at age eighteen (VII 537b2-6). After military training, there are ten years of scientific and mathematical instruction in arithmetic, geometry, stereometry, astronomy, and harmonics (525b-531c). This period is followed by five years of dialectical training (531d ff. and 537-539e2) and then fifteen years in public administration (539e3-540a). At age fifty, one may then turn to philosophy. At this stage, and only at this stage it seems, does one come to know the Good and thus truly becomes knowledgeable, philosophical, good, and capable of ruling the *Kallipolis*.

As for the first eighteen years, matters are more opaque. There seem to be at least four stages of education. Working backward from the military training at age eighteen, there appears to be approximately seven years of secondary or advanced educational training, wherein music, some reading, and some mathematics comprise one side of one's training, and ever more difficult physical exercises, including guided visits to battles on horseback, are offered as part of gymnastics.[15] Throughout these musical exercises, there is a steady diet of memorization and recitation of the appropriate ethically oriented texts of the poets. It is here where there will also be an opportunity for the dispositions and predilections of the youths to manifest themselves. Some will apparently drop out to pursue apprenticeships in the arts and crafts, which seems to occur around the age of twelve in the early fourth century, no doubt influenced by circumstances, interests, proclivities, and likes and dislikes. Prior to that period, there seems to be four or so years of primary schooling in the same vein, with less demanding exercises in both music and gymnastics. From the ages of three to seven, we find something like preschool and kindergarten, where basic storytelling is offered to the youths and elementary exercises are required of all. That leaves the very earliest years as part of one's infancy. Here, with parents and nursemaids keeping track, the children are exposed to fairy tales and baby songs.

Now while Socrates says next to nothing about what happens to the children who enter the educational system, only some will make it to the military training (VII 537a), and he does recognize that there will be a winnowing effect on numbers as these best of the military, as it were, work their way through their mathematical and dialectical studies (537b-c). In the summary paragraphs at the end of book VII, Plato implies that these twenty-somethings who fail to advance to dialectical training lack a certain steadfastness and the synoptic vision to see the affinities among all the sciences and the nature of things. Yet, we can imagine that people will turn to different sciences as they discover that they are most interested in geometry or astronomy. Similarly, there will be dropouts at the remaining stages, that is, those who fail to pass trough dialectical training and those who stop sometime during the fifteen years of public administration.[16] Socrates says little about what experiences the five years of dialectic and fifteen years of state administration will provide one. Are the five years of dialectic spent in the same kind of philosophical study as that which the fifty-somethings engage in, or are they more like the relation of graduate study in philosophy to what one does once one has attained a doctoral degree and begun to develop his or her own research program? It is therefore even more curious why Plato thinks that the years from thirty-five to fifty should be spent in public administration. This stage is by far the longest in the educational cursus and seems inevitably to redirect the synoptic gaze down from the objects of dialectic and the mathematical and astronomical heavens. In the much larger city of Athens, there seem to have been approximately seven hundred city administrators. While the smaller *Kallipolis* requires far fewer, some number of individuals would have to serve as judges, revenue collectors, overseers of various religious and civic festivals, and especially overseers of the educational establishments. But when it comes to these jobs, the needs of *Kallipolis* are not mentioned. Rather, Plato seems to think that serving in these jobs is in some way conducive to coming to knowledge of the Good. One question is whether we can learn something about the sorts of problems that these nascent philosophers deal with; that is to say, how are we to think about the objects of the *techne* that they engage in at this stage? Since, in the chronological order of the fantasy, these folks will be working with mechanisms of the state created by older philosophers (i.e., the founders), we can speculate that they will spend their time learning first how these mechanisms were designed and why, and then solving the problems that they are designed to address, for instance, court cases, decisions about trade and other relations between the *Kallipolis* and the neighbors, whatever tax and revenue collection is needed to finance the activities of the military, religious and educational ministries, and overseeing the ministries. To think about the nitty-gritty details might incline one to conceive of the "objects" of this part of one's life as dwelling in the bottom-half of the line, as it were, unlike say the objects of the sciences studied for the previous ten, which occupy at least the third level. But this, I think, may not be right. Consider their activities instead as settling disputes and worrying about questions of distributive justice and finally as learning to deal with the behaviors, as a type, of the nonphilosophical soldiers, educators, and craftsmen. Then, perhaps, we can say that these fifteen years are spent rather in the study of rhetoric, psychology, sociology, and other social sciences. In this vein, these fifteen years seem more of a propaedeutic to philosophical study than fifteen years of administrative hell. Once again, of course, there will undoubtedly be dropouts during these fifteen years, individuals who will become judges or lawyers or counselors of various sorts.[17]

On the flip side from those who drop out at some point are those who complete the fifty-year course of instruction. They present their own problem, a problem apparent from the outset, since philosophy and guardianship and political rule appear to be different jobs. A philosopher who practices all would be a counterexample to the principle of specialization. On the other hand, it seems unlikely that whatever it is that qualifies the philosopher as a philosopher, the synoptic vision and the disregard for affairs in this world, is also going to serve as a special skill or *techne* that is adequate for managing the affairs of state. Lastly, focusing on what happens to individuals who are selected after their military training, we can perhaps see how difficult it is to contemplate what the one man-one job principle might actually mean in effect. The argument seems to imply that those who turn out to be philosophers are equally best at being guardian-warriors, mathematicians, astronomers, city managers, and so on. On the other hand, if pursuing one's job still relies on the single-minded focus on the task, lest opportunities slip by unpursued, then it is hard to understand how the philosopher who spends perhaps a few years studying geometry can be thought to do that job as well as the geometer who devotes his adult life to his study. Whatever one makes of the different way(s) in which the philosopher surpasses the scientist in knowledge of the scientific discipline,[18] Plato is well aware that none of the sciences prescribed for the would-be philosophers is complete in the sense that all of its truths have been discovered. A single-minded focus on geometry is characteristic of the geometer. The philosopher, on the other hand, is attracted to the study of affinities between sciences and has his or her focus on some synoptic goal. Both, then, have a single, though distinct, focus. Perhaps it is fair to characterize the geometer as having a deeper and broader understanding of the special science, while the philosopher seeks to understand the nature of science itself.

Even more peculiar, what might it mean to think that Plato is committed to the view that one's antecedent nature determines when one stops the climb through the educational and practical cursus? I shall turn to this topic in the next section, but first let me also register the question of what we are to say about the moral improvement, or lack thereof, of those who pursue astronomy or law, but never make it through the whole of the fifty years: Are these dropouts benefited by this cursus scientiarum regardless of whether they persist through to the end of their study and come to know the Good? It seems that they are, at least to the extent that gaining scientific understanding is considerably better than not, for it is part of the intelligible as opposed to the opinable. Equally clearly, the goal seems to be open to all who are selected for further training, despite the limited few who exhibit or develop the desire to pursue the synoptic vision. We do not know what the attrition rate is, but this does not matter. In fact, Plato never talks about who will likely drop out or whether they are silver or gold. It seems that they are tweeners.

If we consider the many remarks in the *Republic* on the principle of specialization and its accompanying doctrine of unique natural aptitudes, it is easy to come to believe that, according to Plato, each individual winds up in the very job that he finds him- or herself in because of antecedent nature. Eudoxus was born to be a geometer, not a philosopher, whereas Plato was born to be a philosopher. Of course, in order for each to wind up in the their respective jobs, there had to be a series of tests which each happened to pass, until the moment came when the former apparently was not good enough to succeed to the next study. A moment's reflection, I think, reveals how utterly implausible this notion is. But the fact that Plato relies on tests or some such device to determine who gets selected for each successive stage highlights that we need not appeal to antecedent nature to explain the distribution of individuals in the jobs they occupy. For we also have available a notion of developed nature that equally well accounts for all these outcomes. One's developed nature is, basically, the pattern of activities and dispositions that have come to be present in one's life owing to both one's nature and nurture, as it were. Nature in this case is understood in a much coarser fashion than the nature we just appealed to in explaining why Eudoxus became a geometer. Broadly speaking, there is little difference between the natural gifts of any scientist or dialectician or city administrator, or maybe even these folks and philosophers. In this respect, the various elements of the intelligentsia resemble the various elements of the artisan class. For while the introduction of the principle of specialization and its accompanying doctrine of unique natural aptitudes seems to imply that some are born to be cobblers and others house builders, by the middle of book IV Plato has undercut this strong reading of the doctrine. It matters hardly at all whether cobblers become farmers or house builders. It appears, then, that having revealed oneself as an artisan, it is an open question which kind of artisan one ultimately might turn out to be.

The difficulties the reader faces in trying to determine why one will migrate into the scientific disciplines rather than pursue philosophy to the (bitter) end raise the question of vocation anew. On the one hand, we can think that many of the would-be philosophers find themselves working in state administration or scientific disciplines because they find that they are called by math or astronomy or the law. Many others will of course resign themselves to their jobs, treating each of these disciplines as something to do, given that they have to do something. The notion of predestination, lurking behind much of Weber's account of vocations, works itself in as a justification perhaps for some. But if we now ask ourselves what Plato has in mind in adducing the principle of specialization, the analogue to both the predestination and the vocational aspects of the problem, we are asking about the design of the state and its educational institutions, a question of sociological or political structure. Does Plato's Platonism commit him not only to predestination but "pre-established harmony" between states, jobs, and natures?[19] Does it commit him to limiting the number of individuals who might enter into primary or advanced education? For instance, are the artisans' children denied all education? And, finally, what does it imply about Plato's conception of the nature of the state? Is the purpose of the educational institutions simply to guarantee that no one who is not a philosopher makes it into a position of rule? This would seem to imply that the fundamental aim of Plato's state design is to guarantee stability, since the state is most at risk when the nonphilosopher is allowed to rule. Or is Plato's aim to try to promote into that position whoever is capable of becoming (and, I would add, willing to become) a philosopher?

3 Institutional Design

The question is about the design of the state in relation to the capacities of the citizens of the state. In this regard, we can distinguish two aspects of the design. On the one hand, there is the need for stability. The educational institutions are designed to promote a unified city (*Rep.* V 462a-b).[20] If unity is to be achieved and maintained, some individuals must come to know the Form of the Good and be able to make the city into an image of that Form. A, if not the, chief threat to unity is lack of stability, in the form of stasis or civil war. One certain prospect for this outcome is to somehow allow a nonphilosopher to enter the ranks of the ruling elite. Equally threatening, given the powers vested in the ruling philosophers, dissension in their ranks must be avoided at all costs. In response to this threat, the designs of the educational system might be to ensure that only those capable of being philosophers obtain political power. Hence, the educational institutions can be quite selective. There is no guarantee that even all those among the silver and golden offspring who might in fact be capable of coming to knowledge of the Good will be admitted to advanced study. Whatever the founders determine to be the number of replacement philosophers, and with some empirical calculation of the rate of attrition that they can expect in the entering class, only a limited number of youths, undoubtedly selected from the offspring of golden parents, need be educated. Insofar as Plato is driven by considerations of the nature of the Forms and the necessity that one who is to rule (and be happy) will need to know the Form of the Good, the focus is on the educational programs that develop that knowledge in a handful of citizens. Provided that the denial of opportunities does not foment stasis among the nonphilosophers (if they think that the promise of social mobility was a lie), and provided that those golden offspring from the silver and golden parents not admitted to the training do not sew discord, the state will remain stably ruled only by philosophers. In this circumstance, we may raise questions about the degree to which the nonphilosophers are happy or whether the conditioning allows them to develop a sense of justice and pursue justice for justice's sake. But a failure to educate them to the best of their ability is not a charge to which Plato feels the need to respond, since they pose little threat to the stability of the *Kallipolis*.

This is not Plato's preferred path to stability. Unity and stability are to be achieved by the promotion of *homonoia* among all the citizens. *Homonoia* will be achieved, in turn, if each class (and its individual members) enjoys the degree or level or kind of happiness appropriate to each (IV 419-421c). This condition is secured when each person performs the task in the state for which his nature is best suited (433a).

This is the second, and critical, aspect of the design of the state: it has to produce a certain outcome of goods for all the citizens, if stability is to be reached through consensus. In response to Adeimantus' objection at the outset of book IV that the guardian rulers will not be very happy (419a ff.), Socrates responds that their goal was not to make them the most happy (in the manner in which Adeimantus thinks of happiness), but rather that their object "... on which we fixed our attention in establishing the state was not the exceptional happiness of any one class but the greatest possible happiness of the city as a whole." Here we do face the question of the status of those individuals who are not philosophers and what Plato envisages with respect to their lives or their degree of happiness. It is agreed by all that most of the citizens in Plato's state will not in fact achieve the happiness enjoyed by the few who come to know the Good. Defenders of antecedent nature think that the reason why most will not come to this knowledge is that most cannot from birth make the climb. Either because they are cognitively defective and thus lack the raw intellectual power to pursue the study of the Good, or because they are born with a desiderative capacity configured in a way in which their desires are channeled from the outset in the pursuit of either appetitive or spiritive satisfaction, most individuals, regardless of what they might learn or hear in the course of their upbringing, that is, regardless of how they might be educated, simply will not choose to pursue philosophy or any of the prerequisite studies that Plato proposes in books II, III, and VII. Against this reading, a reading all concede is available if not the most obvious to take from the text, one can cite a few considerations. First, there is the historical and philosophical record. Socrates appears to have been rather egalitarian in his approach to the educability of the Athenians. While he surely thought that knowledge was extremely hard to come by, and may even have doubted whether anyone had in fact come to know what virtue is, and while he may have thought that the many, owing to the corrupting influences of the democratic political processes in Athens, were almost doomed never to come to such knowledge, Socrates engaged in elenctic and philosophical inquiry with any Greek speaker, including slaves. Second, the psychic metaphysics of the *Republic* suggests that every human soul is fundamentally and essentially rational. Irrespective of the cycle of reincarnation, the character of one's upbringing, and even the genetic inheritance, "[th]e excellence of thought, it seems, is certainly of a more divine quality, a thing that never loses its potency, but according to the direction of the conversion, becomes useful and beneficent, or, again, useless and harmful" (VII 518e).[21]

Finally, there is the theme, highlighted in the Myth of the Metals (III 414c-415e), that just as children born of golden parents are not guaranteed to be themselves of the same metal, so too there is the chance that children born of silver or even bronze parents may in fact turn out to be golden-souled. It is controversial whether or not Plato in the remainder of the argument, and especially in the light of his remarks about eugenics in book V, actually lives up to the promise of the Myth. If Plato does believe that philosophers can come from any class, and if the goal of the state is to promote each to the highest level of achievement he can reach,[22] then the educational institutions will have to embrace, at least at the outset, virtually all the citizens of *Kallipolis*.

It is beyond the scope of this essay to defend the thesis that the design of the state is to promote each citizen to the highest level possible for him or her to achieve. And it is equally impossible to offer a reading of the Myth of the Metals and an account of the Noble Lie in the limited confines of this essay. I do think that there is a clear promise of social mobility in the Myth, and accordingly, I think that all children of *Kallipolis* receive at least elementary education. Among other reasons, if an entire class of children were excluded from the outset and so never received any education, it would be obvious to all that the promise of social mobility was a lie. But more importantly, while Plato's clear focus is to promote an increasingly diminished number to each successive stage of instruction, it is very hard to see how (or why) any of the children and citizens of *Kallipolis* can be exempted from the cultural and ideological milieu that Plato spends books II and III detailing. From the fables and nursery hymns to the tales of the gods and other heroes, to the music that surrounds the festivals and ceremonies of the state, and on to the public architecture and art, all conform to the principles of beauty, symmetry, and order that is *Kallipolis*' ideology (see especially Burnyeat [1999b] and *Rep.* III 401b ff).[23] Plato offers no hint that the songs and hymns sung to the children will vary depending on whether the children are raised by parents in the home or nursemaids in the special crèches of book V furnished to the golden and silver offspring, and it is hard to see how the folklore could vary widely in a state the size of *Kallipolis*. Total culture is just that: no one is unexposed to the revolutionary changes to the musical, moral, and material environment Plato envisages.

Homonoia is secured when each person performs the task in the state for which his nature is best suited (IV 433a). I think that in order to guarantee this outcome, Plato needs to offer every citizen the opportunity for education—not the prospect of certain advancement to even guardianship training after the age of twelve, but merely the chance to exhibit one's talents in early education. That all are so-educated reinforces the prospect for *homonoia* in that the early phases of education, along with the cultural and ideological environment, promotes a more uniform social psychology by controlling, to the extent possible, the emotional development and reactions of the citizens.

Plato thinks that all citizens are better off by having a better set of beliefs about justice and pleasure. It is possible, in other words, that his state sets about to develop better-ordered souls that fall short of knowledge, since the same set of beliefs and emotional responses that allow those who are capable to achieve knowledge of the Good also promotes the better ordering of the souls of those who will not climb so high. All are provided the same first stages of education, for all are better off for having heard the myths and the music and seen the art and, in general, better off for having some education. The length of time one remained in the system might then conduce to both the greater stability of these true beliefs and, perhaps, more focus on the better pleasures.

This distributional outcome of people to jobs is not, I have claimed, the responsibility of Plato's strong commitment to antecedent natures. A good thing, too, since were there such a strong antecedent nature, there would be little reason to put everyone through any education or provide tests: an individual's nature would out, perhaps without any reference to his own efforts, provided that the economic environment provides the appropriate avenues of employment. In its place, read Plato's remarks about nature as largely referring to developed nature, a combination of nature and nurture. In a moment I will explore just how weak or strong a reading of nature's contribution we might arrive at. Some support for the account of developed nature is found in reflection on the path that those selected for advanced study go down. Rather than think their stopping point is predetermined by a fine-grained antecedent nature, we should view their stopping point retrospectively: having seen where each ended up, Plato can write that that occupation was in their nature all along.

4 The Principle of Specialization and Vocations

In many cases, it seems that a strong commitment to antecedent nature is the product of Plato's account of the principle of specialization and its extension to the design of the state and its educational institutions. Here, too, one starts from two questions: What kinds of jobs are needed in the state if it is to be well-functioning and stable? How does one find or develop individuals with the requisite abilities to perform those jobs? Let us begin from the state. Plato arranges his analogy of the state to show that there are certain tasks or jobs that must be performed in a society if it is to flourish. Broadly speaking, there are the tasks of ruling, soldiering, and the commercial activities, the banausic jobs. But Plato paints with finer strokes. The principle of specialization enters the *Republic* with the creation of the first city, the so-called City of Pigs. The creator of this first city is our needs for food, housing, clothing, shoes, and so on. Isolated individuals are unable to provide for these needs and so band together to remedy their lack. Socrates inquires whether each of these four men will contribute their work to the common use of all, for example, the farmer working full time on farming and feeding all four, or whether each will divide his days into four, devoting a quarter of his time to procuring for himself each necessity. Adeimantus answers that the former way is easier: each will perform one task. This is the principle of specialization; one man will do one job. In support of this answer, Socrates remarks: "It would not, by Zeus, be at all strange; for now that you have mentioned it, it occurs to me myself that, to begin with, our several natures are not all alike but different. One man is naturally fitted for one task, and another for another" (II 370a7-b2). This is the principle of unique aptitudes, on which rests the notion of antecedent nature. Why does Plato add this principle? One reason might be that the principle of specialization seems a forgone conclusion, given the setup of the first city. For if individuals were able to provide for their needs by dividing their time, the first city would not have been necessary to begin with. Two additional reasons to think that specialization will make for "better working" (*kallion prattoi*) are then adduced: each job goes better when the worker seizes the relevant opportunities of the moment and when he devotes all his energy to mastering the one task. These "requirements of expertise" amount to at least the recommendation that the worker pay constant attention to his work and that he work long and steadily to master the craft. "The result, then, is that more things are produced, and better and more easily when one man performs one task according to his nature, at the right moment and at leisure from other occupations" (II 370b-c).

Note that not only are the principle of specialization and the principle of natural aptitudes distinct, but there is nothing in either that entails that there is a unique nature or definition or job description, as it were, for any of the crafts. Later (V 455b-c) we learn that one's aptitude is evidenced by facility at learning, easy comportment of one's body to the task, and so on. But like the requirements of expertise, these features all address the worker, not the craft itself. Strictly speaking, we cannot infer anything about the nature of these crafts from the conditions true of us human workers. Still, it is plausible to assume that there is some connection between the way in which we perform jobs and the nature of the jobs we perform. Even so, the purpose behind the introduction of the principle of specialization is not to address us and the ease with which we work, but rather to promote a greater amount of goods that each of us may share.

If the inference from features of human workers to descriptions of jobs to be performed is not entirely licit, I suspect that there are other reasons scholars have embraced the notion that each craft or job has a fixed, specific description or nature. First and foremost, perhaps, is the Platonic Theory of Forms, portrayed vividly in the metaphor of philosophy as butchery: for each one of the crafts, there is a Form or job-Form,[24] as it were, whose definition provides what I have called its job description. There are reasons to be skeptical about Forms of the crafts or any Form that seems dependent on the activities of humans or other creatures; for instance, new crafts or skills constantly come to light, and new and better ways of performing a task seem an inevitable part of our progress. Even when we consider the sciences, it is hard to imagine that Plato thinks that he already knows what the essential nature of each is. This is not to say that there is no Form of Geometry, as it were, whose structure will be revealed when our progress is finished, that is, when the science is complete. It is, rather, to suggest that Plato recognizes that advancements are being made constantly in each science, and that he is not yet in a position to write the job description.

But suppose that there are Forms of each of the crafts and suppose that there are the detailed job descriptions that specify what skills are needed if one is to perform the job. It does not follow from the Theory of Forms itself that there are souls matched to tasks. It is a separate task to determine whether individuals have the antecedent nature to perform those jobs. It sometimes seems as though Plato proposes that we can scrutinize individuals to see what skills they possess prior to their practicing any craft, namely, when they are quite young. Maybe Plato thinks that there is the equivalent of the Scholastic Aptitude Test (SAT) for each job that allows somebody to assign those born with artisanal souls to their respective tasks. Surely this would be a mind-numbing job for the philosopher-rulers, so perhaps this is one of the tasks that the city managers perform. The fact is we simply lack any definitive texts here that tell us how folks sort themselves out into their occupations prior to the age of twenty.

Finally, as we read the dialogue, it sometimes seems that Plato thinks that we can determine which jobs will be needed if the state is to flourish. Believers in the notion that Plato is propounding a detailed blueprint for how to create the *Kallipolis* will incline to such a view. But it faces its own challenges. There is a providential assumption to the effect that there are natural aptitudes for just these jobs and that in the special circumstances there is present in the labor pool individuals with just those aptitudes. Perhaps the top-downing goes even further, such that the well-functioning polis includes all the jobs, and that there is no individual born with an aptitude for whom the state fails to provide a job accordingly. There is neither excess labor nor malcontented individuals struggling to find an opportunity to practice their natural or god-given talents. (One can also imagine, as was true of Athens and is true in the present, that one would need to import talent. Nor does it even follow that there will be folks with those talents—we can envisage jobs simply going unfilled.)

The fortuitousness of this top-down situation emerges from the first moment of city construction in the dialogue, the City of Pigs. What then is the point of adding that individuals have natural aptitudes? We can, I think, find three possible explanations. First, Plato might just think it is true that individuals are born with such aptitudes and he wants to bring this in from the beginning of his enterprise. Second, he might believe that given aptitudes, one who focuses on the single task for which one is fit will produce more goods for the group and thus make the state, that is, the individuals, better off. Finally, he may believe that if one works at the job for which one is naturally fit, one will be happier in one's work. All three explanations are consistent and all three, when combined with the providential design that finds first five and then many more dwellers who have precisely the aptitudes needed by the city, result in a cooperative enterprise where no one's needs goes unmet and each seems satisfied with what they have.

The top-down or providential account leaves us with individuals who are born with specific aptitudes to do jobs that require, in virtue of the kind of jobs they are, constant attention and long single-minded study. It is not necessary to go so far, however. One fallback position sponsors generic antecedent natures: some are born to be craftsmen and some philosophers or soldiers. The basic image here is that of the three classes isolated in the Myth of the Metals. Nothing speaks to whether one will be a cavalryman or an infantryman, an astronomer or a geometer, a maker of statues or a maker of pots. The third, and weakest, and therefore most plausible, account allows that the differences are not even best viewed as job related. Rather, the basic difference is a matter of intelligence or desire. One can carve broadly with this distinction. At bottom, it reflects the belief, or fact, that some people are just smarter than others. (Perhaps philosophers take the lead in thinking that this is true.) Usually, this thesis is deployed in the negative claim that some are not capable of engaging in certain kinds of work; for Plato, some are not capable of being philosophers. The task of the educational system is then understood to be finding those who are not gifted enough and weeding them out. The oracle said, "the city will be destroyed if it ever has an iron or bronze guardian" (415d).

If philosophy is a profession with a well-defined job description including a set of skills that are required by all who practice it, then it may seem more plausible to believe that there are only a few individuals born with the requisite nature to practice philosophy. Of course being born with such a nature does not guarantee that one will end up a philosopher, since nurture can cause even the best among the *Kallipolians* to wind up in a bad place.

> Plato's picture of the virtuous agent in the *Republic* makes his intelligent appreciation of the objective properties of fineness and goodness essential to virtuous action. The virtuous and rational agent, for Plato, is one who is properly responsive to the real value of actions and things. Without a grasp of these true value properties, the person must fail to be appropriately responsive to genuine value. So part of Plato's pessimism in the *Republic* about the virtue of the nonphilosophers rests on his understanding of a virtuous agent as one who is responsive to genuine value. (Bobonich 2002, p. 86)

The idea that only the philosophers have the right sort of values is founded on the premise that only the philosophers have beliefs and knowledge about the Forms and especially the Good. Read strictly, this implies that only when one knows the Good, the Form seemingly known last among all the Forms, does one have knowledge of any Form and hence only then does one live a happy and just life. It is not clear whether prior to this achievement one even has beliefs about Forms. If one hews to so strict a line of interpretation, then it is arguable that no one prior to the age of fifty is happy or just.

I have tried to suggest that there is reason to think that we should not view Plato, or the *Republic*, as a sponsor of the view that philosophy is a profession. I have also tried to draw attention to just how committed we readers must be to the idea that the argument of the dialogue provides us with Plato's detailed blueprint for developing philosophers. Perhaps Plato does believe in a fortuitous or god-given linkage between just the right kind of souls with antecedent natures designed to do certain jobs and the need and availability of just those jobs for a well-designed state in which philosophers rule. But if we consider the number of jobs or disciplines through which the would-be philosopher must pass, and especially if we keep in mind that the longest years of study are spent not on mathematical studies but city management, it is hard to see what discipline contributes most to the synoptic vision. And it is equally hard to see why any study would be unsuitable. Reflection on the course of study reinforces the suspicion that neither the principle of specialization nor the notion of unique natural aptitudes is straightforward. Developed nature, a combination of nature and nurture, is enough. And what seems more plausible an account of specialization is single-minded focus, not performance of a job. The would-be philosopher focuses all his energy on coming to know the Good, treating the various disciplines as means to that end. Eudoxus is not built that way. He, rather, is gripped by geometry and focuses on developing as much of the science as he can. We cannot predict whether Eudoxus will be a philosopher or mathematician, we can only look backward at his choice.

Plato's philosopher-ruler is called by the Good. The right sense of "vocation" is that associated with Weber's charismatic leader and Wolin's epic theorist, an agent of vision and imagination, not a technocrat who details and predicts events in an actual polis. The relevant nature of such a leader is not his antecedent nature but his developed nature. Similarly, the idea that the educational establishment of the state is designed for only a few, perhaps the offspring of golden parents or maybe also silver parents, is again wedded to the wrong sense of vocation. Which class people end up in is a function of the choices exercised throughout the course of an educational cursus whose initial class is everybody. All three parts of the soul are plastic. Doubtless Plato believes that individuals are born with differences in their intellectual gifts and motivational structures. The question seems to me to be whether Plato's political theory is designed to reinforce those differences to secure a handful of philosophers or to give everyone the opportunity to break free from their earlier mindset, whether that is due to a developed or an antecedent nature. *Mutatis mutandis*, the same question can be asked about his readers. And lastly, it can be asked of those of us who spend our life teaching the *Republic*: to what are we called?

Notes

1. They are, respectively, the evolution of the practice of politics in Europe from roughly 1800 to 1918 and the evolution of the discipline of Political Science in the United States especially in the years between the end of World War II and 1968. Wolin's epic theorist trying to change the world is founded on his reading of Plato, and Weber's remark captures the paradox that the descended philosopher recognizes in considering the outcomes of his actions.
2. But see Adams' essay on vocation (1999, pp. 292–317): "What would tend to render the concept of vocation superfluous would be the identification of one's true vocation with the course of life in which one would do the most good" (p. 300). Here Adams is reflecting on consequentialism, not Plato.
3. For the sake of completeness, let me note that the third lexical entry is "the special function of an individual or group."
4. Ibid., p. 83
5. In this respect, they differ from the charismatic leaders. Those called in the sense of the great leaders will concentrate on the use of violence and the control of power or force. They will inevitably be confronted with the hard political choices and in all likelihood be corrupted by the process.
6. As in times past, the proper training for those called in this sense are the great books of Plato, Hobbes, and so on, which allow those who are called to appreciate the nature of the set of problems all political theorists face, as opposed to a set of solutions that purport to address a defined goal of theory. There is no such well-defined goal.
7. Indeed, Wolin thinks that in the hands of their sponsors, they have become the normal science for all of the problems addressed by the "science" of political science, with theory now being regarded as part of a methodology that has been replaced by the behavioral revolution.
8. *Rep.* II 374a-e, III 394d-e, 400e, 406c, 415a-d, 421a, IV 421c, 423c, 423d (cf. 397e), 433a, 434a-b, 435b, 441d, 444b
9. Compare also the neo-Pythagorean account of the late Plato, where dialectic is largely, if not solely, mathematics and any one who cannot do advanced mathematics is disqualified from engaging in metaphysics or epistemology; or those who think that understanding Plato requires a special training in reading what is not in the text, whether because it is between the lines or revealed somehow elsewhere; or excessively analytic types who implicitly or explicitly exclude, both in the classroom or in print, the availability of alternative lines of interpretation

predicated on literary, historical, or non-analytic approaches. A contemporary scholar of ancient philosophy might rewrite, *mutatis mutandis,* the Wolinesque complaint about the way in which his discipline was heading, where sometimes seminal scholars seem to be absent from reading lists, whether it be a Cherniss or a Derrida, or an Irwin or a David Charles.

10. Burnyeat (1999b).
11. Burnyeat is addressing his essay in no small measure to Strauss (1964) and his followers, who emphasize the paradox of genesis in defending their ironic reading of the argument. For a most sensitive discussion of Strauss, see Ferrari (1997).
12. Ober (2001, p. 176).
13. See pages 127–128 *supra* on Weber's understanding of the state.
14. See the classic studies of Jaeger (1943) and Marrou (1956).
15. Marrou conjectures literature, music, and then math.
16. Compare Reeve (1988, pp. 195–97) who associates these dropouts with his sixfold classification of desires.
17. See *Rep.* IV 425b7-e10. There is much, for example, business matters and contracts, that is legislated in Athens that *Kallipolis'* rulers need not legislate about. This, however, does not entail that disputes will not arise nor eliminate the need for contracts.
18. One's position on the nature of the ascent to and descent from the unhypothetical first principle of *Rep.*V 511 is liable to be influenced by one's conception of Plato's epistemology: holists will differ from intuitionists over whether knowledge of the principle entails awareness of all the truths of a field of study or perhaps of all the Forms.
19. See Striker's remark in Brennan (2005, p. 257 n. 9).
20. On the importance of unity (of the city), see Schofield (2006, pp. 212–18).
21. Despite the fact that the context is that of the climb from the Cave, this remark is not limited to those who have left the Cave. Compare the remarks in book X (609–612a) on the true nature of the human soul. All translations derive from Shorey.
22. See Meyer (2005, p. 234), Brennan (2005, p. 248), and Reeve (1988, pp. 170–234).
23. See Burnyeat (1999b) and Lear (1992).
24. Compare the argument in the *Cratylus* 386d8-390a5 leading to the problem of "Name-Forms": Is there a Form of Name itself or (inclusive) are there Forms for each of the names, that is, the common nouns, whose referent, so to speak, is a Form, such as the "Horse" itself, the "Dog" itself?

Bibliography

Adams, Robert. 1999. *Finite and infinite goods.* New York: Oxford University Press.
Bobonich, Christopher. 2002. *Plato's utopia recast.* New York: Oxford University Press.
Brennan, Tad. 2005. Commentary on Meyer. In *Proceedings of the Boston area colloquium in ancient philosophy,* ed. John J. Cleary and Gary Gurtler, 244–263. Leiden: Brill.
Burnyeat, Myles. 1999a. Culture and society in Plato's *Republic. Tanner Lectures on Human Values* 20: 217–324.
Burnyeat, Myles. 1999b. Utopia and fantasy: The practicability of Plato's ideally just city. In *Plato 2,* ed. Gail Fine, 297–308. New York: Oxford University Press.
Ferrari, G. 1997. Strauss' Plato. *Arion* 5(2): 36–65.
Jaeger, Werner. 1943. *Paideia: The ideals of Greek culture,* vol. 2. New York: Oxford University Press.
Lear, Jonathan. 1992. Inside and outside the *Republic. Phronesis* 37: 184–215.
Marrou, H.I. 1956. *A history of education in antiquity.* New York: Sheed and Ward.
Meyer, Susan. 2005. Class assignment and the principle of specialization in Plato's *Republic.* In *Proceedings of the Boston area colloquium in ancient philosophy,* ed. John J. Cleary and Gary Gurtler, 229–243. Leiden: Brill.

Ober, Joshua. 2001. The debate over civic education in classical Athens. In *Education in Greek and Roman antiquity*, ed. Yun Lee Too, 175–208. Leiden: Brill.
Reeve, C.D.C. 1988. *Philosopher-kings*. Princeton: Princeton University Press.
Schofield, Malcolm. 2006. *Plato*. New York: Oxford University Press.
Shorey, Paul. 1930–35. Plato's *Republic*. 2 vols. Cambridge, MA: Harvard University Press.
Strauss, Leo. 1964. *City and man*. Chicago: University of Chicago Press.
Weber, Max. 1946. Politics as a vocation. In *From Max Weber*, ed. H.H. Gerth and C.Wright Mills, 77–128. New York: Oxford University Press.
Wolin, Sheldon. 1960. *Politics and vision*. Boston: Little Brown.
Wolin, Sheldon. 1969. Political theory as a vocation. *The American Political Science Review* 63(4): 1062–1082.

Soul, Soul-Parts, and Persons in Plato

C.D.C. Reeve

Republic IV argues that a human soul has three parts or elements: appetite (*epithumêtikon*), spirit (*thumoeides*), and reason (*logistikon*). Socrates speaks, too, of "others that may be in-between" (443d7-8) the canonical three. While this no doubt allows for some relaxation of strict tripartite-ism, it raises a problem of its own: Why would any other elements or parts there might be have to be "in between" the others? That, of course, is just a special case of the more general problem of explaining what these soul-parts are and how they are related to the soul itself and to the person whose soul it is.[1]

1 Reason

When reason is first introduced, its functions seem to be predominantly practical. It is the element in the soul [1] "with which it calculates" (439d5), the one [2] that is "really wise and exercises foresight on behalf of the whole soul" and so is its proper or appropriate ruler (441e3-5), [3] that "guards the whole soul and the body against external enemies...by deliberating" (442b5-7), and [4] that has "within it the knowledge of what is advantageous both for each part and for the whole, the

---

Philosophy, need I say, is a disputatious subject. So it will come as no surprise that David Keyt and I have often disagreed—including on the topic of his recent publication, "Plato and the Ship of State," as readers of my *Blindness and Reorientation: Problems in Plato's Republic* (New York: Oxford University Press, 2012), will quickly see. But I would never have looked at the simile so closely had it not been for David's characteristically trenchant paper. For that, and for the generous help he gave me with my translation of Aristotle's *Politics*, I offer him this essay in celebration of his fifty-five years of distinguished service to his university.

C.D.C. Reeve (✉)
Department of Philosophy, CB #3125, University of North Carolina-Chapel Hill, Chapel Hill, NC 27599, USA
e-mail: cdcreeve@mac.com

community composed of all three" (442c5-7). Later, however, reason takes on a more contemplative or theoretical characterization. It is the element [5] "with which we learn" (580d9). It is the one [6] that is "always straining to know where the truth lies" (581b6-7), [7] that it is appropriate to call "learning-loving and philosophic" (581b10-11), and [8] that, when it rules in someone's soul, causes him to think that the pleasures of making money and being honored are "far behind" that of "knowing where the truth lies and always enjoying some variety of it while he is learning" and to praise his own life as the most pleasant (581d1-11). When we recall that the philosopher's preferred life is one of contemplating the Forms (519b7-521c8), our confidence might grow that if a fracture or fissure were to open within reason, it would occur between [4] and [5].

That none occurs there—or that none is presented as occurring there—is due, in part at least, to a pair of doctrines. First, "the most important thing to learn about" is the Form of the Good (505a2), since "it is by their relation to it that just things and the others become useful and beneficial" (505a3-4), so that "if we do not know it, ... even the fullest possible knowledge of other things is of no benefit to us, any more than if we acquire any possession without the good" (505a6-b1). The putatively theoretical knowledge described in [5–8] is thus knowledge of something with profound practical import. Put another way, the truth it is always seeking is (or includes) practical truth—truth whose unhypothetical first principle is the Good (508b12-511e5). Second, while justice and beauty are *ambivalent* so that "many people would choose things that are reputedly just or beautiful, even if they are not so, and to act, acquire things, and form beliefs accordingly," goodness is not ambivalent: "no one is satisfied to acquire things that are reputed good, but, on the contrary, everyone seeks the things that are good" and "disdains mere reputation" so that the good is "what every soul pursues and for its sake does everything" (505d5-e2).

The joint import of these two doctrines is that the Good is pursued because every soul wants good things and so wants to know what things are really good, useful, and beneficial—something only knowledge of the Form of the Good can provide. What eventually emerges as the most beneficial thing, however, the one the *Philebus* calls "the [best] good *in a human being*" (64a1), is knowing or contemplating that very Form so that the pleasure of "knowing where the truth lies" emerges as the most pleasant pleasure, and the philosophic life around which it is organized is the happiest (576d6-588a10).

What makes it just and appropriate for reason to rule the soul (or the appetitive and spirited elements) is explained in [2], [3], and [4]. Reason is wise (it has knowledge of the Form of the Good) and exercises foresight on behalf of the whole soul by making use of that knowledge. When it rules, it is not simply its own interests that it considers, therefore, but those of the other parts as well: "when the entire soul follows the philosophic element and does not engage in faction, the result is that each element does its own work and is just, and, in particular, each enjoys its own pleasures, the best pleasures and—to the degree possible—the truest" (586e4-587a2). On the other hand, when "one of the other parts gains mastery, the result is that it cannot discover its own pleasure"—since it does not have access to the only reliable paradigm for evaluating the goodness of pleasures—and "compels the other parts to pursue an alien, and not a true pleasure" (587a4-6). With each part satisfied by the best and truest pleasures available to it, faction is banished, and from "having been many," the reason-ruled soul becomes "entirely one, temperate, and harmonious" (443e1-2). As an ideal of rational order and unity, the Form of the Good thus induces a like order and unity in the soul of the one who loves and contemplates it (500c3-d3).

Though the rational unity that flows from the Good flows into the reason-ruled soul as a whole, the consequences for reason are different from those for the other soul-parts. The following passage begins to explain why:

> We must not think ... that the soul in its truest nature is full of complexity, dissimilarity, and conflict with itself.... It is not easy, you see, for something to be immortal when (*te*) it is composed of many elements and (*kai*) is not composed in the most beautiful way—which is how the soul now seemed to us.... Yet both our recent argument, and others as well, compel us to accept that the soul *is* immortal. But what it is like in truth, seen as it should be, not maimed by its partnership with the body and other bad things, which is how we see it now, what it is like when it has become pure—*that* we can adequately see only by means of rational calculation. And you will find it to be a much more beautiful thing than we thought and get a much clearer view of the cases of justice and injustice and of all the other things that we have so far discussed. So far what we have said about the soul is true of it as it appears at present. But the condition we have seen in it is like that of the sea god Glaucus, whose original nature cannot easily be made out by those who catch glimpses of him, because some of the original parts of his body have been broken off, others have been worn away and altogether mutilated by the waves, while other things—shells, seaweeds, and rocks—have been fastened to him, so that he looks more like any wild beast than what he naturally was. Such, too, is the condition of the soul when we see it beset by myriad bad things. But, Glaucon, we should be looking in another direction ... toward its love of wisdom. We must keep in mind what it grasps and the kinds of things it longs to associate with, because it is akin to what is divine and immortal and what always exists, and what it would become if it followed this longing with its whole being and if that impulse lifted it out of the sea in which it now is, and struck off the rocks and shells which, because it now feasts on earth, have grown around it in a wild, earthy, and stony profusion as a result of those so-called happy feastings. And then you would see its true nature, whether multiform or uniform, or somehow some other way. But we have given a pretty good account now, I think, of what its condition is and what elements it possesses in human life. (611a10-612a6)

The soul is partnered with the body but also with other bad things, which—as the reference to feasting makes clear—are (or include) appetites. As the shells, seaweed, and rocks that have become fastened to him obscure Glaucus' true nature, so these appetites obscure the true nature of the soul.

An earlier passage completes the explanation by telling us in plainer terms what this true nature is:

> The other so-called virtues of the soul do seem to be closely akin to those of the body: they really are not present in it initially, but are added later by habit and practice. The virtue of wisdom, on the other hand, belongs above all, so it seems, to something more divine, which never loses its power, but is either useful and beneficial or useless and harmful, depending on the way it is led around.... If this element of this sort of nature had been hammered at right from childhood, and struck free of the leaden weights, as it were, of kinship with becoming, which have been fastened to it by eating and other such pleasures and indulgences,

which turn its soul's vision downward—if, I say, it got rid of these and turned toward truly real things, then the same element of the same people would see them most sharply, just as it now does the things it is now turned toward. (518d9-b5)

What is struck free of the appetites and so on that gets fastened to it by eating or feasting is the rational part alone, which is the locus of wisdom (442c4-7). Hence, what we would see to be the soul's true nature, were these removed, is reason, which—like the Forms to which it is akin—is uniform, not multiform. The virtues other than wisdom are so-called virtues *of the soul*, apparently, because they are virtues not of reason alone, which is the true soul, but of the soul when it is embodied.

One problem for this way of interpreting these texts is raised by the sentence: "it is not easy ... for something to be immortal when (*te*) it is composed of many elements and (*kai*) is not composed in the most beautiful way." For it seems to allow that even a complex soul could be immortal if it were beautifully put together. However, *te ... kai* is "often used to unite complements," when "the second may be stronger than the first."[2] This is how consistency requires it to be taken here. The sense is "when it is composed of many elements and, moreover, not composed in the most beautiful way." Only one possibility is thus in view—that of a soul that cannot easily be immortal, because it is composed of many elements. To be sure, the complex soul does become "*entirely one*" (443e1-2), when reason rules in it. But the unity it then achieves, since it is "out of many," is not the natural or metaphysical sort of unity that constitutes an absolute barrier to disintegration and belongs to reason alone.

As naturally uniform and unified, reason is akin to the uniform and unified Forms. In flowing into the whole soul, therefore, the rational unity of the good meets in reason its psychological analogue or partner. Nonetheless, even reason can be turned away from the Form of the Good toward the world of becoming, to which the other elements in the soul are akin. It is in this unnatural state that it appears complex and multiform, just as Glaucus does, even though he, too, is really simple and divine. The tripartite soul *is* truly complex. What falsely appears complex is reason maimed by its association with the other soul-parts and the body. As Glaucus is a simple divine being, we—to the extent that we are truly human—are our reason, which is the genuinely human element in us:

> Fashion a single species of complex, many-headed beast, with a ring of tame and savage animal heads that it can grow and change at will.... Now fashion another single species—of lion—and a single one of human being. But make the first much the largest and the second, second in size ... Now join the three in one, so that they somehow grow together naturally ... Then fashion around the outside the image of one of them, that of the human being, so that to anyone who cannot see what is inside, but sees only the outer shell, it will look like a single creature, a human being. (588c7-e2)

If we take this verbal image seriously, reason is not just something immortal and so capable of autonomous existence when separated from the other (mortal) soul-parts but is the true human being rather than a mere (or proper) part of one.[3] Appetite and spirit, by contrast, like the shells, seaweed, and rocks attached to Glaucus, are something of a different order altogether.

Reason—the more divine element in the soul—always has sharp vision, but it can be controlled by vice, that is, by the rule in the soul of appetite or spirit (443c9-444e1). The effect of such rule is to turn the soul downward toward the visible world of becoming, rather than allowing it to look upward toward the intelligible world of being and the Forms to which the soul is akin (525b2-c6). But the psychological power concerned with becoming is belief (534a2-3; also 508d3-8). Hence, the rational part (turned downward) should be responsible for becoming.

Though philosophically felicitous, this conclusion—like the doctrine of the unity and simplicity of reason—can seem textually problematic:

> Haven't measuring, counting, and weighing proved to be most welcome assistants in these cases [of optical illusion and illusionist painting], ensuring that what appears bigger or smaller or more numerous or heavier does not rule within us, but rather what has calculated or measured or even weighed? ... And that is the task of the soul's rational element? ... But quite often, when it has measured and indicates that some things are larger or smaller than others, or the same size, the opposite simultaneously appears to it to hold of these same things.... And didn't we say that it is impossible for the same thing to believe opposites about the same thing at the same time? ... So the element in the soul that believes contrary to the measurements and the one that believes in accord with the measurements could not be the same. But the one that puts its trust in measurement and calculation would be the best element in the soul.... So the one that opposes it would be one of the inferior elements in us. That, then, was what I wanted to get agreement about when I said that ... imitation really consorts with an element in us that is far from wisdom, and that nothing healthy or true can come from their relationship or friendship. (602d6-603b3)

It is to reason, for example, that stick X *appears* longer than stick Y. It is reason that does not *believe* in accord with that appearance that X is longer than Y. If these psychological relations—*appears to* and *believes*—are genuine opposites or contraries, one must be had by one subpart of reason and the other by a different subpart, since "the same thing cannot do or undergo opposite things, not, at any rate, in the same respect, in relation to the same thing, at the same time" (436b9-c2). Whether they are genuine opposites is another question.[4]

An inferior element in us believes, contrary to measurement, that X is longer than Y. In accord with, what are *its* beliefs formed? The only candidate in view is *what appears to reason*. But this appearance cannot be the same as the inferior element's belief, which is only "in accord with" the appearance. Similarly, reason's own belief, as contrary to the appearance, must also be different from it. What appears to reason certainly conflicts in this case with what reason believes. But this conflict is not of the sort that requires psychic division, since perceiving and believing are not the same psychological relation. Hence the passage gives us no grounds for dividing reason into subparts or elements.

The phrase "one of the inferior parts within us" denotes appetite, which is the part that lacks reason (604d8; also 439d7). But spirit, too, is probably included in its denotation, since spirit can be bestial (411e1) and become irrationally angry (441c2). In any case, Socrates himself later cites anger as among the things that appearances and their imitation on the tragic or comic stage "nurture and water, when they should be dried up, and establish as rulers in us when—if we are to become better and happier rather than worse and more wretched—they should be ruled" (606d1-7). That is why we get the odd shift from the soul being ruled by what appears bigger or smaller—that is, by something that is not a soul-part—to its being ruled by something that is such a part, namely, reason. It does not matter what part gets nurtured and watered into ruling the soul. As long as appearances are doing the watering and nurturing, the results will be bad.

Though the text we have been considering does not present us with a divided rational part, it does present us with an inferior part, whether appetite or spirit, that has beliefs. And this is no anomaly. For temperance to exist in the soul, reason, appetite, and spirit must "share the belief that reason should rule" and "not engage in faction against it" (442c9-d2). Moreover, assent and dissent (437b1) are among the opposites that only a divided soul can have simultaneously toward the same thing. It is probably to this text, indeed, that ours refers, with belief treated as equivalent to assent by a soul or soul-part.

A belief can be either what is believed or assented to—a content of some sort—or the cognitive attitude of assent (or dissent) that is held to it. In a fully virtuous, reason-ruled soul, content and assent are always united, since the soul-parts assent in unison to whatever content reason provides. But in a soul ruled by one of the other soul-parts, the two elements in belief can come apart. In the case of a perceptual belief, for instance, the relevant content, as we saw, is an appearance to reason. On the basis of measurement and calculation, reason dissents from this appearance and so believes contrary to it. But this does not mean that the soul's ruling element will follow suit. It may assent to the appearance. Since it rules the soul, its assent will carry the day, affecting subsequent belief, calculation, and action.

So when we ask what part does the believing in the tripartite soul, we have to be clear about which side of belief we have in mind. What makes available a belief's *content* is always the rational part. What determines the *attitude* adopted to that content, whether assent or dissent, is the part that rules in the soul. Since a full belief consists of both a content and an attitude to it, only the rational part forms beliefs autonomously or without help from the other parts of the soul, since only it provides access to content. The other parts, by contrast, form beliefs only in cooperation with reason, which provides them with contents to assent to or reject. What these soul-parts have on their own are not beliefs proper, then, but sub-doxastic dispositions to assent to or dissent from contents. The fact that these dispositions are acquired and shaped by habituation rather than by education proper (522a4-7) is of a piece with this conclusion.

What is true of belief in this regard must also be true of appetite, desire, and any other psychological function that involves content that is broadly cognitive or propositional. The content involves the rational part, while the attitude to it—the assent or dissent, pursuit or avoidance—is determined by the part that rules the soul, which may, of course, be the rational part itself. It follows that nothing in the soul is autonomously capable of any of these cognitive or partly cognitive psychological functions except the rational one. There is a clear sense, therefore, in which the rational element alone is *a* soul.

2 Appetite

Appetite is the element in the soul [1] "with which it feels passion, hungers, thirsts, and is stirred by other appetites, the irrational and appetitive element," and [2] that is "friend to certain ways of being filled and certain pleasures" (439d6-8). It is the element [3] whose rule in a person's soul leads him to say that compared to the pleasure of making a profit, the pleasures "of being honored or of learning are worthless unless there is something in them that makes money" and to give "the highest praise to his own life" as most pleasant (581c1-d3).

It is with the appetitive element, [1] tells us, that the soul feels appetites, which are desires for "the pleasures of food, sex, and drink and those closely akin to them" (436a10-b2). The fact that hunger and thirst are "the most conspicuous examples" (437d2-3) helps explain why [2] characterizes appetites generally as "friend to certain ways of being filled." For the passive partner, at least, even sexual desire might seem to be like that. A cognate characterization is given later on, when "hunger, thirst, and the like" are described as "emptinesses related to the state of the body" (585a8-b1). Though "closely akin" and "the like" are vague phrases, we get the picture. Appetites are desires that can be credibly or intuitively represented as specifically body related. Thus the needs or desires for shelter and clothing, for example, though not in any obvious way sorts of emptiness, are presumably appetites, all the same (369c9-d4).

Because they are body related, appetites can be consistently represented as pulling reason away from the intelligible world of the Forms, where it belongs, down toward the visible world of becoming, which is the body's own natural bailiwick. In the *Phaedo,* the view is expressed in its starkest terms:

> As long as we have a body, and our soul is contaminated by such a bad thing, we shall never adequately attain what we desire—which, we say, is the truth. The body keeps us busy in a thousand ways because of the nourishment it must have—besides, if any illnesses befall it, they impede our hunt for what *is*. It fills us, too, with multifarious passions, appetites, fears and phantoms, and with all sorts of other trash, so that we are really and truly, as the saying goes, never able to think about anything because of it. It is nothing other than the body and bodily appetites, indeed, that cause wars and factions and conflicts. For it is over the acquisition of wealth that all wars take place,[5] and it is because of the body that we are compelled to acquire wealth, since we are enslaved to its service. And so for all these reasons it keeps us too busy to practice philosophy. Worst of all, if we *do* get any leisure from it, and turn to investigate some issue, in the middle of our inquiries there it is again creating uproar, disturbance, and fear all over the place, so that the truth cannot be discerned in a pure way because of it. But, in fact, it has been shown to us that if we are ever going to know anything in a pure way, we must be apart from the body and must look at things by themselves with the soul itself. It is then, it seems, that the thing we desire and whose lovers we claim to be—wisdom—will be ours, and that happens, the argument indicates, when we are dead, not while we are alive. For if we cannot know anything in a pure way when we are together with the body, then one of two things holds: either there is nowhere we can acquire knowledge, or it is when we are dead—since it is then that the soul will be all by itself, separate from the body, and not before. And so, while we are alive, we shall come closest to knowledge, it seems, if we have as little to do with the body as possible and as little association

with it, beyond what is absolutely unavoidable, and do not allow ourselves to be infected by its nature, but remain purified of it, until the god himself releases us. (66b5-67a6)

For a true human being—for reason—it is clearly bad to be embodied and attached to appetite. All the same, while it is embodied, reason has no choice but to see to the welfare of the whole soul and body, since its own welfare depends on theirs.[6] On Earth, at any rate, contemplation requires a village, so to speak. We need food and drink, shelter and clothing, protection from violence and predators, and, no doubt, some love and affection, too.

When we meet the democratic man, this way of understanding appetites suffers a setback:

> He lives from day to day, gratifying the appetite of the moment. Sometimes he drinks heavily while listening to the flute, while at other times he drinks only water and is on a diet. Sometimes he goes in for physical training, while there are other times when he is idle and neglects everything. Sometimes he spends his time engaged in what he takes to be philosophy. Often, though, he takes part in politics, leaping to his feet and saying and doing whatever happens to come into his mind. If he admires some military men, that is the direction he is carried in, if some moneymakers, then in that different one. There is neither order nor necessity in his life, yet he calls it pleasant, free, and blessedly happy, and follows it throughout his entire life. (*Rep.* 561c6-d8)

It suffers another setback when we read the following passage about jokes and comic theater:

> What is forcibly kept in check in our personal misfortunes and has an insatiable hunger for weeping and lamenting—since that is what it has a natural appetite for—is the very element that gets satisfaction and enjoyment from the poets.... If there are jokes you would be ashamed to tell yourself, but that you very much enjoy when you hear them in a comedy, or even in private, and that you don't hate as something bad, aren't you doing the same as with the things you pity? For the element in you that wanted to tell the jokes, but which you held back by means of reason, because you were afraid of being reputed a buffoon, you now release, and by making it strong in that way, you are often led unawares into becoming a comedian in your own life. (606a3-c9)

A hungry, thirsty, randy *appetitive* part is all well and good, as perhaps is one that desires physical training, but what makes a desire to do philosophy, or participate in politics, or to lament or tell jokes an *appetite?* Why think that there is one single part with which a soul does or feels all these?

Socrates uses the verb *epithumein* not just to express what appetite alone does or what a soul or person does with it but in an obviously looser and more popular sense.[7] He describes the three soul-parts as having "three kinds of ... appetites" (580d6-7), Cephalus as having "appetites for discussions and their pleasures" (328d4-5), Thrasymachus as "pretending to have an appetite to speak in order to win a good reputation" (338a5-6), honor-lovers as "having an appetite for honor as a whole" (475b1-2), and even a philosopher or wisdom-lover as having "an appetite for wisdom" (475b8-9). In these texts, an appetite seems to be simply a strong desire of whatever sort. Though we should not overlook this fact or causally spurn the assistance it might provide with how to understand the democratic man or the theater enthusiast, we must be careful not to allow it to let us off too many hooks.

Even if we set aside the apparently problematic appetites as loosely and popularly so called, we still have to explain what it is about the desires for food, drink, sex, and the rest—which *are* appetites in the strict sense—that makes them the contents of a single part of the soul.

Socrates is himself well aware of this problem:

> In just the way a city is divided into three classes, the soul of each person is also divided in three.... It seems to me that the three also have three kinds of pleasure, one peculiar to each, and the same for appetites and kinds of rule.... One element, we say, is that with which a person learns; another, that with which he feels anger. As for the third, because it is multiform, we had no one special name for it, but named it after the biggest and strongest thing it has in it. I mean, we called it the appetitive element, because of the intensity of its appetites for food, drink, sex, and all the things that go along with them. We also called it the money-loving element,[8] because such appetites are most easily satisfied by means of money.... So if we said its pleasure and love are for profit, wouldn't that best bring it together under one heading for the purposes of our argument, and make clear to us what we mean when we speak of this part of the soul? And would we be right in calling it money-loving and profit-loving? (580d2-581a7)

The appetitive part certainly includes unproblematic appetites—sexual desire or passion, hunger, and thirst—as some of its contents, but what makes it a single part of the soul is that its characteristic pleasure and love are for money or profit, since its constituent desires are most easily satisfied by means of it. This does not mean, obviously, that you can drink, eat, or have sex with money. Socrates' point is that money is the best single instrumental means to satisfying these appetites, since you can buy real food, drink, and sex with it. What makes appetite a unified part is that it has or can have a unified goal. Its unity is thus telic or teleological. There is one, single thing that it loves, and it is that which confers on it such unity as it has. The philosophy the democratic man dallies with, we might infer, is the sort that money can buy—for example, from a sophist.

The discussion of appetites, which divides them into necessary and unnecessary ones, reveals the good concealed in this teleological picture of appetite:

> In order not to have a discussion in the dark, would you like us first to define which appetites are necessary and which are not? ... Well, then, wouldn't those we cannot deny rightly be called necessary? And also those whose satisfaction benefits us? For we are by nature compelled to try to satisfy them both. Isn't that so?... So we would be right to apply the term necessary to them? What about those someone could get rid of if he started practicing from childhood, those whose presence does no good but may even do the opposite? If we said that all of them were unnecessary, would we be right? ... Let's pick an example of each, so that we have a pattern to follow.... Wouldn't the desire to eat to the point of health and well-being and the desire for bread and relishes be necessary ones? ... The desire for bread is surely necessary on both counts, in that it is beneficial and that unless it is satisfied we die.... And so is the one for relishes insofar as it is beneficial and conduces to well-being. What about an appetite that goes beyond these and seeks other sorts of foods, that if it is restrained from childhood and educated, most people can hold in check, and that is harmful to the body or harmful to the soul's capacity for wisdom and temperance? Wouldn't it be correct to call it unnecessary? ... Wouldn't we also say that the latter are spendthrift, then, whereas the former are moneymaking because they are useful where work is concerned? ... And won't we say the same about sexual appetites and the rest? (558d8-559b6)

Necessary appetites are thus divided into two classes, those (such as the one for bread) whose satisfaction is both beneficial and essential for life and those whose satisfaction is beneficial and conduces to well-being (but is not essential for life). Both are necessary, because we are compelled by nature to satisfy them both.[9] Appetites are unnecessary, when we are not compelled by nature to satisfy them, because early education and upbringing can get rid of them (or allow us to keep them under control). They also fall into two classes, those whose presence is harmful to the body and those whose presence is harmful to the soul's capacity for wisdom and temperance. The good or benefit that comes from the satisfaction of necessary appetites is associated with money (an association foreshadowed at 442a6-7), as are the harms brought by unnecessary ones (spendthriftiness).

Even unnecessary appetites of the worst sort (because they are lawless) are "probably present in all of us, but they are held in check by the laws and by our better appetites allied with reason" (571b4-6).[10] It is only in "a few people that they have been got rid of or that only a few weak ones remain, while in others they are stronger or more numerous" (571b6-c1). Thus, our better appetites—that is to say, the necessary or moneymaking ones—are assigned a sort of policing role in relation to the unnecessary ones (as they are at 554d9-e2). The fact that they are then allied with reason is further evidence that money is a sort of good, since reason is intrinsically related to an ideal of goodness and rational unity.

Because unity and goodness enter the appetitive part only with the appearance therein of the love of money and the structure that this love imposes on it, we are better able to understand the claim, crucial to the account of incontinence, that thirst is in its nature for drink and not for good drink, and similarly for the other appetites (437d1-438a5). The claim, as we can now see, is that there is nothing intrinsic to hunger—to change to the example Socrates develops in *Republic* book VIII—that makes it either a necessary appetite (essential for life or the promotion of well-eing) or an unnecessary one (non-beneficial or harmful, but eliminable or controllable). It all depends on how training and upbringing have shaped or qualified it. A hunger satisfied by a healthy amount of bread or some other staple is necessary, as is one for relishes or healthy garnishes, whereas one that goes "beyond these and seeks other sorts of foods is unnecessary" (559b8-9). The good drink that thirst is not by nature for is not good-tasting or high-quality drink, but beneficial drink—drink that is good for the relevant person. The unqualified appetites are, in that sense, good-independent. As a result, there is nothing about them that could serve as a unifier of appetite. They are irreducibly many, because they are by nature for irreducibly distinct things—drink, food, sex, and so on.

It is here, surely, that we find an explanation for the claim that appetite's unity is somehow not as tight or natural as that of the spirited part or the rationally calculating one. It is multiform as they, evidently, are not. The unforgettable image of appetite as "a single species of complex many-headed beast," later identified as being "snakelike" (590b1), that has "a ring of tame and savage animal heads all of which it can grow or change from within" (588c7-10), gives vivid expression to this fact. Since lawless and unnecessary appetites, such as cannibalistic or incestuous desires, are described as constituting "the bestial and savage element" (571b3-c5), they are presumably represented by the savage heads, while other appetites—the necessary ones, certainly, but perhaps the lawful but unnecessary ones as well—are represented by the tame heads. A head grows as the appetite it represents empties and craves satisfaction, evidently, only to have another take its place once it is sated or filled, as happens in the appetite-ruled democratic person: "putting all his pleasures on an equal footing, he lives, always surrendering rule over himself to whichever desire comes along, as if it were chosen by lot, until it is satisfied; and after that to another, dishonoring none but satisfying all equally" (561b3-6).

Though the love of money can impose (a degree of) unity on the appetitive element, the discussion of the oligarchic person reveals how circumscribed it is. For the unnecessary appetites perforce still exist in him unmoderated, ready to spring into action when the occasion arises:

> Where someone like that has a good reputation and is thought to be just, something good of his is forcibly holding in check the other bad appetites within, not persuading them that they had better not, nor taming them with arguments, but using compulsion and fear, because he is terrified of losing his other possessions.... Yes, by Zeus, my friend, you will find most of them, when they have other people's money to spend, have [unnecessary] appetites in them akin to those of the drone. (554c12-d7)

As a result, Socrates says, the oligarchic person is not "one but somehow twofold, although his better [necessary] appetites would generally master his worse [unnecessary] appetites" (554d9-e2).[11] He is twofold, notice, because his ruling appetitive part—the one with which he identifies, as we might put it—is itself divided. The (generally overlooked) fact that this divide occurs within the appetitive element is surely important. What is equally important is that it does not split that element into two *parts*, but into a part unified by its love of money on the one hand and a collection of essentially disunited—because unnecessary—appetites on the other.

Socrates' talk of the oligarchic man as not persuading his unnecessary appetites "that they had better not" or "taming them with a word" (554d1-2; compare 442a1) naturally re-raises the question of appetite's cognitive resources. In this case, as opposed to that of belief attribution, the text is somewhat plainer. The dronish or unnecessary appetites exist in the oligarch, we are told, because of "his lack of education" (554b7-8). Moreover, as we saw, it is the education and restraint of appetite "from childhood" (559b9-10) that lead to the elimination of unnecessary appetites or the restriction of their operation to fantasies and dreams. In *Republic* book IV, musical and physical training are identified as what makes the three parts of the soul harmonious and concordant (441e7-442a2), which is exactly what the oligarch's soul fails to be in book VIII: "the true virtue of a single-minded and harmonious soul would somehow far escape him" (554e4-6). But musical training, as the counterpart of physical training, is what "educated the guardians through habits, conveying by harmony a certain harmoniousness of temper, not knowledge, and by rhythm a certain rhythmical quality" and its constituent accounts or stories "cultivated other habits akin to these" (522a4-7). Glaucon's insistence on habits and his contrast of them with knowledge make it plain that the persuasion of appetite and the taming of it with words or accounts are not to be conceived on the model of a two-party conversation. Appetite is persuaded and tamed through the process of being habituated. But there is no need, having recognized this fact, to dumb the process of habituation down unduly. Appetites, like other desires, have intentional contents (hunger is for *food*, thirst for *drink*), and to that extent cognitive ones; they are not blind reflexes. It is on these contents, too, that habituation works, shaping thirst, for example, to be discerning, so that only beneficial drink will arouse or satisfy it.

3 Spirit

Spirit is the part of the soul [1] "with which it gets angry" (439e2-3; also 580d9-10). It is the one [2] that always has as its whole aim "mastery, victory, and high repute" and so is "victory-loving and honor-loving" (581a9-b4) [3], that is, "the natural auxiliary of the rationally calculating element, if it has not been corrupted by bad upbringing" (IV 441a2-3) and that is not seen "partnering the appetites to do what reason has decided should not be done" (440b4-7), but rather "in the faction that takes place in the soul, it is far more likely to take arms on the side of reason" (440e3-4) [4]. When spirit rules in a person's soul, it makes him say that the pleasure of being honored casts the pleasures of making money or of learning into the shade (581d5-7), so that he praises his own kind of life as most pleasant (581c1-11).

The natural tendency of spirit, we learn when it is first mentioned, is to make "the whole soul fearless and unconquerable in any situation" (375b2-3). In a revealing metaphor, spirit is characterized as "the very sinews" of the soul (411b3), the thing that holds it together in the face of an adversity that might otherwise cause it to melt or collapse: the opposite of spiritedness is gentleness (375c7-8) and softness (410d1). Thus, while spirit may not simply be an embodiment of the instinct of self-preservation, it clearly has something in common with it. It is the analogue, after all, of the protective military guardians in a city. Though it is present in everyone right from birth (441a7-8), some people are nonetheless naturally spirited, others are not (411b6; 5, 456a4-5).

A person's spirit can apparently be engaged or sparked directly by events in the outside world (as in the case of Leontius' spirited disgust or Odysseus' instantaneous anger), but it can also be engaged by what occurs within: "don't we often notice on other occasions that when appetite forces someone contrary to his rational calculation, he reproaches himself and feels anger at the thing in him doing the forcing, and just as if there were two warring factions, such a person's spirit becomes the ally of his reason?" (440a9-b4). Moreover, spirit is sensitive not just to the rationality or incontinent irrationality of its own behavior but to its justice. The very sort of painful or life-threatening treatment that would normally arouse spirit, indeed, will not do so when it takes the form of just punishment: "what about when a person thinks he is doing some injustice? Isn't it true that the nobler he is, the less capable he is of feeling angry if he suffers hunger, cold, or the like at the hands of someone whom he believes to be inflicting this on him justly, and won't his spirit, as I say, refuse to be aroused?" (440b9-c4). What is self-reproach when directed toward the incontinent or unjust self, thus, becomes something more like righteous indignation when engaged on behalf of the unjustly treated one:

> But what about when a person believes he is being unjustly treated? Doesn't his spirit boil then and grow harsh and fight as an ally of what he holds to be just? And even if it suffers hunger, cold, and every imposition of that sort, doesn't it stand firm and win out over them, not ceasing its noble efforts until either it achieves its purpose, or dies, or, like a dog being called to heel by a shepherd, is called back by the reason alongside it and becomes gentle? (440c6-d3)

In the cases of incontinent and unjust behavior or treatment, spirit seems to have the whole self as either good or bad in its purview. In the cases of Leontius' disgust and Odysseus' instantaneous anger, it seems more like an ordinary appetite or desire. Socrates himself says of spirit that it initially seemed like "something appetitive." In the end, though, he says, it emerged as something else, somehow more allied with reason, which itself looks to the welfare of the whole soul (440e1-4). In another phrase, it is "the middle element" (550b6), in between appetite and reason, with the result that rule by it is "somehow in the middle between aristocracy and oligarchy" (547c6).

Leontius' appetite wants to look at the naked corpses, but his spirit is "disgusted (*duscherainoi*)" (439e8) by them and turns him away. The question is "what is it disgusted at?" Is it at the naked corpses? Or is it at Leontius himself (or his appetitive part) for wanting to look at them? When, mastered by his appetite, Leontius succumbs to incontinence, what he says to his appetites is "Look for yourselves, you evil wretches, take your fill of the beautiful sight" (440a3-4). This strongly suggests that he himself—as possessing and succumbing to those evil appetites—is his disgust's target. The verb *duscherainein*, used to characterize his attitude to himself and his appetites, confirms this interpretation. Throughout the *Republic*, it is primarily used to express a distinctive evaluative attitude.[12] Thus Glaucon's perfectly unjust man is not, as he should be, "disgusted by doing injustice" (362b5), while the guardians are, as they should be, "disgusted" by—and so unwilling to imitate—the lamentations of famous men at the loss of family and possessions (388a1). Moreover, as the latter example suggests, it is an evaluative attitude directed not so much at (in this case) actions, but at the agent himself for performing them:

> When a moderate man comes upon the words or actions of a good man in the course of a narration, he will be willing to report them as if he were that man himself, and he won't be ashamed of that sort of imitation. He will be most willing to imitate the good man when he is acting in a faultless and intelligent manner, but less willing and more reluctant to do so, when he is upset by disease, passion, drunkenness, or some other misfortune. When he comes upon a character who is beneath him, however, he will be unwilling to make himself resemble this inferior character in any serious way—except perhaps for a brief period in which he is doing something good. On the contrary, he will be ashamed to do something like that, both because he is unpracticed in the imitation of such people, and also because to shape and mould himself on an inferior pattern disgusts him. In his mind he despises that, except when it is for the sake of amusement. (396c6-e1)

What the moderate man is disgusted by and ashamed of—what he despises—is himself for acting like a bad person.

The evaluative vocabulary spirit employs—or that a person motivated by spirit employs on its behalf—is that of justice and injustice, good and bad, shameful (ugly) and beautiful (fine). But its grip on this vocabulary is in an important sense incomplete:

> Then aren't these the reasons, Glaucon, that musical training is most important? First, because rhythm and harmony permeate the innermost element of the soul, affect it more powerfully than anything else, and bring it grace, such education makes one graceful, if one is properly trained, and the opposite, if one is not. Second, because anyone who has been properly trained will quickly notice if something has been omitted from a thing or if it has not been well crafted or well grown. And so, since he feels disgust correctly, he will praise fine things, be pleased by them, take them into his soul, and, though being nourished by them, become fine and good. What is ugly or shameful, on the other hand, he will correctly condemn and hate while he is still young, before he is able to grasp the reason. And, because he has been so trained, he will welcome the reason when it comes, and recognize it easily because of its kinship with himself. (401d4-402a4)

Properly habituated by musical and gymnastic training, the spirited element is in harmony with reason, sticking to its "pronouncements" in the face of adversity (IV 442b10-c2). In this condition, it spontaneously loves and hates in the right way, ensuring that its possessor exhibits "political courage" (429b1-430c4). But to exhibit full-blown courage, more is required: the rational element must be wise, so that its pronouncements, stemming as they do from knowledge of the Good, will be the most genuinely beneficial ones (504c9-505b3).

In his discussion of political courage, Socrates carefully extends the purview of that virtue to include resistance not just to pains and fears, but also to pleasures and appetites (429d1, 430b1-2; compare 412d9-414a6). Leontius' incontinent gazing at corpses is thus a failure of courage: his spirit cannot withstand the tempting appetitive pleasures of looking at pale naked bodies.[13] He is defeated—primarily in his own eyes, hence the self-disgust—by those pleasures much as a Homeric hero is by his opponent. And in that defeat, the honor that goes to victory is lost.

Socrates twice cites the Homeric passage about the triumph of Odysseus' reason over his spirit but never quotes it in full. Like well-brought-up Athenian boys and (perhaps) girls, we are supposed to be familiar with it:

> There devising evils in his spirit for the suitors,
> Odysseus lay awake; and out of the palace issued
> those women who in the past had been going to bed with the suitors,
> full of cheerfulness and greeting each other with laughter.
> But the spirit deep in the breast of Odysseus was stirred by this,
> And much he pondered in the division of mind and spirit,
> whether to spring on them and kill each one, or rather
> to let them lie this one more time with the insolent (*huperphialoisi*) suitors,
> for the last and latest time; but the heart was growling within him.
> And as a bitch, facing an unknown man, stands over
> her callow puppies, and growls and rages to fight, so Odysseus'
> heart was growling inside him as he looked on these wicked actions.
> He struck himself on the chest and spoke to his heart and scolded it:

> Bear up, my heart. You have had worse to endure before this
> on that day when the irresistible Cyclops ate up
> my strong companions, but you endured it until intelligence
> got you out of the cave, though you expected to perish. (*Od*. XX 5–21)[14]

Odysseus is devising evil in his spirit for the suitors because they are *huperphialoi*, which is usually, but not always, something pejorative. When, still in disguise as a beggar, he wants to try to draw the great bow that is, of course, his own, Antinoös responds:

> Ah, wretched stranger, you have no mindfulness, not even a little.
> It is not enough that you dine in peace, among us, who are men of quality (*huperphialoisi*),[15]
> and are deprived of no fair portion, but listen
> to our conversation and what we say? But there is no other
> vagabond and newcomer who is allowed to hear us
> talk. (XXI 287–292)

Whether being *huperphialos* is a bad thing thus seems to depend on relative status, relative honor. Diomedes, a mere mortal, is *huperphialos* for attacking the immortal gods (*Il*. V, 881). The Cylopes, on the other hand, are *huperphialoi* because they are puissant enough to "build a most beautiful wall for the famous city" (Bacchylides 12, 78).[16] If Odysseus were truly a wretched beggar, the suitors would not be insolent in treating him and his household in the way they do, since a fair portion is one proportional to honor and status. Because he is far from wretched, their treatment amounts to an assault on his honor. It is as such that it galvanizes his spirited anger.

The anger ignited by the maidservants is partly derivative from the already smoldering one Odysseus feels at the insolent suitors: the maidservants are going off to sleep with men who are dishonoring him. At the same time—as the simile of the bitch with her puppies reveals—they are *his* property: it is their *master* they are dishonoring and betraying.[17] Unlike intelligence (*mêtis*) or mind (*phrenes*), this anger is instantaneous, unreflective, and uncalculating. It motivates Odysseus quickly to reestablish mastery, achieve victory, and thereby regain honor and high repute.

In the cases of both Leontius and Odysseus, spirit's characteristic love for honor is in play. In the case of Leontius, love is defeated by appetite (he is incontinent, weak-willed); in the case of Odysseus, it is defeated by reason (he is continent, self-controlled). In both men, there is psychological conflict, which the basic characterization of spirit lays at the feet of bad upbringing. For spirit, in contrast to appetite, is the *natural* auxiliary of reason, both allied with it and subordinate to it, unless corrupted. What we want to understand now is why that is so.

Appetite, as we saw, naturally contains unnecessary—because harmful or non-beneficial—appetites that cannot be brought into harmony or unity of purpose. That is why appetite is not naturally on the side of reason. It takes musical and gymnastic training to purge or repress unnecessary appetites, so that only the necessary, beneficial, and reason-allied ones remain as motivators of action. Appetite's unity and harmony with reason is thus an essentially cultural or political achievement.

The basis of appetite's unity as a soul-part is its characteristic love for a single, unified goal (money), which is the best means of satisfying its essentially diverse contents. Reason's unity, too, has its source in its characteristic love for the perfectly unified Form of the Good. On systematic grounds alone, spirit's unity and natural alliance with reason should have a cognate explanation. We noticed earlier that spirit—as what holds the person together and preserves his unity and coherence in the face of threats to it—has significant overlap with the instinct of self-preservation. That is why its virtue, courage, is "a sort of preservation" (*Rep.* 429a5). As a natural conatus for unity, spirit is allied with reason as itself the paramount unifying force. Because it wants to be successful, however, to triumph over what threatens it with dissolution, spirit requires not just conatus but to get things right. It is reason, with its cognitive and ratiocinative capacities, that is best suited to that task. So spirit, given its nature, will not just be allied with reason, but subservient to it, so that what it will first and foremost preserve is "the *correct and law-inculcated belief* about what should inspire terror and what should not" (430b3-5)—a belief that has its source in reason's knowledge of the Form of the Good (442b10-c7).

What becomes of spirit during its subsequent education through music and gymnastic training is what brings honor into the picture. The object of honor, like that of self-preservation, or of the sort of disgust we looked at, is the whole person. At first, this (proto-)person is, as it were, a natural being or product—a human animal. The effect of socialization is to give this animal a second nature. Now it is a (full-blown) person with a social position and status. As a natural being, its preservation was one thing. As a social being, it is much richer and more complex. A sufficiently serious social slight can result in suicidal shame, as it does in Sophocles' Ajax. Honor—being accorded a respect appropriate to one's status—can become more important than animal life itself.

Nonetheless, just as in the case of appetite, the unity that the love of honor brings to the spirited part is imperfectly transmissible to the whole soul. Here the timocratic man is the pertinent example. His spirit-ruled soul is the result of bad education, in which "the true Muse, the companion of discussion and philosophy" is neglected and physical training is honored more than its musical correlate (548b7-c2). Consequently, an appetite for money remains unmoderated in his soul, just as it does in that of the oligarch. On the other hand, his adoration of gold and silver is not out in the open, as the oligarch's is, but secret, indulged only in private (548a5-b2).[18] Its scope in his life, like that of lawless unnecessary appetites in most of ours, is thus more circumscribed. Although nothing is explicitly said about the timocrat's enslavement of his rational element to the pursuit of honor rather than truth, we do know that the effect of such a lopsided education is to make someone the sort of "unmusical hater of argument" (411d7) that is the very opposite of an argument-loving philosopher (*La.* 188c4-189b7; *Phd.* 89d1-91b7)—someone who does not use "argument to persuade, but force and savagery" (*Rep.* 411d7-8). Reason, we may infer, is as coerced in him as is spirit in the oligarch (555a1-6).

People who conceive the good as honor, Aristotle claims, fail to do justice to its somewhat schizophrenic nature. For honor "seems to depend more on those who honor than on the one honored" and so is too superficial to be the human good, which is "something of our own and hard to take from us." Here the honor at issue is *donor-honor*. And about it, Aristotle is surely correct. For if the donors are foolish or imperceptive or vicious, nothing a person does, no matter how meritorious, will be any guarantee of getting it. As Aristotle continues his investigation, *recipient honor* comes into play. Cultivated people, he says, "seek to be honored by practically wise people, among people who know them, and for their virtue" (*NE* I.5 1095b21-30). This is the honor we possess when we have the virtue that rightly attracts donor-honor from right-thinking and right-perceiving donors. It is the honor Plato's philosopher-kings possess. In between these two, Plato discerns a third sort, which is the honor we possess when the virtue we exhibit is itself dependent on those who do genuinely possess recipient honor. This is the sort the honor-loving guardians go for. They reliably do what the truly virtuous do, since they genuinely possess virtue's *manifest* properties—the very ones right-thinking and right-perceiving people look to in correctly bestowing honor. Nonetheless, on the inside, there is something they lack—something that comes not from others, but from themselves.[19] While not as superficial as donor honor, or as deep as recipient honor, this in-between kind does seem substantive enough to count as a genuine sort of human good.

4 Ruling the Soul

A canonical soul-part description specifies: first, an instrumental role or what the soul does by means of the part, whether rational calculation or feeling anger or thirst; second, a characteristic love (truth, honor, money); third, a characteristic pleasure associated with that love; and, fourth, a characteristic type of rule (aristocratic, timocratic, oligarchic). The second, as we have seen, is the key to understanding what makes a Platonic soul-part a unified element in the soul. But it is the fourth that most illuminates what a soul-part is—namely, a unit that can rule the soul by bending the other parts to its will, to its own characteristic love. What most illuminate the different parts, therefore, are the objects of these loves: money, honor, and the (Form of the) Good.

What distinguishes one such object from another is the distinctive sort or degree of unity that a ruling love for it can impose on the soul. How much intra-soul coercion as opposed to persuasion does love for it involve? How much potential for conflict does love for it leave open and in what areas? How much starving or dissatisfaction of the elements being ruled and of itself does it involve? These are the considerations that provide a basis for the claim that, for example, spirit is (as a unifier) in-between appetite and reason. Provided we accept that money is a minimal unifier and the good a maximal one, it also provides a basis for believing that if there were other such unifiers, with corresponding loves, they would be in between the three canonical ones.

Because soul-parts are like this, the sort of conflict that reveals their existence is conflict over rule of the soul—conflict whose resolution identifies the soul involved as, for example, incontinent (Leontius) or continent (Odysseus). For in the harmonious, reason-ruled soul, no such conflict occurs—at least, not in the ideal case. In the ideal case, indeed, soul-*parts* are almost invisible. But rule is a notion at once normative—because rule by any part aims at the real good, even if, as in case of appetite and spirit, it also involves a misconception of that good—and, in a way to be explained, *higher order*. Take the love or desire for money. From the logical point of view, it is a first-order desire, as is the desire for honor or the good. But its existence, like theirs, presupposes that of other desires to whose satisfaction it has (derivatively) an attitude, so to speak. If it rules in a soul, all the soul's other desires and resources will be employed to best achieve its goal, even if, as in the case of money, its goal is a means to satisfying some of them. The sort of conflict that reveals the existence of soul-parts, therefore, always involves something that is *in this sense* higher order.

We are naturally inclined to think of Platonic soul-parts in the context of an overall psychology, and to ask which part performs which psychological function or houses which psychological state or attitude. Which part perceives, imagines, or remembers? Which feels grief, jealousy, shame, or pride? Faced with interaction between soul-parts, we are beset with worries about vicious regresses—does spirit need a rational element of its own in order to listen to reason?—and unexplanatory homuncularism.[20] The fact that the rational part, alone of the parts, is *a* soul should help allay these worries. But it does so by radically reconceiving the very idea of a soul-part. The rational part is alone *a* soul. Appetite and spirit are non-souls, parasites on the rational part, which—like more familiar parasites—can alter their functioning and change their goals. But that is to speak of soul-parts from the eternal point of view. From the temporal point of view, appetite and spirit are, when properly ruled, reason's providers and defenders—the analogues of the producers and guardians in Kallipolis, as reason is itself the analogue of the philosopher-kings.

5 Souls and Persons

The idea that the rational element in the soul—or *rational soul* as we may now more usefully call it—is alone, properly speaking, *a* soul is confirmed by accounts we find elsewhere in Plato's dialogues. Here is one fairly early example:

> Soul is most similar to that which is divine, immortal, intelligible, uniform, and unsusceptible to disintegration, and always remains in the same state and condition as itself. Body, on the other hand, is most similar to what is merely human, mortal, unintelligible, multiform, susceptible to disintegration, and never in the same state as itself. (*Phd.* 80b1-5)

The reason for the difference is that the soul is incomposite, and the body is composite: "what has been put together and is naturally composite is the sort of thing that is susceptible of being divided in the respect in which it was put together; whereas if something is really incomposite, then it alone is really immortal if indeed anything is" (78c1-4). Since only rational soul is incomposite in this way, it would thus seem to be what the *Phaedo* treats as soul itself. As a result, psychological capacities attributed to parts of the incarnate soul in the *Republic* are attributed not to soul but to body (66b5-d3, quoted above). At the same time, souls that have lost the bodies they have on earth—although not perhaps the bodies they have as ghosts or when in Hades—can have the sorts of appetites (81e1), fears (81c11), and types of character (81e2-3) that could hardly be possessed by rational soul alone. Rather than see this as an out-and-out contradiction, we should perhaps see it as prefiguring, if not presupposing, a view like the *Republic*'s. Rational soul is alone a soul—simple, indissoluble, eternal. But, when embodied, it acquires characteristics that disguise its true nature. Thus, when a complex embodied soul is divided "in the respect in which it was put together" with the body, what you get is rational soul, and some other elements, which are not themselves souls but accretions to them.

A later portrait from the *Phaedrus*, which is one of the best known of all, represents reason, spirit, and appetite as a charioteer and pair of horses:

> To say what sort of thing soul is would require a long exposition, and one calling for utterly divine powers; to say what it resembles requires a shorter one, and one within merely human capacities. So let us speak in the latter way. Let it then resemble the combined power of a winged team of horses and their charioteer. Now in the case of gods, horses and charioteers are all both good and of good stock; whereas in the case of the rest there is a mixture. In the first place, the ruler in our case has charge of a pair; secondly, one of them he finds noble and good, and of similar stock, while the other is of the opposite stock, and opposite in its nature; so that the driving in our case is necessarily difficult and troublesome. How then it is that some living creatures are called mortal and some immortal, we must now try to say. All soul has the supervision of all that is soulless, and ranges about the whole universe, coming to be now in one form, now in another. Now when it is perfectly winged, it travels through air and governs the whole cosmos; but the one that has lost its wings is swept along until it lays hold of something solid, where it settles down, taking on an earthly body, which seems to move itself because of the power of soul, and the whole is called a living creature, soul and body fixed together, and acquires the name "mortal"; immortal it is not, as any reason that has been calculated out shows, but because we have not seen a god or adequately grasped one with our understanding, we imagine a kind of immortal living creature that has both a soul and a body, combined for all time. (246a3-d2)

The perfectly winged soul that travels through air or space is entirely nonsolid and bodiless. When it loses its wings, it takes on an earthly body, and the resulting psychophysical compound is called a living creature. But loss of wing power is a matter of degree. The gods that end up on the stars and the planets are also immortal souls that have lost something of their power of flight, but because their horses and charioteer are better than ours, they never sink down to earth but stay up in the heavens.

Though Plato sometimes allows the stars and planets themselves to be called "gods" (*Ti.* 40a2-d5), he is also explicit, as he is the *Republic* and here in the *Phaedrus*, that this is like calling the snake-lion-human complex a "human being." It's harmless enough as long as you don't take it literally. For the stars and planets are psychophysical compounds, and just as rational soul alone is the true human being, so it is the souls of the stars and planets that are alone gods:

> Consider the stars and the moon, the years, months, and all the seasons: what other account can we give except this same one? Since a soul or souls are evidently the causes of all these things, and good souls possessed of every virtue, we shall declare these souls to be gods. (*Lg.* X, 899b3-7)

So it is not the celestial bodies that are immortal, but the souls that have laid hold of them. If we imagine otherwise, it can only be because we do not understand what a god is.

Because the stars and planets are not immortal, they can in some sense be divided into body and soul. Yet, they will never, in fact, come apart into their two components. When the Demiurge addresses them, he explains why this is so:

> Gods, works divine whose maker and father I am, whatever has come to be by my hands cannot be dissolved without my consent. Now while it is true that everything that is put together can be dissolved, still only someone evil would consent to the dissolution of what has been beautifully fitted together and is in good condition. That is why you, as creatures that have come to be, are neither completely immortal nor completely exempt from dissolution. Still, you will not be dissolved nor will death be your lot, since you have received the guarantee of my will. (*Ti.* 41a7-b5)

These manufactured gods are thus a nice intermediate case. They do not have the absolutely indissoluble unity possessed by rational soul, but they do have a type of unity that mortal creatures, whose souls and terrestrial bodies can come apart, lack. Metaphysical unity is all or nothing; psychophysical unity is a matter of degree. Since acquiring a body involves acquiring accretions to rational soul (the pair of horses), the same holds for the unity of a complex soul. Its unity isn't absolute and metaphysical, but mediated by Demiurgic will.

We are used to thinking of souls as immortal, less used to thinking of them as transmigrating. Yet, that, too, is something Plato made a part of his portrait of them. At the spindle of necessity, for example, where souls choose their next incarnations, Er saw the soul that once belonged to Orpheus choosing a swan's life and a swan "changing to the choice of a human life" (*Rep.* 620a3-8). In the *Timaeus*, too, reincarnation retains its prominence:

> Once souls were of necessity implanted in bodies, and these bodies had things coming to them and leaving them, the first innate capacity they would of necessity come to have would be sense perception, which arises out of compelled disturbances. This they would all have. The second would be erotic desire, mingled with pleasure and pain. And they would come to have fear and spirit as well, plus whatever goes along with these, as well as all their natural opposites. And if they could master these, their lives would be just, whereas if they were mastered by them, they would be unjust. And if someone lived a good life throughout his proper span of time, he would at the end return to his dwelling place in his companion star, to live a life of happiness that agreed with his character, but if he failed in this, he would be born a second time, now as a woman. And if even then he still could not refrain from evil, he would be changed once again, this time into some wild animal that resembled the wicked character he had acquired. And he would have no rest from these toilsome transformations until he had dragged that massive accretion of fire-water-air-earth into conformity with the revolution of the Same and uniform within him, and so subordinated that turbulent, irrational mass by means of reason. This would return him to his original condition of excellence. (42a3-d2)

Choice is not mentioned here, which may be a significant difference—although the mechanisms that determine how a soul will be incarnated seem compatible with it. Nonetheless, the picture still presents us with the need to make sense of a single soul that acquires erotic desire and spirit only when it acquires a body, and that can subsequently be embodied in very different sorts of animal bodies, with different consequences for it. It does not take much to see that rational soul is alone well suited to play both these roles. For the complex tripartite soul already has erotic desire and spirit and so cannot acquire them, and if a soul is to learn from an incarnation, or make a choice of another one, or subordinate anything at all to reason, it must have a rational cognitive capacity of some sort.

The mention of a soul's "companion star" refers us to the *Phaedrus*, where souls are portrayed as followers of different gods—or, in the language of the *Timaeus*, as associated with or located on different stars or planets. At a point in their revolutions, these gods "travel to the summit of the arch of the heavens" (247a8-b2). From there they can view "the region above the heavens" and the Forms that dwell in it (247c3-e2). In order to do this, however, their souls must enter that upper region:

> When those souls that are called immortal have reached the top, they travel *outside* and take their stand upon the outer part of the heavens, and positioned like this they are carried round by its revolution, and gaze on the things outside the heavens. (247b6-c2)

At other points in its revolution, such a soul is inside the heavens and so is both embodied and tripartite—although its body may not be of the earthly sort that a human soul takes on when it is incarnated terrestrially: in the *Timaeus*, the bodies of the gods are "mostly fire" (40a2-3). When it travels outside, though, it apparently leaves even these astral bodies (or whatever we are to call them) in some sense behind. It is this sort of soul that is "called immortal." That it is rational soul is clear:

> This region [outside the heavens] is occupied by being that really *is*, that is without color or shape, intangible, and that only the captain of the soul—the understanding—can contemplate, and that is the kind of thing with which true knowledge is concerned. Thus because a god's thought is nourished by understanding and knowledge that is pure, and so too every soul that is concerned to receive what is appropriate to it, it is glad at last to see what *is*, and is nourished and made happy by contemplating what is true, until the revolution brings it around in a circle to the same point. (*Phdr.* 247c6-d5)

Rational soul does not lose contact with its astral body altogether. It continues to be carried around by its revolution. But because of the paths these astral bodies reliably travel, rational soul is able regularly to escape from the realm of body, while yet remaining attached to it.

A human soul that is a particular god's follower also travels to this summit, provided it has trained its appetitive horse well (*Phdr.* 247b3-5)—something not all such souls succeed in doing. But its charioteer or captain—rational soul—can keep itself in the realm of the Forms only intermittently, subject as it is to "disturbance by its horses" (248a4; compare *Phd.* 66d3-7). As a result, it "scarcely catches sight of the things that *are*, while another captain now rises, now sinks, and because of the compulsion exerted by its horses sees some things but not others" (248a4-6). It is how much of the Forms its captain does manage to see—and how often—that determines what happens to it. It may remain on its star or planet, following in the orbit of its god. But whenever "through inability to follow it fails to see, and through some mischance is weighed down with forgetfulness and deficiency, and because of the weight loses its wings, it falls to earth" (248c5-8).

If a soul is good enough not to be sent to earth at all, and remains on its home planet or star, we should presumably imagine its life on the model of that of its god: sometimes, but less reliably, less frequently, and less continuously than he or she, its rational part gets to travel outside the heavens while yet remaining attached to its astral body and so to the spirited and appetitive elements that the horses represent. But even if a soul is not good enough for that, its fall to earth is, so to speak, graduated. In its first incarnation, no soul, however minimal its wing power, is "planted in any wild beast" (248d1). That fate can come only in much later incarnations and only to those whose wings resolutely refuse to grow (249b3-5). Instead, souls are initially planted in terrestrial human beings—snake-lion-human complexes—with different types of characters. Thus, "the one that saw most shall be planted in a seed from which will grow a man who will become a philosopher or a lover of beauty or one devoted to the Muses or prone to love; the second in the seed of a law-abiding king, or someone fit for generalship and ruling," until, in the eight place, we reach the seed from which a Sophist or demagogue will grow, and, in the ninth, a tyrant (248d1-e3). And so it continues through thousand-year cycles of reincarnation and choices of lives, until, after ten thousand years, "each soul returns to the place from which it has come" (248e5-6).

A god's rational soul, while it is initially separate from every sort of body, then, is never subsequently in that condition. Once it is joined to an astral body by the Demiurge, it cannot be separated from it. That is why gods cannot suffer the equivalent of death by having their rational soul come apart from their astral body. We can suffer death. That is one thing that distinguishes us from them. But we do not do so by having our rational soul come apart from our astral body—none of the portraits of soul envisages that. If they did, our souls would be better off than those of the gods, not worse. Instead, we die by having our complex soul come apart from our earthly body: we die on earth, not on our home star or planet. Whether we say that it is our complex soul or our rational soul that gets reincarnated matters only at the very beginning, when what is alone absolutely immortal and simple in us takes on an astral body or whatever sort of body it has on its home star or planet. Thereafter, our souls, like those of the gods, are always complex, always tripartite, and always embodied. Yet, to the degree that we can make sense of that beginning as an event in our lives or the life of our soul, it is our rational soul alone that we must take to be ourselves. That is why, as "an immortal thing," we should be seriously concerned with what happens to us throughout "the whole of time" rather than in the relatively short period "from childhood to old age" (*Rep.* 608c6-d11; also 498d1-7).

In the *Republic*, Socrates identifies rational soul with the human element in the snake-lion-human complex that is a terrestrial human being. In the *Phaedrus*, he is apparently more circumspect:

> I am not yet capable, in accordance with the Delphic inscription, of "knowing myself." ...
> So I inquire ... into myself, to see whether I am actually a beast more complex and appetite-

consumed (*epitethumenon*) than Typhon,²¹ or both a tamer and a simpler creature, sharing some divine and un-Typhonic portion by nature. (229e5-230a6)

The question he raises is one we would think better posed by leaving human beings out of the picture altogether. For while we might concede that rationality is something that human beings have a portion of by nature and might even concede that there is something divine about it, we would surely hesitate to concede that it is all there really is to being a human being. Appetite and spirit—to stick to things already in play—seem equally important.

"Person," to be sure, is something of a term of art, but if we agree that a person is "an intelligent being, that has reason and reflection, and can consider itself as itself, the same thinking thing in different times and places" (Locke 1979 [1690], p. 335), then there is much to be said for thinking that only rational soul—only the soul's rational part—is a person. For as portrayed, in any case, rational soul must in some way remember what happens to it in its many different incarnations, whether in animal or human bodies and especially in those glimpses it catches of the Forms when it is, as it were, as out of body as it is possible for it to be:

> For a soul that has never seen the truth will not take human shape. For a human being must comprehend what is said in accord with a Form, arising from many perceptions and being collected together into one through calculation; and this is a recollection of those things that our [rational] soul once saw when it traveled in company with a god and treated with contempt the things we now say *are*, and rose up into what really *is*. (*Phdr*. 249b5-c4)

The answer to Socrates' question, then, is that he is a person, a rational soul. This person is by nature simple or incomposite, but by Demiurgic fiat, it is part of the sort of appetite-spirit-reason complex that is a human soul and is so, moreover, even when the terrestrial body it inhabits is that of another species of animal.

Notes

1. Translations of the *Republic* are based on Reeve (2011).
2. Smyth (1980, pp. 667, 2974).
3. Aristotle also claims that we are—or are most of all—our understanding (*nous*), which is the divine element in our souls (*NE* IX.4 1166a16-17; X.7 1178a2-8).
4. A question answered affirmatively by Burnyeat (1999).
5. Compare 373d7-e8.
6. Suicide is not an option, except in exceptional circumstances, for reasons canvassed at *Phd*. 61d3-c8.
7. Noticed by Lorenz (2006).
8. At 553c5; implied at 442a6-7.
9. This is relevant to the claim that every "soul pursues" what is really good and "for its sake does everything" (505d7-e2).
10. Notice that the cognate phrase "the fine and good appetites" (561b9-c1) must refer to strict, not loose and popular, appetites.
11. He is probably relying on a claim introduced earlier in connection not with souls but with cities: "in all constitutions, change originates in the ruling element itself when faction breaks out within it; but if this group remains of one mind (*homonoountos*; compare *homonoêtikês* at554e5), then—however small it is—change is impossible" (545d1-3).

12. The one exception is 475b11, where *peri ta mathêmata duscheranionta* means "to be choosy or fastidious about learning things."
13. If we know anything about the historical Leontius, it is that he was infamous in Athens for his love of boys as pale as corpses, suggesting that the appetite attributed to him is sexual in nature. But we know this only if the *Leôtrophidês* of the dramatist Theopompus is indeed our Leontius, who must have been sufficiently infamous for something, in any case, for everyone involved in the conversation to know what Socrates is talking about.
14. Lattimore (1975).
15. See Russo et al. (1992, p. 179).
16. See Campbell (1992, p. 183).
17. "Odysseus' rage at the maidservants reveals the possessiveness of the master beneath the beggar's disguise, and may also hint at sexual jealousy, since it was not uncommon for powerful nobles to have sexual relations with their female servants (1, 429–433). In this sense (even though Odysseus did not intend sexual relations with the maids), they 'belonged' to him, which makes his extreme anger here more understandable" (Russo et al. 1992, pp. 108–9).
18. Honor, as something conferred by others on the basis of what they see, has trouble providing the motivation needed to rule out private appetitive indulgence.
19. It is this fact that explains spirit's particular attachment to what is *kalon* (fine, noble, or beautiful)—an idea that Lear (2006) fruitfully explores.
20. See Williams (2006, pp. 108–117).
21. Typhon (or Typhoeus) was a dragon with a 100 snake heads, whose voice was at times like that of a lion. He was the last obstacle between Zeus and the kingship of the gods (Hesiod, *Theogony* 820–868). The adjective *atuphou* ("un-Typhonic") may mean "lacking in pride."

Bibliography

Burnyeat, Myles. 1999. Culture and society in Plato's *Republic*. *The Tanner Lectures on Human Values* 20: 223–227.
Campbell, David. 1992. *Greek lyric*, vol. 4. Cambridge, MA: Harvard University Press.
Cooper, John M. 1999. The psychology of justice in Plato. In *Reason and emotion*, ed. John Cooper, 138–150. Princeton: Princeton University Press.
Lattimore, Richard. 1975. *The Odyssey of Homer*. New York: Harper and Row.
Lear, Gabriel Richardson. 2006. Plato on learning to love beauty. In *The Blackwell guide to Plato's Republic*, ed. Gerasimos Santas, 104–124. Oxford: Blackwell Publishing.
Locke, John. 1979 [1690]. *An essay concerning human understanding*. Oxford: Clarendon.
Lorenz, Henrik. 2006. *The brute within*. Oxford: Clarendon.
Reeve, C.D.C. 2003. Plato's metaphysics of morals. *Oxford Studies in Ancient Philosophy* 25: 39–58.
Reeve, C.D.C. 2011. *Plato: Republic*. Indianapolis: Hackett Publishing Company.
Russo, Joseph, Manuel Fernández-Gailano, and Alfred Heubeck. 1992. *A commentary on Homer's Odyssey*, vol. 3. Oxford: Clarendon.
Smyth, H.W. 1980. *Greek grammar*. Cambridge, MA: Harvard University Press.
Williams, Bernard. 2006. The analogy of city and soul in Plato's *Republic*. In *The sense of past: Essays in the history of philosophy*, ed. Myles Burnyeat, 108–117. Princeton: Princeton University Press.

Just City and Just Soul in Plato's *Republic*

Gerasimos Santas

No one doubts that the isomorphism between just city and just soul is fundamental to Plato's ethics and political philosophy in the *Republic*. From the many applications of the concept of justice (to societies, institutions, laws, judgments, persons, actions, desires, and intentions), Plato selects two for investigation, just society and just person. He relates them in a unique way as being isomorphic to each other and uses the isomorphism to deduce a definition of a just person from his definition of a just city (book IV) and to give analyses of four kinds of unjust persons (book VIII). Other applications of the concept (e.g., just laws and just actions) are apparently treated as derivative from these two primary applications.

No one doubts that Plato's analysis of the psyche is also central. The tripartite analysis is used in his programs of primary and higher education (implicitly in books II and III, explicitly in book VII); it is used to define the virtues and vices of individuals (books IV and VIII), and it is used in the justice-health analogy (book IV), in the proofs that we are worse off being unjust (democrat and tyrant, books VIII and IX), in the analysis and ranking of pleasures (book IX), and in the evaluation of works of art and in the myth of the afterlife (book X). There is no similar consensus that the functional theory of good and virtue is also fundamental. I will bypass this lack of universal recognition here (having given textual evidence of the uses of the functional theory throughout the *Republic* recently)[1] and take it as a hypothesis that these three theories are main building blocks of Plato's ethics and politics in the *Republic*, namely, the isomorphism of just city and just soul, the

---

An earlier draft of this chapter was read at a conference in honor of David Keyt in 2006. I wish to thank the audience particularly Marc Cohen and Charles Young for the helpful comments. I am especially grateful to David Keyt from whose work—marked by an admirably close reading of texts, great clarity of reasoning and statement, and superior craftsmanship—I have been learning for a long time. I am honored to contribute this essay to the volume.

G. Santas (✉)
Department of Philosophy, University of California, Irvine, HBO 2, Irvine, CA 92697, USA
e-mail: gxsantas@uci.edu

tripartite analysis of soul, and the functional theory of good and virtue. Of course one would have to add the metaphysics and epistemology of the middle books, but I leave these mostly out of this discussion, though not out of view or reference.

In this essay, I use these three building blocks together, which to my knowledge no one has done, to throw light on some main interpretive controversies: in particular whether the parts of the soul are faculties or agents and whether all the citizens or only the philosophers in Plato's ideal city can be just. I argue that there is strong evidence that the parts of the soul are faculties rather than agents, that all the citizens in Plato's completely good city can be just, and that Plato's ethics is better without the parts of the soul as agents and without the ethical elitism of supposing that only the philosophers can be just.[2]

It is helpful to remember how the three building blocks are mainly related, at least in Plato's exposition of his theory: the functional theory of good and virtue is used as a premise in the construction of the just (indeed, completely good) city; the just city is used in turn as a premise in the derivation of the definition of a just person; and the analysis of the soul and the isomorphism are also used as premises in that derivation.

1   The Functional Theory of Good and Virtue

I confine myself here to some main points relevant to this investigation. Plato presents us with a definition of two kinds of function: "The work [*ergon*, function] of a horse or anything else is that which one can do only with it or best with it" (*Rep.* I 353e). I call the first kind of function "exclusive," illustrated by the two organs of eyes and ears; I term the second "optimal," illustrated with the artifact of pruning shears (the example of a horse is harder to place—we do not know whether he is speaking of domesticated horses or horses in nature). Virtues (and vices) are then generally characterized as qualities that enable things with functions to perform their functions well (and vices cause them to do so poorly). And things with functions are said to be good instances of their kind when they perform their functions well or have the appropriate virtues (I 352E-4c).[3]

Plato illustrates exclusive functions with natural organs and optimal functions with artifacts (a seemingly pluralistic conception of functions still in play in modern philosophy of biology).[4] The important point to note is that Plato finds functions in nature as well as in human artifacts; indeed, we know that most, if not all, organs of plants and animals have unique functions that only they can perform. The concept of exclusive function is immediately applied to another natural entity, the psyche itself, and several such functions are attributed to it: only the soul can deliberate, plan, make a body alive, perhaps move it, and so on.[5] As the last example shows, a thing can have several functions and accordingly several virtues, as indeed we find later for cities, souls, and bodies. Virtue is characterized relative to functions, and so, as defined, the concept does not apply to things without functions; things that have virtues must have functions. Further, even though we have two kinds of functions, virtue is characterized in the same way for both artifacts with optimal functions and natural objects with exclusive functions.

From these points, I think we can infer that if justice is a virtue of cities, then cities must have functions, and their justice cannot be understood independently of their functions; it is likewise with any other virtues cities can have. Similarly, if justice is also a virtue of the soul, then the soul must have functions and its justice cannot be understood independently of its functions, and so with any other virtues a soul has. We can reach the same conclusion in another way: when the functional theory is applied to the city and then it is put together with the isomorphism between the virtues of the city and of the soul, the two together imply that the soul must have functions that correspond to the functions of the city; the two together require not only that the soul has parts corresponding to the city's parts but also psychic functions corresponding to the city's social functions.

2 The Isomorphism Between Just City and Just Soul

One might grant that Plato uses the functional theory to discover justice in the city, but deny that the functional theory plays any role in the account of the virtues of the soul. To discover justice in the human soul, Plato does not use (at least not explicitly) a functional procedure, as he did for justice in the city,[6] but a shortcut made possible by his assumption that a just soul is isomorphic to a just city; this shortcut enables him to deduce an account of the just soul from his account of the just city and an independent argument for his division of the soul (IV 434-42). But for the reasons just given (viz., the isomorphism), the functional theory must be in the background in the case of the soul as well. Moreover, the close analogy between the tripartite city and the tripartite soul (city and soul have "the same kinds, equal in number," IV 441c) that the isomorphism presupposes and the analogy between justice in the soul and health in the body indicate that Plato thinks the human soul comes with a *natural* division of parts and psychic labors (functions) unique (and exclusive) to each part; further, the human soul can be educated so that its parts are matched optimally to the psychic functions of an individual to provide for, defend, and govern herself[7] just as the city comes with a *natural* division of abilities and talents and can be designed and legislated so that its talents are optimally matched to its social functions of providing, defending, and governing itself.

The isomorphism also requires that the cryptic formula of justice—that in both city and soul justice obtains when "each [part] is doing its own"—must have the same interpretation in both cases (IV 441d)[8]: if a city is just when each (relevant) part of the city is doing that civic function (of the three general civic functions of provisioning, defending, and ruling) which it can by nature and education do best (i.e., optimally), then a soul is just when each (relevant) part of it is performing that psychic function (of the corresponding three general psychic functions of providing, defending, and ruling oneself) which it can by nature and education do best (i.e., optimally). The functional theory is still in play, I think, in the division of the soul by exclusive functions, in the account of a just soul by optimal functions, and in the defense of justice in the soul by the justice-health analogy.

The isomorphism has been the subject of a great deal of discussion and controversy.[9] A crucial passage setting out the isomorphism is worth quoting in full:

> But now let us work out the inquiry in which we supposed that, if we found some larger thing that contained justice and viewed it there, we should more easily discover its nature in the individual man. And we agreed that this larger thing is the city, and we constructed the best city in our power, well knowing that in the good city it would of course be found. What, then, we thought we saw there we must refer back to the individual and, if it is confirmed, all will be well.… That seems a sound method.… Then, said I, if you call a thing the same whether it is big or little, is it unlike in the respect in which you call it the same or like? Like, he said. Then a just man too will not differ at all from a just city in respect of the very form [kind] justice, but be like it. Yes, like. But now the city was thought to be just because three natural kinds existing in it performed each its own function, and again it was temperate, brave, and wise because of certain other affections and habits of these three kinds. True, he said. Then, my friend, we shall expect the individual also to have these same kinds in his soul, and by reason of identical affections to these with those in the city to deserve correctly the same names. (IV 434d-5c)

At first sight, it looks as if the basis for this conclusion is a linguistic principle of univocality: "if you call a thing the same whether it is big or little, it is like, rather than unlike, in the respect in which you call it the same… then a man too will not differ at all with respect to the very form justice, but will be like it." But the principle seems false of natural languages, including English and Greek. There are many counterexamples to it in English and Greek, for example, "sharp" as in "sharp knives" and "sharp notes," and *aischron* (shameful) in Greek, according to Plato's Callicles (*Grg.* 482). Moreover, as David Keyt has noted, Plato himself does not apply it to just actions and just persons: at *Republic* book IV 443e, Socrates says that actions are just in so far as they produce and preserve a just psyche, so just actions are defined by a causal relation to a just soul, not by just actions being isomorphic to a just soul (Keyt 2006a).

Rather than a linguistic principle of univocality ("that a formula that defines a term in one application defines it in all applications"), Keyt suggests a more subtle principle at work:

> [I]f (i) two systems have the same number of parts, if (ii) the parts of the one system can be paired one to one with parts of the other on the basis of the kinds to which the parts belong, if (iii) these kinds of parts are the seats of certain affections, and if (iv) the one system has a quality in virtue of its parts having such an affection, then (v) the other system has the same quality if its parts have the same affection. (Keyt 2006a, p. 349)

This is clearly a great and sound advance over using the principle of univocality alone, as I and many others have done. Keyt's interpretation is closer to the text (by taking the whole text into account, not just the opening statement, as well as later texts); it avoids falsehoods and provides more direction for an interpretation of both sets of Platonic virtues, social and individual.

The principle is intricate and we must keep clear its various elements, especially when we apply it to cities and souls: we have two systems, one a city and the other a human soul; there are parts of the city and parts of the soul; then we have kinds, and a part of the city can belong to the same kind as a part of the soul and can be paired accordingly; further, the parts of either system can be seats of "affections"; and finally, each system can have a quality (a virtue or vice in this case) by reason of affections of its parts, which can be "identical" to a quality the other system has by reason of similar affections of its corresponding parts.

We can reasonably infer from the definitions of the social virtues already at hand what some of the "affections" are by reason of which the social virtues are present in the city; thus the city is courageous when its defenders preserve in all circumstances correct beliefs expressed by the rulers about what the city should fear. More generally, it is by reason of each class performing its optimal function (the function for which it is best suited by nature and education) that the city is just. We can similarly infer what some of the affections of parts of the soul are from the subsequent definitions of the psychic virtues; thus we can infer that a human being is courageous by some part in her soul preserving in all circumstances the correct beliefs held by another part about what she should fear.

But what are the three kinds to which the three parts of the city and the three parts of the soul belong? It is essential to answer this question if the basis for pairing a part of the city with a part of the soul one to one is that they both belong to the same kind, and this pairing is necessary for the account of what the psychic virtues are and how social and psychic virtues are "the same." This need can be seen in the incomplete definition of psychic courage I just gave. How can we determine which parts of the soul correspond to which parts of the city, so that we can define courage as being present in both by reason of similar affections of corresponding parts? How did Plato determine this?

Now, I think there are stronger (very strict) and weaker interpretations of Keyt's principle of isomorphism. The strictest interpretation is based on the inscription analogy Socrates gives in book II 368d: here we have not only sameness of structure between the two inscriptions (what isomorphism surely entails) but also sameness of parts (something not entailed by sameness of structure); the lowercase letter "a" and the uppercase letter "A" are both letters and indeed the same letter, "alpha."[10] I think the principle of isomorphism can also be satisfied by a less strict interpretation, according to which the structure is the same but the parts are not the same in that strong sense. An example would be a house and the architect's plans according to which the house was built; if we look at the front elevation of the house, we see a door in the middle of the first floor and two windows on the second floor symmetrically placed above the door; we can decide whether the builder followed this part of the architect's plan faithfully because we can match the windows (of the house) to the pictures of the windows (in the plan), the door to the picture of the door, and their corresponding relations. But a door and a picture of a door are obviously not both doors or both pictures of a door; the picturing relation is sufficient for matching parts of one system to parts of another. And there might be other relations among parts of one system and parts of another, which might guide us in matching parts of one system to parts of another, one to one.

The functional theory can work with a less strict interpretation. We have, to begin with, the similarity among the three general functions of city and individual: provisioning the city and provisioning oneself, defending the city and defending oneself, and ruling the city and ruling oneself. Then we have the similarity in optimal functions that guides the matching of social and psychic parts: for example, spirit may be matched to the military class because they are both best suited to defend the wholes of which they are parts; reason and men with inborn high intelligence can be matched because they both are best suited (with appropriate educations) to govern the whole of which they are parts.

3   Parts of the Soul: Agents or Faculties?

The strict interpretation (based on the inscriptions analogy) and some inferences can be one source of the agent interpretation of parts of the soul (see Keyt 2006a, p. 50). On this strict model if, for example, the relevant parts of the city are agents, then it seems that the parts of the soul must be agents. Of course the relevant parts of the city are not necessarily individual persons, though presumably a group of persons can be an agent. The parts of the city are collections of persons, each group collected on the basis of innate capabilities (and appropriate education) for one or another of the three general social functions (provisioning, defending, and governing the city); the three general social functions of the city and the innate capabilities (distributed by the "natural lottery")[11] for performing these functions well guide the collecting of the persons of the city into three groups, and this is the sense in which these groups are natural and not arbitrary.[12] It is to these groups, so collected, that the three parts of the soul correspond. This suggests that the three parts of the soul are also groups, each group collected on the basis of innate capabilities for the three general psychic functions (of providing for, defending, and governing oneself); these groups of the soul too, I believe, Plato thinks are natural. But groups of what?

Well, we find Plato giving different characterizations of the parts of the soul and parts of the city in different places. Just before he argues for the division of the soul, Socrates (whose dialogue in the *Republic* represents Plato's position) says:

> Is it not necessary to admit this much, that the same kinds and qualities that exist in the city are to be found in each one of us. They could not get there from any other source. It would be absurd to suppose that the element of [high] spirit was not derived in cities from the citizens … or love of learning … or love of money. (book IV, 435c)

So perhaps the three kinds are three kinds of love: love of learning, love of honor, and love of money (see also II. 374d-376c, VIII 544d, IX 580c-581b). Rulers and reason can be paired because both love learning, defenders and spirit because both love victory and honor, and artisans and appetite because both love money. Of course to see what this implies, we need to understand what Plato thinks this love is—his term in all these passages is *philia* (not the *eros* of the *Republic* which unlike the *eros* of the *Symposium* is only sexual, in these passages at least). And if *philia* presupposes beliefs, as it seems to do in the *Republic*, then it is natural to think that Plato attributes beliefs to each part of the soul since each part has *philia* for something; and if each part has beliefs, then it has cognitive powers; and consequently, each part seems to be an agent.[13]

We can reach a similar conclusion from Plato's view that any part of the soul can rule an individual. Ruling surely requires cognition and reasoning. And if ruling requires cognition and reasoning, then it seems that every part of the soul can have beliefs and can reason. As in the case of loving, once more it looks as if spirit and the other parts of the soul are agents. Bobonich is quite explicit that on Plato's view, every part of the soul can have desires and goals and can reason; only reason proper, however, can reason about the Forms, a fact which presumably distinguishes it from the reasoning that appetite can engage in (Bobonich 2002, pp. 219–20).

But if we look at Plato's initial division of the soul, this conclusion becomes problematic: the Odysseus example, Plato's last example in the long argument for the division of the soul in *Republic* book IV, 441b-c, would be useless in showing that spirit and reason are distinct, if spirit can reason. And notice that the reasoning here has nothing to do with Forms, since Odysseus' reasoning is entirely about his past and his future; it is reasoning about the sensible world, which spirit here cannot carry out; and if it cannot reason about Forms (something granted by all), it cannot reason at all. Similarly, if appetite can reason, then Plato's first example, of a man thirsting and refusing to drink on the basis of reasoning, would be equally useless in showing that appetite and reason are distinct parts of the soul; and once more in that example, the reasoning that appetite does not carry out is about sensible objects. In the original argument for the partition of the psyche, these examples do their work in the argument only if appetite and spirit cannot reason about sensible objects (as well as about Forms). Aside from the paradoxical consequences of supposing that parts of the soul are agents,[14] Plato's main argument for partition suggests that the parts are faculties or capabilities for distinctive psychic activities, not agents.

Plato sets up what is at issue in the analysis of the psyche as follows:

> … whether we do all these things with the same thing, or whether there are three things and we do one thing with one and one with another—learn with one part of ourselves, feel anger with another, and with yet a third desire the pleasures of nutrition and generation and their kind—or whether it is with the entire soul that we do each of them…. " (IV 436a-b)

This question sets up two and only two alternatives:

(a) We learn, we feel anger, and we desire the pleasures of nutrition and generation with the whole soul, or
(b) We learn with one part of the soul, we feel anger with another part, and we desire the pleasures of nutrition and generation with a third part.

But the agent interpretation gives an answer which is a third alternative not contemplated in the question:

(c) We learn, feel anger, and desire the pleasures of nutrition and generation with one part of the soul; we learn, feel anger, and desire with a second part of the soul; and we learn, feel anger, and desire with a third part of the soul
   (Bobonich 2002, p. 220, except that he leaves out "feeling anger").

This alternative does not appear to be coherent as an answer to that question. And it has many problems of its own, such as distinguishing *these* three parts from each other, divisions within divisions, and lack of unity. It may even commit Plato to the view that there are several just and/or unjust persons within a person, since agents, like parts, can be Platonically just or unjust by his definition of psychic justice.

Here is the first part of Plato's answer to Socrates' question, based on the principle of contrariety and the case of men who thirst but refuse to drink:

> Is it not that there is a something in the soul that bids them drink and something that forbids, a different something that masters that which bids? I think so. And is it not the fact that that which inhibits such actions arises when it arises from the calculations of reason, but the impulses which draw and drag come through affections and diseases? Apparently. Not unreasonably, said I, shall we claim that they are two and different from one another, naming that in the soul by which it calculates [reasons] the calculating [reason] and that by which it [erotically] loves and hungers and thirsts, and feels the titillation of other appetites, the irrational [arational] and appetitive.... (439c-d; Shorey translation, the last sentence modified to show that literally a part of the soul is named here after what it does, its function)

Here I take Plato to be giving us what he thinks are the kinds to which the parts of the soul primarily belong, the kinds that tell us what they are, what they *always* are, and what they are by *nature*. I take him to think that he is discovering a natural division of the psyche—natural in the sense of a division into innate or inborn psychic parts according to *innate* psychic capabilities: reason is that psychic part by which we reason. When he asks a few lines later (IV 439e) whether "spirit" is a third part, he repeats the phrase he used to describe spirit when he introduced the whole issue at book IV 436a-b: "that by which we feel anger" and invents (at 441a) a name for it, literally "the anger-kind" (*thumoeides*, a name of the psychic power as distinct from the psychic activity which is its exclusive function), usually translated spirit. "That by which we feel anger" is what spirit is by nature, but what we feel anger at is contingent and depends on our learning and experience. Similarly, drink is the object of thirst by nature, but what we like to drink (hot, cold, sweet, good, or bad drink) is contingent and depends on learning (V 437-9a).[15] Again, "that by which we reason" is what reason is by nature. Reason too has a natural object, "to know where the truth lies" (581b), while some things we reason about are learned and contingent (the oligarchic man reasons about how to produce and maintain wealth, the timocratic how to attain victory and honors). In all three cases— reason, spirit, and appetite—the parts are initially characterized by what they do by nature, by their natural capabilities or functions, and/or by their natural objects.[16]

Further, I think his calling the appetitive part arational (*alogiston*) in the very sentence in which he names reason and appetite after what they do (IV 439d), is strong evidence that he is using the concept of exclusive functions, and that the appetitive part cannot reason. He makes a similar move in his last example of the division, the Odysseus example, when he calls Odysseus' feeling anger unreasoning (*alogistos thumoumenoi*, 441c). He is using the example to isolate feeling anger (or perhaps getting angry) itself before there is any reasoning mixed with it (which is more difficult to isolate in an adult, as distinct from an infant in Glaucon's example). The whole point of the example is that feeling anger itself is not identical with (or similar enough to) reasoning, and so the capability to do one and the capability to do the other are not identical capabilities (or even similar enough). Plato's initial division of the soul favors heavily the interpretation that the parts of the soul are, to begin with—inborn or by nature—faculties or psychic capabilities rather than agents, in the question by which he sets up the issue, in his examples, and in his answers to that question.

It is mainly in subsequent passages, when he is mostly speaking of the educated and experienced psychic powers of adults, that we find some evidence that he thinks of the parts as agents: in his image of the embodied soul as a man, lion, and many-headed beast, for example (IX, pp. 588–89; cf. Keyt 2006a, p. 350); in his attributing desires and pleasures to all three parts; and in supposing that a man who is ruled by a dominant desire for wealth is ruled by the appetitive part of the soul.

In Plato's account of psychic temperance, the only direct evidence for the agent interpretation that I know of (book IV at 442d) is in Plato's account of psychic temperance, in his statement that all three parts of the soul have "common opinion" that reason should rule. And though this evidence cannot be completely neutralized, context should be kept in mind. In this case, the most relevant context is his previous account of how a guardian can be so educated as to have the holistic virtues of justice (the particular order of reason ruling, spirit defending, and appetite being ruled) and temperance (agreement on that order or harmony among the parts in that ordered functioning). When we look back at that educational program, we can see that there is a division of labor in it, some activity aiming at habituation and some at cognitive learning:

> Then is it not, as we said, the blending of music and gymnastics that will render them [reason and spirit] concordant, intensifying and fostering the one [reason] with fair words and teachings and relaxing and soothing and making gentle the other [spirit] by harmony and rhythm?[17]

The agreement among the parts of the soul on reason's rule, psychic temperance, can be achieved by these two aims of Platonic education, and purely cognitive agreement among the parts is not necessary.

Whenever Plato speaks of parts of the soul, we need to consider whether he is speaking of the faculties as already educated (not always by his educational program, of course), as mixed with learning and experience (as he does most of the time because he is speaking of adults or children of some experience), or as what they are by nature (as he does in the initial division of the soul). It is essential to remember that Plato allows for the development of the inborn parts of the soul and for interaction among these parts to produce conduct. Plato's psychology is not static, but developmental and interactive. He fully realizes that "the [adult] human soul is an achievement," the result of experience of the world, education, and interaction among its parts.

The oligarch's ruling desire to produce and maintain wealth above all is an educated desire and the result of appetite and reason working together. This desire has been placed by some commentators in the appetitive part of the soul (Irwin 1995; Bobonich 2002), inferring that appetite can think, if not about the Forms, then about means and ends and overall sensible goods, since the oligarch, along with the democrat and the tyrant, is said by Plato to be ruled by the appetitive part. But rule by the appetitive part can be understood in terms of the person taking the satisfaction of appetites as his ultimate end and using reason only to find out the necessary or efficient means for satisfying appetites. The oligarchic man's reason finds that wealth is that means; the democratic man reasons that it is freedom and equality; the tyrant takes the means to be power. The resulting dominant and ruling desire, for wealth or freedom and equality or power, is a mixture of appetite and learning. The various psychic rulings are done by developed, experienced, and interacting psychic parts. Even a simple appetite for hot drink is already a mixture of thirst and a bit of learning: I am thirsty and I like hot drinks.[18] It is not necessary to suppose that each part of the soul by itself and as it is by nature produces action (say, drinking hot milk), since the parts can interact with each other to do so.[19] In Plato's portraits of characters, such as the timocratic and the oligarchic men, reason and spirit or reason and appetites already work together, but these two characters use reason "as a slave," only to figure out ways and means to victory or wealth and even to discipline the appetites (VIII 553e). Their conduct is the result of developed and experienced faculties interacting with each other. In order for the timocratic man to reason about ways and means to victory and honor, it is not necessary that his spirit has reason in it—a second reason in addition to reason he has to begin with! Or that the oligarchic man's appetite has reason in it, in addition to the reason he already has, like everyone else. Even for Plato, this seems like a prolific and futile proliferation, though occasionally his language does suggest it when he speaks of educated and experienced parts of the soul.

Commentators often go to books VIII and IX "to fill out" the analysis of the psyche in book IV, but they overlook the fact that in the later books, Plato is often speaking of the faculties as already educated, experienced, and interacting with each other. He is not speaking of thirst simply as thirst, or hunger simply as hunger (unless he explicitly so specifies), but of these desires as already mixed with learning, experience, and education. Just as an adult's body is the result of development—of growth, nutrition, and exercise—so an adult's psyche is the result of learning and experience. The educated and experienced parts of the soul of an adult can indeed look like agents, but that is because they are developed and can be the result of that development and interaction. The education, experience of and interaction among inborn parts of the soul that Plato himself provides, accounts well enough for speaking of these developed parts as if they were agents.

I think that each inborn part of the soul is complex, but it is complexity in each of the original inborn or natural psychic parts, not to be conflated with agent complexity that is the result of development and interaction. We can see this complexity within a psychic part in the trouble Plato has from the beginning in finding a unified principle for appetite. There is a multiplicity of psychic functions and natural objects that he groups together: erotically loving (i.e., lusting, with sex as the object), hungering for (solid) food, thirsting for drink, and even "other similar appetites" (IV 431d). Later in book IX 580d, he calls the appetitive part "multiformed" and, apparently for convenience of reference, proposes to call it the "lover of money" since money is the major means for satisfying all these appetites. But this way of referring to it is actually misleading—it has led readers into thinking that appetite is an agent who can think. The invention of money was a recent development in Plato's time, and it is highly implausible to attribute to Plato the view that Homo sapiens are born with an appetite for money. The desire for money is clearly a cultural construct involving much learning, only a tiny bit older in biological time than the desire for a Cadillac. Plato would have been better off seeking some reference to the body as a unifying principle for the appetitive part; for instance, that appetite, as distinct from the other parts and as distinct from the desires of other parts, always has some bodily source (e.g., organs), and its object is related to a bodily need or a bodily satisfaction. Elsewhere, I have suggested that the unifying principle for the appetitive part is relative to the need of provisioning oneself (parallel to the economic need of provisioning of the city): appetites signal bodily needs and motivate their satisfaction, though the signals are imperfect or incomplete regarding what would satisfy the need, how much of it, and how frequently (inborn appetites by themselves are almost blind on all these three things and need learning). And it is this very imperfection of appetite that makes it rational and best for it to be ruled by reason.[20]

There is a passage in book V that reveals Plato's approach to understanding psychic parts:

> Shall we say that powers belong to that kind of existing things by which we ... can do what we can do.... In a faculty (power) I cannot see any color or shape or similar mark such as those on which in many other cases I can fix my eyes in discriminating in my thought one thing from another. But in the case of a faculty I look to that only—that to which it is related and what it effects, and it is in this way that I come to call each one of them a faculty, and that which is related to the same thing and accomplishes the same thing I call the same faculty, and that to another I call other. (477c-d)

He gives as obvious examples the powers of sight and hearing: sight is the power by which we see colors and shapes in objects (the power itself has no color or shape), and seeing is what it accomplishes; hearing is a different power because it is related to different objects, sounds, and it accomplishes a different thing, hearing. Socrates then applies this principle to distinguish knowledge and opinion as different faculties or powers: the former relates to Forms as its objects and accomplishes knowing (cognitive states that are always true); the latter relates to sensible things and accomplishes opining or believing (states sometimes true, sometimes false). This must be a distinction within the faculty or psychic part of reason (since, among other things, the states have truth values in either case), and it shows that Plato tries to understand psychic powers by the objects they are related to (presumably characteristically or by nature, as thirst is for drink) and by what they accomplish when the faculties work on those objects (presumably their exclusive functions). In this principle, we again see the functional theory at work, this time relying on exclusive natural psychic functionings, in conjunction with the natural objects of these functionings, to understand psychic powers.

Can we go back and see if this principle is at work in the division of the soul in book IV? I think so, but of course we must distinguish the role of this principle from the role of the principle of contrariety. The latter, in conjunction with psychic conflicts, can lead us to divide the self or soul, in cases where we cannot account for the conflict by reference to the state of the external world (e.g., my finances in the example of caviar and champagne) or by dividing the object or aspects of it (as in loving and hating different parts or properties of a car) or by dividing time (sometimes I want it and sometimes I don't). But once we do divide the self into (let us say) two parts, we still need to understand the nature of each part—the principle of contrariety is not sufficient for individuating the parts. And here is where the principle of identifying a psychic power by its characteristic objects and exclusive functions comes into play. In the case of reason, Socrates characterizes it by its exclusive activity, reasoning or calculating, and in the case of thirst, by its natural object, drink and the psychic activity of moving toward the object (rather than away from it as in fear (see Miller 1999, for motions of the soul, literally)). Even so, it can still be difficult to characterize the nature of each part. To return to the appetitive power, it has, after all, three different kinds of objects: liquids, solids, and sex. We can group the first two as food or nutrients, but how do we group together nutrients and sex, especially when different physical systems are involved?[21]

I think that Keyt's isomorphic principle is compatible with the parts of the soul being faculties or powers, rather than agents. And though our texts provide some support for each interpretation, too many grave paradoxes face the agent interpretation (well brought out recently by Bobonich himself, 2002, pp. 254–258, and Keyt 2006a, p. 350): on the agent interpretation, a person has no center of consciousness and no unity of self, and there is a proliferation of powers and agents. It may even lead to several just or unjust agents within a person! Further, the agent interpretation weakens Plato's most fundamental reason for his definition of psychic justice: that reason and only reason can think at all, and so it alone can think about the good of the person. If all three parts of the soul can reason, why should one of them rule and the others obey? Why is that condition just and why is it better for the agent?[22]

All these difficulties, together with the ambiguity of the evidence, suggest strongly that we adopt the interpretation of parts of the soul as faculties, especially if the interpretation is coherent and does not have similar difficulties. Plato's initial division of the soul suggests distinctive psychic powers. When we take the functional theory as a premise for understanding the nature of the psychic parts as innate psychic powers with characteristic functions and objects, as well as a premise for the division of the city into natural classes, we can have a coherent and consistent interpretation of Keyt's principle of isomorphism. The division of the city is based on inborn capabilities of citizens for the three general functions of cities—provisioning, defense, and ruling the city; and the division of the soul is also based on inborn capabilities of souls for the three general functions of souls— provisioning, defending, and ruling oneself. The social and psychic functions are similar enough to be of the same kind, and so are the social and psychic capabilities required for the optimal performance of these functions. Given these similarities, parts of the city and parts of the soul can be matched, and the virtues can be similarly defined: for example, reason and persons of inborn high intelligence can be matched because they are better suited, with appropriate educations, to rule the city and the soul, respectively, than the other (relevant) parts of the city and soul.

4   Is Plato's Completely Good City Intellectually, Politically, and Ethically Elitist?

Some commentators who argue that the parts of the soul are agents also take the view that in the good city, only the philosophers can be just and virtuous (e.g., Cooper, Irwin, Bobonich). How closely these two views are connected is not clear. Few dispute that only the philosophers (persons who can know Platonic Forms, *Rep.* V) can have wisdom, if wisdom requires knowledge of the good (what I call intellectual elitism), and few dispute that the completely good city is politically elitist (the paradox of the philosopher king that only men who have such knowledge are fit to rule). But these commentators go beyond this intellectual and political elitism to an ethical or moral elitism: in the completely good city, only the philosophers can be just and, more generally, virtuous (Cooper 1999; Bobonich 2002, pp. 41–88).[23]

Ethical elitism seems to me to be grossly paradoxical and to wreck Plato's argument that justice makes a man happy or happier than injustice. It is paradoxical because according to it in Plato's completely good city, the vast majority of the population would not or could not be just—certainly the artisan class as well as the warrior class. Even if a perfect or high compliance rate may not be part of the definition or essence of a just city, and even if its justice is to be found primarily in its institutions, there is still something strange in supposing that a city is completely just but the vast majority of its citizens are not just—especially if its citizens lack by nature a level of ability (to acquire knowledge of the Form of the Good) required for being just.[24] Moreover, such a city might be grossly deficient in stability and not because, as Plato says (VIII 545d), there might arise dissension within the ruling class, but because the vast majority of its citizens could not have justice in their souls.

The view that the vast majority of the citizens in Plato's completely good city would not or could not be just would also wreck Plato's argument that one is better off or happier being just rather than unjust, at least if this argument is meant to answer Thrasymachus' or Glaucon's challenge. Plato's argument is supposed to provide a rational motivation for being just, a greater such motivation than the motivation for being unjust; but now (on the view in question) this argument, even if completely successful, applies only to a tiny minority, the philosophers. The argument is irrelevant to the motivation of the rest of the citizens, for they still may be motivated by the desire for happiness, but now being just plays no role in this motivation. There is no evidence whatsoever in books I and II that Thrasymachus or Glaucon, or indeed Socrates himself conceived of the challenge to show that justice pays as so severely limited in scope—to show that for a few very naturally talented and highly educated individuals, justice pays.

To be sure, since Plato has two kinds of justice—justice for the city and justice for the individual—which though isomorphic to each other are still two different standards of justice, ethical elitism might not be so paradoxical, if we distinguish the just citizen from the just person. The view can allow that all citizens in Plato's city can be just (they have political justice—the justice of the polis) in the sense of each doing that social work for which she/he is best suited by nature and education (see 434b-c, where Plato says or implies that persons who move from a social function they are best at to another, or who multifunction, are doing injustice). Ethical elitism claims that it is only psychic justice that the philosophers alone can have, while other citizens can have political justice since this does not require that *they* have wisdom. Even so, ethical elitism still wrecks Plato's argument that justice pays; for in that argument, both in the health-justice analogy of book IV and in the pleasure arguments of book IX, it is clear enough that psychic justice is what is at stake: in all these arguments, the issue is whether Plato's psychic justice is better or pleasanter for us. And in Glaucon's challenge, that is clear enough too: it is whether justice in one's soul makes one happy that Glaucon wants to know (358b). This is how Plato himself sets up the challenge. But according to ethical elitism, psychic justice is still irrelevant to the vast majority of the citizens' motivations in the completely good city and to the question how we should live. Do we not have here a kind of Sachs' fallacy of irrelevance, only in an even more radical form, since if this is Plato's view, it can never be fixed?

An extreme symptom of ethical elitism is the supposition that the three characters Socrates sets up for comparison with respect to pleasure (in IX, 580d-81d) are the three types of citizens in his ideal city, the philosopher rulers, the defenders, and the providers (Bobonich 2002, pp. 47–48, 68).[25] The alternative view is that they are the philosopher, the timocratic man, and the oligarchic man of book VIII, the latter two being indisputably unjust men by Plato's definition of psychic justice. But according to this symptom, the defenders of Plato's just city, in books III and IV, are the same as the timocratic men of book VIII, and the providers the same as the oligarchic men. This seems consistent enough with ethical elitism since the defenders and the providers do not have psychic justice. But this supposition still faces the objection that it wrecks Plato's argument that justice pays, and now it is an even bigger wreck since it supposes not merely that the defenders and providers of the completely good city are not just but that they are psychically *un*just by Plato's own definition of psychic justice. Not only do the defenders (if identified with the timocratic men) and the providers (if identified with oligarchic men) lack justice because they lack wisdom, they are also unjust in that they have a disorder in their soul (spirit or appetite rule, instead of reason).

I think this extreme symptom may betray a conflation. The defenders and the artisans in Plato's completely good city are characterized (in books II, III, IV) by their ability by nature (and subsequent appropriate education) to perform a social function, to defend or provide for their city, whereas the timocratic and oligarchic men (in books VIII and IX) are characterized by what part of their soul rules and what is their dominant value (what they believe is their chief good). Thus, the definitions of the defenders and of timocratic men are different, and it is an open question whether those best able by nature to defend the city would or need to have their psyches so structured that spirit rules and their dominant or ultimate value is victory and honor. Similar is the case with the providers and oligarchic men.

Further, textual evidence (from books III, IV, and VIII) is against this extreme symptom, perhaps decisively so. If we look at the definition of the social virtue of the defenders, (social) courage, it is said to be the ability or power to preserve under all conditions (or the preservation in action under all conditions of) correct and lawful beliefs, provided by the legislators (rulers of the city), about what the city should and should not fear (IV 429c-d, 430b). Presumably the rulers provide such beliefs on the basis of their social wisdom, knowledge of what is good for the city as a whole in its internal and external relations. To be courageous, the defenders need not believe that victory and honor are the dominant or ultimate goods of life, as the timocratic men believe by definition; nor is spirit ruling their soul part of the definition of the defenders. Further, such a belief is not part of the Platonic education of the defenders; nor is sprit ruling the soul an intended result of their Platonic education (III 412c-14b). Indeed, Plato's account of the education of the defenders (in book III) and his account of how a young person becomes timocratic (book VIII 549c-50b) are so different; one may well suppose that these two characters could not possibly be the same.

But let us finally consider the pivotal proposition itself that on Plato's view, the defenders and the artisans of his completely good city would not or could not be psychically just. Aside from its unpalatable consequences (paradox and the wrecking of the argument that justice pays), what is the textual evidence for it? And is it decisive or compelling?

The only passage that I know of that a series of commentators (beginning with Cooper 1999, p. 140, and argued for also by Irwin and Bobonich) cite as direct evidence is IV 441e4-6: "Does it not belong to the rational part to rule, being wise and exercising forethought in behalf of the entire soul, and to the principle of high spirit to be subject of this and its ally?" (Shorey trans.). This comes immediately after the formal principle of psychic justice, deduced from the isomorphism and the formal principle of city justice: "We must remember, then, that each of us also in whom the several parts within him perform their own task—he will be a just man and a man who minds his own affairs" (441d-e). So it seems that in the former passage, Plato is filling in the formal principle of psychic justice by assigning to reason "its own" task (in my language, the optimal matching of psychic part and psychic task), namely, ruling, apparently giving his most fundamental ground why that is the best assignment, which together with the other two optimal assignments makes a person just. His fundamental ground is "being wise and having forethought for the entire soul." We may note that for this to be a good ground for the assignment of ruling to reason, either the other parts of the soul cannot at all be wise and exercise forethought for the entire soul (the faculty interpretation according to which these things are exclusive functions of reason) or the other parts can do these things but not as well as reason can (optimal function with perhaps the agent interpretation of parts).

Of course this passage (441e4-6) is put together with the subsequent definition of wisdom (442c) as being possessed "by that small part" (reason) and as "knowledge of what is beneficial for each [part of] and for the whole [soul]." And in turn, these two passages are put together with passages from books VI and VII (especially VII 534b8-c5) to show that on Plato's view, one cannot have knowledge of any other good unless one knows the Form of the Good. Knowledge of the Form of the Good is a necessary condition for the wisdom in our passage, and since only the philosophers can have the latter, only the philosophers can be just.

The confluence of these passages may seem decisive in favor of ethical elitism, and apparently it has seemed so to many. But I think there are reasons for serious doubts, apart from the unpalatable consequences drawn above.

For one thing, the functional theory gives us reason to believe that the view conflates a thing performing its optional or exclusive function *and* performing it well, and as a result conflates the virtues of justice and wisdom or supposes that they are so closely related that justice requires wisdom. My eyes are seeing but they may be seeing well or poorly, well by their appropriate virtues, poorly by their vices; I may be pruning my roses with the optimal instrument for doing so, but my shears may be sharp or dull at the edges and I prune well or poorly. Similarly, my reason may be performing its exclusive functions of judging, reasoning, or calculating, but it may be doing so well or poorly. Similarly, my reason may be in charge of my life (performing its optimal function of ruling), in setting the purposes of my life and choosing effective means to them, but it may be doing so well or poorly; and it does it well if it has wisdom and not so well if it lacks wisdom, but it can be ruling in either case. When my reason rules, my spirit helps to carry out the injunctions of reason, and my appetites are obedient to reason on what, when, and how much to eat, drink, and be merry, then I am a just person according to Plato's definition of psychic justice. Whether I also have wisdom that enables my reason to rule well is an open, further question.[26] If I have wisdom, my reason rules well. But perhaps my reason can still rule well if it has only true opinion (as Socrates apparently had only true opinion about the good in the *Republic*) and I can still be just.[27]

It may be objected that Plato himself seems to conflate a thing performing its proper function and performing it well and consequently in the relevant cases seems to conflate justice and wisdom. There is a grain of truth to this, but it does not support the charge that Plato conflates justice and wisdom. It is true that on Plato's theory of justice, the city having optimal matching of parts to functions will result in these functions being performed better than they would be without the optimal matching. This is how he argues for the principle of social justice the first time it comes up (II. 370a-e): his comparison is between a city organized by division of labor by natural talent and a city without division of labor or with division irrespective of talent, and his conclusion is that the city's needs will be better satisfied, the corresponding functions better performed, with the first model. Given the isomorphism, the corresponding conclusion can be drawn about the organization (through experience and education) of the complex human soul: the soul as a whole will perform its functions better with division of psychic labor by psychic parts on the basis of the natural capabilities of these parts, than it would otherwise. In this sense, justice too enables a soul or a city to perform its functions better, and in this sense justice, like temperance (though for different reasons a soul will perform its tasks better as a whole if it has no structural conflicts, no internal stasis, but harmony), is a holistic virtue, unlike wisdom and courage that are located in parts of the city or parts of soul and enable those parts to perform their functions well, that is, to perform better than they would without these virtues. But this gives us no reason to conflate justice and wisdom or to suppose that justice requires wisdom or that Plato conflated these things. It is of course true that a part, the rulers or reason, will perform its function well if it has wisdom, but that performing well involves a different comparison from the performing well that justice enables the whole city or whole soul to do. There is no conflation of justice and wisdom or of a part performing well by a virtue belonging to that part and a whole performing better by a virtue belonging to that whole.

Aside from the functional theory itself, which plainly distinguishes between what the function of something is and whether it performs that function well, the view I am supporting too has textual support: namely, in Plato's definition of justice itself, there is no reference to wisdom either of the city or of the individual, at least in its formal parts. This is especially true of Plato's account of the justice of the city in IV 433a-34c: in that whole discussion (of formal social justice and its full definition), there is no reference whatsoever to social wisdom; the definition is entirely based on the principle of optimally matching natural capabilities of citizens to the main city functions. Isomorphically, the same thing should be possible for psychic justice. And indeed, in the formal part of the definition of psychic justice, there is no reference to wisdom.[28]

Now it may seem strange to suppose that we can understand someone's justice without any reference whatsoever to any of her cognitive states. But the view I am supporting does not do that, for it allows that the just person can have true relevant beliefs, perhaps even *reasonable* true relevant beliefs. And of course Plato makes a strong distinction between knowledge and belief (strong in the sense that there can be no knowledge of changing sensible objects). So it seems a possible interpretation of his view that a person may be just through knowledge of the Form of the Good or with true beliefs about the Form of the Good (as Socrates himself says that he has only beliefs about the Form of the Good) or through true beliefs about what is good in this world for the city or for oneself. And this view has indeed been held by several commentators, and it has been the chief traditional means of combating ethical elitism as an interpretation of Plato's *Republic*.

Some main evidence for this interpretation is Plato's definition of social courage, the courage of the city as located in the defenders of the city; they can be courageous through true belief from the rulers about what the city should fear (IV 429b-c, 430b). This has often been discounted as being only "political" civic courage (430c) rather than courage within the soul, and it is indeed true that this is a virtue of the city. But this virtue is located in persons assigned to defend the city, as social wisdom is located in persons assigned to rule the city. These two social virtues are unlike the holistic social virtues of justice and temperance; if a city is Platonically just, it does not follow that its citizens have Platonic justice in their souls, and the same is true of Platonic social temperance. But if a city is Platonically courageous, it does follow that some of its citizens are courageous— namely, its defenders. The city is courageous when its defenders preserve in all circumstances correct beliefs from the legislators about what the city should fear. They can do this because they are born high-spirited and receive an education and training with the aim of attaining the ability to so preserve in all circumstances such beliefs.[29] In giving his account of social courage, Plato considers the souls of the defenders twice, first to address their education and then to define the quality they have by which the city is courageous. To be sure, this definition does not explicitly refer to the beliefs they must have, the preservation of which would be psychic courage, namely, true beliefs about what they should fear for themselves. The contents of the two beliefs, the belief taken from the rulers and the belief taken from reason, have different objects: the object of the former is what the city should fear, and the object of the latter is what a person should fear. But Plato tells us explicitly and forcefully that the rulers and the defenders must identify their interests or good with the interests or good of the city (III 412d-e), and this is essential for doing their job well; from this we can reasonably infer that what the rulers and defenders should fear for themselves is the same as what they should fear for the city. And this is well supported by Plato's claim that the defenders must preserve the belief about what the city should fear "in all circumstances." The brave man "preserves it both in pain and pleasures and in desires and fears and does not expel it from his soul" (IV 429cd).

Moreover, it seems paradoxical to suppose that the defenders of the city—who are courageous as soldiers in battle, risking their lives, and indeed preserving beliefs about what the city should fear "in all circumstances"—would not need to have correct beliefs about what they should fear for themselves.[30] The same holds for the non-holistic virtue of social wisdom, which is located in the rulers: the city is wise by the rulers being wise, and their wisdom consists in knowledge of what is good for the city in its internal and external relations; but since they too and above all identify their good with the good of the city, the wisdom by which they are psychically wise must have the same content. It is not possible for the rulers to be wise without being wise as persons, as it is not possible for the defenders to be courageous without being courageous as persons.[31]

To all this we may add that even Plato's philosophers must use a lot of, or perhaps use entirely, at best true beliefs rather than knowledge when they rule, since their laws and policies and directives will be about sensible things, and according to the Divided Line (VI 509d-510a), no one can have knowledge of sensible things; a lot of the philosophers' wisdom, at least the wisdom they use when they rule, is going to consist of at most true beliefs rather than knowledge.[32] Indeed, when we look at Plato's two accounts of wisdom in book IV, we see that they are about sensible cities and persons in this world, not about Platonic Forms: social wisdom is about "the city as a whole and the betterment of its relations within itself and with other states" (428d), and individual wisdom is "knowledge of what is beneficial for each [part of the soul] and for the whole, the community composed of the three" (442c). Cities and souls are not Forms, they are changing things in our changing world. It is quite possible, I think, that in book IV Plato was willing to call reasoned true beliefs about these changing things *sophia*, and this is I think compatible with his sharpening the concept of *episteme* later so that its objects can only be

Forms and compatible with his important assertion in book VI that unless one knows the Forms and the Form of the Good, one could not "know" about the good of cities and souls.

5 The Virtues and Vices of Isomorphism

There is no doubt that Plato chose to investigate two most important applications of the concept of justice—justice of city-states and justice of persons. But the isomorphism is not the only way to understand the relation between just persons and just cities; they may be related non-accidentally in at least two other ways.

One way is to suppose that a just city is a city composed of just persons; this gives explanatory primacy to the concept of a just person: we first define just persons and then give an account of a just city, not as Plato does but as a city composed of just persons as already defined. It is difficult to see how this can be a correct or fruitful way to understand a just city or a just society, since it would seem to render the nature of its institutions, its constitution, or its economic system, for example, irrelevant to its justice. It seems to imply that if a city is composed of just persons, it is a just city no matter what its institutions are.[33]

The other non-Platonic way of relating the justice of society to the justice of individuals in it is to suppose that a just individual is one who subscribes to the principles by which a society is just. Here the justice of society is given explanatory primacy over the justice of individuals: we first define a just society and then give an account of a just individual as one who has a strong and normally effective desire to act in accordance with the principles that make a society just. This is the way Rawls proceeds,[34] going back to an anti-Platonic tradition that begins perhaps with Aristotle. In fact it goes back to the *Republic*, since this is the way the justice of persons is related to the justice of society in Thrasymachus' and Glaucon's theories.[35] This seems to be the dominant tradition that justice is primarily and essentially a social virtue, unlike perhaps such other virtues as wisdom and courage, which may be more plausibly thought to be primarily and essentially virtues of individuals.

Perhaps the greatest advantage of the Rawlsian way of relating the justice of persons to the justice of societies is that it assures us of a coherent and unified theory of justice: there is only one standard of justice, the justice of society, and a just person is one who subscribes to that standard. But in Plato's theory, there are two standards of justice: one of cities and one of persons. And the isomorphism by itself does not imply that a person who has Platonic justice in her soul will also obey or subscribe to the constitutions and laws that make a city Platonically just, or conversely. There seems to be a gap between a just citizen and a just person even in Plato's completely good city: a just citizen is one who performs that social function for which she/he is best suited by nature and education, that is, one who subscribes to and obeys Plato's principle of social justice, but a just person is one in whose soul each part is doing that psychic function for which it is best suited by nature and education. From the definitions alone at least, there is no built in assurance that a just citizen in Plato's ideal city will be also a just person, or conversely. This is a gap like the Sachs' gap, but it seems to exist even within Plato's own completely good city. It is not, however, quite like the David Sachs gap, a gap between Platonic psychic justice and common standards of social justice or common standards of just and unjust behavior.[36] It is a more radical problem than the Sachs' problem, since it arises within Plato's own ideal theory, that is to say, within the completely good and so completely just city. Indeed, it is this gap that makes possible ethical elitism.

So what advantages did Plato see in defining a just person as an image of a just society (his actual order of exposition), or a just society as an image of a just person (possibly his real view)?

One advantage perhaps is that his actual procedure enabled Plato to project a publicly observable social structure onto the mystery of the human soul: if the justice of the city consists in a division of social labors which matches optimally inborn abilities of citizens to the city's functions, the justice of the person will consist in division of psychic labors which matches optimally natural psychic parts to the person's functions. Here the isomorphism can be viewed at least as a heuristic principle, to help us understand the structures and functionings of the human soul and discover its virtues.

A second advantage is that the isomorphism provides a strategy for the defense of justice. Plato defense of his *social* justice is that it promotes[37] the good or happiness of the city as a whole *most*: that particular social ordering is best and so rational and just. This is a recognizable version of a fundamental principle of teleological ethical theories that the right is what maximizes the good: the social structure that Plato calls just promotes the good of the city as a whole most, and so it is rational and just. Now if the same functional theory of good and the isomorphism are used to construct psychic justice, then we can have a corresponding defense of *psychic* justice: this psychic order most promotes the good of the person as a whole, and so it is rational and just. Thus, the isomorphism, the common functional theory of good, and the analogy from social to psychic justice, taken together, give Plato a heuristic device for understanding justice in our souls and some leverage in the defense of psychic justice: the same theory of functional good and the same teleological principle are applied to cities and persons. And a reasonable and recognizable defense of a conception of social justice, that it most promotes the good of the society as a whole, is used as leverage for a similar defense of an analogous conception of psychic justice.

As for the Sachs-like gap within his ideal theory that Plato's isomorphism seems to create, I think we can begin to see its solution in the causal relations Plato *also* envisages between just (or unjust) men and just (or unjust) cities—something we can see most clearly in book VIII but also in books II, III, IV, and VIII. Very roughly speaking, within ideal theory, the gap is closed by Plato's educational institutions. It is partly the aim of the completely good city that it will educate its citizens to have the virtues of citizens and of persons, as we can see in Plato's education program for the guardians and his higher educational program for the rulers. This is ideal theory. But Plato also has going causal relations between unjust constitutions and unjust persons: roughly speaking, timocratic men will try to create timocratic constitutions to live under, and timocratic cities will try to educate their citizens to be timocratic men, and similarly with the other constitutions. Here too, as in ideal theory or as part of it, we have the isomorphism and causal relations working together. For the Sachs problem itself, created in part by the isomorphism, we have some recent interesting solutions, one of them by David Keyt himself.[38]

Notes

1. Santas (2006, pp. 133–41). For a defense of the functional theory, see also Coumoundouros and Polansky (2008).
2. An objection can be made at once to my procedure: that there are major controversies of interpretation about all these three building blocks, so that at best I will be using controversies to try to resolve controversies. Can such a procedure be helpful? I think it can, mainly because these three blocks have not to my knowledge been used together to interpret the work and also because we need to understand the grand theories of the book, and building blocks help us to order Plato's ideas.
3. See Santas (2001, pp. 66–75) for an extended discussion. It should be noted that I distinguish the abstract theory of function and virtue from its immediate application to the soul in book I; the failure of the latter (for the reasons that Socrates gives at the very end of book I) is no evidence that the abstract theory itself is abandoned, especially in view of the evidence I give of its use throughout the *Republic*. See Santas (2006, pp. 133–41).
4. See Preston (1998).
5. *Rep.* I. 353d; see also Miller (1999).
6. I track this functional procedure in Santas (2001, pp. 75–90).
7. These three psychic functions correspond to the three general functions of the city, to provide, defend, and govern itself, and are necessary to suppose because the virtues of the individual require individual functions and the isomorphism which requires similar virtues and parts thus presupposes similar functions. Plato found divisions and organization in natural systems (organisms) and supposed them to be there for the best, I think. His division of the city into three classes has seemed to some to be somewhat arbitrary and the corresponding division of the soul into corresponding three parts all too convenient. But the attribution to the city of three general functions—economy, defense, and government—each of them complex, while not completely free of arbitrariness, is rooted in the initial supposition that individuals are not self-sufficient and the city comes into being to remedy that. The corresponding general psychic functions—providing for oneself, defending oneself, and governing oneself—each of them complex, also seem reasonably comprehensive needs of each individual, that is, general needs with respect to which the individual is not self-sufficient. For an excellent recent discussion of the origin of these general functions and the division into parts, see Joshua Weinstein (2004, pp. 79–196).
8. In saying that the formula must have "the same interpretation," I agree in part with David Keyt (in 2006a, p. 350), who says that "the definitions of justice and the other virtues must carry over word for word from polis to psyche." See my next sentence in the main text. I argue below that the isomorphism does not entail a strong sameness of parts but only of structure; the parts of the city and the soul can correspond to each other without being the same in the strong sense in which the letters of the smaller and larger inscription can be the same letters. I think Keyt is correct if we take the inscriptions' analogy strictly, but I think the differences between parts of the city and parts of the soul are too great for the inscription analogy to work strictly.

9. See, for example, Julia Annas (1981), N. P. White (1979), and Bernard Williams (1997).
10. See Keyt (2006a, p. 349), for an illuminating discussion of the strictest interpretation.
11. The myth of the metals is a symbol for the natural lottery; it is false if taken literally, but true if taken as a symbol that intelligence and other natural assets such as high spirit are distributed differently and unequally by the natural lottery. The phrase "natural lottery" is taken from Rawls; it should be kept in mind, though, that on Plato's view, the inborn distributions of talents might not be random, given the teleological creation of the *Timaeus*. Cornford calls the myth of the metals "the noble lie," but it is no lie on Plato's part if it is taken symbolically and not literally.
12. Natural, inborn differences among human beings, such as differences in intelligence and spirit, play important roles in any theory of justice. Rawls' theory tries to compensate for some of them by his principles of fair equality of opportunity and even the difference principle. Plato's theory institutionalizes inborn differences in intelligence and spirit, by making them a basis for the selection of rulers and defenders, but it blindfolds inborn differences in gender.
13. For my view of Plato's treatment of *philia* in the *Republic*, especially book V, see Santas (1988, pp. 89–97). But this holds for persons; whether it can be applied without alteration to parts of the soul is an open question.
14. The costs of partition of the soul into agents are well laid out by Bobonich (2002, pp. 252–58). Notice that these are the costs of partitioning into agents, not the costs of any other partitioning. I am not at all disputing the paradoxes of partitioning into agents. I dispute the interpretation that such partitioning is into agents.
15. This long passage is usually explained by commentators as trying to avoid a Socratic objection (to the partitioning) that what we desire is always something good (apparent or real). But while Plato is indeed trying to avoid this objection, the passage tries to isolate thirsting not only from goodness but also from many other (indeed an indefinite list of) attributes of an object, such as hot or cold, sweet or bitter. We are better off with the supposition that he is trying to isolate thirsting from any learning about the object of thirst: thirsting is just for drink (liquid nutrition); that is its natural object.
16. In *Rep*ublic IX 580d, when Plato brings in the tripartite division as it was made in book IV and uses it in the pleasure arguments, he repeats these primary characterizations of the parts of the soul.
17. IV 441e-42a; cf. the more extended passage on Platonic education to which Socrates refers, III 411e-12a. Bobonich (2002) has long discussions of the communication among the parts of the soul as agents. Communication among the parts as agents is attractive because it is like communication among persons, with which we are familiar. But if the parts of the soul are agents, the same communication issues arise within each one of them. We are better off with deliberation and causal models of communication, which can work with psychic parts as faculties and in which only reason needs to be capable of thinking. See Modrak (2008).
18. See Plato's long argument, IV 437d-39c, just before his first example of appetite versus reason, to separate, by abstraction, thirst for drink from thirst for drink of some particular kind—not only good drink, but also hot or cold drink, bitter or sweet. The appetite for some hot milk is already a mixture of appetite and learning. See Modrak (2008) for a review of the evidence in earlier and later books of the *Republic*.
19. In his initial question at IV 435e, Plato seems to count reasoning itself or desiring itself or feeling anger as psychic actions; he uses *prattein* twice in that one sentence; so he may think that a faculty by itself can produce psychic action, if desiring, feeling anger, and thinking are such (presumably psychic) actions.
20. Santas (2001, pp. 123–24, 126–28). In all controversies about the analysis of the psyche, we must distinguish complexity within a part, such as plurality of appetites within the appetitive part, from the very different complexity of agency. Since Aristotle's criticism of Plato's divisions, a fear of an infinite regress of divisions has almost blinded us to the fact that each psychic part is indeed complex, in the case of appetite obviously so. The question here is not its obvious complexity but what its unifying principle is. The case of spirit is similar. It is

division of agents that we need to fear, since it has more divisions built into it. To allay the fear of infinite division, we need not deny the complexity of each part, but to distinguish the initial conflict and division from others—a path that Lorenz usefully takes in his recent book (Lorenz 2006). There need not be similar contrariety within each part that would oblige us to divide again similarly; contrariety within each part can be explained not by further division of soul but by facts about the external world; if I hunger for caviar and thirst for champagne but cannot have both, that can be accounted for by my financial situation and we need not further divide the soul because of that conflict. Even if we had to make further but different divisions, though, there is no a priori reason to believe that such divisions can never end, just as there is no good a priori reason to believe that the human soul has just three *simple* parts or empirical evidence that Plato thought that. Look at his division of the body in the *Timaeus*; why would he suppose that the human soul is far less complex?

21. Freud too had a hard time with this, first supposing that hunger and libido are two different basic instincts in *Three Essays on the Theory of Sexuality* and, later, beginning with *Beyond the Pleasure Principle*, trying to group them together after all under the heading of self-preservative instincts—lumping together preservation of the individual and preservation of the species.
22. Bobonich (2002) distinguishes between reason and the other parts by supposing that only reason can reach the Forms and appreciate nonsensible value properties, while the reasoning of the other parts is only about means to ends and perhaps sensible goods, and that only those persons whose reason reaches the Forms can appreciate virtue for its own sake. I gave reasons above why in Plato's main argument for partition, in his first and last examples of conflict, we must suppose that appetite and spirit cannot reason about sensible things.
23. David Keyt, who holds the agent view in (2006a), refutes ethical elitism; Keyt in (2006b, pp. 202–204).
24. Compare Rawls (1971, pp. 4, 8–9, 453) on the concept of a "well-ordered society" or "a perfectly just society." If that concept is analogous to Plato's "completely good city," at least with respect to justice (if not with respect to a complete social ideal), the paradox almost amounts to a contradiction.
25. I call it an extreme symptom because it is not, I think, an essential part of ethical elitism, and it depends on Bobonich's particular interpretation of how the three types of persons are characterized in the pleasure arguments of book IX. Plato's characterizations allow Bobonich to put this up as a possible interpretation, but I think it is too big a defect in Plato's ideal theory of justice for it to be correct, and Plato's language also allows a different interpretation.
26. Aside from the direct textual evidence, another reason for supposing that justice requires wisdom may be a somewhat silent assumption that Plato in the *Republic* still holds to some version of the unity of virtues, perhaps the reciprocity thesis, that if a person has one virtue she/he has them all. As far as I know, there is no direct statement of this view in the *Republic*. This is a complex issue that I do not directly address here. But I think that in this case, Plato's silence on the matter is quite telling. If he held the view of the *Protagoras* or the *Laches*, why not say so, especially since in the *Republic* he undertakes a far more fundamental analysis of the social and individual virtues? In any case, since in the *Republic*, unlike the early dialogues, we have elaborate definitions of the virtues, anyone holding some unity of virtues' thesis must show how this is related to the definitions. For the most recent discussion of this point, see Devereux (2006).
27. Even if my reason has false beliefs, it can still be ruling in the sense that my reason makes the choices, with spirit helping to carry them out and appetite obeying; even then I would be just, even if my choices were disastrous, for I would have exactly the order in my psyche that Plato specifies as justice. One might suppose that if my choices were disastrous and made me unhappy, this could not possibly be Plato's justice. But does Plato really hold in the *Republic* that justice *all by itself* is sufficient for happiness?
28. For further textual support of the view that the lower classes in Plato's ideal city can be just, see Keyt (2006b, pp. 202–204).
29. The instability of true belief of the *Meno* is now compensated for by a rigorous education and training—or so now Plato thinks.

30. The language of belief is also used in Plato's definition of social temperance. See the most recent discussion of the true belief interpretation; see Devereux (2006).
31. The gap between the courage of the city and the courage of persons was brought to my attention by Charles Young, and is supported by Socrates' qualifying remark at IV 430c, that it is political courage that he defined. This gap focuses on what true beliefs the defenders need to have for the city to be courageous and what the city should fear versus what beliefs persons need to have for them to be courageous and what they should fear for themselves. I am arguing that for the defenders, the former beliefs must include the latter beliefs: the defenders could not be courageous in all circumstances without having also correct beliefs about what they should fear for themselves. But it is true that Socrates' quick account of psychic courage (IV 442b-c) is not revealed in Socrates' account of the courage of the defenders, namely, that it is one's spirit that preserves the commands of reason about what one should fear and not fear for oneself, perhaps because the analysis of the psyche was not at hand when Socrates defined the courage of the defenders. Still, once we know the two accounts, we can see, I think, that for the defenders to be courageous in defense of their city, they must have courage in their souls. And of course it is also true if one has courage in one's soul, this will show up in other circumstances than fighting.
32. We can see the inclusion of beliefs in Plato's own basic ground why reason should rule in a person and why the philosophers should rule in a city: only it or they can have wisdom "and forethought" about the whole soul or whole city. Obviously forethought cannot be strict Platonic knowledge; and is not forethought involved in every choice, action, law, or social policy? It is noteworthy that every single proposal Socrates makes for the completely good city—about private property and wealth and about gender, for example—is stated in presumably true beliefs, not on strict Platonic knowledge.
33. It is true that a just city with perfect compliance ("a well-ordered" just city—to use Rawls' phrase for an ideally just society) would be composed of just persons, and it might also be true that one can reasonably doubt that a city is just if it has very low (say, 25 %) compliance. Even so, perfect compliance is not a necessary condition of a city being just, although very low compliance would affect its stability and raise questions about the citizens' perception of its justice.
34. Rawls (1971, pp. 1, 7–17, 436).
35. This is quite explicit in Thrasymachus: persons are just insofar as they act according to the laws of their societies, and these laws are just if obedience to them promotes the interests of the ruling party. Similarly, in Glaucon's contractarian theory, a person is just insofar as he obeys just laws, laws that are in accord with the fundamental contract (an agreement by all neither to do nor suffer harm).
36. Nor is it a problem of a just man in an unjust society or circumstances, as in the case of the historical Socrates. In Rawls' terms, it is not a partial compliance problem, such as civil disobedience.
37. That is, more than the known alternatives, which are the other models of organization for the city that Plato considered (everyone doing everything to satisfy their needs or division of labor without regard to natural talent—Adam Smith's model).
38. See Keyt (2006a, pp. 351–355).

Bibliography

Annas, Julia. 1981. *An introduction to Plato's* Republic. Oxford: Clarendon Press.
Benson, Hugh (ed.). 2006. *A companion to Plato*. Oxford: Blackwell Publishing.
Bobonich, Christopher. 2002. *Plato's utopia recast*. Oxford: Clarendon Press.
Cooper, John. 1999. The psychology of justice in Plato. In *Reason and emotion*, ed. John Cooper, 138–150. Princeton: Princeton University Press.

Coumoundouros, Antonis, and Ronald Polansky. 2008. Function, ability and desire in Plato's *Republic*. *Philosophical Inquiry* 30(4): 1–14.
Devereux, Daniel. 2006. The unity of the virtues. In *A companion to Plato*, ed. Hugh Benson, 325–340. Oxford: Blackwell Publishing.
Irwin, Terence. 1995. *Plato's ethics*. Oxford: Oxford University Press.
Keyt, David. 2006a. Plato on justice. In *A companion to Plato*, ed. Hugh Benson, 341–355. Oxford: Blackwell Publishing.
Keyt, David. 2006b. Plato and the ship of state. In *The Blackwell guide to Plato's* Republic, ed. Gerasimos Santas, 189–213. Oxford: Blackwell Publishing.
Lorenz, Hendrik. 2006. The analysis of the soul in Plato's Republic. In *The Blackwell guide to Plato's Republic*, ed. Gerasimos Santas. Oxford: Blackwell Publishing.
Modrak, Deborah K.W. 2008. Desires and faculties in Plato and Aristotle. *Philosophical Inquiry* 30(3): 163–174.
Miller Jr., Fred D. 1999. Plato on the parts of the soul. In *Plato and Platonism*, ed. J.M. Van Ophuijsen, 84–101. Washington, DC: Catholic University of America Press.
Price, A.W. 1995. *Mental conflict*. London: Routledge.
Preston, Beth. 1998. Why is a wing like a spoon? A pluralist theory of function. *Journal of Philosophy* 95(5): 215–254.
Rawls, John. 1971. *A theory of justice*. Cambridge, MA: Harvard University Press.
Santas, Gerasimos. 1988. *Plato and Freud*. Oxford: Basil Blackwell.
Santas, Gerasimos. 2001. *Goodness and justice*. Oxford: Blackwell Publishing.
Santas, Gerasimos (ed.). 2006. *The Blackwell guide to Plato's* Republic. Oxford: Blackwell Publishing.
Singpurwalla, Rachel. 2006. Plato's defense of justice in the *Republic*. In *The Blackwell guide to Plato's* Republic, ed. Gerasimos Santas, 263–282. Oxford: Blackwell Publishing.
Weinstein, J. 2004. *Thumos and tripartition in Plato's* Republic. Ph.D. dissertation, The Hebrew University.
White, Nicholas P. 1979. *A companion to Plato's* Republic. Indianapolis: Hackett Publishing Company.
Williams, Bernard. 1997. The analogy of the city and the soul in Plato's *Republic*. In *Plato's* Republic: *Critical essays*, ed. Richard Kraut. Lanham: Rowman and Littlefield.

Virtue, Luck, and Choice at the End of the *Republic*

Mark L. McPherran

> Human life occurs only once, and the reason we cannot determine which of our decisions are good and which bad is that in a given situation we can make only one decision; we are not granted a second, third, or fourth life in which to compare various decisions. (Milan Kundera, *The Unbearable Lightness of Being*)

The *Republic* famously ends with a consideration of the previously dismissed question of the rewards of justice by first proving the soul's immortality (*Rep.* X 608c-612a) and then arguing for the superiority of the just life in what appear to be purely consequentialist terms. Plato begins by affirming Adeimantus' story (II 362d-363e) that the gods reward just souls and punish the unjust during the course of their earthly lives (X 612a-614a), and then—just as Cephalus feared (I 330d-331a)—the gods do the same in the afterlife (X 614a-621d; see J. Lear 2006, p. 39). In the world as it is, the *reputation* of being just—though often ill accorded—correctly reaps the external rewards that it typically does; but regardless of one's earthly reputation, the gods are fully aware of who is just and who is not, always loving the former and always hating the latter (X 612d-e; cf. II 362e-363e). Hence, although we might believe that those who are actually just are neglected in favor of those who are only seemingly just when the former are visited by conventional evils (e.g., poverty, disease), these events must be understood to be only apparent evils: they are either beneficial punishments for previous errors or they assist the recipient in some other fashion. Besides such disguised benefits, however, the gods visit easily recognizable goods on the just person insofar as he or she resembles the gods by being good (X 612e-613b).

Happy as this account is, critical readers often find it a silly bedtime story—or worse—lacking in philosophical depth and charm. For in the context of the *Republic*'s justice-advocating project as a whole, book X can appear to be "gratuitous and

M.L. McPherran (✉)
Department of Philosophy, Simon Fraser University, 8888 University Drive,
Burnaby, BC V5A 1S6, Canada
e-mail: mark_mcpherran@sfu.ca

clumsy," to quote Julia Annas (1981, p. 335). This is particularly true because of the way book X spells out the postmortem rewards of justice by deploying the odd story of Er's near-death experience, a myth whose "vulgarity seems to pull us right down to the level of Cephalus, where you take justice seriously when you start thinking about hell-fire" (ibid., p. 349). It is this myth and this sort of sensible reaction to its contents that I want to consider here.

The Myth of Er provides a last glimpse of the *Republic*'s gods as they dispense justice in the hereafter, but it is difficult at best to know how to view this particular story in the light of Plato's categorical denigration of mimetic writing.[1] It is, however, both in theme and in detail similar to Plato's other eschatological myths that display a willingness to use pain and pleasure as inducements to virtuous behavior for those nonphilosophical individuals who are not yet prepared to pursue virtue for its own sake (*Phd.* 107c-115a; *Grg.* 523a-527e; *Phdr.* 245c-257b). These are myths that are to be taken as true in their essentials (e.g., *Grg.* 522b-523a, 526d-527c); each is an allegory—a *hyponoia* (*Rep.* II 378d-e)—and, as such, has an "underthought" that might be revealed. Moreover, in this particular case, Socrates also emphasizes the need to *heed* the message of Er's story, whatever it might be (X 621b-d; and see 618b-619a). Nevertheless, its complex portrait of the long-term rewards for striving after justice is, again, often found to be depressing, not reassuring (e.g., Annas 1981, pp. 350–53). For although there are tenfold rewards for the just and tenfold punishments for the unjust, there are also non-redeeming, everlasting tortures for those who, because of their impious and murderous behavior, have become morally incurable (X 615c-616b; cf. *Grg.* 525b-526b). True to the theological principle established in book II that "God is not the cause of all things, but only of the good things" (whatever it is that causes bad things, that cause is not divine; *Rep.* II 380c6-10, III 391e1-2), Plato then explicitly attempts to relieve the gods of all responsibility for the future suffering we might experience in our next incarnation by means of two insulating episodes. First, there is a lottery that determines one's order of choice in picking that new life, and then one is offered the chance to browse through and select from a range of future lives (X 619e; cf. *Odyssey* 1.32-41). An individual soul's choice of what will prove to be a happy life of justice depends both on the apparently random fall of the lots (617d-618b, 619c-d) and on that soul's ability to select its next life wisely. Unfortunately, it is unclear if the lottery is rigged in some fashion, and a soul's degree of practical choice-making wisdom is constrained by its prior experiences, experiences that were in turn the result of even earlier, seemingly chancy, and relatively ignorant choices. Hence, even the souls that have lived lives of just action—but performed their actions out of habit rather than genuine understanding—will arrive at the lottery having forgotten the sufferings that preceded the narcotic, memory-erasing rewards they received in Heaven. As a result, most of these souls will make hasty, unfortunate choices in picking their next incarnations and so will suffer further torments in the future (617d-621b). Particularly noteworthy on this score is the first soul in the life-choice line. Despite—or perhaps because of—the rich variety of lives laid out before him, he rashly chooses the life of a man who is fated (*heimartos*; 619c1) to eat his own children (619b-c).

Finally, aside from the apparently random work of the lottery, Plato never articulates the many sources of evil mentioned in book II: sources against which even the gods are powerless and which might, for all we know, thwart the expected happiness of our next lives.[2] So although the last lines of the *Republic* encourage us to race after justice so that we may collect our Olympian rewards (X 621b-d), it is understandable that some might still find Thrasymachean shortcuts a better moral strategy in the choice insistent here and now.

It is exceedingly hard to determine how Plato meant for us to read this myth: perhaps all its details of colored whorls and lotteries are only entertaining bits of window dressing, not to be taken as contributing to a philosophically coherent eschatology (Annas 1981, pp. 351–53). This is poetry, after all, and it is, again, composed within the framework of a dialogue that distains poetry. On the other hand, it may be possible to read Er's tale as alluding to the beneficial initiations of Eleusis but now connected to the true initiation and *conversion* provided by philosophical dialectic (Morgan 1990, p. 150). There are also reasons to suppose that the Myth's display of whorls, Sirens, and Necessity is symbolic of the metaphysical elements of the *Republic's* middle books and are thus meant to impress the message of those books on each soul prior to its next choice of life and its drink from the River of Forgetfulness (X 620e-621c). The message of those books is that the happiest life is the life of justice and the Good and so ought to be chosen for that reason alone.[3]

The essential message that Plato intends does seem to come through loud and clear, however: no god or *daimôn* can be blamed for whatever predicament we may happen to find ourselves in when we put down Plato's text. Moreover, by placing the determinants and outcomes of our present choices in the lap of the gods of past choice (*Lachesis*) and future necessity (*Atropos*), whether Plato intends this effect or not, readers can find themselves put off by all such *deus ex machina* and thus inclined to recall the truly pious aspirations of philosophy developed over the preceding nine books. If so, they will perhaps find themselves encouraged and emboldened to dismiss the cheap motivations of carrot and stick outlined in book X, seemingly for the benefit of the vulgar many.[4] The end of the *Republic* can thus be read as returning us to the stern Socrates of book I who urges us to choose the path of justice *simpliciter* and damn the consequences (cf. *Cri.* 48a-49e). To this, however, his pupil has now added in eight books of subsequent argument a more rigorous moral and religious message that grounds that choice in a transcendental aspiration and assimilation to an unseen perfect Justice apprehended by collegial, all-good gods.[5]

With this happy, albeit speculative, solution to the place of the Myth in the philosophical economy of the *Republic*, we must, however, face as best we can the problem it poses for Plato's own conception of moral responsibility (and the attached Problem of Evil).[6] That is, Plato clearly intends to keep the gods clear of any responsibility for *our* wrongdoing and consequent suffering, but the muddled insulating mechanisms he installs to place such responsibilities in our laps call into question the *Republic*'s entire project of articulating a theory of justice. For, one wonders, how can there be any sort of human justice without our possessing real, coherent responsibility for the character from which our actions—for whose consequences we will later pay—spring? Moreover, how can the *Republic* make any legitimate impact on its readers, if its readers cannot be held morally responsible for their reactions to that very text? Do we not generally forgive our own freshmen when they recoil from their first encounter with *Kallipolis*, finding it an anti-Spring Break dystopia?

The pivotal section of the *Republic* generating our concern runs as follows:

> Now when ... [the souls] arrived they were straightway bidden to go before Lachesis, and then a certain prophet (*prophêtês*; 617d2-3) first marshaled them in orderly intervals, and there took from the lap of Lachesis lots and patterns of lives and went up to a lofty platform and spoke, "This is the word of Lachesis, the maiden daughter of Necessity. 'Souls that live for a day, now is the beginning of another cycle of mortal generation where birth is the beacon of death. Your *daimôn* will not be assigned to you by lot; you will *choose your own daimôn*. Let him to whom falls the initial lot first select a life to which he shall be bound by necessity (*anagkê*; 617e3). But virtue knows no master; each will possess it to a greater or less degree, depending on whether he values it or distains it. The blame is his who chooses. God is blameless (*anaitios*; 617e5).'" So saying, the prophet flung the lots out among them all, and each took up the lot that fell by his side, except himself [Er]; him they did not permit. And whoever took up a lot saw plainly what number he had drawn. And after this again the prophet placed the patterns of lives before them on the ground, far more numerous than the assembly. They were of every variety.... But there was no determination of the quality of soul, because *the choice of a different life inevitably* (*anagkê*; 618b3) *determined a different character*. But all other things were commingled with one another and with wealth and poverty and sickness and health and the intermediate conditions. (X 617d-618b; my emphasis)

Every commentator of the Myth of Er has rightly understood Plato's insertion of the lottery to be his way of initially absolving the gods of moral responsibility for each soul's choice of a life and the consequences that accompany that choice. Blame for one's placement in the life-choice queue will then be placed on *tuchê*, commonly translated as "luck" or "chance" (619c-d). Any doubts on that score can be settled by looking at book V 460a, where the marriage lottery—albeit a "sophisticated" lottery, meaning a "fixed" one—is introduced with the explicit aim of deflecting blame from the guardians onto *tuchê*. It is also possible to suppose that the lottery is introduced as a mechanism that will ensure as fair a distribution of life-choices as is practically possible (although such a supposition would appear to undermine the gods' providential power and goodness). We are, then, to understand the mysterious prophet to cast in one throw a collection of markers with numbers or other indicators of the sort we moderns find in large delicatessens and government offices, with the assembled souls then each simply *choosing* the closest marker in order to determine that soul's own place in the life-choice queue. Interestingly, Plato does not explain why no soul attempts to acquire a lower-numbered marker that falls near another soul (as might happen in a jostling, big city deli, especially if Plato's would-be tyrant of 619b-c were there). The solution to this puzzle is evident, however. Lachesis is a deity—the goddess of lots—and that deity has implicitly ordered each soul to choose the closest marker. But then this scenario seems to offer the souls less choice than we might have thought.

Once confronted with the final selection of a life, each soul inspects a series of life-paradigms and picks one. This is a decision whose consequent life experiences will reconfigure each agent's character, that is, the ordering of that soul's three component parts, thereby determining whether the soul will be driven primarily by its appetites, spirited part, or intelligence in a human or nonhuman form. This, however, seems often a purely reactive, emotionally driven selection and so not a relatively unconstrained choice. For example, and in what is perhaps a last slap at the poets, Plato tells us that the soul "that had once belonged to Orpheus" adopted the life of a swan in order to avoid being conceived by and born to the kind of being—a female human—that had caused his previous death (620a). The choice of a life, we are meant to see—at least for nonphilosophers—is a somewhat automatic *reaction* to the kind of suffering experienced in one's previous incarnation. It is clear that Plato means to emphasize this fact, for otherwise he would not go on at length, offering one example after another of famous and relatively intelligent individuals who—despite their rich experiences of life—make choices that have all the appearance of being "rebound" selections (619e-620d). For example, besides the case of Orpheus, we are told that both Ajax and Agamemnon chose animal lives—the life of a lion and an eagle, respectively—because of what they suffered at the hands of other humans (620a-b). But as we saw above, this account then seems to result in an infinite regress of states of moral responsibility, since every choice of a life springs from the character of a soul whose condition is the result of the consequences of its presumably constrained prior choice and so on (Dorter 2003, p. 131). Worse yet, the sketchy model of deliberation we are given makes a mystery of the disembodied soul, for if it is not *Orpheus* who chooses to become a swan but *the soul* that once was Orpheus, we are left to wonder about the identity and nature of this soul in itself prior to and subsequent to its incarnation into swanhood (Thayer 1988, pp. 372, 378; Halliwell 2007, pp. 458–63). The most plausible account of it in view of Plato's remarks at 618d would identify it with our reason alone—reason that is able to deliberate and choose a new life. But do we or Plato really want to credit the souls of birds and beasts with the same rational faculty that *we* possess?[7] And if here the soul *is* pure reason, then what sort of pleasures and pains could this purified soul have experienced during its previous thousand years of reward and punishment? That is, if the soul in the afterlife is reason alone, then how can it possess lower-level appetites or desires to reward or thwart? This problem may explain why Plato does not spell out these rewards and punishments in any degree of satisfying detail.[8]

Despite all of this, some commentators have chosen to accept Plato's story at more or less face value, and so find him in the cosmic context he mythologizes to be advocating the idea that even if "... our choices are always determined by an infinite regress of previous choices, at least this chain of causality is not an empty, meaningless, blind necessity, but follows from the rational nature of the universe" (Dorter 2003, p. 135). For although the rewards and punishments of Tartarus and Heaven might on many occasions influence the appetitive and spirited parts of a particular soul, it remains possible for each soul's rational part to choose its next life wisely and to then prevent it from drinking too deeply from the River of Unheeding (619b, 619e; 621a).[9] And while our reason may itself be structured and strongly influenced by its prior life choices, the pick of a particular life by a soul's reason is free in a sense compatible with causal determinism. After all, goes this line of thought, this choice is made by our truest self, namely, reason (Dorter, pp. 137–38). However, I remain unconvinced by this sort of approach, although that does also leave me at this juncture with not much more than a "record of honest perplexity" (to recall Gregory Vlastos's view of the first part of the *Parmenides* [Vlastos 1954, p. 343]).

The problem, as I see it, begins with the casting of lots. Here we must ask why Plato employs a prophet, and why he fails to name him. The best answer to this second query is, presumably, that any identification of the prophet would make suspect the prophet's motivations, and this would then cast doubt on the apparent randomness of his throw. Next, we must have a *prophet* because Plato requires a divine being of some kind—this is a non-mortal realm (whether it be extraterrestrial or not), after all, and so Plato requires an immortal of some sort to do the job of lot casting and soul instruction. However, a full-blown divinity would thwart the entire purpose of insulating the gods from any responsibility for our next-life suffering; hence, Plato adopts a lesser divinity for the job. Is this move successful? The answer, alas, has to be "no."

Plato mysteriously undermines his insulation project by describing the lot caster as a *prophet* and, thus, as a being who can, in theory, know in advance the outcome of his toss. The semidivine prophet could, then, influence his toss in a nonrandom way. But, still, it might be objected that we cannot be sure that the prophet does anything more than the minimum a prophet might be expected to do, namely, "speak on behalf, or under the influence, of divine authority/inspiration" (Halliwell 1988, p. 183). So, our prophet might not know the outcome of his toss, or even if he does, that need not mean that he would influence that toss.[10] But although this point does blunt the force of the worry that Plato's use of the term "prophet" causes, it does not entirely dissipate it. For a reader is bound to notice that the prophet does more than merely *speak* for the god Lachesis: he *acts* as well. And if, then, the point is to thoroughly insulate the gods from any moral responsibility for our bad choices, why label this being a "prophet" in the first place? Why not just call him "the tosser" or "the croupier"? Or why not install a lottery tumbler or other device that might better reassure us that random, non-intentional forces and not divinities are at work in the arrangement of the life-choice queue?

More worrisome, perhaps, is the fact that for the audience Plato's prophet addresses—the disembodied souls *and* Plato's own ancient readers—the casting of lots (*klêroi*) was not a way of making a decision via random selection; rather, it was a way of allowing *the gods* to decide an issue.[11] Moreover, the meaning of "*tuchê*," cited at 619c5 as a force the tyranny-choosing soul will blame, is easily construed as "divine providence" and not the random, contingent, spontaneous, and indeterminate chance that was recognized (if not endorsed) by the early atomists and others.[12] So, then, it appears as though on a deeper reading the ordering of the life-choice queue is not random but takes place through a providence Plato is unwilling to expose and explain (and, in addition, results from Lachesis' implicit order to pick the closest marker). Still, we might be reassured by this reading, precisely because it *does* implicate wise(er) beings in the process of our future life choices. On the other hand, though, one would expect that if the lottery is being manipulated, the first choice would go to a *philosophical* soul, not to one who was virtuous merely through habit and who might thus go on to make a monumental, child-abusing error.

A graver stumbling block appears once we arrive at the head of the queue, where each soul in that cohort is presented with a collection of life outlines. These paradigms have inscribed on them the major, more or less *external*, life events with which one would have to cope, such as the fact that one will be wellborn or not, and whether one will at some point in that life become wealthy or poor, healthy or ill, and so on (617e-619b). To the gods' credit, the prophet announces that it is possible for even the very last soul in the queue to discover a life token that would yield a satisfactory life experience, if that life were to be lived with serious intent (619b). However, we should worry that since at any one moment there are many more nonphilosophers than philosophers on the earth, the souls will be selecting out of a pool of lives that includes a large number of nonphilosophical life tokens and only a few philosophical ones (617e-618a). Moreover, their choices will occur in a haphazard and/or reactive way, and hence, the chance of one's having a maximally happy future life is directly proportional to one's place in the suspiciously organized queue.

In any event, we are at least told that the assembled souls are warned to choose a life only after a careful, deliberative inspection of the outlines before them (619b). But despite this warning, some souls are stubbornly negligent and thus choose lives without engaging in sufficient rational consideration, lives that cause them grave unhappiness—as, again, illustrated by the first unfortunate soul in the queue (who rashly chooses the life of a child-eating tyrant [619b-c]). When we wonder how this individual could have overlooked such a glaring, painful, and evil episode, Plato explains that this overhasty soul was one of those whose previous life had been virtuous merely through habit and, hence, was someone still under the spell of his pleasure-filled thousand-year rewards (619c).[13] In this tranquilized state, he is overcome by foolish, blind greed (*laimargia*; 619c1) and so snatches up what seems to be an attractive life of power and luxury. The problem here, of course, is that this story requires that the externals of the life one chooses—such as riches and political power—when allied to a particular sort of soul *necessitate* a particular character state that then *necessitates* the performance of an action that one ought not to perform both absolutely and in terms of consequentialistic self-interest (618c-d, 619b-c, 620a). One is stuck choosing one's *future* choices in a state of relative ignorance. This is especially true, given that souls commonly drink too deeply from the River of Unheeding (under their new *daimon's* influence), forgetting all the educational conversations they had with their fellow souls during their previous week of leisure in the meadow (614d-616b; 621a-b). To avoid a completely deterministic system, however, Plato posits that it is possible for the soul's rational part to choose its next life well, provided certain conditions are met. If that soul is ruled by the rational part and *if* that part possesses a knowledge of how external factors such as wealth will affect its future character states and actions, that soul can overcome its past habits and so constrain its spirit (*thumos*) and appetites (e.g., mastering its fears [see 616a]) and thus can choose its next life wisely.

One solution to this dismal picture might perhaps be this: the necessity that Plato speaks of at 617e3, 618b3, and 619c1 may also be a contingent one. That is, the fateful requirement that the first soul who chooses a tyrant's life eat his own children might be a necessity that comes into play only after *that* particular soul picks *that* particular life. On this interpretation, the soul selects a tyrannical life-token that contains no clear signs of what will come to pass if that particular soul does pick that particular token. But subsequent to that choice, the factors that necessarily attend a tyrannical life—those a more philosophical soul might have spotted more readily—come into play and thus make inevitable its grisly family dinner.[14]

Unfortunately, readers of Plato know that he endorses the asymmetry of good and bad character states, that is, that "the voluntary acquisition of a bad character is no more possible than the voluntary performance of a bad action," and that he thinks that an action that flows from a character state is voluntary if and only if that character state is voluntary (Ott 2006, pp. 66–68). However, Plato also holds that no one acts unjustly except in a fashion contrary to his or her rational will (*Prt.* 345e; *Laws* V 731c-d, IX 860d-861b). As the *Timaeus* has it, for example, "… no one is willingly evil. A man becomes evil, rather, as a result of one or another corrupt condition of his body and an uneducated upbringing" (*Ti.* 86d-e; see also 87b). The result is a more detailed version of the vicious circle I alluded to earlier in this essay. Plato wants to absolve the gods of any responsibility for our suffering, but the cost is that he must embrace an apparently deterministic eschatology according to which the choice of a life by a nonphilosopher dictates the sort of character state that then dictates—or at least severely influences—courses of action that mandate that soul's future suffering or rewards that in turn dictate its subsequent choice of a life-paradigm and so on.

Still, we might suppose that although the Myth postulates that various external features of a life such as health and wealth can mould a nonphilosopher's character, this influence need not follow a rule of causal necessity in every case. We might, for example, take the Myth to claim that there are regular and predictable effects of such external influences that are not wholly deterministic, although they allow for prediction and post hoc explanation. So when Plato says that evil actions are involuntary, perhaps we need not understand him to hold that we cannot do other than what we do when we act badly, as a determinist would have it. What he could mean is that we violate our own deepest will and preferences when we act in such ways and yet still maintain a degree of responsibility over how our characters are formed.[15]

Now, it is true that Plato does hold out this possibility of free deliberation and consequent responsibility for the truly philosophical souls gathered before the Throne of Necessity. They can "reason out which life is better" (618d) and so choose the best, most just life. Plato makes this alleged possibility vivid by contrasting the first, unsatisfied, soul to choose with a glimpse of the last soul to choose, namely, that of Odysseus.[16] In confirmation of the prophet's earlier claim that even the last soul in line will be able to descry a satisfactory life, Odysseus is able to find the life token of an ordinary private individual; one that he says he would have picked even if he had been first in line. Socrates explains in what appears to be a laudatory tone that this Odysseus had been relieved of his prior love of honor by his earlier sufferings—presumably those portrayed in the *Odyssey*. Odysseus the Cunning, it seems, has been transformed into a more virtuous and philosophically reflective individual (*pace* Morgan 2000, p. 207) by means of the purification that suffering and punishment provide (see, e.g., *Grg.* 523a-527e). He thus looks "for a long time" for the life token of a private individual who "did his own work" (620c)—the very definition of justice the preceding books of the *Republic* had articulated. True to Socrates' stern advice to Glaucon at 618b-619b, by choosing the mean over the extremes, Odysseus has found a life that will lead him to life experiences that will increase his justice and, thus, his overall happiness (cf. 621d).

Still, though, while it is all very well to *postulate* that such souls can escape the causal chains the Myth employs, one is still left to wonder how a nonphilosophical soul could ever make the sort of choice that would convert it into a philosophical soul.[17] Yet, if the Myth of Er is to offer intelligent but nonphilosophical souls such as Thrasymachus a motive for becoming truly just by becoming philosophical, it must at least make some attempt to address this bootstrapping problem. As it is, we seem to be left almost where the *Meno* ends: our souls might become virtuously philosophical by means of *Kallipolis*' educational program, but we will choose such a life in the afterlife only by means of some fortuitous, providential *theia moira* (cf. *Rep.* VI 492a, 492e-493a).[18] In the case of Odysseus, this *theia moira* takes the form of his being third to only Zeus and Athena in his possession of wisdom, and a man who faces ten years of sufferings at sea, imposed by the god Poseidon. But this then suggests that the gods are back in the hot seat of responsibility from which Plato wanted to unseat them.

It will not do, then, to hold simply, as Dorter (2003) does, that all the souls' choices are free in a sense because they are "made by our truest self, namely, reason," since the ability of that very element to make something we would want to call a "choice"—a choice significantly unencumbered by the influence of not only *thumos* and appetite but character (one's degree of ignorance, intellectual habits, and so on) as well—appears to have been too severely compromised by the sorts of prior experiences that Er spells out. It seems that for Plato, we simply are not free in the fashion that he himself requires.

Still, perhaps I am misreading the real function of the Myth. Jonathan Lear, for example, has argued that those who are disappointed by the Myth because they take it to be a sign that Plato is admitting argumentative defeat are misplacing their disappointment (Lear 2006, pp. 40–42). He contends that "Plato has used myth not to argue for an actuality, but to cover the universe of possibilities," of which there are three: (1) nothingness, (2) death as removal to another sphere of existence, or (3) death as removal to another sphere of existence followed by reincarnation (ibid., p. 41):

> One way or another, these are the ways things have to be—unless, that is, there is a fourth possibility: namely, that the world is essentially a bad place, an occasion for despair. In this world there would be an afterlife in which the just would be mocked and tortured by malevolent gods. Virtually all of the rhetorical power of the *Republic*—the allegories and myths, the arguments and images—is designed to cure the reader of the temptation to think this is a real possibility. Reality and intelligibility itself are structured by the Good. Thus while there may be grounds for *pessimism*, there can never be grounds for *despair*. (Ibid., pp. 41–42)

I have, unfortunately, provided an argument that Lear's confidence in this last claim is itself misplaced. If the third alternative for the afterlife as spelled out by Plato is in fact a true allegory, then in the light of that possibility, I might well despair of ever getting off the many-thousand-year wheel of painful incarnation Plato has thus set in motion. Where, then, does this leave us?

I suggest that although it is hard to determine Plato's designs at this point, we are supposed to be left with the strong impression—whether it is founded in a genuine Platonic commitment to the Myth's reality or not—that we must still in the here and now continue to believe that we are forced to make morally significant choices on the fly, that these choices have long-term consequences that extend beyond this present life, and that since more future pains are guaranteed for the unjust than for the just, we have instrumental reasons for being just in the present moment. For if nothing else, pain interferes with the ready acquisition of the wisdom we require to be truly happy. We can then understand the Myth of Er as an allegory of the lives we are already leading. Its motif of a prenatal life can be interpreted as "a stark emblem of the inescapably self-forming consequences of ethical agency, a magnified image of how at every moment ... the individual soul/person is intrinsically responsible for what matters most about its existence" (Halliwell 2007, p. 469; Albinus 1998, p. 99). At the very best, we can live in hope of modeling ourselves after Plato's reformed Odysseus and, thus, hope that in the furnace of personal suffering, our prior conceits will be eradicated. At the worst, we will hurt our children and then blame *tuchê*, the gods, or the uncaring universe. But, Plato has warned us that the choice—such as it is—is ours alone, so far as we can tell, at any rate. Ancient readers who understand Plato's picture of the afterlife as having disguised and not solved the problems of morally responsible choice and evil are thus left with reasons for performing what still *appear* to be unconstrained rational choices.[19] Modern readers can then both admire and commiserate with Plato on the size of the problem he raised but did not solve. And if the master can write dialogues that are aporetic, then perhaps it is acceptable for us to write aporetic philosophy papers. And if philosophy begins in wonder, then perhaps it is acceptable to now and again end there as well.[20]

Notes

1. See Morrison (1955) and Stewart (1905) for detailed discussion of the Myth. Morgan (1990, p. 152) notes that the precise sources of the Myth " ... are beyond our grasp. There are doubtless Orphic, Pythagorean, and traditional elements" (cf. Stewart 1905, pp. 152–69). Morgan (2000, p. 208) claims that the Myth has the sort of correct form that Plato thinks he can use to replace traditional myth in his reformed Kallipolis.
2. The role of chance that seems implicit here, though, suggests that Plato may have had his later *Timaeus* view of the causes of evil in mind, causes that he locates in the disorderly motions of matter (see Cherniss 1971; cf. *Phdr.* 248c-d.) The *Republic* does at least make clear that human evil is a consequence of our having souls that are maimed by their association "with the body and other evils" (X 611c1-2; cf. 611b-d, I 353e; *Phd.* 78b-84b; *Tht.* 176a-b; *Laws* X 896c-897c); e.g., not even the *Republic*'s rulers are infallible in their judgments of particulars,

and so Kallipolis will fail due to the inability of the guardians to make infallibly good marriages (given their need to use perception; *Rep.* VIII 546b-c). Such imperfection is, however, a necessary condition of human beings having been created in the first place, a creation that Plato clearly thought was a good thing, all things considered.
3. See Johnson (1999) for this reading.
4. Annas (1982) appears to come to this view of the effect of the Myth, moderating her earlier (1981, pp. 349–53) assessment. This, however, raises the issue of the intended audience of the *Republic*; on which, see below.
5. However, note Else (1972) who distances Plato from the authorship of book X.
6. Dorter (2003, p.132). Stewart (1905, p. 169) holds that with the Myth of Er, Plato is attempting (for the first time in Western philosophy) to "reconcile Free Will with the Reign of Law."
7. I suppose Plato can maintain that animal souls possess the same rational faculty as we, but that their diminished rational capacities result from their souls having taken a very deep drink from the River of Unheeding (619b, e; 621a).
8. See note 13.
9. In this case, however, Dorter seems to think that the soul has all three of its parts present to it; but this seems at odds with the evidence outlined above that only the rational part of the soul is present during the period in which it makes its life choice.
10. Thanks to Mark Ralkowski for this point. Of course, if the prophet does know the potential outcome of the toss, then it might seem incumbent on him to influence his toss for the greater good.
11. See, e.g., *Laws* III 690c; VI 756e-758a; cf. *Ti.* 34b-36d; 46c-47e.
12. Those who recognized this sense of chance include Thucydides (perhaps), Jocasta in Sophocles' *Oedipus Tyrannus* 977–78, and Euripides *Helena* 267–69; *Troiades* 469–71.

Regarding tuchê, see, e.g., Berry (1940, pp. 26–27). As he notes (p. 8), in its original sense, *tuchê* had little to do with chance in causality but always designated a result that found its cause in divinity. In Pindar's *Olympian* 12, for example, we are told that "saving Fortune" is the "child of Zeus the Deliverer" (12.1-2; cf. 8.67); in Aeschylus *Agamemnon* 661–80, "*tuchê*" designates the work of an unknown god, while at *Libation Bearers* 59–60, we read "Among mortals good fortune (*eutuchia*) is a god and more than a god." Only later did "*tuchê*" begin to be used to mean "chance" by those who might postulate wiggle room in a cosmos otherwise under the causal thumb of divinity (ibid., pp. 8–9). Halliwell (2007, p. 470, n. 37) observes that "*Tuchê* is glimpsed only in the margins of the *Republic*: see esp. VI 492a-c, IX 579c, 592a, X 603e."

Taylor (1999, pp. 185–87) discusses Democritus' and Leucippus' assertion that all things do not happen by chance but for a reason (the Principle of Sufficient Reason) and by necessity (see, e.g., DK 67 B1) and its relation to other evidence that would allow random chance to play a causal role (e.g., Aristotle *Phys* II.4 196a24-28). Long (1977, pp. 63–88) argues that the later atomists' (e.g., Epicurus' and Lucretius') references to chance and the atomic "swerve" "do not imply ... that sheer contingency or spontaneous events play a part in nature along with necessity" (p. 85).

See, e.g., *Rep.* V 460a8-10, Aristotle's *EE* VII.14 1247b4-9 and b28-29, and his *Physics* II.4 195b36-196a17 and observe that "*tuchê*" can bear the sense of "Fate" or "Necessity" (and see Taylor [1999, esp. pp. 186–88] who comments on Aëtius I.29.7: "Democritus and the Stoics say that it [i.e., chance] is a cause which is unclear to human reason"). Aristotle appears to distinguish two senses of *tuchê* at *Rhetoric* I.5 1361b39-1362a13—where some events due to *tuchê* can be either due to or be contrary to nature—and *EE* VII.14 1248b3-7, where he distinguishes divine (god-caused) good fortune from the irrational sort (at *On Divination in Sleep* 2 463b12-22, Aristotle uses "*tuchê*" to describe the operation of tossing dice).
13. But here one *must* ask: *Why* does Plato postulate a Heaven that rewards mere habitual virtue (especially if this myth is written for a philosophical audience)? If the point is to make virtue attractive to the nonphilosophical many, why mention the later sufferings of those who are virtuous only through habit? If the point is to make philosophy attractive to the nonphilosophical, why reward the nonphilosophical with anything? And if the point is to spell out the

rewards of any-old virtuous life to the nonphilosopher, why not do so *at length* and in *luscious detail*? We know well what such souls want to hear. For example, when asked about the afterlife, the late Anna Nicole Smith—a figure from popular American culture —proclaimed to a reporter for the *Los Angeles* magazine that "I think heaven's a beautiful place. Gold. You walk on gold floors." Finally, if the point is to emphasize that the just *are* to be well rewarded, why not make their reward a permanent one (as suggested at the end of the *Timaeus*)? (Though this last worry may simply be a consequence of an overriding commitment to reincarnation on Plato's part.)

14. Thanks to Julia Annas for this suggestion.
15. Thanks to Nicholas Smith for this point.
16. Thanks to Toph Marshall for this point. Note how placing Odysseus last in line brings the tale of Er full circle, back to the mention of the "tale told to Alcinous" in the *Odyssey* (614a). Halliwell (2007, pp. 447–48) elaborates on the Odyssean motifs of the Myth, such as the Sirens. We see here in the Myth, perhaps, the kind of proper poetry that is to be distinguished from the sort rejected by Plato in books II and III.
17. Here the puppets of the *Laws* (I 644e, VII 803c-804b) come to mind. One might read these texts as suggesting that Plato's final view was strictly deterministic: we just *are* puppets of the gods, gods who "pull *all* of our internal strings." However, a close look at those texts shows that Plato imagines that we might freely employ our "golden string of judgment" in order to rule over those other stringlike internal forces.
18. Forster (2007) argues that Socrates understood all his positive moral convictions to be gifts of the gods in some sense.
19. If we suppose that the intended audience of book X are all philosophers already (or consider themselves so, at least—especially after their having plowed through the first nine books), we have one speculative solution to our initial puzzle, namely, that book ten is *not* a proleptic encouragement that employs heavenly rewards to urge its nonphilosophical readers to become virtuous by becoming philosophers. Rather, book X would be Plato's way of reassuring his *already*-philosophical readers that all is well *with them*, especially if they should find themselves bothered by the fear of death and the equally lowly but all-too-human worry concerning afterlife payoffs. This would more closely align the Myth of Er with the myth at the end of the *Phaedo* (107c-115a), which is said to serve as a kind of incantation against the fear of death (114d-115a). See also the myth of the *Phaedrus* at 246a-257a (on which, see Griswold [1996, pp. 87–136]).
20. Thanks to Sylvia Berryman and Nicholas Smith for their comments on an earlier version of this essay. I am also indebted to Mark Ralkowski for his very useful response to the version of this essay I presented in Tucson, Arizona, February 2007, to the Twelfth Annual Arizona Colloquium in Ancient Philosophy ("Socrates and Plato on the Nature and Teaching of Virtue"). The essay also benefited from being presented to the Classical, Near Eastern, and Religious Studies Visiting Speakers Programme, University of British Columbia, September 2007, and the International Plato Society meeting, World Congress of Philosophy, Seoul, August 2008.

Bibliography

Albinus, Lars. 1998. The Katabasis of Er. In *Essays on Plato's Republic*, ed. Erik Nis Ostenfeld, 91–105. Aarhus: Aarhus University Press.
Annas, Julia. 1981. *An introduction to Plato's Republic*. New York: Oxford University Press.
Annas, Julia. 1982. Plato's myths of judgment. *Phronesis* 27: 119–143.
Berry, E.G. 1940. *The history and development of the concept of theia moira and theia tuchê down to and including Plato*. Chicago: The University of Chicago Libraries.
Burkert, Walter. 1985. *Greek religion: Archaic and classical*. Cambridge, MA: Harvard University Press.

Cherniss, Harold. 1971. The sources of evil according to Plato. In *Plato*, vol. 2, ed. Vlastos Gregory. New York: Anchor Books.
Dodds, E.R. 1951. *The Greeks and the irrational*. Berkeley/Los Angeles: University of California Press.
Dorter, Kenneth. 2003. Free will, luck, and happiness in the Myth of Er. *Journal of Philosophical Research* 28: 129–142.
Else, Gerald. 1972. The structure and date of book X of Plato's *Republic*. Heidelberg: C. Winter.
Ferrari, G.R.F. 2008. Glaucon's reward, philosophy's debt: The Myth of Er. In *Plato's myths*, ed. Catalin Partenie, 116–133. Cambridge, UK: Cambridge University Press.
Forster, Michael. 2007. Socrates' profession of ignorance. *Oxford Studies in Ancient Philosophy* 32: 1–35.
Gifford, E.H. 1905. *The Euthydemus of Plato*. Oxford: Clarendon.
Griswold, Charles. 1996. *Self-knowledge in Plato's Phaedrus*. University Park: Pennsylvania State University Press.
Guthrie, W.K.C. 1950. *The Greeks and their gods*. Boston: Beacon.
Guthrie, W.K.C. 1971. *Socrates*. Cambridge, UK: Cambridge University Press.
Halliwell, Stephen. 1988. *Republic X*. Oxford: Aris & Phillips.
Halliwell, Stephen. 2007. The life and death journey of the soul: Interpreting the Myth of Er. In *The Cambridge companion to Plato's Republic*, ed. G.R.F. Ferrari, 445–473. New York: Cambridge University Press.
Johnson, Ronald R. 1999. Does Plato's Myth of Er contribute to the argument of the *Republic*? *Philosophy and Rhetoric* 32(1): 1–13.
Lear, Jonathan. 2006. Myth and allegory in Plato's *Republic*. In *The Blackwell guide to Plato's Republic*, ed. Gerasimos Santas, 25–43. Oxford: Blackwell Publishing.
Long, A.A. 1977. Chance and natural law in Epicureanism. *Phronesis* 22: 63–88.
Moors, Kent. 1988. Named life selections in Plato's Myth of Er. *Classica et Medievalia* 39: 55–61.
Morgan, Michael. 1990. *Platonic piety*. New Haven: Yale University Press.
Morgan, Michael. 1992. Plato and Greek religion. In *The Cambridge companion to Plato*, ed. Kraut Richard. New York: Cambridge University Press.
Morgan, Kathryn A. 2000. *Myth and philosophy from the Presocratics to Plato*. Cambridge, UK: Cambridge University Press.
Morrison, J.S. 1955. Parmenides and Er. *The Journal of Hellenic Studies* 75: 59–68.
Ott, Walter. 2006. Aristotle and Plato on character. *Ancient Philosophy* 26: 65–79.
Richardson, Hilda. 1926. The Myth of Er (Plato, *Republic*, 616b). *The Classical Quarterly* 20: 113–133.
Schils, Gretchen. 1993. Plato's Myth of Er: The light and the spindle. *Antiquité Classique* 62: 101–114.
Stewart, John Alexander. 1905. *The myths of Plato*. New York: MacMillan and Company.
Taylor, C.C.W. 1999. The atomists, chap. 9. In *The Cambridge companion to early Greek philosophy*, ed. A.A. Long, 181–204. New York: Cambridge University Press.
Thayer, H.S. 1988. The myth of Er. *History of Philosophy Quarterly* 5(4): 369–384.
Vlastos, Gregory. 1954. The third man argument in the *Parmenides*. *Philosophical Review* 63(3): 319–349.

The Grounds of *Logos*: The Interweaving of Forms

Christopher Shields

> Plato's view of a 'meaning' is simple. The name 'circle' which I now utter *means* the Form 'Circle', an eternal and unchanging object of thought. —Francis Cornford (1960)

1 Interwoven Forms and the Simple Semantic Theory

Cornford's easy assimilation of Forms to meanings is understandable. After all, says Plato, "*Logos* comes to be for us because of the interweaving of Forms with one another" (*Sph.* 259e5-6; *dia gar tên allêlôn tôn eidôn sumplokên ho logos gegonen hêmin*). Assuming for now something we will come to query, that the *logos* he has in view here is a *statement*, Plato's view about the relation between statements and Forms may indeed seem simple, perhaps, some may suspect, even simple minded: the semantic values of words making up the statements of our natural languages are Forms, with the result that statements come about when we combine those Forms, those meanings, in suitable ways with one another. So, just as Plato

---

In his stimulating, philosophically adroit exposition of a paradox of knowledge and the mutability of Forms in Plato's *Sophist*, David Keyt (1969, p. 13) comments more fully in a similar vein on the close connection between thought and language in Plato's thought: "Knowledge, a Platonist might argue, implies thought; thought is simply 'a dialogue of the soul with itself' (*Sph.* 263D6-264B4); so thought implies language. Language in turn requires general names with fixed meanings; or, to put it another way, it requires fixed concepts to which general names are attached. But this is one of the roles that Forms play in Plato's philosophy … the Form of horse is the meaning of the word 'horse'." Because Keyt's observation provided the initial impetus for the investigations leading to the present chapter, it is an especially fitting pleasure to offer this essay to him, with gratitude and admiration, in a volume dedicated to his honor. Keyt's unremittingly philosophical engagement with the works of Plato and Aristotle has served as a model to many—and will, no doubt, continue to do so for many years to come.

C. Shields (✉)
Lady Margaret Hall, University of Oxford, Oxford, OX2 6QA, UK
e-mail: Christopher.shields@lmh.ox.ac.uk

says, *logos* comes about for us only by the interweaving of Forms. His weaving metaphor,[1] one echoed in several key passages of Aristotle,[2] is, on this approach, transparent and immediately intelligible: propositions are the whole cloth woven of the semantic threads of Forms. As different weaves yield different patterns from the same stock of thread, so different propositions result from different weavings of the same Forms. Language, in its indefinite variety and unending complexity, finds its underlying semantic structure in the woof and warp of Forms.

If Cornford's appeal to the semantic character is for these reasons understandable, then it is also distressingly quick and monodimensional. For Plato's remark about the interweaving of Forms has impressed his readers as no less elusive than rich.[3] Even if we assume, in keeping with one central strain of scholarship on Plato's *Sophist*, that the *logos* Plato mentions here is something broadly semantic in character, we are not licensed by Plato's contention to infer directly that Forms are meanings, and propositions the tapestries made of them. Indeed, as I shall argue, Plato's point of view about the relation of Forms to meanings in this passage is both less direct and more consequential than Cornford's simple, direct assimilation of Forms to meanings would suggest. For, importantly, Plato regards it as an immediate corollary of his view that if Forms had not been woven together with one another, our language and thought would be bereft of meaning; but that is to say, then, that if the Forms were not interwoven, language, and indeed thought, would not exist at all. So, according to Plato, if the Forms did not weave together with one another, you could not be reading this paragraph, as, undoubtedly, you are. Hence, Plato may conclude that the reader of this essay tacitly accepts not only the existence of Forms but also their freestanding semantic interrelations, whatever those may be. In this sense, Plato's contention constitutes an existence argument for Forms, an indirect one to be sure, but an existence argument all the same.

Indeed, if we trace this same train of thought a bit further, we can appreciate why Plato intimates that we must all acknowledge the interweaving of Forms lest we fall into an immediately self-undermining semantic endeavor: if Plato is right about the interweaving of Forms, then any purported denial of his dictum makes sense only by implicitly granting the thesis it seeks to undercut. This, presumably, is what Plato means when he contends that to deny the interweaving of forms is to speak nonsense—literally, in his idiom, to say nothing at all (*legoien an ouden*; *Sph.* 252b5).[4] The same contention seems more or less expressly advanced by Plato when he argues that those who deny the communion (*koinonia*; 252b9) of Forms "need not wait for us to refute them: as the saying goes, their foe comes from within their own household" (*Sph.* 252c5-7). He castigates those who deny communion and goes so far as to liken them to the ventriloquist Eurycles,[5] because "they undermine themselves, carrying about a voice of contradiction from within" (252c7-9). Their view, he concludes, is in fact the most utterly ludicrous of all (*panton katagelastotata*; 252b8).

This is decidedly strong language from Plato, language consonant with the force of his convictions about the relations of Forms with one another. In view of these considerations, Plato's claim about the interweaving of Forms emerges as arrestingly ambitious, even radical.[6] After all, as he frequently shows himself well aware, not everyone is prepared to acknowledge the existence of Forms, and so for such people, posterior questions concerning their relations with one another simply do not arise. Even so, Plato implies, Form deniers implicitly embrace the commitments they eschew, insofar as their very denials rely upon the obtaining of the commitments they seek to reject. Such, then, is the richness of Plato's remark.

The elusiveness of the remark is reflected in the variety of interpretations it has elicited from Plato's exegetes and critics. Even within the semantic interpretation at its most circumscribed, [7] scholars have understood Plato to be making a variety of distinct, nonequivalent points, all in different ways concerning the requisites of sentence meaning. Upon reviewing these understandings, it becomes clear that only one interpretation does justice to the precision and compactness of Plato's text. It also becomes clear, for allied reasons, that the semantic approach itself does at best partial justice to Plato's conception of the fundamentality of Forms to thought. What is left unexplained on this approach is the still more elusive question of *why* Forms should be required for sentence meaning. What is left unexplained, in fact, is precisely what interweaving (*sumplokê*) should consist in.

When we explore this question, I contend, we come to a deeper appreciation of Plato's metaphysics of meaning: he thinks that Forms comprise an *intensional sense structure*,[8] and that this structure moves us to a commitment well beyond anything one might regard from the standpoint of pure logic, or indeed from the standpoint of semantic theory narrowly conceived, in the manner of Cornford, as involving Forms as meanings and statements as the combinations of such meanings. Plato's suggestion is rather that Forms, as meanings, must stand in metaphysical relations to one another, relations including, among others, necessary cross-predication, necessary exclusion, and necessary super- and subordination. It is this structure, I will suggest, to which he alludes with his metaphor of *interweaving*.

If this proves correct, then an immediate corollary results: Plato's contention regarding the interweaving of Forms constitutes a transcendental argument for their existence. Were there no Forms, language and thought would be impossible; language and thought are actual and so possible; hence, Forms, as the necessary grounds of this possibility, exist.

Although this *existence* argument does seem to animate Plato's claim about the interweaving of Forms in the *Sophist*, this is not his first concern when characterizing their interweaving with one another. Rather, he means to establish that they do in fact have, of necessity, freestanding metaphysical and semantic relations with one another. This is a point some writers in the semantic tradition have failed to appreciate, partly, again, because they have failed to attend to the precision of Plato's language.

2 Positioning Plato's Remark

Plato's contention regarding the interweaving of Forms occurs within the larger context of his investigations in the *Sophist* into division and definition, predication and existence, negation and falsehood, and, more generally, into the parceling of reality into kinds.

In the long middle section of the dialogue, after the preliminary attempt to define the sophist by means of the method of division (*Sph.* 218e-231e), Plato engages in some of his most intricate and demanding discussion of the notions of *being* (*to on*) and nonbeing (*to mê on*), both individually and in relation to one another, and then again with respect to their roles in predication, both positive and negative. In this section, he launches a series of abstract, sometimes abstruse arguments all circling a series of tightly knit topics:

- Problems pertaining to nonbeing and what is not (237d-241c)
- Problems pertaining to being and what is, which are held to be no less demanding than those pertaining to what is not (242-251e)
- Problems brought about by some "late learners," about whom Plato is disparaging, pertaining to the possibility of saying that one thing is many things (251a-c)
- Problems pertaining to the mixing of kinds, including five very important kinds (*megistê genê*), namely, being, motion, rest, sameness, and difference (251d-257a)
- Problems about negative expressions, difference, statements (*logoi*), names and verbs, appearances, and, once again, true and false statements (257b-264b)

In the middle of this last section, the Eleatic Visitor reminds Theaetetus that it had been established earlier that some Forms combine with one another, while others do not (259d9-26a3; cf. 251d5-252e8, 255e8-257a12; cf. 254c4-5). He does so, he suggests, to underscore his view that the sophist's failure to show false speech and thought impossible results *inter alia* from his failure to grasp the ways in which nonbeing (*to mê on*) can be mixed with other Forms (260b2-c4).

It is in this connection that he introduces his contention about interweaving. It makes sense for him to do so, because he has been tussling with the sophist about being and nonbeing and also about positive and negative predication. Given that he has charged the sophist with failing to come to terms with the manner in which Forms can and cannot mix with one another, he has implicitly accepted the assumption that they do mix in some ways and in other ways not, and, indeed, that their doing so is required for discourse of any kind. He then introduces a striking, sweeping claim about interweaving in general. We may label this claim, with Ackrill (1955/1997, p. 72), statement (**S**):

> (**S**) *Logos* comes to be for us because of the interweaving of Forms with one another (259e5-6).

Immediately noteworthy is the fact that (**S**) occurs as a premise in a truncated argument. The relevant passage, taken together, is:

> The untwining (*to dialuein*) of each thing from every other is the complete disappearance of all *logoi*. For *logos* comes to be for us because of the interweaving of Forms with one another (259e4-6).

As the Eleatic Visitor would have it, (**S**) provides a reason for thinking that without the interweaving (*sumplokê*) of Forms with one another, *logoi* would be annihilated, presumably because the lack of interweaving would result in the isolation of each Form from every other, where such isolation precludes the existence of *logoi*. Thus, untwining is sufficient for the disappearance of all *logoi*, while interweaving is necessary and sufficient for communion (*koinonia*), which we will provisionally introduce as the contrary of untwining (*to dialuein*).⁹ So, interweaving is necessary for *logos*.

What is *logos* in this connection (*Sph*. 259e6; cf. 260a5 and 260a7)? A fair bit turns on the question, but we cannot be confident about its answer on narrowly lexical grounds: *logos* might, in principle, mean any number of different things, ranging from various semantic items in the neighborhood of *meaning* to various non-semantic notions, including, for example, *reasoning, reckoning, account*, or *explanation*. Or, it might simply mean something linguistic, like *sentence*. Crucially, even if we suppose, as I shall urge, that it means *statement*, that too is already ambiguous, straddling *sentence*, regarded as a token or type of some natural language utterance, or *proposition*, taken as something expressed by a sentence in the indicative mood, perhaps also the sort of thing able to be believed, hoped, or simply thought. To complicate matters, suppose that *logos* does mean *statement*. Then there is a further question as to what precisely we lose if Forms fail to interweave with one another. That is, one might naturally think that if *logos* means *statement*, and the unweaving of Forms makes *logos* disappear, then Plato must finally be understanding interweaving as necessary for sentence *meaning*. Possibly, however, he might be thinking not that interweaving is necessary for *meaning* but rather for truth and falsity; this is because the abolition of truth and falsity would equally result in the lack of *logos* understood as an assertoric statement. For, one might reasonably suppose that if there is no truth or falsity, then neither are there true or false sentences, with the further result that there are not assertions of truth or falsity, and so no assertions at all.¹⁰

As I have suggested, we cannot determine this matter before reflecting on the sorts of considerations Plato adduces on behalf of (**S**). Indeed, in the abstract, without exploring the context of the utterance, we cannot know what Plato takes himself to be saying. Consequently, the semantic interpretation, however initially natural and finally apt it may prove, cannot be assumed without argument. It is really just one of several possible approaches. Awareness of this fact, in turn, should prepare us to appreciate that the semantic interpretation is itself already open to a variety of nonequivalent formulations.

3 A Problem for Plato

One way to assess Plato's intended meaning is to reflect upon an important problem that has captured the attention of his readers. This problem pertains to the example Plato employs to illustrate and support (**S**). He says (261e12-263b11):

Eleatic Visitor: I'll say a statement (*logos*) for you by putting together a thing (*pragma*) with an action (*praxis*) through a noun (*onoma*) and a verb (*rhema*). You then tell me what it is a statement of.
Theaetetus: I'll do so to the best of my ability.
Eleatic Visitor: "Theaetetus sits." —Not a long statement to be sure?
Theaetetus: No, a rather modest one.

Eleatic Visitor: Your job is to tell me both about whom the statement is and whose it is.
Theaetetus: Clearly it is about me and it is mine.
Eleatic Visitor: How about another?
Theaetetus: What sort?
Eleatic Visitor: "Theaetetus (with whom I am currently conversing) flies."
Theaetetus: And this too one should say belongs to no one other than me and is about me.

Plato's prime illustration of a *logos* is then[11]:

- (**I**): Theaetetus sits (*Theaitêtos kathêtai*).

There is, however, this problem: Plato speaks of the interweaving of Forms *with one another* (*sumplokê eidôn tôn allêlôn*), in the plural, and yet his illustration evidently mentions just one Form. As Guthrie tidily sums up the situation: "This sentence has caused great difficulty, for at 263a the statement 'Theaetetus is sitting' is given as an example of a *logos*, yet it exhibits not a combination of Forms but of a single Form with a particular" (Guthrie 1978, p. 161). More precisely, and in the present context more pressingly, according to the *simple meaning theory* of Cornford, Forms are the meanings of words, while statements are interwoven meanings, that is, interwoven Forms. So, (**I**) seems a wholly inadequate illustration of (**S**). Indeed, it takes only a little reflection to see that matters are still worse than Guthrie and others have suggested: on the simple meaning theory of Forms, (**I**) positively refutes (**S**). Plato introduces (**I**) as an especially clear instance of a *logos*, where every *logos* is meant to involve the interweaving of Forms. Yet (**I**) does not—again according to the simple meaning theory of Forms—involve the interweaving of anything with anything else and certainly not the interweaving of some Forms with any other Forms. It seems to follow that (**S**) is false and shown to be so by (**I**).

From this perspective, (**I**) is much worse than an inept illustration. It seems a case of Plato exhibiting a rather bald confusion with respect to his own theory of Forms. If so, Plato's introduction of (**I**) reflects rather badly on his understanding of his own position. It is not surprising, then, to find William and Martha Kneale contending in their *Development of Logic* that Plato "never dealt clearly with the distinction between singular and general statements" (1962, p. 20). What we see in the interplay of (**S**) and (**I**) is simply an unhappily stark symptom of this lack of clarity.

At any rate, we should conclude something along these lines if we adopt the simple meaning theory. Even so, commentators working within the tradition of semantic interpretation have responded to this problem fairly indulgently, not least by understating its severity. Some have apologized for Plato implicitly, by suppressing his view in an undertranslation of his Greek (Cornford 1960, p. 300), while others have apologized for him explicitly, by treating him as if he had somehow unwittingly *overstated* his own position regarding the interweaving of Forms (Ross 1951, p. 115). As one example of undertranslation, Cornford omits "with one another" (*allêlôn*; *Sph.* 259e5) and proceeds to represent Plato as adhering to a weakened version of (**S**), namely, what we may call (**S'**): "He has said that 'all discourse depends on the weaving together of Forms' (259E), *i.e.* at least one Form enters into the meaning of any statement" (Cornford 1960, p. 300).

Cornford's omission seems a wholly misplaced expedient. Not only does it fail to represent accurately what Plato actually says, but it purchases him very little in the process. For even if we assume that he had really intended (**S'**) and not (**S**), we will find ourselves coming upon our same problem only a little downstream: an identity statement is no less a *logos* than a singular predication. Consider, that is, statements of the form "George Eliot is Mary Anne Evans." This, no less than (**I**), qualifies as a statement (*logos*). Yet it violates (**S'**) as surely as (**I**) violates (**S**) (still, of course, on the assumption of the simple semantic theory). Nor will it do to rule identity statements out of consideration by fiat. For in that event, we might as easily have disallowed singular statements from consideration by the same sort of fiat. Nothing would be gained in either case by our doing so. On the contrary, we would only have succeeded in misrepresenting Plato's actual view.

Much the same can be said about an instance of a second apologetic strategy, one best typified by Ross. On his approach, it is acknowledged forthrightly that (**S**) is false. Still, on this approach, its falsity is to be treated as a mere overstatement of a defensible view in its proximity. The correct view, Plato's true view, is rather (**S"**) that "all subjects of statements except proper names stand either for Forms or for things described by Forms" (Ross 1951, p. 115). The thought would then be that for any statement, with the exception of those with a proper name in the subject position, the subject either stands for a Form or at least for something described by a Form.

Somehow Ross' view seems wrongly put by him. For even proper names may refer to objects, to use his idiom, described by Forms. Indeed, (**I**) seems to be one such case: "Theaetetus" refers to Theaetetus, and he is "described," as Ross says, by the Form of Being Seated. Perhaps, however, Ross means rather, somewhat more periphrastically, "Forms will always be implicated in any *logos*. Either the subject will stand for a Form (e.g., 'Justice is a virtue.'), or, failing that, as when the subject is a proper name, it will stand for something that is described by a Form (e.g., 'Solon is just.')." If so, then, first, his view will tend to collapse into Cornford's, and, more importantly, it will in any case fall prey to the same objection. That is, (**S"**), no less than (**S'**), is forced to treat statements involving identity as non-statements. Yet an identity statement is a *logos* no less than a singular or a general predication is a *logos*. So, once again, the corrected view offered to Plato is incorrect and is shown to be so by the existence of identity statements. So, again, not much is gained by attempting to render Plato's view acceptable by the device of underrepresentation. The net result merely postpones the day of reckoning. Strikingly, neither Cornford nor Ross adheres to the precision of Plato's actual statement of (**S**) and neither, in consequence, comes to terms with it. So, ultimately, neither serves Plato's final aim at all well, because each in his own way makes his view vague or imprecise.

4 Introducing Precision

Ackrill introduced precision into the discussion of (**S**) when he refused to countenance these deflationary strategies. Although he did not advance the point about identity statements introduced above against Cornford and Ross, his objections to them were very much in keeping with this sort of response. When surveying their views, Ackrill contended, correctly, that Plato's (**I**) illustrates not the thesis that every meaningful sentence presupposes the existence of at least one Form, or the thesis that except for statements with proper names a Form always plays some role describing some subject, but rather that *logos* comes about because of the interweaving of Forms—in the plural—with one another (Ackrill 1955/1997, pp. 72–74). He then counseled, again correctly, that rather than rushing to rescue Plato from an unfortunate infelicity of illustration, we might instead work harder to understand how Plato might suppose his illustration to fit his principle. In short, Ackrill saw no reason to rescue Plato from Plato and instead sought to rescue him from his apologists.

In place of preemptory apologetics, Ackrill advocated understanding the relation between (**S**) and (**I**) by urging reflection upon the arguments Plato offered on behalf of (**S**) or at least on behalf of theses in the immediate neighborhood of (**S**).[12] To this end, he looked to Plato's discussion of Form intermixture (*summeixis*). For even if intermixture (*summeixis*) and interweaving (*sumplokê*) are different sorts of relations among Forms, surely Forms must be related to each other at least to the extent that one could draw some data from Plato's remarks about one of these relations to the application of the other. This would be especially so (although Ackrill does not suggest that it is so) if one relation were a species of the other. Perhaps, for instance, interweaving is a kind of intermixing. In that case, anything said of intermixing (*summeixis*) would automatically hold of interweaving (*sumplokê*) as well.

In any event, Plato entertains three theses with respect to the relations Forms might bear to one another (*Sph.* 251d-252e):

(1) Every Form combines with every other.
(2) No Form combines with any other.
(3) Some forms do and others do not combine with one another.

He rejects the first two, extreme theses, and ultimately endorses the last, moderate thesis.

As Ackrill observes, the most relevant thesis relating to the interweaving of Forms is (2), against which Plato advances two arguments. In the first instance, he contends that philosophers of all stripes would be speaking nonsense or saying nothing at all (*legoien an ouden*) if there were no intermixture of Forms at all (*medemia summeixis*). Moreover, those who advance (2) undermine their own case even as they speak: their refutation emerges from an enemy within their own household (252c5-7), because they refute themselves even as they endeavor to make their case.

How they manage to do so, however, is a bit unclear. Indeed, applying Ackrill's exacting standards to himself, we find that he ascribes to Plato in this connection a view not expressed by Plato in the *Sophist* or elsewhere, at least not overtly, namely, that "the very statement of (2) involves a contradiction." Which contradiction? As Ackrill himself hastens to add, "It is not of course that they straightforwardly both assert and deny *summexis* (intermixture)." Rather, "The thesis 'No Forms combine with one another' is held to be self-refuting because its meaningfulness presupposes that some Forms do combine." Finally, then, "Plato's conclusion, that there are connections between Forms, rests upon the simple fact that some sentences are meaningful and some are not" (Ackrill 1955/1997, p. 75).

There is something importantly right about Ackrill's contention but also something troubling. He is right that Plato's treatment of (2) provides important data regarding his attitude toward the interweaving of Forms. Still, it is troubling that Ackrill seems to offer three nonequivalent diagnoses about the self-undermining character of (2), the thesis that no Form combines with any other. First is the suggestion that any expression of (2) involves a contradiction—though what contradiction that is Ackrill does not say, preferring only to say which contradiction it is not. Next is the suggestion that no assertion of (2) could be *meaningful* if (2) were true, since precisely what (2) denies, namely, that at least some Forms combine with other Forms, is a necessary condition of the meaningfulness of statements. Finally there is a third, nonequivalent suggestion that (2) is shown to be false, ultimately, by the fact that some sentences are meaningful and others are not. In sum, Ackrill offers Plato three nonequivalent arguments for the falsity of (2): one from contradiction, one from the conditions of meaningfulness, and, finally, one from the (putative) general fact that some sentences are meaningful and others are not. In so doing, he establishes none of these objections uniquely.

In order to develop and secure the sort of strategy Ackrill advocates, it is thus necessary to consider why Plato should be so confident that the advocates of (2) are doomed to self-refutation. In particular, one should like to know, *in this dialectical context*, why the advocates of thesis (2) should be compelled to acknowledge that even in offering a *logos*, they sow the seeds of their own downfall. In this connection, we shall see that the simple semantic theory of Cornford comes up short—even while a more subtle and satisfying semantic thesis emerges. Hence, although Cornford's easy assimilation of Forms to *meanings* is unsustainable, a more general thesis about *meaningfulness* does indeed emerge from Plato's presentation of the interweaving of Forms in the *Sophist*.

5 A Platonic Sense Structure

In raising these questions about Ackrill's understanding of Plato's attitude toward (S), I do not mean to suggest that he has somehow misconstrued Plato's approach to its eventual grounding but that he has underconstrued it. Indeed, if we proceed further along Ackrill's same line of explication, I contend, we come to a deeper appreciation of Plato's true attitude toward the wellsprings of (S) and so to the interweaving of Forms with one another.

To begin, then, two complementary features of Ackrill's approach seem fruitful and worth pursuing further. First is his suggestion that to understand the relation between (S) and (I), we must first plumb Plato's motivations for advancing (S). Second is his suggestion that in order to make progress in this direction, we should focus first on Plato's independent remarks about the intermixture of Forms. For while Plato in fact uses a fair number of discrete terms regarding Form-to-Form relations in the *Sophist*—including combining or commonality (*koinônia*), connecting (*prosaptein*), blending together (*summeignushthai*), joining or fitting together (*sunarmottein*), being consonant with (*sumphônein*), partaking (*metalambanein*), and participating (*metechein*)—he seems to have some root ideas about their manner of association. Some Forms seem of necessity mutually predicable; others seem of necessity mutually unpredicable of one another; some seem of such a nature that if one, F-ness, is predicated of something other, then a second Form, G-ness, must also be predicated of that same thing; and still others will be such that if F-ness is predicated of something other, then G-ness cannot be predicated of that thing. Without tracing out these fine-grained relations, we may conclude that if at least some of them obtain, then (2) is false, that is, some Forms will combine with some others.

As we have seen, Plato offers the judgment that those who deny *all* of these sorts of association find themselves engaged in a self-undermining enterprise. Consider, more fully:

> Eleatic Visitor: Further, now, these people meet with the most ludicrous of all results by following the account of those people who will not allow one thing to share in the quality of another.
> Theaetetus: How so?
> Eleatic Visitor: Because they are compelled when referring to anything to use the words 'being' and 'apart' and 'from the others' and 'by itself' and any number more. They are powerless to avoid using them or from connecting them in their statements, and so have no need of others to refute them; their enemy is in their own household, as the saying goes, and, like that extraordinary Eurycles, they carry out their own refutation within themselves.
> Theaetetus: True: your comparison is most apt. (*Sph.* 252b8-d1)

Despite Theaetetus' pliant agreement, it is unclear precisely why Plato thinks that this is so. Still less is it clear why his opponent should be compelled to acknowledge an enemy lurking in his own household.

Evidently Plato has some general argument of the following sort in mind:

(i) Suppose someone, perhaps Antisthenes,[13] insists that no Form has a share in any other. Call this thesis *the discreteness contention* (**DC**).
(ii) A necessary condition of the possibility of (**DC**) is not-(**DC**).
(iii) So, if Antisthenes asserts, or seeks to assert (**DC**), then he has implicitly accepted not-(**DC**).
(iv) If (iii), then anyone who asserts (**DC**) refutes himself.
(v) So, anyone who asserts (**DC**) refutes himself.

This is why the enemy of Antisthenes comes from within his own household: he need not await any refutation from without, since he has already done that job well enough himself.

One obvious point about this argument is that it is indirect, in the sense that those who deny interaction also presuppose its truth. It is thus, as Ackrill noted, plainly in keeping with a similar sort of indirect proof of Aristotle's, namely, his elenctic proof for the principle of noncontradiction in *Metaphysics* IV 4, even to the point of sharing some of its same language. If the parallel is apt, then there is one further point of note, namely, that Aristotle's proof is avowedly indirect because it *must* be indirect. Whatever the ultimate status of his proof, Aristotle rightly notes that no direct proof for the principle of noncontradiction could avoid circularity (*Met.* 1006a2-6).

Further, just as there is a question about the precise grounds of Aristotle's contention that all attempts to deny the principle of noncontradiction succumb to some form of self-undermining, so there is a question in the *Sophist* as to why Plato feels himself secure in alleging self-refutation against those who affirm (2). This is, then, a question as to the grounds of (ii), the claim that a necessary condition of the possibility of (**DC**) is that not-(**DC**). We have implicitly already considered a number of nonequivalent possibilities, mainly in the realm of statement meaning. Some suggestions, not mutually exclusive are the following:

- If (**DC**) is to be *meaningful*, then not-(**DC**).
- Any assertion of (**DC**) is, unbeknownst to those asserting it, a *contradiction*.
- If (**DC**) is to be asserted, it must be asserted *as true*, but then it must be the case that some statements are true and others false, which in turn requires not-(**DC**).
- If (**DC**) is to be assertoric at all, then not-(**DC**).

So, since one or the other (or all) of these grounds must be in place in order for anyone to assert (**DC**), a necessary condition of the possibility of (**DC**) is not-(**DC**).

Let us consider the often-mooted suggestion that Plato's (ii) depends immediately upon considerations pertaining to logic. It is in principle possible that Plato has such a claim in view, but he does not advance it in any plain terms. He does say, in an allied passage, that those who maintain (1), the claim that every Form combines with every other, implicate themselves in the greatest of impossibilities. They will be forced to say, for instance, that *motion rests*. Those saying such things, according to Plato, are implicated in the most extreme impossibilities (*tais meigstais anagkais adunaton*; *Sph.* 252d9-10). This prompts Ackrill to say: "These we can observe to be self-contradictory, logically impossible" (Ackrill 1955/1997, p. 74).

If this were so, then one might legitimately import analogous considerations to (2), by suggesting that those who deny any sort of combination of Forms are implicated in a contradiction of logic. That would, it seems, provide the securest possible grounds for (ii).

Unfortunately, in neither case do principles of logic apply. As regards (1), Ackrill is not entitled to appeal to logical impossibility: whatever its demerits, the statement "motion rests" is not a contradiction of logic. On the contrary, its logical form is perfectly unobjectionable. Indeed, as I will suggest, it is precisely its being a nonlogical impossibility that gives the claim its force and interest. For the present, however, we may simply note that any attempt to locate a form of logical impossibility in (1) as a basis for finding the grounding (ii) in pure logic stalls. For the impossibility to which Plato appeals in (1) is entirely nonlogical. Consequently, any movement in that direction would serve only to obscure the kind of impossibility Plato has in view in either case, by proposing peremptorily a kind of impossibility unsuited to his purposes.

Better, perhaps, then is the suggestion that (ii) is self-undermining due to considerations of meaningfulness. Here, put in its most direct formulation, the suggestion would be that anyone who asserts (**DC**) implicitly denies the possibility of meaning. Hence, (**DC**) is meaningful only if it is, according to its own terms, not meaningful; hence, it is self-undermining. If that is correct, however, the self-undermining character of any denial of (2) results not from a contradiction, at least not a contradiction in logic, but rather from some nonlogical incompatibility resulting from any denial of the intermingling of Forms: those who deny (2) do not contradict themselves but rather rob their own assertions of meaning even as they speak.

Why so? To be sure, on its surface, the statement "Forms do not interweave with one another" seems perfectly meaningful, even if it proves to be false, and indeed even if it proves to be necessarily false. If we permit ourselves to become exercised about the possibility of false judgment, as Plato does to very good effect in both the *Sophist* and *Theaetetus* (*Sph.* 236d5-264b10; *Tht.* 167a6-8, 187c7-200c7; cf. *Rep.* 478b5-478c2; *Euthd.* 284b1-284c6; *Cra.* 429c6-430a5), then we should not be inclined to do so because we think that necessarily false judgments are *meaningless*. It is easy to understand the meaning of the statement $7+5=11$, even though it is necessarily false; indeed, to grasp that it *is* necessarily false seems first to require that we have understood its meaning. Looked at this way, any immediate or direct appeal to the meaninglessness of (**DC**) requires, at the very least, significant amplification.

The relevant amplification begins by reconsidering what I have termed the *simple semantic theory* characteristic of the framework of interpretation evidently embraced by Ackrill in common with the targets of his criticisms. Perhaps appeals to meaning in this connection are unsatisfying because they seem to rely too readily on the easy thought that Forms *are* meanings.[14] Perhaps, that is, the simple semantic theory is our culprit. For, after all, if Plato shows that those who deny the interweaving of Forms run afoul of the strictures of meaning only because they fail to appreciate that Forms *are* meanings, then he shows only that those who deny the simple semantic theory must adhere to some other theory of meaning in order to avoid self-refutation. Needless to say, most philosophers have been independently inclined to do so anyhow; indeed, most think it is a mistake to suppose that anything at all like the simple semantic theory is worth taking at all seriously and (in partial consequence) not one in any case appropriately ascribed to Plato.[15] This would, as a matter of the dialectic currently before us, include even those who were happy to admit the existence of Forms. So far, then, we have been given no reason to ground (ii) in any considerations pertaining to the meaningfulness of discourse.

Still, there is a possible route to grounding (ii) in claims pertaining to meaning, and it is one that acknowledges that the simple semantic theory of Cornford is hopelessly inadequate to the task. We might instead take a cue from Keyt who, while seeming initially to agree with Cornford in expressing the simple semantic theory, in fact points to a deeper and more illustrative connection: *logos* need not mean merely statement meaning.[16] Instead, it might refer to statements in common with *rational discourse in general*, a possibility made vivid by Plato's suggestion that thinking (*dianoia*) and discourse or statement (*logos*) are the same thing, except that what we call thinking is an inward dialogue of the soul carried by the mind with itself without spoken sound (*Sph.* 263e4-5; cf. *Phil.* 38c5-38e8; *Tht.* 189e6-190a6). This suggests that the stakes are in fact higher than any narrow investigation of statement meaning might portend. For if thought is somehow internal language, where in fact Plato affirms a parallel between belief (*doxa*) and statement (*logos*), the first internal and silent and the latter voiced and public (*Sph.* 263e10-264a3), then he is equally saying that without an interweaving of Forms we cannot so much as think.

That is a strident claim, and not one plausibly unpacked in terms of the relation between words and Forms, where words are items in natural languages and Forms are their semantic values. Rather, it suggests the more general and ambitious thought that without Forms and their relations *to one another*, the very enterprise of rational inquiry cannot get underway (cf. *Prm.* 135). This is why, indeed, the Eleatic Stranger generalizes his remarks about statement meaning to the enterprise of philosophy taken as a whole: "If we were robbed of *logos* (namely, as one of the kinds of things that exist [*tôn ontôn hen ti genôn einai*]), then, what is worst of all, we would be robbed of philosophy" (*Sph.* 260a5-7).

Altogether, then, these remarks suggest that what is in view is not the simple semantic theory advocated by Cornford but rather something more general. Plausibly, I will suggest, this more general condition of thought is something less atomistic than Cornford contends, but something broadly semantic in character all the same. Plato seems to be relying, namely, on what we may call the thesis of *intensional sense structure*.

This thesis finds its clearest manifestation in Plato's development of (**I**), the very illustration which gave rise to our reconsideration of his attitude toward the interweaving of Forms. Plato contrasts the true statement (**I**) "Theaetetus sits," with the false statement "Theaetetus flies." His treatment of the false statement has occasioned very many different interpretations.[17] According to the most compelling interpretation, owing to Brown,[18] Plato's account of falsity in this passage requires understanding his approach to be given in terms of a "limited incompatibility range" of predicates. That is, when someone utters the false statement "Theaetetus flies," he commits the error of "saying different (*heteron*) things from the things that are" (*Sph.* 263b7), where, crucially, he has already distinguished what is *only* or *merely* different (*monon heteron*) from what is positively contrary (*enantion*) (257b1-c3). The false speaker (and, let us remember, the false thinker) predicates of a subject a feature which is different from the features had by the subject (else his predication would be true). His proposed predicate is thus excluded from the class of predicates in fact applying to the subject.[19]

This exclusion may, however, happen in a number of nonequivalent ways, and Plato is under no obligation to select one uniquely. After all, some falsehoods are necessary falsehoods and some merely contingent; further, some necessary falsehoods are logical falsehoods, and others are merely metaphysical or categorial. So, the exclusion may occur *either* because a feature predicated is *inconsistent* with a feature had by the subject *or* because that feature is simply of such a nature as to be precluded from instantiation by a feature had by that subject *or* because it happens to be different from the set of properties in the set of properties holding of the subject. If I say that Theaetetus is pale, when he is dark, then I say what is incompatible with his being pale (though, again, no logical contradiction is involved in the *logos Theaetetus is pale and dark*).[20] Less obviously, if I say that *Theaetetus stands* while he sits, we can judge that what is predicated is different (*heteron*) because sitting and standing are not truly co-predicable. If I say, more bizarrely, that Theaetetus is a three-sided figure, then I say something excluded by some obtaining categorial feature of his, namely, that he is a human being, something categorially incompatible with his being an abstract entity. Neither of these last two facts is a consequence of logic, but each results from the freestanding relations obtaining between Forms with one another. In short, some Forms will not permit themselves to be coinstantiated together, while others marry happily. Their proclivities in these respects derive not (only) from the principles of logic that they, in common with everything else, must respect. Rather, Forms marry or repel one another due to their own intrinsic natures.

Crucial to the current discussion is the fact that Plato is advancing (2), and so ultimately (ii), as a point about the structure of Forms taken corporately, not taken atomistically. When he rejects (1) and (2) in favor of (3), he makes a series of related points: *some* Forms, of necessity, bear some relations to other Forms; some Forms, of necessity, do not bear certain relations to other Forms; all Forms, of necessity, bear some relations to *all* Forms; and all Forms, of necessity, do not bear certain relations to any Forms. This yields a rather more complex argument than we have seen so far for (ii), the claim that a necessary condition of the possibility of (**DC**) is that not-(**DC**). This more complex argument is one which, like the simple semantic theory that it replaces, is in fact semantic in character but, unlike that simple theory, does not rely upon any commitment to the claim that there is a one-to-one correspondence of predicates to Forms. Forms, according to the thesis of an intensional sense structure, *may* be meanings, but they need not be. What is central to the argument is that Forms bear freestanding, nonlogical relations to one another, both categorial and semantic in character. This is the thesis of their standing in an intensional sense structure.

As regards Plato's commitment to (ii), the claim that a necessary condition of the possibility of (**DC**) is that not-(**DC**), all that matters is that Forms are implicated in meaning, in the sense that their relations to one another make meaningful discourse possible. His thought is rather that for *logos* to be possible, whether in the exterior realm of language or in the interior realm of thought, freestanding *metaphysical and semantic relations* between Forms must obtain. Meanings which are determinates under a determinable must, when predicated, carry in their wakes the meanings which are superordinate to them: nothing can be said to be green without also being colored. Plausibly, no speaker or thinker has the ability to predicate greenness of grass who does not equally have the ability to predicate *being colored* of grass; indeed, anyone without that ability seems unable to think the more determinate *logos*. In the same vein, meanings preclude their contraries when predicated, when, that is, they have contraries: nothing said to be white all over can also be said at the same time to be black all over. Moreover, this same observation obtains whether the contraries in question are polar opposites or mere determinate features under a shared determinable: nothing said to be red all over can at the same time be said correctly to be green or black all over. Plato's suggestion is that neither language nor thought—*logos* in general—creates these forms of superordination or subordination but must instead adhere to them. Because they are given as conditions for the possibility of *logos*, and because their being given is rooted in the interweaving of Forms, all *logos* come to be for us because of an interweaving of Forms with one another.

To make his argument for (ii) explicit, then, if the discreteness contention (**DC**) is to avoid saying nothing, and so if it is to say anything determinate at all, it must be the case that freestanding intensional relations obtain between the semantic values of the predicates of our language; but if such relations obtain, then we may conclude that the discreteness contention is false—not as a matter of logical necessity, nor even as a matter of metaphysical necessity given directly. Rather, the prize of *logos* is won only because *logoi* reflect the intensional sense structure required for their possibility. It is in this way that those who pretend otherwise meet with an enemy from within their own household: theirs, like every domain of *logos*, is a household founded upon a freestanding, nonlogical metaphysical necessity, one these detractors are unable to deny. When they try to formulate a *logos* to the contrary, whether in speech or thought, they undermine their own campaign. This is why, then, Plato uses the caustically strong language in which he indulges: their view is the most ludicrous of all (*pantôn katagelastotata*; *Sph.* 252b8). They may as well be uttering the *logos* in speech *I am not speaking* or worse, thinking the *logos* in thought *I am not thinking*.

With this enhanced understanding of Plato's motivations, we may return, at last, to our initial problem. It has seemed to many that Plato's illustration (**I**) *Theaetetus sits* hardly illustrates the doctrine it was introduced to illustrate, namely, (**S**), that *logos* comes to be for us because of the interweaving of Forms with one another (259e4-6). We now see that his plural locution is fully intended: Plato's remark is no excusable overstatement; still less must we suppress features of (**S**) to make (**I**) conform to it. On the contrary, (**I**) illustrates (**S**) precisely because in every *logos*, more than one Form is in play. Every statement, whether voiced or silent within the soul, is assertoric; hence, every statement is truth evaluable. What makes truth evaluability even possible? How are statement-making *logoi* to be parceled into the true and the false? According to Plato, what makes *logos* in general possible is that determinate semantic content is possible; but determinate semantic content is in turn possible only if various necessary relations between semantic values obtain. Crucially, these necessary relations respect logical strictures but extend also to the freestanding relations between Forms, relations which involve their standing in nonextensional, nonlogical relations with one another: *logos* requires, beyond logic, the antecedent existence of an intensional sense structure, a structure of meanings whose own autonomous relations are required for the very possibility of meaningful thought and discourse. We might say, then, that when Forms provide meaning, they provide more meaning than even Cornford imagined: he was right that Forms *involve* meaningfulness; but the meanings Forms involve prove to be systemically enmeshed rather than simple and atomistic, because they are complex both in their internal decompositional sense structures and their noncontingent, nonlogical relations to one another.

6 Conclusions

Plato thinks that *logos* comes about because of the interweaving of Forms with one another. It was natural, almost unavoidable, to understand him initially just as Cornford had done, imagining him to be maintaining that Forms are meanings, with the result that woven meanings constitute the statements we make, aloud in speech and silently in thought. There emerge two mistakes in this natural understanding. First, we should not suppose, with the simple semantic theory, that Forms are meanings; surely, at the level of the lexical, they are not. Fortunately, if we attend to Plato's own examples in the *Sophist*, we see that he has not intended a doctrine so narrowly atomistic. Second, less obviously but also more importantly, we do not go about weaving Forms together ourselves, as if by an act of semantic stitching. For on this approach, without our efforts, Forms would fail to bear their antecedently given necessary relations. This is way Plato gives every indication that he regards the interweaving of Forms as given to us rather than as effected by us.

We would overreact badly to these realizations, however, if we corrected ourselves by concluding that Forms are altogether irrelevant to the semantic features of thought and language. Plato makes no such concession. On the contrary, he demands that those prepared to deny the interweaving of Forms justify their success in assertion. When they attempt to do so, Plato insists, the voice which refutes them is their own. Alas, they may not even take refuge in silence: their silent *logos* is *logos* all the same. When Plato says that *logos* comes about for us through the interweaving of Forms with one another, he means nothing less than that rationality itself requires the existence of antecedently given Forms standing in independent metaphysical and semantic relations to one another. Without Forms standing in such relations, we could not engage in rational discourse—we could not, indeed, be rational beings. So deep is Plato's attachment to (**S**): *logos* itself, he believes, comes to be for us because of the interweaving of Forms with one another (259e4-6).[21]

Notes

1. Plato uses the word in several different contexts, only sometimes in connection with Forms, language, truth, and falsity. Interestingly, the word is concentrated in Plato's later works, occurring five times in the *Politics* (though not in semantic contexts, perhaps 281a3 is relevant), three times in the *Sophist*, and once each in the *Laws*, *Theaetetus*, and *Symposium*. See esp. *Tht.* 202b5; *Sph.* 240c1, 259e6, 266c6. All translations are my own.
2. In Aristotle, talk of interweaving is often, though not always, corelated with the requisites of truth and falsity. In this sense, his dominant diction is closest to Plato's use of the term in the *Sophist*. Cf. *Cat* a16-18, 1b25, 2a6-9, 13b10-13; *Int* 21a5; *Top* 113a1, 147a33, 153a30, 154b16; *An* 428a26-29, 432a11; *Met* 1027b30, 1065a22.
3. The literature on *Sophist* 259e4-6 is extensive. In addition to Ackrill's (1955) seminal article, some especially useful discussions are Cornford (1960), Ritter (1910), Peck (1962), Lorenz and Mittlestrass (1966), Heinaman (1982), and Silverman (2002). Guthrie (1978, pp. 161–62) provides a succinct overview of some of this literature, without attempting to advance the issue it engages.

4. Ackrill (1955/1997, pp. 75–78) appropriately makes much of this point, not least by connecting it in an illuminating way with Aristotle's use of the same locution in *Met* IV.4.
5. Eurycles was a ventriloquist, mentioned by Aristophanes (*Wasps* 1015–20), whose name was given eponymously to ventriloquists in general. In some contexts, he was represented as being able to project his voice into the bellies of others, so that (evidently) he could represent them as refuting themselves by a second voice from within even as they spoke; in others, including scholiasts on Aristophanes, he is also represented as having prophetic powers. See Musurillo (1974, p. 237)
6. This suggestion runs directly counter to the deflationary treatment offered by Heinaman (1983), who thinks that scholars who ascribe theses concerning *meaning* to Plato are misguided: "I believe that such an interpretation is too optimistic and that Plato's view is less sophisticated than scholars would like to admit" (p. 175). If the considerations of the current chapter are apt, then scholars have been, on the contrary, rather too shy when characterizing the stridency of Plato's view.
7. Ackrill (1955/1997) crystallizes this tradition in an exceptionally clear article, first reviewing and criticizing the main proponents of the tradition before him, but then extending it in a fruitful direction. I suggest below in Sect. 4 that however far it is extended, this tradition leaves some important aspects of Plato's conception of the relation between Forms and *logos* unexplored.
8. I use the phrase "intensional sense structure" to characterize the semantic theory proposed by Katz (1990); its precise application to the *Sophist* I make clear in Sect. 4. Very roughly, for now, an intensional sense structure, in Katz's contemporary Platonist philosophy of language, is a system of intensions with a decompositional structure in virtue of which individual senses bear determinate, noncontingent, nonlogical relations of superordination, subordination, and categorial compatibility and incompatibility to one another. Katz contends:

    We postulate that the sense of the syntactic simple 'woman' is complex, consisting of the sense of 'human', the sense of 'adult', and the sense of 'female'. On this postulation of decompositional sense structure for 'woman', the redundancy of 'a woman who is female' is immediately accounted for with the same intuitively obvious notion of redundancy that accounts for the redundancy of expressions like 'a woman who is a woman'. This case is exactly parallel to that in which Chomsky postulated an underlying syntactic structure in order to extend the account of subject and direct-object relation in sentences like 'John loves Mary' to sentences like 'John is easy to please' and 'John is eager to please'. By parity of reasoning, we postulate an underlying semantic structure in order to extend the account of redundancy in expressions like 'woman who is a woman' to expressions like 'woman who is female'. Decompositional postulations require a grammatical locus for the unobservable complex senses they postulate; so we are led to taking the step of positing that grammatical structure contains an underlying level of sense structure. (pp. 64–65)

    Further, says Katz: "Semantic properties and relations like analyticity and analytic entailment, which also depend on sense containment, can be accounted for on the same decompositional hypotheses used to account for redundancy and superordination" (p. 65).
9. Plato's diction in this important passage is somewhat peculiar: *to dialuein*, without an accompanying preposition, tends to mean simply *disintegrate, dissolve*, or *destroy* (*Phd.* 80b4, 80c4, 88b1; *Rep.* 609c2; *Ti.* 68d5; *Phil.* 32a2; *La.* 201c3), though it is also used, punningly, in the *Sophist* at 252d4 by Theaetetus to mean *solve*. Two especially helpful passages are *Gorgias* 524b3-4, where it means *separation* or *disentangling* (*scil.* of the soul and body, which are said to continue to exist once separated), and *Statesman* 281a6, where *dialutikê* is introduced as an antonym of interweaving (*sumplokê*), which is in turn said to be a kind of intertwining: *to men tês huphês sumplokê tis esti pou* (*Pol* 281a3). Taking those references together with the appearance of the preposition *from* (*apo*) in the current passage, it seems reasonable to understand Plato as intending something in the neighborhood of *unbraiding* or *untwining* by *dialuein*. This suggestion gains some further confirmation from the use of *apochôrizein* at 259c1.

10. Heinaman (1983, p. 176) asks: "So the first problem is this: does communion of Forms explain the truth or the meaningfulness of statements?" He answers (p. 185): "I conclude that the communion of Forms accounts for the truth of statements, not their meaning. And so the suggestion that the doctrine of communion of Forms lays down conditions for meaning rather than truth must be rejected."
11. Cornford (1960, p. 303 n. 1) comments on what he takes to be a shift in the meaning of *logos*, from "discourse" to "statement" in the course of this discussion. There seems to be no reason, however, to detect any such shift: given that *logos* at 262d14 is taken to illustrate its usage at 259e6, it must take the same meaning there; and given that there is no indication that Plato has shifted his diction in the intervening passage, there is for the same reason no reason to suppose that he has shifted his meaning and then shifted it back again.
12. Ackrill (1955/1997, p. 78): "These few remarks must suffice to indicate how a *sumplokê eidôn* is presupposed by any and every statement, including those about Theaetetus. Plato admittedly does not argue the point in connection with the Theaetetus examples, which are used in the discussion of a different topic. Still, it is a related topic, since it does involve the incompatibility of two predicates."
13. It is possible, as many scholars have suggested, that Antisthenes is to be counted among the late learners ridiculed at *Sophist* 251c. In fact, however, we cannot be secure about that judgment. See Cornford (1960, p. 254). In the present context, let us introduce him as a foil.
14. Cf. note 1.
15. For a judicious review of the relevant evidence, see Crivelli (2008). In a similar vein, most philosophers have been inclined to deny that predicates can be identified with properties. For a clear and useful, if ultimately unpersuasive, discussion of the case against identification, see Mellor (1997). Mellor argues: ". . . universals are not to be understood semantically as meanings, references, or extension of predicates. This does not of course prevent there being obvious connections between universals and predicates. For example, to every property there obviously corresponds a possible predicate applying to all and only particular with that property. But it does not follow from this, and is not obviously true, that to every actual predicate there corresponds a single property or relation" (p. 255).
16. See note 1.
17. See Moravcsik (1962), Keyt (1973), Frede (1967), Brown (2008), and Crivelli (1993) and (2008).
18. Brown (2008). Brown follows Keyt (1973) in referring to one standard account as the "Oxford Account" and a second as the "Incompatibility Account." Briefly, according to the Oxford Account, the false *logos* "Theaetetus flies," like every other statement composed of a noun and a verb, is false when *the verb* signifies everything that is *other* (*heteron*) than what Theaetetus *is* (i.e., everything other than what obtains with respect to Theaetetus). The Incompatibility Account maintains that this same *logos* is false when what *the verb* signifies is *incompatible* with what Theaetetus is (i.e., it signifies something incompatible with what obtains with respect to Theaetetus). The Incompatibility Account supposes without warrant that what is different or other (*heteron*) is positively incompatible. The Oxford Account does not suffer that shortcoming but implicitly and without warrant supplies a universal quantifier by suggesting, as it must, that the verb signifies *everything* that is other. Brown's limited account makes sense of the examples, which involve incompatibilities (or, as I would prefer, Forms whose natures necessarily preclude co-instantiation) while not introducing the textually unwarranted universal quantifier.
19. This much remains correct about the "Extensional Account," as it is called by Crivelli (2008), that is, the account offered by Crivelli (1993), namely, that a statement composed of a noun and a verb is false when "the object signified by [the noun] is other than everything of which the action signified by [the verb] holds." This is correct as far as it goes, though, according to the interpretation offered in the text, it does not go the full distance alone. In general, the alternatives advanced as mutually exclusive in the literature cited in notes 28 and 29 are often, in fact, not mutually exclusive but rather different forms of difference.

20. To be clear, there is a contradiction in the triad: (i) Theaetetus is pale; (ii) Theaetetus is swarthy; and (iii) Nothing is such as to be pale and swarthy (i.e., all over). Note, however, that this merely relocates the question of incompatibility to (iii), which is not a logical contradiction but a metaphysical incompatibility given rise by the natures of pallor and swarthiness.
21. I am grateful to Dominic Bailey, Rachel Singpurwalla, and Fred Miller for comments on an earlier draft of this essay. I am also deeply indebted to Paolo Crivelli for his generous and instructive discussions concerning the topics it engages.

Bibliography

Ackrill, J.L. 1971 (reprint). Plato and the copula: *Sophist* 251–59. In *Plato 1: metaphysics and epistemology*, ed. Gregory Vlastos, 210–222. Garden City: Anchor Books.
Ackrill, J.L. 1997. *Essays on Plato and Aristotle*. Oxford: Clarendon.
Bostock, David. 1984. Plato on 'is-not' (*Sophist* 254–9). *Oxford Studies in Ancient Philosophy* 2: 89–119.
Brown, Lesley. 1999. Being in the *Sophist*: A syntactical enquiry. In *Plato 1*, ed. Gail Fine, 455–478. New York: Oxford University Press.
Brown, Lesley. 2008. The *Sophist* on statements, predication, and falsehood. In *The Oxford Handbook of Plato*, ed. Gail Fine, 437–462. New York: Oxford University Press.
Brown, Lesley. 2010. Definition and division in the *Sophist*. In *Definition in Greek philosophy*, ed. David Charles, 151–171. New York: Oxford University Press.
Burnyeat, Myles. 2002. Plato on how not to speak about not-being. In *Le Style de la pensée*, ed. Monique Canto-Sperber and Pierre Pellegrin, 40–65. Paris: Belles Lettres.
Cornford, Francis M. 1960 (reprint). *Plato's theory of knowledge*. London: Routledge and Kegan Paul.
Crivelli, Paolo. 1993. Plato's *Sophist* and semantic fragmentation. *Archiv für Geschichte der Philosophie* 75: 71–77.
Crivelli, Paolo. 1998. Allodoxia. *Archiv für Geschichte der Philosophie* 80: 1–29.
Crivelli, Paolo. 2008. Plato's philosophy of language. In *The Oxford handbook of Plato*, ed. Gail Fine, 217–242. New York: Oxford University Press.
Crivelli, Paolo. 2011. *Plato's account of falsehood: A study of the Sophist*. Cambridge: Cambridge University Press.
Denyer, Nicholas. 1991. *Language, thought and falsehood in ancient Greek philosophy*. New York: Routledge.
Denyer, Nicholas. 2010. Critical notice of Richard Gaskin, *The unity of the proposition*. *Australasian Journal of Philosophy* 88: 173–179.
Ferejohn, Michael. 1989. Plato and Aristotle on negative predication and semantic fragmentation. *Archiv für Geschichte der Philosophie* 71: 257–282.
Frede, Michael. 1967. *Prädikation und Existenzaussage*. Göttingen: Vandenhoeck und Ruprecht.
Frede, Michael. 1990. Plato's *Sophist* on false statements. In *The Cambridge companion to Plato*, ed. Richard Kraut, 397–424. New York: Cambridge University Press.
Frede, Michael. 1996. The literary form of the *Sophist*. In *form and argument in late Plato*, ed. C. Gill and M.M. McCabe, 135–151. Oxford: Clarendon.
Gaskin, Richard. 2008. *The unity of the proposition*. New York: Oxford University Press.
Guthrie, W.K.C. 1978. *A history of Greek philosophy vol. 5: The later Plato and the academy*. Cambridge: Cambridge University Press.
Heinaman, Robert. 1982–1983. Communion of forms. *Proceedings of the Aristotelian Society* 83: 175–190.
Katz, Jerrold. 1990. *The metaphysics of meaning*. Cambridge, MA: Massachusetts Institute of Technology.

Keyt, David. 1969. Plato's paradox that the immutable is unknowable. *Philosophical Quarterly* 19: 1–14.
Keyt, David. 1973. Plato on falsity. In *Exegesis and argument*, ed. E. Lee, A. Mourelatos, and R.M. Rorty, 285–305. Assen: K. Van Gorcum & Company B. V.
Kneale, William, and Martha Kneale. 1962. *The development of logic*. New York: Oxford University Press.
Lewis, Frank. 1975. Did Plato discover the *estin* of identity? *California Studies in Classical Antiquity* 8: 113–142.
Lorenz, K., and J. Mittlestrass. 1966. Theaitetos flieft, zur Theorie wahrer und falscher Sägtze bei Platon. *Archiv für Geschichte der Philosophie* 48: 113–153.
Mates, Benson. 1979. Identity and predication in Plato. *Phronesis* 24(3): 211–229.
McDowell, John. 1982. Falsehood and not-being in Plato's *Sophist*. In *Language and Logos*, ed. Malcolm Schofield and Martha Nussbaum, 115–134. New York: Cambridge University Press.
Mellor, D.H. 1997. Properties and predicates. In *Properties*, ed. D.H. Mellor and Alex Oliver, 255–269. New York: Oxford University Press.
Moravcsik, Julius M.E. 1962. Being and meaning in the *Sophist*. *Acta Philosophica Fennica* 14: 23–78.
Musurillo, Herbert. 1974. The problem of lying and deceit and the two voices of Euripides, *Hippolytus* 925–31. *Transactions of the American Philological Association* 104: 231–238.
Peck, A.L. 1962. Plato's "Sophist": The *sumplokê tôn eidôn*. *Phronesis* 7: 46–66.
Ritter, Constantin. 1910. *Neue Untersuchungen über Platon*. Munich: Ayer Co Publishing.
Ross, W.D. 1951. *Plato's theory of Ideas*. Oxford: Clarendon.
Silverman, Alan. 2002. *The dialectic of essence: A study of Plato's Metaphysics*. Princeton: Princeton University Press.
Szaif, Jan. 1996. *Platons Begriff der Wahrheit*. Munich: Karl Alber.
Vlastos, Gregory. 1981. An ambiguity in the *Sophist*. In *Platonic studies*, ed. Gregory Vlastos, 270–322. Princeton: Princeton University Press.

Accidental Beings in Aristotle's Ontology

S. Marc Cohen

Aristotle, as is well known, proposes an ontology of substances and accidents. Substances, such as a man or a horse, are the basic, independent entities in this ontology; accidents are the dependent entities that inhere in the substances. Accidents are usually thought of as the properties[1] of substances, and on the whole this is a reasonably accurate way to think about them. A horse, for example, is a substance, and pallor, perhaps, is a property (an "accident") of that horse. But that is not the end of Aristotle's story. For in addition to the substance and the property, he thinks that there is something else—an accidental being, I will call it—that is intermediate between the substance and the property. In the case of our example, Aristotle would use the expression "the pale horse," or sometimes, without specifying which substance enters into the compound, simply "the pale [thing]" to pick out this intermediate entity.

In the interests of maintaining a deflationary ontology, it would be tempting to suppose that the expression "the pale [thing]" does not pick out something distinct from both the substance, the horse, and its property, pallor; it simply picks out the substance, albeit not in the same way that the simple expression "the horse" does.

I am grateful to David Keyt for graciously inviting me to contribute this essay to the present volume. David was the Chair of the Department of Philosophy at the University of Washington when I was hired there in 1973, and he has remained my treasured colleague ever since. During these nearly forty years, we have read and commented on one another's work, and spent one delightful summer co-authoring a paper.

An earlier version of this essay was presented at the April 2012 meeting of the Pacific Division of the American Philosophical Association as part of a special memorial session celebrating the work of Gareth B. Matthews. Gary and I were friends and colleagues for over forty years, and my debts to him, both personal and intellectual, are enormous. His influence will be evident throughout this essay; I dedicate it to his memory.

S.M. Cohen (✉)
Department of Philosophy, University of Washington, Seattle, WA 98195, USA
e-mail: smcohen@uw.edu

But, as we will see, this is not the approach that Aristotle takes. For him, accidental beings are neither substances nor properties. They are typically picked out by definite descriptions such as "the F" or "the FG" where "F" is replaced by an adjective and "G" is replaced by a noun, or by noun phrases of the form "Fa," where "F" is replaced by an adjective and "a" is replaced by a proper name. Examples are *the pale*, *the musical man*, and *seated Socrates*.

Accidental beings have been noted in the literature for some time now, the *locus classicus* being Matthews (1982). Here is what he said about them:

> Aristotle's picture of an accidental unity is that of an ephemeral object—an object whose very existence rests on the accidental presence, or compresence, of some feature, or features, in a substance. (p. 224)

Such objects are ephemeral because they last only as long as their components are united, only as long as the accident in question is present in its host substance. The musical man did not come into existence until the man became musical; seated Socrates ceased to exist when Socrates stood up.

Aristotle is very clear about this. In discussing the topic of coming-to-be in the *Physics*, he considers the case in which a man becomes musical. Here is what he says:

> the man survives, but the unmusical does not survive, *nor does the compound of the two, namely the unmusical man*. (190a19-21, emphasis mine)[2]

This compound, the unmusical man, is something that goes out of existence when the man becomes musical and comes into existence when the man loses his musicality. The man and the unmusical man are clearly distinct entities, on Aristotle's view, since they have distinct identity and persistence conditions.

In Matthews' view, Aristotle's positing of these ephemeral objects is a concomitant of his understanding of the semantics of definite descriptions, an understanding that is very different from a more recent, basically neo-Fregean, one. On the more recent view, the expressions "Socrates" and "Socrates seated" have the same reference, but different senses. That is, these expressions pick out one and the same man, although they do so in different ways. As it is sometimes put, Socrates and Socrates seated are the same man under different descriptions. But on Aristotle's understanding, the difference is not just semantic but ontological. For he takes pains to point out (*Top* I.7 103a23-31) that Socrates and Socrates seated are only the same in a sense and are strictly speaking not the same at all.

No doubt it was this feature of accidental unities such as *seated Socrates* and *the musical man* that led Matthews to dub them "kooky objects." For if seated Socrates is not just Socrates under another description, then seated Socrates must be a very kooky object indeed, one whose identity conditions do not correspond to those of any "straight" object that we are inclined to recognize.

The fact that such objects are kooky did not lead Matthews to despise them, however. On the contrary, he shows how Aristotle is able to appeal to them in dealing with puzzles that we characterize today as involving substitutivity of co-referential expressions in opaque contexts (*SE* 24 179a33-b22). The puzzle is this: How can it be that one knows Coriscus but does not know the masked man, when Coriscus is the masked man? Aristotle's answer is, in effect, that Coriscus and the masked man are only accidentally the same and are not strictly speaking identical. Aristotle thus accepts the principle of substitutivity of co-referential expressions but refuses to allow that the expressions "Coriscus" and "the masked man" are co-referential. Rather, they denote distinct objects that are only accidentally the same. Aristotle is quite explicit about accepting the principle of indiscernibility of identicals only in this strengthened form: "[O]nly to things that are undifferentiated in substance and one in being is it generally agreed that all the same attributes belong" (*SE* 24 179a37).[3] Coriscus and the masked man may be one in number, but they are not one in being, and so we cannot infer that they have all the same attributes, especially the attribute of being known by you.[4]

In previous writings (e.g., Cohen 2008) on this topic, I have adopted Matthews' terminology, referring to such entities as *the pale man* or *seated Socrates* as kooky objects. But in this essay, I have retreated to the less pejorative-sounding "accidental beings." For I want to make two claims about accidental beings that I hope will make them seem somewhat more attractive, or at least not as strange as they might at first appear to be. First, they can help us resolve a long-standing dispute in Aristotelian scholarship, and, second, they can be located within a more familiar latter-day conceptual scheme.

The long-standing dispute concerns the nature of the so-called non-substantial individuals of Aristotle's *Categories*. As you will recall, in that work Aristotle posits a number of basic categories, each of which is populated by both universals and particulars (or individuals[5]). Just as the category of substance contains both universals, such as *man* and *animal*, and particulars, such as *this man* (*ho tis anthrôpos*), so the category of quality contains both universals, such as *pallor* and *color*, as well as particulars, such as *this pale* (*to ti leukon*). The status of these particulars or individuals in the non-substance categories has been a matter of great dispute over the years. There have been basically two lines of interpretation.[6] The traditional interpretation holds that these entities are indeed particulars, that is to say, non-shareable, non-repeatable entities peculiar to the particular substances in which they inhere. A minority interpretation, championed by Owen (1965), holds that these entities are individuals only in the sense that they are the lowest-level members of their categories, but that they are shareable and, in that sense, universal. On the traditional interpretation, the expression *to ti leukon* picks out a *trope*, that is, a particular bit of pallor that is peculiar to a particular substance, say, Socrates; on Owen's interpretation, it picks out a determinate pale shade that may well turn up elsewhere in the world than on the surface of Socrates.

The literature on this dispute is enormous, and I have no intention of trying to summarize it here. Rather, what I hope to show is that each side of the dispute is partly right and partly wrong. The trope theorists are right to maintain that non-substantial individuals are not universals but wrong about what it is that makes them particulars. The Owen side is right to say that Aristotle allows universals to inhere in particular substances but wrong to suppose that this requires non-substantial individuals to be universals.

I am going to assume that the traditional interpretation is correct at least in holding that individual non-substances are indeed non-repeatable particulars.[7] This alone makes it clear that they are at the very least ancestors or close cousins of the accidental beings under discussion, if not the very same entities.[8] The question is what light this sheds on the *Categories*.

The ontology of the *Categories* exhibits two different kinds of ontological dependence: the dependence of universals on particulars and the dependence of non-substances on substances. In Aristotle's terminology, the former is the dependence that things *said of a subject* have on the subjects of which they are said; the latter is the dependence that things *in a subject* have on the subjects in which they inhere.

Individual substances, or primary substances (*prôtai ousiai*), as Aristotle calls them, are the ultimate foundational entities in the ontological scheme—they underlie both substance universals (which Aristotle calls secondary substances) and non-substance universals. But they do so in different ways. The dependence of secondary substances on primary substances is immediate: horse exists because there are horses, not because of the existence of something else that in turn depends on the existence of horses. But the dependence of universal non-substances on primary substances is mediated. The particulars on which the universal, pallor, immediately depends are not particular substances, but particulars in the category of quality, such as *this pale (thing)*, each of which in turn depends on the substance in which it inheres, say, this particular horse.

There are thus two steps to the dependence of non-substance universals on primary substances, which is what makes them doubly dependent.[9] First, there is the dependence of universals on particulars, and, second, there is the dependence of non-substances on substances. Particular non-substances thus play an intermediate role in the ontological scheme of the *Categories*; universal non-substances (i.e., property universals) are dependent on them, and they in turn depend on particular substances.

This intermediate role that particular non-substances play in the *Categories* is precisely the role that Aristotle assigns to accidental beings in the *Metaphysics*.[10] In *Metaphysics* Z.1, after claiming that substances are the primary beings, Aristotle goes on as follows:

> And all other things are said to be because they are, some of them, quantities of that which is in this primary sense, others qualities of it, others affections of it, and others some other determination of it. And so one might even raise a question about *walking (to badidzein)*, *being healthy*, or *sitting*, whether each of these things is existent, and similarly in any other case of this sort; for none of them is either self-subsistent or capable of being separated from substance, but rather, if anything, it is that which walks (*to badidzon*) or sits or is healthy that is an existent thing. Now these are seen to be more real because there is something definite which underlies them (i.e., the substance or individual) .... (1028a18-28)[11]

Notice that in addition to the property of walking (*to badidzein*) and the substance (e.g., Coriscus) that does the walking, there is an intermediate entity, *the walker* ("the walking [thing]," *to badidzon*). That there are three entities here and not just two is made clear by the fact that Aristotle takes pains to point out that *the walker* is "more real"[12] than the property of walking because of the substance (say,

Coriscus) that underlies it. The existence of the property of walking is dependent on the existence of substances, but the dependence is not immediate. Rather, there is such a thing as walking because there are walkers, and there are walkers because there are substances "underlying" them. An accidental being, such as a walker, cannot exist unless there is a substance (a man or a horse) with which it coincides. Notice that the relation between the accidental being and its "parent" substance (as Frank Lewis calls it) is coincidence, not identity. The walker is not identical to the substance that underlies it; rather, it coincides with that substance.

What is the point of introducing these intermediate entities? Why is the dependence of a non-substance such as walking on substances mediated by accidental beings? Why can't walking depend on substances right from the start? The answer seems to me to be the following: walking is a universal, and (as the *Categories* makes clear) universals depend on there being particulars that they are said of. The particulars that the universal, walking, is said of are items in the same category as walking. Hence, those particulars are not substances (for the relation between walking and the substances which walk is that of being *in a subject*, not being *said of a subject*). The intermediate entity is thus a particular case of walking, which in turn owes its existence to the particular substance that is engaged in that particular case of walking.

Notice that it is the particular substance, not the property, that gives the intermediate entity its particularity. No matter how closely Callias manages to approximate the walk of Socrates, the walk he produces will still be the walk of Callias, not the walk of Socrates. The two may walk the same way, but they cannot be the same walker. The point will be important below when we turn to the non-substantial individuals of the *Categories*.

We can encapsulate the aforementioned levels of dependence involving accidental beings by means of the following two schemata. Where F is a predicate from a non-substance category, and F things are accidental beings:

- Schema 1: F-ness exists because F things exist.
- Schema 2: F things exist because some substances are F.[13]

When we place these two schemata side by side, however, there appears to be an important difference between them. For the dependence in Schema 2 (the dependence of accidental beings on substances) is asymmetrical; an accidental being (an F thing) cannot exist apart from the substance it coincides with, but the substance does not similarly depend on its coinciding with that F thing. However, it seems doubtful that the dependence in Schema 1 (the dependence of properties on accidental beings) can be similarly asymmetrical. Rather, the dependence here seems to be two-way. Just as F-ness cannot exist unless there are F things, neither can F things exist unless F-ness does. Walking cannot exist unless there are walkers, but walkers cannot exist unless walking is what some substances do.

It thus appears that in explaining the existence of accidental beings, we must appeal to the very universals whose existence the accidental beings are supposed to explain. This lack of asymmetry in Schema 1 seems to make the entire explanatory framework hopelessly circular.

That the dependence claimed in Schema 1 should be reversed also seems to be supported by Frank Lewis' account of what he calls "accidental compounds." Lewis (1985, p. 85) claims that accidental compounds (such as *Socrates seated* or *the generous one*) "are constructed out of individual substances and accidents." An accidental compound, Lewis tells us, "is an entity of the form $a+\varphi$, where a is an individual substance, φ is an accident of a, and the '+' notation introduces the primitive operation of compounding" (ibid.). And if accidents (i.e., properties) are among the components of accidental compounds, then, contrary to Schema 1, it would seem that accidents are prior to those compounds since (as Aristotle insists[14]) a compound is always posterior to its components.

We are now faced with two serious difficulties. For not only does Aristotle's effort to ground the existence of properties on that of substances via intermediate accidental beings seem doomed to failure, but my account of accidental beings as playing the same explanatory role as the non-substantial individuals of the *Categories* seems equally flawed. For it is clear that the non-substantial individuals of the *Categories* do play the grounding role that the accidental beings of the *Physics* and *Metaphysics* now seem to be incapable of.

Fortunately, there is a solution to these difficulties, for they both depend on a conflation of two different notions of priority and dependence that Aristotle takes pains to distinguish.[15] On the one hand, there is priority in formula or definition (*kata logon*); in this sense, the parts of a definition are prior to the definition constructed out of those parts. On the other hand, there is priority in nature and substance (*kata phusin kai ousian*); in this sense, one thing is prior to another if it is capable of existing independent of the other. Here is how Aristotle applies the distinction:

> [I]n formula ... the accident is prior to the whole, e.g. musical to musical man, for the formula cannot exist as a whole without the part; yet musicalness cannot exist unless there is someone who is musical. (*Met* Δ.11 1018b34-36)

Clearly, the priority that Schema 1 requires of accidental beings is priority in substance, not priority in definition. Indeed, Aristotle himself marks this distinction with the very example we have been discussing:

> [N]ot all things which are prior in definition (*tôi logôi*) are prior in substance (*têi ousiai*). For those things are prior in substance which when separated from other things continue to exist, but those are prior in definition out of whose definitions the definitions of other things are compounded ... white is prior to the white man in definition, but not in substance. For it cannot exist separately, but is always along with the compound thing; and by the compound thing I mean the white man. (*Met* M.2 1077b1ff)

In the relevant sense of priority, then, an accidental being, Lewis' $a+\varphi$, is prior to its component accident, φ. So by Aristotle's lights, at least, the charge of circularity can be avoided.

This is all well and good, but one may still be left with a feeling of bewilderment. It is easy to see why accidents are prior in definition to the accidental compounds of which they are components but harder to see how priority in substance is supposed to work. It is easy to see how the existence of accidents depends on that of accidental beings since, according to Aristotle, accidents cannot go uninstantiated. But how is the required asymmetry possible? Why doesn't the existence of accidental beings similarly depend on that of accidents? How can the white horse exist unless whiteness does too?

This question actually lies at the heart of the dispute between Aristotelian and Platonic metaphysics, and for that reason is too large for a thorough discussion within the confines of this essay. But Aristotle gives us a few clues in the remainder of the passage just quoted:

> [I]t is plain that neither is the result of abstraction prior nor that which is produced by adding posterior; for it is by adding to the white that we speak of the white man. (1077b10-11)

Aristotle characterizes the accident "white" as "the result of abstraction," as he also characterizes numbers, lines, and planes. There is thus a sense in which we must first have the physical objects from which we abstract these things before we can do the abstracting. Whatever that sense is, it is the sense in which substances and accidental beings are prior to and independent of the accidents we abstract from them.

Aristotle seems to think that if accidents were not in this sense posterior to accidental compounds, they would be available as components from which to construct those compounds. At any rate, a few lines earlier he makes the corresponding point about these geometrical examples:

> But how can lines be substances? Neither as a form or shape, as the soul perhaps is, nor as matter, like body; for we have no experience of anything that can be put together out of lines or planes or points, while if these had been a sort of material substance, we should have observed things which could be put together out of them. (1077a32-6)

A pale horse is no more capable of existing in a world in which pallor does not exist than a cube is capable of existing in a world in which there are no squares, but that does not deprive the compounds of their ontological priority. Just as cubes are not constructed out of squares, neither is a pale horse constructed out of pallor. A pale horse may be analyzed, à la Lewis, as this horse + pallor, but it is not constructed out of those ingredients. The accident is only a definitional, but not an ontological, constituent of the compound. The accidental compound is ontologically prior to the accident that is one of its (definitional) constituents. This is precisely what makes Lewis' formulation, "accidental compounds are constructed out of individual substances and accidents," so misleading.

I hope that I have by now made it at least plausible to think that accidental beings should be assimilated to, or are at the very least close cousins of, the non-substantial individuals of the *Categories*. But one may still resist this assimilation on the grounds that these two kinds of beings are categorially different. Non-substances, one might say, are properties, or property-like entities, whereas accidental beings are not properties—they are things that *have* properties. The accidental being, the pale horse, has the property of being pale, whereas the non-substantial individual, this pale, does not have the property of being pale—it *is* that property.

There are two problems with this objection. First, it assumes that because a universal in the category of quality, such as *pallor*, is a property, so too an individual in that category, such as *this pale*, must be a property. What is wrong with this assumption is that it takes for granted that we have some independent idea of what such an individual, non-repeatable, non-shareable property could possibly be. Second, the objection assumes that we can learn everything we need to know about the *Categories* by reading the on substance and quality and can pretty much ignore the rest. However common this assumption may be, it is still a mistake. If we look at some of the other categories, non-substantial individuals start looking a lot more like accidental beings.

Consider the category of relatives (*ta pros ti*). It includes such items as a master, a slave, the wing of a bird, the rudder of a boat, a head, and a hand. Presumably fathers and daughters also go into this category. But these do not seem to be dependent entities in the same way that qualities are. It is tempting to say that what Aristotle calls relatives are actually substances, or at least parts of substances, and not ontologically dependent entities. But if we want to get Aristotle right, we should resist this temptation, for he insists that they are not substances. Socrates the man is a substance, but Socrates the father is not.

Notice how smoothly things go, however, if we think of relatives as accidental beings. Socrates the man and Socrates the father are distinct, but coincidental, objects. The first is a substance, the second is a relative. The substance can exist without the relative that depends on it, but not conversely. A father cannot exist if the man that he inheres in does not exist. On this reading the items in the category of *ta pros ti* are not *relations*, like fatherhood or being larger than, but the things that *instantiate* these relations. That is, Aristotle's relatives are *things related*—things that are fathers or that are larger than something. These things are not substances; rather, they are the accidental beings that coincide with substances.

Consider another non-substance category, that of place. Which things belong to this category? Places, one might at first suppose. But this cannot be correct, for it is not plausible to maintain that a place is incapable of existing apart from the substance that is located at it. Coriscus is in the Lyceum, and he can exist apart from the Lyceum. But surely the Lyceum also can exist apart from Coriscus, indeed, apart from there being any substances at all located there. A more careful look at the example Aristotle gives us when he introduces this category (2a1), however, suggests a different story. For he lists *in the Lyceum* (rather than the Lyceum itself) as an example of an item in this category. This suggests that the members of the category of place are not *places* but *things placed*. (It is actually a misnomer to name this the category of "place"; Aristotle in fact calls it the category of *where*.) So an example of something in this category might be *the one in the Lyceum*. This, of course, is something whose location is its essence, but which happens to coincide with Coriscus for as long as the latter is in the Lyceum, and whose existence depends on that of Coriscus. Once again, the best interpretation of what Aristotle has in mind as an individual in a non-substance category is that it is an accidental being.

What are the consequences of this identification, or near identification, between accidental beings and non-substance individuals for our interpretation of the

Categories? As I mentioned earlier, the latter have been traditionally understood to be *tropes*, that is, particular instances or bits of properties or relations. One of the main objections to this interpretation has been the philosophical unattractiveness of tropes themselves, as it is difficult to conceive of what a bit of pallor or fatherhood might be. Trope theorists seem to be willing to live with this difficulty as part of the price of avoiding any commitment to universals.

But Aristotle himself had no such hostility to universals. In this respect, my understanding of accidental beings is the same as Frank Lewis': an accidental compound is an entity of the form $a+\varphi$, where a is an individual substance and φ is a universal non-substance. The particularity of $a+\varphi$ comes from a, not from φ. For that reason it would be better to say that Aristotle's non-substance individuals are particular exemplifications of properties rather than tropes.[16] For what makes these things individuals, or particulars, is that they inhere in particulars. But if it is the particularity of Socrates that makes the pallor of Socrates a particular, then the key ingredients in this entity, the pallor of Socrates, will just be pallor (a universal) and Socrates. The particularity of the non-substantial particular is contributed by its component substance. What makes the pallor of Socrates distinct from the pallor of Callias, even though the two are indistinguishable in color, is that Socrates and Callias are distinct substances. So the pallor of Socrates is neither a universal nor a trope, but the particular exemplification of pallor in Socrates.

Actually, there is one further complication, and that will lead, as a kind of bonus, to a brief answer to my second question: Do these curious entities, accidental beings, turn up at all in a more familiar conceptual framework?

The additional complication is time. For typically a substance will have an accidental property for only a short time, or at one time but not at another. So there are really three key ingredients: a substance, a property, and a time (or a period of time). My proposal is that these three things provide the identity conditions for accidental beings. More formally, we need to revise Lewis' formulation slightly: an accidental being is an entity of the form $a+\varphi+t$, where a is an individual substance, φ is an accident, and t is a time.

Immediately, accidental beings start looking more familiar—they start looking like events. If we follow the lead of Kim (1983, 1991) and Bennett (1988), we will say that "an event is the instantiation, at a time, of a property by a substance" (Bennett 1988, p. 88). An event is thus a particular that has a substance, a property, and a time as its constituents. The substance, property, and time in question are essential to its being the very event that it is. The lunar eclipse that occurred in North America on February 20, 2008, for example, has the moon as an essential ingredient. Had it been the sun that was eclipsed on that day, or had the moon been eclipsed a day earlier, that would have been a different eclipse.

This may at first not seem to work for accidental beings such as *the red thing* that comes into existence when a lobster is cooked. For a red thing does not seem to be an event. But consider. The red thing exists for precisely as long as its underlying substance—the lobster—is red. It is thus something whose existence begins when the lobster turns red and ends when the lobster either ceases to be red or ceases to exist. That is, its career coincides exactly with the lobster's period of being red. It thus has as its constituents a substance (the lobster), a property (redness), and a period of time. These are precisely the constituents of an event. The only apparent difference is that its temporal constituent is a stretch of time rather than a point. But even that is only apparent since most events last for a stretch of time, however short. So an accidental being, such as a red thing, has a strikingly event-like structure. Aristotle himself thought of a color as either a state (*hexis*) or a condition (*diathesis*), depending on how long lasting and firmly established it is.[17] But states and conditions are themselves event-like entities.[18] So the red thing in question is the exemplification of redness by the lobster for the duration of its being red.

In conclusion, when non-substantial individuals and accidental beings are conceived of as particular states of substances or events involving substances, they fit perfectly into Aristotle's program of showing how and why primary substances are the basic realities, the things on which ultimately everything else depends. For a universal to exist, there must be instances of it: horse does not exist unless there are horses; pallor does not exist unless there are pale things. Where the universal is in the category of substance, states and events are not yet part of this picture of ontological dependence. There is no need to introduce "horse-things" into the ontology since a horse-thing would just be a horse, an individual in the category of substance. But for universals in non-substance categories, the situation is different. A universal in the category of quality, such as pallor, cannot exist unless there are pale things, individual instances of pallor. These pale things are themselves just the states that particular substances are in when they are pale. And these states are particulars, not universals, for each of them has a particular substance as a constituent. A pale thing, or *to ti leukon*, as the *Categories* called it, is not merely a determinate shade of color, such as Ghastly Pale #23, but a particular instantiation of such a shade. What makes it particular is that it has a particular substance as a constituent. And this is why, as Aristotle says (*Cat* 5 2b6), "if the primary substances did not exist it would be impossible for any of the other things to exist."

Notes

1. I am using "property" here in the modern sense of a characteristic or feature of an object, not in Aristotle's technical sense of an *idion* (Latin *proprium*), i.e., a characteristic or feature that is proper or peculiar to that object.
2. Translations throughout are from *The Complete Works of Aristotle: The Revised Oxford Translation*, edited by Jonathan Barnes (Princeton, 1984).
3. The strengthened principle also appears at *Phys* III.3 202b15: "For not all of the same [predicates] belong to all things whatsoever that are the same, but only to those whose being is the same."
4. Caveat: Aristotle's solution to these puzzles is only partially successful. For details, see Cohen (2008, p. 13).
5. In this essay I will not worry about whether it is important to distinguish between individuals and particulars and will use the two expressions interchangeably.
6. For more details on this issue, see Matthews (2009) and Cohen (2012).
7. This is the position taken by Matthews and Cohen (1968). We called such items as *this white* "unit qualities" and noted that they were indeed "queer entities" or "philosopher's entities,"

and that "Aristotelian unit qualities are not embodied in our non-philosophical ways of talking" (p. 647). Rereading these lines now, I can see how even then we were thinking of them along the lines of the accidental beings that we came to call "kooky objects." I still think we were right to say that they are not embodied in the nonphilosophical ways of talking that we mentioned in that paper; but it now seems to me that they are less queer than we then supposed, as I will try to show below.
8. This connection between the accidental beings of the *Metaphysics* and the things *in a subject but not said of a subject* of the *Categories* is seldom explicitly noted. Lewis (1985, p. 59) comes close when he writes "φ is in *a* if and only if there exists the accidental compound of *a* with the accident φ." But Lewis' biconditional holds where φ is universal (and therefore *said of a subject*), and so it is noncommittal with respect to *a*'s particular exemplification of φ (which is not *said of a subject*). For more on this connection, see Cohen (2008).
9. Here I disagree with Lewis (1985, p. 53), who insists that all such dependencies for Aristotle are immediate, or "one-step."
10. The intermediate role of accidental beings has been well explored by Code (2010), whose work on this topic has greatly influenced my own.
11. The translation of the phrase *tauta de mallon phainetai onta* is controversial. Where Ross and Barnes in the Revised Oxford Translation have "these are seen to be more real," Bostock has "these things more clearly are." Although I prefer the former translation, my interpretation does not require it. For even if there is no explicit commitment here to such "degrees of reality," it is still clear, even on the Bostock translation, that Aristotle distinguishes the accidental being *the walking thing* (*to badidzon*) from both the property of *walking* (*to badidzein*) and the underlying substance.
12. Or at least "more obviously real." See previous note.
13. Schema 1 appears in Code (2010); Schema 2 is implied by but never explicitly formulated in that paper.
14. *Phys* VIII 256a13ff, *Met* Z.3 1029a5-7, *Met* Z.15 1040a18.
15. *Met* Δ.11, especially 1018b34-36 and 1019a2-3; see also *Met* Z.10 1034b20-33, *Met* M.2 1077b1ff.
16. I am following the distinction between tropes and exemplifications found in Bacon (2011).
17. *Cat* 8 8b27, 9a31, 9b12-27.
18. One might object that states and conditions, unlike events, are shareable (two people can be in the same state; one may have a recurring condition). But so long as we restrict ourselves to particular states and conditions, the similarity seems indisputable.

Bibliography

Bacon, John. 2011. Tropes. In *The Stanford encyclopedia of philosophy*, ed. Edward N. Zalta. URL = http://plato.stanford.edu/archives/win2011/entries/tropes/
Bennett, Jonathan. 1988. *Events and their names*. Indianapolis: Hackett.
Code, Alan. 2010. Aristotle and existence. Paper presented at the Pacific Division meeting of the American Philosophical Association.
Cohen, S. Marc. 2008. Aristotle's ontology: Kooky objects revisited. *Metaphilosophy* 39: 3–19.
Cohen, S. Marc. 2012. Nonsubstantial particulars. A supplementary note to Aristotle's *Metaphysics*. The *Stanford encyclopedia of philosophy*, ed. Edward N. Zalta. URL = http://plato.stanford.edu/archives/sum2012/entries/aristotle-metaphysics/supp1.html
Kim, Jaegwon. 1983. Events as property exemplifications. In *Action theory*, ed. Myles Brand and Douglas Walton, 159–177. Dordrecht: Reidel.
Kim, Jaegwon. 1991. Events: Their metaphysics and semantics. *Philosophy and Phenomenological Research* 51: 641–646.

Lewis, Frank. 1985. *Substance and predication in Aristotle*. Cambridge: Cambridge University Press.
Matthews, Gareth B. 1982. Accidental unities. In *Language and logos: Studies in ancient Greek philosophy*, ed. Malcolm Schofield and Martha Craven Nussbaum, 223–240. Cambridge: Cambridge University Press.
Matthews, Gareth B. 2009. Aristotelian categories. In *A companion to Aristotle*, ed. Georgios Anagnostopoulos, 144–161. Oxford: Wiley-Blackwell.
Matthews, Gareth B., and S. Marc Cohen. 1968. The one and the many. *The Review of Metaphysics* 21: 630–655.
Owen, Gwilym Ellis Lane. 1965. Inherence. *Phronesis* 10: 97–105.

Is There Room for Plato in an Aristotelian Theory of Essence?

Frank A. Lewis

> It is not obvious why Aristotle should have chosen as his illustration of the identity of a *kath' hauto* term with its essence a class of *kath' hauto* terms which he does not believe in, the Ideas. The reason doubtless is that the argument in a29-b11 conveys a covert criticism of the ideal theory. (Ross 1924, II p. 177 on *Metaphysics* Z.6 1031a29.)
>
> It is unfortunate that he has thus improved the occasion by a fling at the Platonic theory, but his own view, that terms *kath' hauta* are identical with their essences, appears clearly enough. (Ross 1924, I p. xcix)
>
> The reasoning of the chapter [i.e., *Metaphysics* Z.6] is weak, and to an unusual degree verbal and dialectical. Its meaning is rendered difficult to seize by the fact[s] that … the argument for the identity of 'self-dependent terms' with their essence is conducted with reference to one particular kind of supposed self-dependent terms, the Platonic forms. (Ross, ibid.)

In *Metaphysics Zeta* 4, Aristotle begins his discussion of how the notion of *essence* contributes to the larger project in *Zeta* of "giving the what-is-it"—that is, of giving a definition—of *substance*.[1] After some initial, ultimately inconclusive attempts at defining the essence of a thing, his main concern in Z.4 is with determining what things have an essence, in particular, what *level* of things have an essence. There is, first, the exclusive, "black-and-white" view: only those things that are suitably primary can have an essence, and nothing else can. Later in the chapter, he takes a more relaxed, inclusive view: strictly speaking, only things that are suitably primary have an essence, but there is a reduced (and related) notion which applies in other cases.[2] In Z.5 too, Aristotle presses the exclusive notion of essence, even while allowing that other more relaxed cases also exist.

This chapter was largely finished before the invitation came to contribute to the volume in honor of David Keyt, and it was only after selecting this as the appropriate chapter for the occasion that I realized that it already contained, as so often before, a use of Keyt's published work (see n. 51 below). It is a pleasure to have found such ready evidence of my debt to him.

F.A. Lewis (✉)
School of Philosophy, University of Southern California, Los Angeles, CA 90089-0451, USA
e-mail: flewis@usc.edu

Aristotle's interest in levels persists in Z.6. The main thrust of the chapter is to argue in favor of a broadly *structural* point about essences: for a certain privileged class of entities—primary substances, which are "said in virtue of themselves"—each thing is *essentially* the same as, that is, I shall suppose, it is *identical* with, its essence.[3] We can perhaps see this identity as a condition on what properly counts as an essence, or as the essence *of* something, in the strict sense.[4] (Equally, it is a condition on what things strictly speaking count as *having* an essence.) At a certain level, we reach a set of entities that are fundamental, so that to the question "what is the essence of this item?" the only possible answer is: itself. But the Identity Result that is the main topic of the chapter does *not* hold for the wrong cases of essence, at the wrong level. It remains to show that the result does hold for what he says are the primary cases.

The distinction between primary and secondary is a recurring feature of Aristotle's metaphysical theory and is central to the theory of essence, in which the fundamental cases of essence form a metaphysical and definitional base on which other reduced cases are built.[5] The distinction is reflected in the very sequence of the arguments that pass under review in the first half of Z.6. Aristotle sketches an initial sameness argument in the opening lines of the chapter (the "Basic Argument", 1031a15-18) and appends a brief excursus. The Basic Argument itself is preliminary, even dialectical, and for this reason, it can be vague about two key issues. In these lines, nothing is said to clarify either the *scope* of the sameness thesis or the *variety of sameness* involved. The excursus that follows (1031a19-28) takes up the question whether and in what way an accidental compound, the pale man, may be the same as its essence. Since the pale man is not a primary entity in Aristotle's (perhaps in anyone's) ontology, the argument usefully pares away the items that have an essence in only a reduced sense and are not identical with their essence. There follows the "Elaborated Argument" (a28-b3), in which Aristotle fixes on a class of items that, in their owner Plato's ontology, do count as primary and, in consequence, (a) genuinely enjoy an essence in the primary sense and (b) are duly identical with their essences.

For us, the main interest will be in what appears to be the "arm's length" strategy Aristotle uses in arguing for these last conclusions. The Elaborated Argument is indirect in the obvious sense that it proceeds by reductio of the opposing view, that certain primary substances, which are "said in virtue of themselves," are nonidentical with their essence.[6] But the argument is also indirect, or perhaps oblique, in a way that has challenged some of Aristotle's commentators. For in the Elaborated Argument, as elsewhere in *Zeta*, he proceeds on the basis of the views of others, even while arguing for conclusions that are central to his own, Aristotelian project. Aristotle frames his argument, not *propria persona*, but speaking on behalf of the Platonist, for whom the things "said in virtue of themselves" will be Platonic Forms. Must not this resort to Platonism, however temporary, restrict or otherwise undercut Aristotle's arguments? On perhaps the least optimistic appraisal, Aristotle's arguments are *impure* and rest essentially on Platonic assumptions that he himself does not accept.[7] But if he does not accept one or more assumptions needed for his arguments, how can the arguments increase his confidence in their conclusion?

Alternatively, Aristotle may have some other, ulterior motive—perhaps a covert criticism of Plato, as Ross and others suggest.[8] If his arguments have Plato as a target, and if the Platonic assumptions Aristotle himself does not accept are discharged at the end, then his arguments start impure but end with *purity regained*. But the path to purity is not easy. One problem is technical. On some accounts, apparently, the very views of Plato that Aristotle means to criticize are essential to the argument for his, Aristotle's, own conclusion: but if some Platonic assumptions remain undischarged, then the argument for sameness is impure after all.[9] At the same time, it is not clear that criticism is in Aristotle's mind at all, at least not for the duration of his arguments for identity. Aristotle seems to say that his "Identity Result" holds whether or not (Platonic) Forms exist, *but all the more if they do*:[10] but how, if Plato is a target, can Aristotle in the same breath claim him as an ally?

Recent commentators have been kinder to Aristotle. In this gentler vein, I shall argue that his arguments are *pure* and essentially contain no assumptions that Aristotle himself cannot accept. On this view, as we shall see, the reference to Platonic Forms is not essential to his arguments.[11] Nor, in these arguments at least, does he have any polemical point in mind. On the contrary, Aristotle co-opts Plato in the passage in the way he co-opts other philosophers elsewhere, with a view to establishing broad metaphysical principles that hold *across* ontologies. In the search for "big tent" principles that are ontologically neutral in this way, he can appeal for support not just to Plato but to Democritus (see H.2), to Anaxagoras (the treatment of *nous* in *De Anima* III.4), or even to one of his own other selves in the *Categories*, for example, *Metaphysics* Z.1 and, somewhat differently, Z.3 (where the *Physics* is also relevant), or in the *De Sophisticis Elenchis* (*Metaphysics* Z.5 on why the snub does not strictly speaking have an essence), or in the *Analytics* (*Metaphysics* Z.17). In this spirit, as I hope to show, there is room even for Plato in an Aristotelian theory of essence.

1 Purity in the Engagement with Plato

1.1 The Basic Argument for Sameness

Plato—more exactly, a Platonic ontology, since Plato himself is nowhere mentioned by name—makes its official appearance in the discussion of essence midway through Z.6; but Plato's influence is at work throughout the segment on essence, if (as I suspect) he is the author of the assumption that governs the segment, that the substance of a thing is its essence:[12]

x is the substance of y if and only if x is the essence of y.

The Governing Assumption in Z.4-6

The "Governing Assumption" is one of the four received opinions reported in Z.3 that shape *Zeta*'s inquiry into substance (1028b33-6): it is this assumption that motivated the inquiry into essence in the first place (see also Z.4, 1029b1-3). The assumption is deeply entrenched in Aristotle's own metaphysical theory: in addition to its reappearance at the beginning of Z.6 (1031a18) and twice again in the same chapter, it reappears three or four times more elsewhere in *Zeta-Eta*.[13]

Burnyeat is at pains to note that Aristotle does not straightforwardly assert the Governing Assumption in Z.6.[14] His point that "the idea remains an unasserted hypothesis" in the chapter, however, may be misplaced: in ordinary-language contexts, "If P, then Q" can often be a compressed form of modus ponens—"If P, then Q; and P; therefore, Q."[15] My own view is that Aristotle will think the Governing Assumption acceptable in any metaphysical theory that recognizes the notions of the essence and the substance of a thing. So put the Assumption on the "big tent" side of the ledger—consistent with its being part of the discussion that is conducted within a framework of received views rather than in Aristotle's own partisan terms.

The Governing Assumption is a premise in the Basic Argument, sketched at the very beginning of Z.6, which Aristotle suggests may or may not point to the sameness in some sense of a thing with its essence:

> Whether each thing and its essence are the same or different, needs to be looked into. For it is somewhat relevant to the study of substance: for (first) (*te*, a17) each thing is thought to be not other than its own substance, and (second) (*kai*, a18) its essence is said to be each thing's substance. (1031a15-18)

That is to say, if as people commonly suppose, (i), each thing is the same as its substance, and if as they also think, (ii), a thing's substance is also its essence (the Governing Assumption), then on the opinions of record at any rate, it follows that (iii) each thing and its essence are the same.

The argument as a whole constitutes Aristotle's Basic Argument for the sameness in some sense of a thing with its essence. As we shall see, however, there is work to be done before the conclusion can be stated in a form that Aristotle will find acceptable. His primary goal in the chapter is to establish the identity in certain cases of a thing with its essence. While he has reasons of theory for maintaining a sameness result in this more refined form, these interests emerge at best indirectly and only in the second half of his discussion.[16] Instead, at the beginning of the chapter, as the passage quoted shows, he is anxious to justify inclusion of the topic at this point in *Zeta*, by pointing to its connection even in its rough and ready form with the larger inquiry into substance.[17]

One point above all stands out in the Basic Argument. The argument is clearly nonpartisan: both the Governing Assumption, (ii), and the opening premise, (i), are cited anonymously, as "received opinion," and not as fact that Aristotle himself is ready to endorse. Later in the chapter, in what amounts to an elaboration of the Basic Argument that he puts into Plato's mouth at 1031a28-b3, Aristotle comes closer to naming names. But (I will argue) Aristotle does more than offer an argument that Plato might find acceptable. The later, elaborated argument will be one that, in essentials, he and Plato can both accept in support of the conclusion, subject now to the needed refinements, that each thing is not other than its essence.

Accordingly, the basis of the Basic Argument in received views leaves room for the thought that the Argument is also, in a certain way, provisional. In order to find an argument that Aristotle and his ally of the moment, Plato, will find acceptable, the opening premise, (i), and the conclusion, (iii), alike *must be restricted to entities that are suitably primary*. At the same time, the opening claim about substance and sameness in (i), where the variety of sameness is left vague, can be firmed up into an identity claim:

Where x is the substance of y and y is a primary substance, $x=y$.

The Identity Premise

Similar transformations apply to the conclusion, (iii), which is sharpened to become the principal conclusion of the chapter, that in the case of primary substances at least, a thing is *identical* with its essence[18]:

Where x is the essence of y and y is a primary substance,[19] $x=y$.

The Identity Result

In the later Elaboration of the Basic Argument, Aristotle argues in favor of the Identity Result for the case in which the primary substances in question are Platonic Forms; on certain reasonable assumptions, including (again) the Governing Assumption, that a thing's substance is also its essence, it transpires that Platonic Forms are indeed identical with their essences. Aristotle makes common cause with the Platonist in part, I suspect, because he sees Plato as one of the authorities for the Governing Assumption. More than this, however, I suggest, he thinks he also has Plato's support for the opening idea, (i), that each (primary) thing is no other than its substance—if Plato is not to be enlisted as one of the sponsors of the Basic Argument as a whole.[20]

Here is an informal sketch of how the shared ideas underlying the Identity Premise will go. (Aristotle himself supplies a more formal defense of the Premise in the Elaborated Argument.) We start with the class of things "said in virtue of themselves"—items that can be defined and explained without reference to some distinct entity. Among these, in turn, are included the primary substances, which have no nature or substance prior to them. For Plato and Aristotle alike, this is part of what it means for something to be a primary substance. How, then, can there be a substance *of* a primary substance? In general, if one thing is the substance of some distinct second thing, the first must be prior to the second, in at least the sense of "prior" already before us. So there can be the substance *of a primary substance*, only if the original primary substance and the substance of that substance are identical, so that neither is prior to the other.

For a more formal look at these ideas, we must turn to the details of the text in the middle of Z.6. As we shall see, the overt engagement with Plato in this part of the chapter constitutes a much more elaborate argument in support of the Identity Thesis, in place of the Basic Argument with which the chapter began. Aristotle's Elaborated Argument, and the support lent to it by Plato's theory of Forms, is our next topic.

1.2 Plato and the Elaboration of the Basic Argument

Aristotle initiates the alliance with Plato in the following terms:

> But in the case of things said in virtue of themselves, is it necessary that they are the same <as their essences>, (a29) for example, if there are certain substances than which there are no other substances or natures <that are> prior, of the kind that some say the forms (*ideas*) are? (a31) For if the good itself and the for-good to be (*to agathôi einai*) will be different, and animal <itself> and the for-animal <to be>, and the for-being <to be> and being <itself>,[21] (b1) (first) (*te*) there will be other substances and natures and forms (*ideas*) in addition to the ones recognized [namely, in Plato's theory], and (second) (*kai*) these will be prior and more substances [Jaeger's text], if essence is substance. (1031a28-b3)

We are to suppose that there exists a class of entities described as "substances than which there are no other substances or natures <that are> prior"—primary substances, for short—and that examples of these include Plato's Forms. Primary substances, in turn, are examples of "things said in virtue of themselves." Aristotle does not say which the primary substances are in his own ontology: at this stage, he borrows his examples from Plato.[22]

Now for the details of the argument. Let G be the Platonic Form of the Good and suppose that G is essentially good: reproducing Aristotle's term for the essence in question,

(1) The for-good to be (*to agathôi einai*) is the essence of G.[23]   A

Aristotle's argument takes aim at the view that, contrary to the Platonic version of the Identity Result,

(2) G ≠ the for-good to be.[24]   A

Against the targeted view, he sets down first a fundamental assumption about substance:

(3) For each substance in a certain class of substances (in fact, the "primary" substances), there is no substance or nature prior to that substance. (a29)   A

Next comes an assumption central to the Platonic theory of Forms, along with a consequence:

(4) Platonic Forms are primary substances of the kind mentioned in (3) (a29-31). In particular, G is a primary substance of that kind.   A

Accordingly,

(5) There is no substance or nature (a29-31), and no Platonic Form in addition to the Platonic Forms usually recognized (b1-2), which is prior to and more of a substance than G.

From (3) and (4)

Aristotle also tacitly helps himself to an assumption featuring the relation, "*x* is the substance of y," together with notions of priority and of the degrees of substance that (presumably) he and Plato will share:

(6) x is the substance of y and $y \neq x$, only if x is prior to and more of a substance than y.   A

In particular,

(7) The for-good to be is the substance of G and G≠the for-good to be, only if the for-good to be is prior to and more of a substance than G.

A final assumption connects the essence-of and substance-of relations in the familiar way:

(8) x is the essence of y if and only if x is the substance of y. (1031b2-3, cf. a18, b31-2)

The Governing Assumption

As we have seen, the Governing Assumption appears in Z.3 as one of the received opinions that shape *Zeta*'s inquiry into substance.[25]

We can now proceed against the targeted view (2), that G ≠ the for-good to be. First, given (1) and (8), we have

(9) The for-good to be is the substance of G.

Given (9) and the nonidentity in (2) together with the priority principle, (7), it follows that

(10) There is some substance or nature or Platonic Form [= the for-good to be] that is prior to G and more of a substance than G. (b1-3)

(5) and (10) are the two halves of a contradiction:

(11) There both is and is not a substance or nature or Platonic Form that is prior to G and more of a substance than G.

By reductio on (2), then,

(12) The for-good to be = G,

as required.[26]

On the present account, Aristotle co-opts Plato in support of his own Identity Result, by relying on a cluster of assumptions most or all of which are thoroughly at home in a Platonic theory of Forms. But why should the non-Platonist care, given that the desired result rests even in part on assumptions that are local to Plato's theory? Assumption (6), about priority and the degrees of substance, is not at issue here; it formalizes views about what it means for a thing to be a substance or for one thing to be the substance of another, and it is at least as much part of Aristotle's theory as it is of Plato's.[27] Aristotle and Plato can also agree to the underlying assumption, (3), that a primary substance has nothing prior to it. From (3) together with the introduction of Platonic Forms in (4), Aristotle derives the Platonic thesis,

(5), that there is no substance or nature prior to a Platonic Form or more a substance than a Platonic Form is. But Aristotle can plausibly argue that (5) holds *mutatis mutandis* in any ontology that includes a class of primary substances, which are "said in virtue of themselves"; however, the various ontologies may differ in other respects. In this sense, the reference to Platonic Forms in (1) and (4) is inessential to the argument. In principle, Aristotle is free to replace both with assumptions instantiating to his own choice for entities that are suitably primary and even with assumptions that do not instantiate to any particular set of entities at all.[28] Apart from these two, or their counterparts in some other ontology, the only remaining assumption is (8), which is the lead assumption of the entire segment.

It follows that Plato is present in the argument in only a very weak sense. The premise-set to the argument, as it stands, includes assumptions that mention Platonic Forms and that are, strictly, unacceptable to Aristotle on that account. But the use of Plato's Forms is not essential to the argument, and the reference to Plato comes down to (what is here) the triviality that while Aristotle and Plato agree over the identity of things that are suitably primary with their essences, they disagree over the existence or otherwise of Platonic Forms. On this story, the engagement with Plato is *pure* and stops well this side of compromise.

But purity is not Aristotle's only option. It is not beyond credibility, for example, that he should quote Plato approvingly for a conclusion that can be reached only on the basis of assumptions Aristotle himself rejects: such a use of Plato would be *impure*. An interpretation of this sort appears in Burnyeat et al. (1979), where the assumption that essence is substance—on the view I have been pressing, yet another statement of the Governing Assumption, that "its essence is said to be each thing's substance," from the beginning of the chapter (1031a18, cf. Sect. 1.1)—is taken to be a statement of Platonic separation. [29] On this reading, according to Burnyeat, "[T]he argument uses Platonic machinery to extract a conclusion the Platonist will have to accept if he once says that Form and essence are distinct." Notably, however, this account lacks an explanation of what about the argument recommends its conclusion to Aristotle, given the (on his terms) wildly Platonic slant of its assumptions.

Yet, a third kind of account attempts to meet the difficulties of impurity by supposing that while the argument apparently begins in impurity, this is only as a means to *purity regained* at the end. On a view of this sort, the assumptions essential to the initial steps of the argument include an assumption Aristotle rejects, but it is present there only because it is the target of a reductio argument and will eventually be discharged.[30] An account of the argument along these lines appears in Cherniss (1944, pp. 334–36). Cherniss holds that the argument is simultaneously an attack on Platonic separation and a proof of the identity of a thing with its essence. According to the argument as he reconstructs it, if (a) a thing and its essence are not identical, and if (b) essence is substance, then (c) there exists a set of Forms prior to the Platonic Forms generally recognized. Since Plato must find this result unacceptable, he must (if Cherniss is right) both reject separation and embrace Aristotle's Identity Thesis.

This account is troubled on at least two scores. First, it requires an unlikely gloss on (b), identical to that found in Burnyeat et al. (1979) two paragraphs back: by "essence is substance," according to Cherniss, Aristotle means that an essence is a *separate* substance; more fully, it is itself a Form and separate from what it is the essence of, in the way that the usual run of Platonic Forms supposedly are both the essence of and separate from the things that fall under them. But there is no explicit reference to Platonic separation in this part of the text.[31] At the same time, as before, it is hard to see a covert reference to separation in the claim that essence is substance, which is more naturally taken as one of the assumptions that guide the argument of *Zeta*.[32]

It is also hard to see how on Cherniss' account the argument achieves its twin goals of refuting separation while establishing identity. Since on Cherniss' view Aristotle's intentions are hostile, Aristotle will use the falsity of the conclusion (c) to reject the assumption (b) glossed as the claim that Forms are separate. Suppose we grant Aristotle this anti-Platonic point, so that (b) goes. How can he simultaneously reject (a) in order to obtain the positive conclusion he wants, that Forms are *identical* with the things they are the essence of? We can reduce only one assumption to absurdity at a time, and without an argument that the failure of separation implies identity, the Identity Result must remain moot. As predicted, then, if the argument serves Aristotle's alleged anti-Platonic purposes, it is difficult to see how it also gives him the desired Identity Result.[33]

Of the three options we have surveyed—purity, impurity, and purity regained—purity remains the most attractive. Even granting purity in the engagement with Plato, however, the question remains: Why the engagement with Plato at all? In part, the reasons are ones of strategy. In later parts of *Zeta*, Aristotle undertakes a major revision in the metaphysical theory of individuals and their kinds found in the *Categories*. By keeping his questions about essence within the confines of Plato's ontology, Aristotle spares himself the need to sort through here the complications that separate not just Plato but also his own views elsewhere from the new theory distinctive of *Metaphysics Zeta*.[34]

In addition to simplicity, the use of Plato also gives Aristotle the advantage of drama. For Aristotle, I have argued (Sect. 1.2), the Identity Result flows directly from what it means to be a primary substance, independently of partisan questions of which entities fill the role of primary substance in a given ontology. The use of Plato conveniently dramatizes the fact that the case in favor of the sameness thesis is not "loaded" by the presence of distinctively Aristotelian assumptions; on the contrary, it does not sink the case for the thesis even when the argument on its behalf is couched in Platonic terms. In itself, the Identity Result is a "big tent" principle that stands independently of its application to Aristotle's choice for primary substances and independently of his own, "partisan," conclusion that Aristotelian forms are identical with their essences.[35]

Once this initial round of arguments in favor of his Identity Result is done, in the lines immediately following, Aristotle apparently drops discussion of the identity of things that are suitably primary with their essence. He turns instead to a discussion of the consequences of the two being "severed" one from another, in particular, the consequences of the supposed "severance" of Platonic Forms and their essences. The relevance of severance and its consequences to Aristotle's larger theme is not immediately apparent: severance and its place in the wider argument are our topics in Sects. 2.1 and 2.2.

2 "Severance": How Platonic Separation Is Not a Target

2.1 "Severance" and Its Consequences: 1031b3-11

In the next stretch of argument, Aristotle launches abruptly into a discussion of the consequences of the assumption that the Platonic Form and its essence, G and the for-good to be, are "severed from" one another:

> And, on the one hand,[36] if they are severed from one another, then of the ones [= Plato's Forms] there will not be knowledge, and the others [= the essences] will not be beings (by "severed," I mean if neither the for-good to be belongs to the good itself (*mête tôi agathôi autôi huparchei to einai agathôi*), nor does to be good<belong>to it [= the essence of good]): (b6) for (first) (*te*) there is knowledge of each thing whenever we know its essence, (b7) and (second) (*kai*) the same holds equally of the good and of the others, so that if not even the for-good to be is good, then neither is the for-being<to be>a being, nor the for-one<to be>one: (b9) in the same way, either all the essences are, or none is, so that if not even the for-being<to be><is a>being, neither<is>any of the others. (b11) Again, that to which<the>for-good to be[37] does not belong is not good. (1031b3-11)

Aristotle is silent about the source of the "Severance Assumption" and about why it merits discussion here. But he does explain what he takes it to mean: (i) "neither the for-good to be belongs to the good itself" (b5, cf. 11) (ii) "nor does to be good<belong>to it [= the essence]" (b6, 8). That is, we will suppose:

(13) The for-good to be is not the essence of G,

and

(14) The for-good to be is not good.[38]

The Severance Assumption

The two-piece Severance Assumption, composed as it is of (13) and (14) together, is problematic in a variety of ways. In the first place, the consequences to which the Assumption is said to lead at 1031 b6-7 and b7-10 are presumably altogether unacceptable. Inevitably, interpreters have been led to suspect controversy with Plato. If severance is the same as (or at least a close counterpart of) Platonic separation, and if the effect of the arguments is to overturn Platonic separation, then the alliance with Plato struck in previous lines is now abruptly shattered. The distancing from Plato is more violent than in the argument explicitly directed against the theory of Forms later at b15-18, where Aristotle prepares for conflict with Plato by saying that the Identity Result for which he has been arguing—arguing, as we have seen, with Plato's help—holds if Platonic Forms exist, but also even if they do not (b11-15). At the same time, if Platonic separation is both the initial assumption and the ultimate target of the arguments, there need be no worries over purity—for the distinctively Platonic assumption at the head of the argument is to be discharged by reductio at argument's end.

If the Severance Assumption does invoke the Platonic theory of separation between Forms and sensibles, then the conclusion that Platonic Forms will not be known will seem reminiscent of the argument in the first half of Plato's *Parmenides* that if Forms are separate from sensibles, they cannot be known by us. Is Aristotle constructing, at the level of Platonic Forms and their essences, a counterpart to Plato's argument concerning sensibles and the Forms that (arguably) are their essences?[39]

It tells against these suggestions that when Aristotle explains what he means by "severed" at b4-6, his explanation seems quite distant from Platonic separation. Aristotle's (13) and (14) appear in the argument *by stipulation*: these together are just what he means by "severing a Form from its essence." But if the conjunction of (13) and (14) tells us how we should understand Aristotle's Severance Assumption, the question arises: What justifies his adopting the Assumption, so understood, in the first place? And what support does the Assumption offer for the Identity Result for which he is arguing?

I will argue that Severance has a place in the discussion because, taken together with a fundamental principle from a framework that arguably Plato and Aristotle have in common, it forms the basis of a fresh round of reductio arguments in favor of the identity of a Platonic Form with its essence. The negations of each of the two components of Severance, together with the fundamental principle, combine to again make the case for the identity of a thing and its essence. In this way, Severance is present in the argument strictly for purposes of reductio: both parts of Severance are admitted into the discussion solely in order to be ejected from it. I describe the details of this strategy in Sect. 2.2.

2.2 A Fresh Argument for Identity: Severance and a Principle from the Theory of Izzing and Having

The Severance Assumption introduces a fresh round of reductio arguments as part of a larger argument designed once more to support the identity of a Platonic Form with its essence. A key component of the argument is a principle set out by Alan Code, which, arguably, is part of the theory of Izzing and Having:[40]

(15) $X = Y \leftrightarrow X$ Is Y and Y Is X.

Code regards (15) as a definition and part of an "ontological framework common to Plato and Aristotle."[41] Thanks to this common background, even if the reference to Platonic Forms is uncongenial to Aristotle, the argument will be pure and will not essentially depend on Platonic assumptions Aristotle rejects.

The argument goes as follows. Plausibly, we can instantiate from (15) to G and the for-good to be in the ontology of Platonic Forms and their essences:

(16) The for-good to be = G ↔ the for-good to be Is G [= the for-good to be is good] and G Is the for-good to be [= the for-good to be is the essence of G].

(16) suggests how the two components, (13) and (14), of the Severance Assumption, repeated here,

(13) The for-good to be is not the essence of G,
(14) The for-good to be is not good,

may have purchase on the identity or nonidentity of a Form and its essence. Thus, if Aristotle can show that the negative claim in (14) is false, this will give the first conjunct on the right-hand side of (16),

(Unneg-14) The for-good to be is good.

And if he can show that (13) is false, this will give the second conjunct:

(Unneg-13) The for-good to be is the essence of G.

Given this twofold assault on Severance, we can now use (16) to give the desired Identity Result, that G = the for-good to be.

On this account, the reductio arguments against Severance in (13) and (14), together with principle (15) from the theory of Izzing and Having, are the main components in a fresh argument in favor of the Identity Result reached in earlier lines.

This may be the point at which to counter two kinds of objections to the key principle, (15). First, (15) has the apparent analogue in set theory, $\forall x \forall y (x=y \leftrightarrow x \subseteq y \ \& \ y \subseteq x)$: does the parallel require us to adopt an extensional view of Aristotle's kinds or Plato's Forms—that is, to think that they have the identity conditions of sets? In a word, no. Each of two kinds Is the other, by (15), just in case they are identical; and from the identity, it follows trivially that they are coextensive. But this last entailment does not hold in the opposite direction. From the fact that the two kinds are coextensive, nothing follows: not that they are identical, nor that each Is the other. On the contrary, all and only men are capable of grammar (say); but it is not the case either that man Is grammatical or that the grammatical Is (a) man, much less that the two kinds, man and the capable of grammar, are identical. Instead, man Has the capacity for grammar, and in general, for Aristotle, propria are coextensive with, but not essential to, their subjects.[42] So sameness of extension is not enough for identity; it must also be the case that each of two kinds Is the other, if we are to conclude that they are identical.

It is not clear that a similar remedy is open to Plato if, as on some accounts, in his theory Platonic Forms are exclusively Izzers, and only sensibles Have their predicables. Plato will need some device to avoid saying that where two Forms, Man and Capable of grammar (say), are coextensive, each also Is the other. He may even have to accept help from Aristotle and allow that Having can also be a Form-Form relation, if he is simultaneously to accept (15) in his theory and to avoid an extensional view of Platonic Forms. For present purposes, I will assume that Plato has the needed device to hand.

A second objection sets (15) against a fundamental doctrine from the *Categories*, along with what seems an obvious point signaling Izzing as the converse of Aristotle's said-of relation:

(15) X = Y ↔ X Is Y and Y Is X.
(a) Socrates (a *Categories*-style primary substance) is not said of Socrates (*Categories* 5, 3a36-37, *apo ... tês prôtês catêgorias oudemia esti katêgoria*).
(b) X Is Y ↔ Y is said of X.

From these three premises, it follows immediately that

(c) Socrates ≠ Socrates.[43]

Given the fundamental doctrine in (a) and the seemingly obvious point about converses in (b), it seems that (15) must be false. There are independent reasons, however, for laying the blame instead at the feet of the seemingly obvious point in (b). Thus, as before, assume the truth of (a) and (b) and add a third claim, (d), from *Metaphysics* Δ.18:

> ... that which is per se (*kath' hauto*) too necessarily is said in many ways: in one, <its> what it is to be is per se to each thing, for example Callias is per se Callias and what it is to be for-Callias. Δ18, 1022a25-7

The result is an inconsistent triad:

(a) Socrates (a *Categories*-style primary substance) is not said of Socrates.
(b) X Is Y ↔ Y is said of X.
(d) Socrates Is Socrates.

Given the textual credentials of (a) and (d), we should abandon the claim about converses in (b) and thereby retain our faith in (15).[44]

I conclude that Plato and Aristotle can overcome the objections to (15). At the same time, (15) works correctly for the cases of interest in Z.6. For Plato, contrary to (13) and (14), the for-good to be Is G,[45] and G Is the for-good to be; by (15), accordingly, G = the for-good to be, as required.

It remains to follow the details of Aristotle's attack on the two components, (13) and (14), of Severance: these arguments are our next topic.

3 Goodbye to Severance, and in Defense of Uniformity

3.1 The Applications of Uniformity: Fallacy, or True Platonic Doctrine?

Aristotle sees two negative, and uncongenial, consequences of (13) and (14): (Platonic) Forms will not be objects of knowledge, contrary to the Platonic view that Forms above all, or even Forms alone, are the objects of knowledge; and no essence will exist. First (1031 b6-7),[46] if (13) is true, and if we know each thing when we know its essence, then G and Platonic Forms generally will be unknowable.[47] In the remainder of the passage (b7-11), Aristotle uses the second assumption, (14), to reach the complementary result, that no essence exists.[48]

The chief point of controversy concerns this last argument, from (14),

(14) The for-good to be is not good,

to the conclusion that essences do not exist. Aristotle argues, first, that if the essence of good is not good, then (by a principle of uniformity) for any X, the essence of X is not (an) X; and second, that if the essence of being is not a being, then (by uniformity again) no essence exists. Of the two would-be applications of uniformity featured in this stretch of argument, the second has been viewed with skepticism by Aristotle's critics; unexpectedly, I will argue, Aristotle can reasonably call upon Plato as an ally against the charge of fallacy.

I begin by repeating the relevant part of Aristotle's text:

> And, on the one hand, if they are severed from one another, then ... the others [= the essences] will not be beings ... (b6) for ... the same holds equally (*homoiôs echei*) of the good and of the others, so that if not even the for-good to be is good, then neither is the for-being to be a being, nor the for-one to be one; (b9) in the same way (*homoiôs*), either all the essences are, or none is, so that if not even the for-being to be <is a> being, neither <is> any of the others. (1031b3-11)

The argument rests on applications of different versions of a uniformity principle, which Aristotle states in undifferentiated form: "the same holds equally of the good and of the others" (b7-8). First (b6), if the for-good to be is not good, as (14) asserts, then in general, for any Form, X, the for-X to be is not (an) X, in particular, the for-Being to be is not (a) Being. But, second (b9, taking up the conclusion of the first installment of argument, but with a fresh application of uniformity), if the for-Being to be is not (a) Being, then in general, for every Form, X, the for-X to be is not (a) Being. That is, absurdly, no essence of a Platonic Form exists.

An initial objection to Aristotle's reductio argument, due to Bonitz and echoed in Bostock, questions the second application of uniformity, which purports to show that if the for-Being to be is not (a) Being, then for any Form, X, the for-X to be is not (a) Being.[49] If Aristotle intended uniformity to work in the same way here as in the first part of the argument, then as Bonitz complains, he would be entitled to conclude, as before, only that for every Form, X, the for-X to be is not (an) X.

It may seem that Bonitz's objection is groundless because, as Ross suggests, he has simply failed to recognize two different applications of uniformity. Lest this response seem too easy, we might press Bonitz's objection a step further. Someone might argue that, while the first kind of uniformity is privileged, what Aristotle takes to be a second kind of uniformity is a fallacy. In contemporary predicate logic, we know that by the rule of Universal Introduction (UI), along with the appropriate restrictions, from

My horse's head is the head of my horse,

we can validly infer,

Is There Room for Plato in an Aristotelian Theory of Essence? 257

($\forall x$)(x's head is the head of x):

take anything you like, its head is the head of it. It does not follow, however, that by UI,

($\forall x$)(x's head is the head of my horse) –

take anything you like, its head is the head of my horse. (On the contrary, take anything you like, its head is its own, and only *my* horse's head is the head of my horse.) As an application of UI, the move I am objecting to is certifiably fallacious, because it violates the restriction that the "instantiating constant," "my horse," in the premise may not appear in the universally quantified conclusion.

The logic is the same in the target case in Aristotle. To

The for-Being to be is not (a) Being,

we can apply the rule of UI to conclude that

for any Form, X, the for-X to be is not (an) X,

along the lines of the first application of uniformity. But the application of UI to produce the second purported conclusion,

for any Form, X, the for-X to be is not (a) Being,

is fallacious, for the same reason as before: the instantiating constant, "Being," in the premise may not also appear in the conclusion. So perhaps Bonitz is right: only the first, but not the second, is a legitimate consequence of Aristotle's uniformity principle.

In fact, however, Bonitz is not right. On the account just given, uniformity is assimilated to the logical rule of Universal Introduction. But uniformity is not a matter of logic alone. Rather, it is the application of an "all or nothing" principle, to the effect that with respect to a given domain of entities and a given property, F, either everything in the domain has F or nothing does:

($\forall x$)Fx v ($\forall x$)~Fx.

This "all or nothing" principle has different consequences, depending on what property we take F to be. Two choices are relevant here:

(17) "Fx" = "the for-x to be is (an) x"
(18) "Fx" = "the for-x to be is (a) Being."

The argument of 1031b3-11, quoted at the head of this section, now falls into place. Suppose, first, that the for-good to be is not good, as in the target claim, (14), and that the "all or nothing" uniformity principle is understood in line with (17),

(Uniformity-1). Either for every Form, X, the for-X to be is an X or for no Form, X, the for-X to be is (an) X.

Given (14), that the for-good to be is not good, the first disjunct of Uniformity-1 must be false; by disjunctive syllogism (DS), then, no Form, X, is such that the for-X

to be is (an) X. In particular, the for-Being to be is not a being. This gives the result of the first half of Aristotle's reductio.

At the same time, the "all or nothing" principle may also be applied with (18) as our choice for "Fx,"

(Uniformity-2). Either for every Form, X, the for-X to be is (a) Being or for no Form, X, the for-X to be is (a) Being.

We begin with the conclusion to the first leg of the argument, that the for-Being to be is not (a) Being. On this assumption, the first disjunct of Uniformity-2 must be false, so that by DS again no Form, X, is such that the for-X to be is (a) Being. This gives the conclusion to Aristotle's reductio.[50] Given that this result is absurd, and if the two Uniformities 1 and 2 are sound, we are in a position to deny the initial assumption (14), that the for-good to be is not good, as required.

Both applications of uniformity in this two-part argument are defensible. But the defense is not merely that these are different applications of uniformity. There is the further point—which Ross does not mention—that the two applications of uniformity are not a matter simply of logic. If they had been, Bonitz would be right. In fact, however, they rest on the propriety or impropriety of the relevant "all or nothing" principle, which is a matter not of logic, but of the *content* of each principle. Arguably, the relevant principles will hold across ontologies and will govern whatever counts as a primary substance in Plato's and in Aristotle's ontology alike.

In fact, Plato and Aristotle can agree over stronger principles of uniformity, which drop the second, negative disjunct in (Uniformity-1) and (Uniformity-2). Plato, for example, can reasonably claim that for any Form, X, its essence *is an X*: this is a candidate for a "categorial," or "formal," property that belongs necessarily to all Forms, in virtue of their status as Forms.[51] Again, for any Platonic Form, X, its essence *is a Being*: this, again, is arguably a categorial property of all Forms across the board. These two claims take to be true for every Form what in the two halves of Aristotle's reductio is assumed to be false for G and for Being. To avoid an inconsistent premise-set in the two halves of his argument, Aristotle limits himself to weaker versions of uniformity, namely, the disjunctive (Uniformity-1) and (Uniformity-2).

Similar considerations apply to the primary substances in Aristotle's ontology. Whether with Z.4 we think that the primary substances are the *genous eidê* (the lowest species of the different genera),[52] or (as in the official theory) that they are Aristotelian forms, it seems that for any primary substance, X, its essence both Is (an) X and Is (a) Being.[53] As before, arguably, it is a categorial feature of primary substances across the board that each has the properties noted. This is enough to support the essentially weaker disjunctive uniformity principles, (Uniformity-1) and (Uniformity-2).

With one notable exception, these different Platonic and Aristotelian ideas essentially involve the notions of primary substances and their essences and only incidentally engage the details of their authors' differing ontologies. One exception to purity, however, stands out (I owe the point to Alan Code). Both applications of uniformity presuppose the existence of a Platonic Form of Being—to be faulted not for its status as a Platonic Form but because, for Aristotle, there is no widest genus, being. Aristotle's argument, then, is at best conditional in form. Beyond this one concession to Plato, no other assumptions are essential to the use of uniformity that Plato would embrace but which Aristotle would reject. Once we allow Plato's widest genus, Being, the appeals to uniformity are not idiosyncratic to Plato, but unsuitable for anyone else or (merely) unsuitable within Aristotle's own theory. Not only, then, are the arguments not bad, as Bonitz thought, but also, as before, the use of assumptions Aristotle shares with Plato conveniently dramatizes the point that his conclusion is—as close as may be—a "big tent" view, which applies across ontologies.

3.2 Fallacy Again, or More True Doctrine?

Our passage ends with a one-line argument to supplement the argument just given:

Again, that to which the essence of good does not belong [*hôi mê huparchei agathôi einai*] is not good. b11.

An important first step in seeing the point of the argument is to resist reading Aristotle's sentence as a universal generalization: for *every* x such that the essence of good does not belong to x, x is not good.[54] As Ross suggests, Aristotle has a particular case in mind: we are to suppose that the for-good to be does not belong *to the Platonic Form*, G,[55] so that it, G, is not good. So the argument has as its premise our old friend, (13):

(13) The for-good to be is not the essence of G.

It follows, Aristotle suggests, that

(19) G is not good.

On this reading, the argument has the appearance of a fresh reductio: its point, presumably, is to discredit the nonidentity theorist's (13) (to this point, targeted only by the argument from knowledge at 1031b6-7) by showing that it leads to (19). But two problems remain. On what grounds should we find (19) unacceptable? At the same time, second, like its immediate predecessor, the argument seems vulnerable on purely logical grounds.

We can discuss this second objection first. The effect of (13) is that G is not essentially good. But, Frede and Patzig (1988) complain, it is a fallacy to suppose that if a thing is not essentially good, then it is not good at all: it may be accidentally good.[56] So the inference to (19) is apparently an instance of an invalid argument schema, and even if (19) is unacceptable, it is hard to see how this fact can be used to undermine (13).

As before, however (Sect. 3.1), not every instance of an invalid argument schema is itself invalid. This is why the restriction to Plato's Forms is important, for there are grounds in Plato's theory for finding the move from (13) to (19) compelling. For

Plato, arguably, at least in a large range of cases, whatever is true of a Platonic Form is essentially true of it: in the theory of Izzing and Having, a Form Is whatever it is (within that range of cases). Hence, if the for-good to be does not belong to G, that is, if G is not essentially good, then Plato can legitimately infer in (19) that G is not good at all. Arguably, for Aristotle too, properties of primary substances of the kind on display in (13), if they hold of their subject at all, do so essentially, and the inference to (19) is again without blame.

But, next, is (19) unacceptable, as required? For Plato and Aristotle alike, uneasiness about (19) rests on a deeper-seated aversion to the premise, (13). As before (n. 45 above), in the shared theory of Izzing and Having, Plato's claim that the Good Is good, or that Man Is (a) man, made within a Platonic ontology of (Platonic) Forms, has a direct counterpart in an Aristotelian ontology of kinds and (Aristotelian) form—independently of the more parochial assumptions that separate a Platonic and an Aristotelian ontology. So Aristotle's reductio holds good: both philosophers have as good a reason for rejecting (19) as they do for rejecting the premise, (13). In the body of theory that Plato and Aristotle share, both lines get swept away together. With the dispatch of (13) (in this section), and the dispatch of its partner, (14) (Sect. 3.1), Aristotle has shown that both components of the Severance Assumption are false.

It remains to recapitulate the relevance of Aristotle's arguments against (13) and (14) to his larger aims in *Zeta* 6. Now that (15) and (16) are defeated, his argument from Severance (Sect. 2.3) is complete. Aristotle is free to apply the principle (15) from the theory of Izzing and Having, in conjunction with the defeat of the two halves of Severance, in a second, major proof of the Identity Result that is his main concern in the chapter.

3.3 Aristotle on How Plato's Forms Are Inessential to His Argument

In the lines at 1031b11-15, Aristotle appears to sum up the net profit (or loss) from his involvement with Plato. But his conclusion is obscured by various issues of translation and interpretation. Dogmatically, I give my translation first, then append Burnyeat's version of the second half of the passage beginning at b14:

> It is necessary therefore that the good and the essence of good be one, and the beautiful and the essence of beauty, and whatever is said not per aliud, but <is> per se and primary: (b14) and this would be sufficiently established, even if [Platonic] Forms do not exist, but all the more perhaps if there are [Platonic] Forms. (1031b11-15)
>
> ... (b14) It is enough if they are this [sc. if they are primary things which are in their own right what they are said to be], even if they are not *eidê*, and perhaps all the more so if they are *eidê* [*or* ... even if there are no *eidê*, and perhaps all the more so if there are *eidê*]. (b14-15, Burnyeat 2001, p. 27)

(i) Burnyeat's translation of and gloss on b14, *kai gar touto hikanon an huparchêi*, follows the standard account: "It is enough"—that is, we get the desired Identity

Result—"if (*an*=*ean*) they are this" or, perhaps, "if this condition is met" [= the condition from b13 to b14 that the items in question are suitably primary]. The back reference seems sufficiently awkward to make tempting the reading *huparchoi* in Ab and in Alexander for *huparchêi* (on this reading, *an* □ *ean*): the meaning would then be "This would be sufficiently established, whether or not Plato's *êide* exist," where the "this" refers back to the Identity Result mentioned in the previous lines.

(ii) By "*eidê*," I suppose that Aristotle means Platonic Forms. Burnyeat wonders whether Aristotle's word here means (a) "Platonic Forms" (a shift from his use of the Greek, "*idea*," everywhere else in the surrounding text), or (b) "species" (in line with the earlier "*genous eidê*" in Z.4), or finally, (c) "Aristotelian forms." In favor of (c), and against (a), is what Burnyeat describes as otherwise the mystery of why Aristotle would think that his Identity Result holds more firmly *in the case of Plato's Forms* than for his own primary substances.[57]

But (iii) if we adopt my reading under (i) above (finding a reference to Plato's Forms, as in [a] above), Aristotle is not saying that the Identity Result holds in any case for primary substances, but even more firmly for Platonic Forms; rather, the Result is adequately established whether Plato's Forms exist or not—but more firmly, *if Platonic Forms do exist*.

The alliance with Plato in Z.6, then, comes to this. Aristotle's arguments in the chapter, couched as they are in terms of Platonic Forms, offer one further supporting case for the desired Identity Result—and this is still support, even if in fact Plato is wrong in thinking that Platonic Forms exist.

Notes

1. A near-finished draft of this chapter was read at a conference on Substance and Essence at Oxford in Summer 2005, and a later version still to an audience in Los Angeles; I am grateful for the helpful comments from the audience on both occasions. Thanks also to David Charles for characteristically generous discussion and to Norman Dahl and Alan Code for their comments on the later version.
    All citations are from Aristotle's *Metaphysics* and in particular from Z.6, unless otherwise indicated. All translations are my own unless otherwise noted.
2. The black-and-white view is set out with some firmness at 1030a11-17, only to be followed immediately by a conciliatory statement of the more relaxed view at a17-27; the contrast between the two kinds of view is repeated throughout the remainder of the chapter.
3. As I emphasize in the main text below, the brand of sameness Aristotle intends is left unclear at the opening of Z.6, but with the help of the Pale Man arguments at 1031a19-28 in excluding an unwanted weaker notion, he later settles on essential sameness; this I take it comprises our identity, coupled with a restriction to primary entities, which qualify for having an essence in the strict sense. For an opposing view, see Dahl (2003) and Charles (2011, see Appendix).
4. Cf. Wedin (2000, ch. VII)
5. The substance-of relation, the definition-of relation, and the essence-of relation are all three subject to variation in degree; see Lewis (1984). For how the notion of essence is articulated within Aristotle's own ontology, see Loux (1991, ch. 7) and Lewis (1995/1999, p. 529).
6. Aristotle assumes for purposes of reductio that a given primary entity, x, is not "essentially the same" as its essence, y; from this, if n. 3 is right, and given the restriction that x and hence

plausibly y too are primary entities, it follows that x is not identical with y. If, as Aristotle's reductio suggests, it results in the end that x and y are identical, the restriction to primary entities ensures that they are also essentially the same.
7. Burnyeat et al. (1979), see Sect. 1.2.
8. According to Ross (1924, II, p. 177), Aristotle has in mind the "covert criticism" of Plato that because the Platonic Form is neither a particular good thing nor the essence of good, and because insuperable difficulties arise if we "separate" the Form from the essence of good, we should make do with essences and stop believing in Forms. Against this, however, Aristotle may well think that the essence of particular good things makes the Platonic Form superfluous; but he has in mind here the different point that even granting that the Form of Good exists, *it*, the Form, cannot in turn have some distinct entity as *its* essence. That is, he is concerned with whether (and on what terms) the Form itself can have an essence, not whether there exists an essence of particular good things. The second option tried out in Bostock (1994, pp. 107–8) follows Ross; perhaps to adjust for the criticism of Ross just given, Bostock goes on to say explicitly that Aristotle is concerned with the essence of all good things, and not (as appears at first sight) with the essence of the Form, cf. n. 23 below.

Finally, it is not clear whether, in Ross's view, *the very same argument* that establishes Aristotle's sameness result also refutes the separation of (Platonic) Form and essence and promotes the case of essences over that of (Platonic) Forms. It may well be that the criticism Ross envisions is only incidental to the argument Aristotle gives: if so, the criticism has the same status as the objections Aristotle himself levels against Plato at b15–18, which do not even pretend to be simultaneously a proof of the sameness result.
9. It is not ruled out on logical grounds that one and the same reductio argument should simultaneously refute Plato and establish Aristotle's desired conclusion about the relation of a thing to its essence: if the target Platonic assumption is (an instance of) *the negation of* the desired sameness result, and if everything else goes right, the desired result can be obtained by negating the target Platonic assumption, with no special Platonic assumptions remaining. In practice, however, not all the special Platonic assumptions are discharged, and the argument remains impure: see the discussion of Cherniss (1944, Sect. 1.2). A different attempt at purity regained, in connection with the argument involving "severance" at b3–11, appears in Frede and Patzig (1988, pp. 96–97); see n. 39 below.
10. So, perhaps, 1031b14-15; see Sect. 3.3.
11. Compare, for example, the third option tried out in Bostock (1994): Aristotle hopes that his argument "will establish that, where X is a fundamental substance as specified, then X and the essence of X must be identical, *whatever* the fundamental substances turn out to be" (p. 108, his emphasis). What place is left for Plato, if this last view is correct? Plato can be included, consistently with the requirements for purity, in the way nicely summarized by Burnyeat (2001, p. 27): " ... the argument will serve his purpose provided that the only feature of the Forms used to derive the conclusion is that, by hypothesis, they are primary things which are in their own right what they are said to be. The conclusion then stands whatever the baseline of one's ontology may be." On some readings, including Burnyeat's, this is much what Aristotle himself says at 1031b14-15, but the translation and interpretation of the passage is under dispute; see Sect. 3.3. Other advocates of purity include Dancy (1975, p. 100), Wedin (2000), and Lewis (2003). The "big tent" view advocated here has its ancestry in Code's "general metaphysics" (Code 1997).
12. On the question of Platonic authorship, see *Met.* M.5, 1080a1, cf. A.6 988a8-11, A.7 988b4-5. At M.5 1079b15-17, Aristotle says that (contrary to Plato?) Plato's Forms cannot be the substances of sensibles. And some of the arguments in Z.14 take Plato to task on the related idea that certain Forms are the substance of other Forms ("the form man is *not accidentally* composed of animal," 1039b7-9, 9-10, 12-13, 15-16); he suggests at the end of the chapter that similar arguments apply to the relation between (Platonic) Forms and sensibles.
13. See the apparent attribution to Plato at Z.6, 1031b2-3 (included in the quotation in Sect. 1.2), and yet a further appearance in Z.6 at b31-2. The assumption is also stated explicitly in Z.10 and 13, in H.1, and perhaps also in Z.7: Z.10, 1035b14-16, Z.13, 1038b14-15, Z.7, 1032b1-2; see also the unqualified assertion in H.1, 1042a17.

14. Burnyeat (2001, p. 26), cf. also Frede and Patzig (1988, II p. 88), who add that perhaps the Platonic antecedents of the idea make any proof of it superfluous. Presumably, then, on the Frede-Patzig view, Aristotle endorses the Assumption, while Burnyeat holds that he abstains with respect to it. But it is hard to see how Aristotle can hold the Assumption at arm's length in Z.6 or anywhere else in the segment on essence (unless—which I doubt—for purposes of reductio), given his statement of his agenda for the bulk of *Zeta* at the beginning of Z.3.
15. Here, I appropriate a point made in a different connection by Gareth Matthews (the point is also recognized in LSJ s.v. *ei*, BVI, and *eiper*, II).
16. See Bostock (1994, pp. 112–13) and esp. Loux (1991, ch. 3). I have in mind Aristotle's desire to avoid an infinite regress, together with the reasons he gives elsewhere for finding a regress objectionable: if an essence is infinitely long, then it will have no cognitive value, *An. Post.* I.22 82b37-83a1, cf. 84a25-26; see also *Metaphysics* α.2 994b16-18 with Alexander *in Met.* 160.30-161.1. On Aristotle's antipathy in general to infinite regresses, see also Kung (1981, p. 255 with nn. 48 and 49).
17. These efforts to highlight the connection with substance are noteworthy, in view of indications that Z.6 is, in origin at least, "semidetached" from the surrounding discussion in Z.4–5 and its continuation in Z.10 (supposing with the current orthodoxy that Z.7–9 are themselves an addition); see Burnyeat (2001, p. 26).

    Ironically, Aristotle's very efforts in the Basic Argument to secure relevance for his question about sameness have been thought to make the question itself pointless: Pelletier (1979, p. 289). According to the redundancy objection, given (i) and (ii) above in the main text as premises, it appears to follow trivially that each thing and its essence are the same. How can this conclusion, so easily obtained, require the kind of inquiry Aristotle proposes in his first sentence and carries out in exquisite detail in the remainder of the chapter? Pelletier himself suggests that we can avoid pointlessness, if in contrast to the contemporary notion of identity, the relation of sameness that Aristotle thinks holds between a thing and its essence is not transitive: on this view, the remainder of the chapter has point, only because the opening argument is invalid. A less drastic response to the redundancy objection is that Aristotle quotes the premises of the Basic Argument as received opinion, not fact: the conclusion to the argument is not assured, until the premises are on a more solid footing. More than this, both premise (i), that each thing is the same as its substance, and the conclusion, (iii), that each thing and its essence are the same, are provisional in nature (see two paragraphs below in the main text); formulating each in a form Aristotle will find acceptable, I take it, is part of the point of the Elaboration of the Argument conducted in Plato's name at 1031 a28–b3.
18. For the use of identity here, see note 3 above.
19. The stipulation that *y* be suitably primary is not present in the Basic Argument, which is preliminary to the more detailed work later in the chapter, where Aristotle will want to differentiate the primary cases in which the Identity Result holds from other cases in which it does not. But the needed restriction is signposted almost immediately with his "on the one hand" (*men*) at 1031a19, answered by "on the other hand," (*de*) at a28, where primary cases are introduced. Notably, Aristotle does not explain in this chapter what in his own "official" theory will count as a primary substance (for speculation about the reason for his reticence, see the comments toward the end of Sect. 1.2).
20. Burnyeat (2001, p. 26) thinks the precedent for (i) is in the *Organon* at *An. Post.* I.21 83a24-32. I do not know if he would agree in finding Plato to be a common ancestor for the *Organon* passage and for *Metaphysics* Z.6 alike.
21. For the "itself" supplied twice over in angle brackets at a32, see Ross (1924, II, p. 177).
22. Aristotle sidesteps the question whether things other than primary substances are also "said in virtue of themselves." So he is able to avoid the complication that in his own theory of form and matter, the form-matter compound (which is "said in virtue of itself," A.7 1017a22-3) is a substance but not a primary substance and importantly, *not* subject to the identity result of Z.6 (cf. Lewis 1984 and Appendix). I say more on his apparent policy of avoiding reference to form and matter at the end of this section.
23. Surprisingly, Aristotle does not explicitly state (1), although what I take to be its denial (= [13] in Sect. 2.2) appears later at 1031b5-6. It is likely that Aristotle's term for the essence

in question serves as an implicit assertion of (1): "the for-good to be" [*to agathôi einai*] may convey simultaneously the ownership of the essence ["what it is *for the good* to be <good>"] as well as its content ["what it is <for a thing> *to be good*"]. (For more on the ownership-content distinction in this context, see [Lewis 2013] Chap. 3, # 3.) As to ownership, my (1) runs counter to Bostock (1994, p. 108), who argues that the essence in question is the essence of —that is, belonging to—*a good thing*, that is, *any* good thing, cf. n. 8 above, rather than the essence that belongs to G itself.

24. Cf. note 6 above.
25. Z.3, 1028b33-6, cf. Z.4, 1029a1-3; (cf. also the opening paragraph of Sect. 1 and note 13 above)
26. Again, see note 6 above.
27. See Sect. 1. Arguably, both assumptions are applications of a general causal principle ("A cause is equal to or greater than its effect") that Aristotle and Plato alike accept without question. (For the application to Plato, imagine that Plato will think that his Forms are primary substances, and that the sensibles that depend on them are substances to a lesser degree.) The causal principle is discussed in Lloyd (1976).
28. With this conclusion, compare the quotation from Burnyeat (2001) and see note 11 above.
29. Burnyeat et al. (1979) on 1031a31-b3. The notetaker on this occasion is identified as Burnyeat: the later views of Burnyeat by himself on issues of purity in Burnyeat (2001) are quite different.

"Arguing from false premises" is discussed without enthusiasm by Aristotle in the *Topics* V.11: it is identified as a fourth kind of fallacious argument at 162b11-15.

30. For the record, this cannot be the view recorded in Burnyeat et al. (1979) (cited in the previous paragraph in the main text), for the contributors recorded there deny that the argument is intended as a reductio of Plato's views; in our terms, then, their account is straightforwardly impure.
31. Even the subsequent talk of taking a thing and its essence "apart from" each other—supposing we were to think this a reference to Platonic separation—is introduced only as part of the set of arguments that follow beginning at b3. But any connection between these arguments and Platonic separation is contested in Sect. 2.1.
32. See notes 13 and 14 with the associated main text above.
33. For another attempt at purity regained, see the interpretation Frede and Patzig (1988, II, pp. 96–7) give of the arguments in connection with separation at 1031 b3; see note 39 below.
34. See, for example, note 22 above.
35. One further bonus of purity is surely friendship: Plato and Aristotle see amicably eye to eye on the issues currently before them. But Aristotle can also view Plato as a philosophical foe in the hunt for substance: one signal place in which the relationship between the two is tested is the account of substance and universals in Z.13; see Lewis (2013).
36. Note the *men*, at b3. There is no corresponding *de* (no "other hand").
37. Following Ross (1924, II, p. 178)
38. The reading of [ii] as (14) is guaranteed by the parallel passage at b8. The first clause, [i], is more difficult to decipher; one constraint on how it is read is that it supply a suitable assumption for the argument at b6-7 that G is therefore unknowable. I see three possible translations. (a) Bostock translates "being for a good thing does not belong to goodness-itself": that is, he explains, the essence is not identical with the (Platonic) Form, but neither does the Form have an essence as a constituent (in the way, perhaps, that an Aristotelian form-matter compound will do). On this reading of [i], on the assumption that to know a thing is to know its essence, where either the thing is identical with its essence or, more weakly, has its essence as a constituent, it follows from [i] that G is unknowable. (b) "G is not essentially good" or, perhaps, (c) "the for-good to be is not the essence of G" (for the reading of *huparchei* here, cf. Z.13 1038b10 and Code (1978) and Lewis (2003, n. 26); on either reading, presumably, G has no essence at all, so that if to know a thing is to know its essence, G is unknowable, b6-7).
39. On the account offered by Frede and Patzig (1988, II, pp. 96–7), Aristotle's assumption that a Form is "severed" from its essence is the basis for an argument on behalf of his own conception

of essence and simultaneously part of an attack on "certain Platonists," if not on Plato himself. We are to assume a version of Platonism on which

(i) (Platonic) Forms are the essence of the relevant sensibles.

Suppose, next, contrary to what Frede and Patzig take to be Aristotle's true view, that

(ii) In general, things are separate from their essences

(the sense of "separate" here is given at b4-6), so that, by (i) and (ii),

(iii) Forms are separate from the relevant sensibles.

By parity with (iii) or, perhaps, by instantiation from (ii), we have

(iv) The essence of a Form will itself be separate from that (Platonic) Form.

Given the various absurdities that follow from (iv), we must deny the premise, (iii), on which (iv) rests. That is,

(v) Forms are not separate from the sensibles of which they are the essence.

More generally, contrary to (ii),

(vi) In general, things are not separate from their essences.

In this argument, Aristotle is imagined arguing the absurdity of separating things from their essences for the special case of (Platonic) Forms and their essences. But if no special Platonic assumptions remain when he moves from the special case to the general conclusion (unless they are concealed in the different arguments to absurdity), the argumentative strategy is a successful example of purity regained.

Unfortunately, the route to purity is again illusory. In the first place, we cannot reject (iii) without rejecting one or other of the assumptions on which (iii) rests. As before, however, we are not entitled to reject both at once. But if (ii) is the assumption to go, we are left with (i)—the assumption that Forms are the essences of the sensibles that fall under them. Alternatively, we can eliminate (i) and the attendant commitment to Platonism—but no conclusion now follows to force the rejection of (ii) and the separation of things from their essences.

There is also a difficulty regarding the correct disposal of (ii). If (ii) is false, then it is not the case that things in general are separate from their essences. But the desired conclusion, (vi), puts the negative in a different place, giving it narrow scope with respect to the universal quantifier. So (vi) is not in any case a proper conclusion to the argument.

40. Code (1980), cf. *Metaphysics* D4 in his (1986, p. 414). In the theory of "Izzing and Having," Plato and Aristotle alike recognize two basic modes of predication, one (roughly) connecting a subject essentially to what is predicated of it and the other connecting them accidentally: for example (two cases Plato and Aristotle agree over), Man Is (an) animal and Socrates Has generosity, or (in Aristotle's book but hardly Plato's) Socrates Is (a) man, and Man Has grammar. (In these cases—but not, perhaps, universally, for reasons explained later in this section—Izzing and Having are the converses of the said-of and in relations respectively in Aristotle's *Categories*.) Other basic claims in the theory that will command assent from Plato and Aristotle alike, for all the differences between their two positions, are noted in note 45 below, and for the full theory, see (Code, op. cit.).

41. While Code views (15) as a definition, it is not hard to see how one might argue in support of (15). Going from left to right, we suppose that Izzing is reflexive. Then if $X = Y$, and given that X Is X, we know that X Is Y and that Y Is X. Going from right to left, the structure of an Aristotelian genus-species tree inclines us to think that Izzing will be asymmetric: for example, man Is an animal but not vice versa. But this and similar examples are preserved if we think that the relation is antisymmetric: that is, that X Is Y and Y Is X, only if $X = Y$.

42. *Categories*.2,3; *Topics* I.5 102a18-22

43. This argument is based on a comment in discussion by Paolo Crivelli.

44. The textual evidence for (d) from $\Delta.18$, quoted above in the main text, suggests that Izzing is reflexive; it also speaks against restricting the field of the relation to universals. For any X, therefore, whether $X =$ man (say) or $X =$ Socrates, X Is X. At the same time, the relation, X is said of Y too is reflexive—but only where X is a universal. The upshot is that the proposed biconditional, (b), is false; only the conditional in the right-to-left direction can be true since—what is not the case with Izzing—entities in the domain of the said-of relation must be universals.

Against the reflexivity of the said-of relation—I owe the point to audience members in Los Angeles—it may be objected that where X is said of Y, Y is a *subject* or *hupokeimenon* to X, and it is hard to think that $X=Y$ so that X is *hupokeimenon* to itself. To this, I answer that where X is said of Y, and X and Y are both universals, as stipulated, we must find *some individual substance*, s, such that s is *hupokeimenon* to both X and Y. Harmlessly, then, X is said of X, and there exists some individual substance, s, such that s is *hupokeimenon* to X and $s \neq X$.

45. Plausibly, Izzing is subject to a form of *reflexivity* (nn. 41 and 44 above), so that the Aristotelian kind, man, Is (a) man; and in any theory that recognizes Platonic Forms, the Platonic Form, G, Is good. But if G Is good and has the for-good to be as its essence, then by general principles about essences, the for-good to be will be the *cause* of G's being Good (see, perhaps, Z.17 1041a28), and by certain general causal principles Plato and Aristotle share (n. 27 above), the for-good to be Is therefore itself good.
46. Following Ross, I will suppose that the two results are proved separately: Ross (1924, II, p. 177), see also Bostock (1994, p. 109), and note 48 below.
47. This first argument is incomplete as it stands, but perhaps we are to supply the thought that if the for-good to be is not the essence of G, as (13) asserts, then G can have no essence at all; if then to know G is to know its essence and if G has no essence, then G cannot be known. There is a different account in Bostock (1994, pp.109–10). See also Frede-Patzig (1988, II, p. 95), who take not (13) by itself but the entire assumption that a Platonic Form and its essence are "taken apart" from each other (as I see it, the conjunction of [13] and [14]) to be the premise of the argument.
48. On the "two argument" view adopted in the main text, Aristotle proves the same result, that essences do not exist, twice over, first (and elliptically) en route to the conclusion that forms cannot be known (n. 47 above), and then for a second time, apparently independently, for its own sake. Alternatively, he gives just a single argument: after warning us first of the connection between knowing a thing and its essence, he goes on to argue for the one conclusion, that no essence exists; from this, there follows almost immediately, given the advertised connection between knowledge and essence, the second conclusion, that no Form can be known (so, perhaps, Burnyeat et al. [1979] on b3–4). On this second view, which sees only one argument, with two intertwined conclusions, Aristotle uses assumption (14) to reach both conclusions, and (13) is put to work only in the one-line argument that follows at b11 (Sect. 3.2).
49. Bonitz (1848–9, II, pp. 317–8), cf. Bostock (1994, p. 110)
50. With the different choices that are open here, we can compare an example from Aristotle's ethics and theology. If the virtuous man imitates God, and God thinks only himself, should we conclude that (a) the virtuous man only thinks himself or (b) that the virtuous man thinks only God? (Answer: How do you define imitation? Is it with respect to the property, thinking oneself, or the property, thinking God?)

    The "all or nothing" claims in this part of Z.6 can be compared with the similar uniformity assumption at Z.13 1038b12-13, for which see Code (1978, p. 70) and Lewis (1991, pp. 313, 344).
51. Recall here that Platonic Forms are causes, and that "the cause is equal to or greater than its effect" (Lloyd, 1976), cf. note 27 above. My appeal to "formal" or "categorial" properties rests on their use in a different context in Keyt (1971).
52. Cf. B.1, 995b29-31, 3, 998b14-999a23; for the choice of *genous eidê* in Z.4, see especially 999a14-16 and also *PA* I.4 644a24-5. In favoring the *eidos* here, note that Aristotle is dropping the candidacy of the *genos* in Z.3, cf. H.1 1042a13-15 (and for the debate between the two options, see again the passages cited from *Beta*).
53. If X is a primary substance, then by the Identity Result of Z.6, $X=$ the essence of X. But it is a theorem of the theory of Izzing and Having that X Is X; accordingly, the essence of X Is X, as required. Similarly, the primary substance, X, is a being, so that the essence of X too is a being, by the Identity Result noted.
54. Cf. Bostock's gloss (using the contrapositive), "the essence of a good thing belongs to *everything* that is good" Bostock, (1994, p. 110, my emphasis). This reading may explain why Bostock finds the argument oddly motivated.

55. See Ross (1924), II, p. 178 and especially 169 on Z.4 1030a1-2. On the preferred reading, the negation *mê* (in contrast to *ou*) is conditional rather than general in force; or if it is general, it is still restricted to (Platonic) Forms.
56. Frede-Patzig (1988, II, pp. 97–8). Frede and Patzig say that Aristotle certainly rejects the inference; they also say that the argument rests on the earlier assumption that a Platonic Form and its essence are to be "taken apart," and also calls that assumption into question. But they do not explain how the assumption is called into question, given what they take to be Aristotle's view that the inference is invalid.
57. Burnyeat (2001, p. 27). It is telling that Ross (1924, II, p. 178) dismisses this as a contemptuous aside on Aristotle's part.

Appendix

I append here more detailed comments on two recent contributions to the secondary literature on Z.6.

I am thoroughly in agreement with one main theme of Dahl 2003—that the various inferences in the target passage 1030a28-b3, quoted in Sect. 1.2, should be "appropriately generalizable"—insofar as this means validating them in Aristotle's own theory as well as in Plato's. This puts us both on the side of purity in our approach to Z.6.

Beyond this lies disagreement. I am not sympathetic to extending the project of "appropriate generalization" so that the sameness result of Z.6, suitably understood, applies to the composite material substance and what counts as its essence (strictly, suitably asterisked to show that this is a different relation, with different logical properties, its essence*, Lewis 1984, pp. 96–118, Code 1985, pp. 118–19). According to Dahl, if the sameness result includes this further case, then the sameness relation in question must be sameness in substance or formula, but *not* also numerical sameness. That is, the relation does not imply identity, as I suppose. But if the sameness result is restricted, as I think, and does *not* apply to the compound material substance and its essence, then the sameness relation can be correspondingly more stringent and can imply identity.

Is it right that the conclusion of Aristotle's Elaborated Argument applies also to the compound material substance and its essence, so that use of the weaker sameness relation is triggered, as Dahl supposes? Although the compound material substance is a substance, it is not a primary substance, and it does have a substance prior to it, namely, its constituent substantial form, which also is its essence*. So the compound material substance apparently is disqualified out of hand for the Elaborated Argument, which Aristotle expressly restricts to entities that are *primary*. Dahl is well aware of the difficulty (p. 164) and attempts to counter it by pointing out that (a) the substantial form is itself dependent on its parent compound material substance. He adds that (b) the various passages in *Zeta* that apparently make form primary substance can be interpreted differently, and that anyway (c) what goes elsewhere in *Zeta* need not hold for this chapter.

I do not think that (c) can bear much weight: for all the fluidity in Aristotle's thought in *Zeta*, we should not want to encourage a Protagorean interpretive stance, where a new Aristotle presents himself in each chapter. And Dahl is not above bringing in the results of Z.17, for example, and the notion of a thing's essence as the cause of its being, in order to supply assumptions to make his version of the Elaborated Argument go. I am also not in sympathy with (b): think of Z.16, for example, on why an individual substance cannot be a primary definable. At the same time, with respect to (a), Aristotle does not discuss how the existence conditions for a given form introduce a dependency on compound material substances. It bears noting, however, that a given substantial form is not (existentially) dependent on a given compound material substance but requires only that there be *some compound material substance or other* in which the form is enmattered. On the other hand, a given compound material substance is (essentially) dependent on a given substantial form—without that very form, the substance could not exist. So the dependency in the two directions is not of equal strength.

At the same time, I also do not agree that the weaker sameness result, with its attendant hospitality to the compound material substance, is required, as Dahl claims it is, if we are to have an acceptable account of Aristotle's discussion of severance at 1031 b3-11 (Sects. 2.1 and 2.2). There is no such requirement, if the argument using (15) in Sect. 2.2 succeeds.

Finally, a fresh attack on the view that the variety of sameness at work in the Elaborated Argument entails identity has been launched in Charles (2011). On the identity reading, Aristotle means to establish that Plato's primary entities—which here go proxy for whatever entities are primary in a given ontology—are *identical* with their essences. Success here, however, may bring a heavy price. Like its (linguistic) definition, the essence of a given primary entity is composed of parts, and these parts will be in some sense prior to *the essence* to which they belong; by the Identity Result, then, these parts will be prior also to *the entity that was supposedly primary*. Among the different remedies that might be set in place to meet this objection, Charles suggests (with Dahl 2003) that essential sameness between a primary entity and its essence does not after all require that they be identical. But is it clear that essential sameness is sufficiently weak so that the unwanted inference does not go through? In particular, the relation must not be that of "being one and indistinguishable in being," *SE* 24 179a37; cf. *Phys* III.3 202b14-16, which would appear to license this and other troublesome inferences. Be this as it may, Aristotle suggests elsewhere that the thing defined—equally, then, the entity of which the essence is being given—will have parts that correspond exactly to the parts in the definition (*Met Z.*10 1034b20-22): so the puzzle remains, independently of the exigencies of Z.6. At the same time, the proposed solution itself appears to be open to the fresh difficulty that there may now exist a multiplicity of essences associated with a single given Platonic Form—multiple essences of the Good (say)—so that the Form of the Good can have an essence, and *that* essence have an essence, and so on, for all we know, ad infinitum (cf. 1031b28-1032a2, leading to the regress at a2-4). These essences for the one Form will all be essentially the same and so, presumably, indistinguishable in content—but they will remain numerically distinct. My own sense is that no definitive answer to these problems is yet in prospect.

Bibliography

Bogen, James, and James E. McGuire. 1985. *How things are*. Dordrecht: Springer.
Bonitz, Herman. 1848–9. *Aristotelis Metaphysica*. 2 vols. Bonn: A. Marcus.
Bostock, David. 1994. *Aristotle Metaphysics Books Z and H*. Oxford: Oxford University Press.
Burnyeat, Myles. 2001. *A map of Metaphysics Zeta*. Pittsburgh: Mathesis Publications.
Burnyeat, Myles, et al. 1979. *Notes on book zeta of Aristotle's Metaphysics*. Oxford: Sub-Faculty of philosophy.
Charles, David. 2011. Some remarks on substance and essence in *Metaphysics Z. 6*. In *Episteme, etc.: Essays in honor of Jonathan Barnes*, ed. Ben Morison and Katerina Ierodiakonou, 151–171. Oxford: Oxford University Press.
Cherniss, Harold. 1944. *Aristotle's criticism of Plato and the academy*. Baltimore: Russell and Russell.
Code, Alan. 1978. No universal is a substance: An interpretation of *Metaphysics* Z.13, 1038b8-15. *Paideia* MCMLXXVIII, ed. G.C. Simmons, pp. 65–74.
Code, Alan. 1980. Aristotle on the sameness of each thing with its essence. Paper read before the Society for Ancient Greek Philosophy.
Code, Alan. 1985. On the origins of some Aristotelian theses about predication. In *The way things are: Studies in predication*, ed. J. Bogen and J.E. McGuire, 101–131. Dordrecht: Reidel.
Code, Alan. 1986. Aristotle: Essence and accident. In *Philosophical grounds of rationality: Intentions, categories, ends*, ed. Richard Grandy and Richard Warner, 411–439. Oxford: Oxford University Press.
Code, Alan. 1997. Aristotle's metaphysics as a science of principles. *Revue Internationale de Philosophie* 201: 345–366.
Dahl, Norman O. 2003. On substance being the same as its essence in *Metaphysics* vii 6: The argument about Platonic Forms. *Ancient Philosophy* 23(1): 153–179.
Dancy, R.M. 1975. On some of Aristotle's first thoughts about substance. *Philosophical Review* 84: 338–373.
Frede, Michael, and Gunther Patzig. 1988. *Aristotles "Metaphysik Z."* 2 vols. Munich: C. H. Beck.
Keyt, David. 1971. The mad craftsman of the *Timaeus*. *Philosophical Review* 80 (2): 230–235.
Kung, Joan. 1981. Aristotle on thises, suches, and the third man argument. *Phronesis* 26: 207–247.
Lewis, Frank A. 1984. What is Aristotle's theory of essence? *Canadian Journal of Philosophy*, suppl. 10: 89–131.
Lewis, Frank A. 1991. *Substance and predication in Aristotle's Metaphysics*. Cambridge: Cambridge University Press.
Lewis, Frank A. [1995] 1999. Substance, predication, and unity in Aristotle. *Ancient Philosophy* 15: 521–49. Reprinted in *Aristotle: Critical assessments volume 1*, ed. Lloyd P. Gerson, 286–317. London/New York: Routledge.
Lewis, Frank A. [1999] 2000. The hitchhiker's guide to *Metaphysics Zeta*. *Proceedings of the Boston Area Colloquium in Ancient Philosophy*, vol. XV, ed. John J. Cleary and Gary M. Gurtler. Leiden: Brill Academic Publishing.
Lewis, Frank A. 2003. Friend or foe?—Some encounters with Plato in Aristotle *Metaphysics Zeta*. *Modern Schoolman* 80: 365–390.
Lewis, Frank A. 2005. A nose by any other name: Sameness, substitution, and essence in Aristotle, *Metaphysics* Z.5. *Oxford Studies in Ancient Philosophy* 28: 161–199.
Lewis, Frank A. 2013. *How Aristotle gets by in Metaphysics Zeta*. Oxford: Oxford University Press.
Lloyd, A.C. 1976. The principle that the cause is greater than the effect. *Phronesis* 21: 146–151.
Loux, Michael. 1991. *Primary ousia: An essay on Aristotle's Metaphysics Z and H*. Ithaca: Cornell University Press.
Pelletier, Francis Jeffrey. 1979. Sameness and referential opacity in Aristotle. *Nous* 13: 283–311.
Ross, W.D. 1924. *Aristotle Metaphysics*. 2 vols. Oxford: Oxford University Press.
Wedin, Michael. 2000. *Aristotle's theory of substance. The Categories and Metaphysics Zeta*. Oxford: Oxford University Press.

Metaphysics Z.11 and Functionalism

Cass Weller

It is no longer as fashionable as it once was to find in Aristotle's *De Anima* adumbrations of materialist functionalism with regard to psychological states, so the criticism I offer in what follows is both a postmortem and an inoculation against future outbreaks. I begin with a general and dogmatic discussion of matter's form dependency and contrast this with matter's independence of form in the materialist functionalism ascribed to Aristotle. I then turn to consider a passage in *Metaphysics* Z.11 where Aristotle seems to commit himself to the compositional plasticity of biological kinds. Here he acknowledges that because the only humans we encounter are made of flesh, we are limited in our ability to abstract the form in a way that we are not in the case of artifacts such as spheres variously made of wood and bronze (1036a31-b7). The suggestion seems to be that humans could have been made of other materials. If so, then humans and animals generally would appear to be members of natural kinds that are functional kinds. The form of a frog would then be a system of capacities to do what frogs characteristically do, realizable in appropriate materials, although not limited to the materials it is actually realized in. The kind frog would thus be compositionally plastic. It would be multiply realizable in different materials. This view has the same shape as materialist functionalism. Minds are functional entities whose states are defined by their roles in cognition and behavior but are multiply realizable in different natural materials with intrinsic natures of their own that are not functionally defined. Whether Aristotle is countenancing this sort of compositional plasticity for humans and biological kinds generally in the passage at 1036a31-b7 is the question to which we will return.

I submit this essay in honor of David Keyt, esteemed friend and colleague for many years.

C. Weller (✉)
Department of Philosophy, University of Washington, Seattle, WA 98195, USA
e-mail: cjwr@u.washington.edu

1 Aristotle's Anti-reductionism: Matter Depends on Form

What deeply unites the *Categories* and the *Metaphysics*, despite the obvious differences, is an anti-reductionist attitude toward the concrete individuals of ordinary experience. In the *Metaphysics* Aristotle quite explicitly positions himself between the extreme reductionist tendencies of both Platonism and pre-Socratic materialism. In the case of Platonism the Forms constitute a system of self-subsistent objects upon which the existence of everything else depends. What makes a given tree a tree does not depend at all on the fact that there are trees. What makes the tree a tree would exist even if there were no particular trees.[1] In the case of pre-Socratic materialism, some basic material(s) or discrete entities constitute a system of self-subsistent objects of which anything made of anything is made. What makes a given tree a tree, that is, what it is made of, does not at all depend on the fact that there are trees. Aristotle, in contrast, treats trees as basic substances. And even if philosophical analysis reveals a more fundamental tree-making aspect, what makes it a tree would not exist unless there were trees. The fact that Aristotle's terms of analysis are "form" and "matter" can be misleading. The organizational level of matter is always correlative to the form of the object in question. Even in the case of an artifact, which is compositionally plastic, what it is made of is specified at the level of organization relative to the function of the artifact. The matter of the blade of an ax is iron or more generally metal, but not earth, air, fire, and water. What is of crucial importance is that for Aristotle the term "matter" does not designate an ultimate ontological sort to be studied by the scientists of matter. It is not a species of being coordinate with mind as Descartes understood it. Aristotle's physics is not the science of matter as such.[2] Nor is his psychology the science of the mind.

The fact that "matter" is a correlative term has a number of significant consequences, two of which I will mention now. (1) The material ultimately composing a given sublunary individual substance is not the matter of that individual and does not provide an ultimate subject of which the form of that individual is predicated. Socrates is not so many pounds of ultimate material of which the form man is predicated. (2) The materials composing individual substances are not ontologically more basic in the following sense. Facts at the level of the ultimate material do not determine facts pertaining to the form-dependent features of an individual substance. Socrates does not supervene on whatever he is ultimately composed of. It does not matter whether ultimate material is prime matter or a mixture of earth, air, fire, and water. In *De Anima* and the *Metaphysics*, form is prior to the materials composing an individual substance. The form or essence of a paradigmatic individual substance is, abstractly considered, a system of interlocking vital capacities including metabolism, reproduction, percipience, motivity, and desire. These capacities are not, however, to be understood on the Lockean model of dispositional physical properties. The solubility of salt in water is a disposition grounded in the ontologically more basic microstructure of salt. For Aristotle, in contrast, the functions that make up the form or essence of an individual substance are more ontologically basic than the elemental bodies that in an extended sense constitute the bodies of individual members of that species. They are not mere functional features that contingently characterize something more ontologically basic. To put it more starkly, for Aristotle natural kinds are functional kinds. There are no function-independent natural kinds. Even the elementary bodies – earth, air, fire, and water – are functional kinds specified in terms of their active and passive powers. (cf. *Cael* III.8 307b18-23.) But there is no further prospect of supposing that the material structure of earth, for example, grounds its dryness and coldness.

In contrast to this picture, the point of materialist functionalism regarding the mental is to reconcile psychological properties with a monistic ontology in which only Galilean/Newtonian matter matters. Psychological properties are functional properties that depend on ontologically more basic physical states. Moreover, those who subscribe to materialist functionalism typically understand this dependence by supposing that there is a level of facts which is the object of the most fundamental science of matter and which fixes the facts at all other levels of organization. Any difference in functional/psychological facts must be reflected in a difference at a lower level of basic physical facts. This is neither ontological nor explanatory reductionism, but is nevertheless a kind of reductionism, insofar as causality at every higher level of organization is dependent on the causality at the lowest level.[3] That is, while the causal laws at higher levels of organization retain their explanatory autonomy and are not to be derived from laws at the lowest level, causal determination, however probabilistically glossed, nonetheless really occurs at the lowest level. The conjunction of S's believing that X over there is sweet and S's desire for something sweet is the explanatory cause of S's moving in the direction of where X is believed to be, only if there is an ontologically more basic level of causation at which events constituent in the macroevent are causally determinative of the macroevent. The idea is to preserve the autonomy of psychological explanations and the metaphysical respectability of mental properties without sacrificing either an austere materialist ontology or the ideal of mechanistic explanation.

At this level of abstraction, we can see that materialist functionalism and the views of Aristotle are fundamentally incompatible in ways in which I have already begun to touch on. If Aristotle is right and the doings of earth, air, fire, and water (or anything else you pick) do not by their own powers causally determine metabolic, reproductive, or perceptual processes, then even this weak form of reductionism is false. The necessities attaching to these materials are inadequate for causal determination at the higher level. More specifically, those attempting to turn Aristotle's explicit anti-Platonism and inadvertent non-Cartesianism regarding the soul into proto-functionalism fail to recognize that the relation of form and matter, most tellingly in the case of sense perception, is neither the relation of functional properties supervening on physical kinds nor the relation of token identity between mental events and physical events, which are only contingently mental in that they realize functionally defined mental events.[4]

In keeping with the considerations I have thus far advanced, two broad strategies have emerged for showing that ascription to Aristotle of proto-functionalism fails, one from above, one from below: (1) show that for Aristotle, as for Descartes, tokens of mental event types are essentially mental and that individual psychological subjects are essentially psychological,[5] and (2) show that for Aristotle there is nothing to play the role of the physical, that is, the soul-independent categorical base upon which the mental contingently supervenes.[6] Aristotle's matter is not the seventeenth-century's matter.

From the other side, it is crucial for those defending the ascription to Aristotle of materialist functionalism regarding percipience or vitality that they block the strategy from below by establishing that the material kinds that realize percipience and vitality are logically independent thereof.[7] Of course, if living kinds are functional kinds defined solely in terms of what they do without reference to the material kinds realizing them, there is every reason to believe that the materials composing them are as logically independent of what they compose as the material kinds realizing artifacts are of the artifacts they realize. A bench is compositionally plastic. Benches can be made of different materials. There is nothing in the nature of what a given bench is made of that ties it to benches. So if living kinds are compositionally plastic, they too can be assumed to be made of material kinds that are only contingently related to the living kinds they compose.[8] The point can be put more starkly. An individual of a compositionally plastic kind is made of a material kind whose essence is independent of the compositionally plastic kind it realizes.

2 The Appearance of Compositional Plasticity in *Metaphysics* 1036a33-b3

In addition to the familiar passages from *De Anima*[9] staking out anti-Platonic/Cartesian grounds and providing an apparent toehold for functionalist readings, there is a passage at *Metaphysics* 1036a33-b3 that appears to encourage readers to believe that Aristotle endorses just the sort of compositional plasticity that would establish the contingency between constituent material and functional form.[10] Shields[11] (1999), for one, has put the passage back in play as part of a broader strategy to revive the case for Aristotle's paternity of materialist functionalism. Here then is the passage in question:

> In the case of things which are found to occur in specifically different materials, as a circle may exist in bronze or stone or wood, it seems plain that these, the bronze or the stone, are no part of the essence of the circle, since it is found apart from them. Of things which are not seen to exist apart, there is no reason why the same may not be true, e.g., even if all circles that had ever been seen were of bronze (for nonetheless the bronze would be no part of the form); but it is hard to effect this severance in thought. E.g., the form of man is always found in flesh and bones and parts of this kind; are these then also parts of the form and the formula? No, they are matter, but because man is not found also in other matters we are unable to effect the severance.[12] (*Met* Z.11 1036a30-b3)

One must initially concede that Aristotle does appear to be raising the question of whether humans could be made of different materials. He wonders why in defining a circle we abstract from the specific material types circles are made of, but not when we define a human being. As a possible answer, he floats the idea that we only ever encounter humans in one sort of material and that our failure to abstract is due to our lack of imagination. This would suggest at least a flirtation with the idea that biological kinds as functional kinds are compositionally plastic and by implication that mental state types, at least the sensory and emotional, are compositionally plastic. Aristotle's subsequent discussion in Z.11 of the dos and don'ts of abstraction is, at the very least, puzzling. I will return to closer examination of the text, but for the moment let us play out the possibility that Aristotle is flirting with compositional plasticity. I do not take the following discussion to be determinative since it simply plays out the assumptions, or if you like, interpretative prejudices, of my previous discussion in Sect. 1, only in more concrete terms.

Suppose then that Aristotle is raising the question of compositional plasticity. Would he then be inviting such questions as whether humans could have been made of rubber, whether rubber could do and suffer what flesh and bones do and suffer? Clearly not, if this were to affirm the possibility of artificial humans, since they would be only homonymously human and not members of a subspecies of humankind. I am assuming that if the form of MAN or the human soul is realizable in some material, then the resulting concrete individual is a human without qualification (*haplôs*). A wooden sphere and a brazen sphere are both equally spheres, that is, they are spheres synonymously. So suppose instead that in addition to flesh and bone people, there were ab initio, unbeknownst to Aristotle, rubber people living in some remote place on earth or on some other planet. Now, even supposing that the rubber people were humans or persons (*anthrôpoi*), would they and we be *anthrôpoi* synonymously? We, I think, would deny that they were human on the grounds that "human," in this context at any rate, is a natural biological kind term and not a functional kind term. The rubber people might be rational animals, but they would not be members of the biological kind to which we belong. Aristotle does not even have an obvious way of making this distinction between human beings and persons. And in any case, even without bothering to construct Aristotle's identity conditions for a species, we can confidently presume that confronted with the question of whether to include rubber people in the species man Aristotle would decline.

A more serious case remains to be considered, whether humans could have been made of rubber in the sense that the world's current animal life, *mutatis mutandis*, might have made its way around in rubber instead of flesh and bone. The issue turns on spelling out the *mutatis mutandis* clause. Let's suppose the ecosystem adjusted so that what is done by and to flesh and bone in ways relevant to animal life is done by and to rubber. Now in order for flesh and bone to do and suffer what they characteristically do and suffer qua flesh and bone, which includes growing and mending, they must be parts of a living organism, undetached animal parts, to coin a phrase. A heap of lifeless flesh is only homonymously flesh as a corpse is merely homonymously a body. One might use the detached and dried-out femur of a bear for various purposes, but the quantity of bone this instrument is made of is really only ex-bone. Antecedently, flesh and bone only come to be when certain materials present in the organism are transformed in processes that only occur in living organisms.

This leaves us with a dilemma regarding the rubber people. Either the rubber in the rubber people can stand alone as rubber outside living organisms or it cannot. If it can, then either it can do and suffer *extra vivo* what flesh and bone do and suffer only in vivo (in which case we have to countenance the prospect of free occurrences of quasi-living pieces of rubber that break and tear and chafe and itch and mend and grow, and so countenance a nonstarter) or it only possesses its flesh- and bonelike dispositions in vivo, in which case rubber *extra vivo* would be rubber only homonymously, contrary to the hypothesis that rubber can stand alone as rubber. On the other alternative, if the rubber which is to play the role of flesh and bone cannot stand alone as rubber outside a living organism, it is not clear that we are talking about rubber at all rather than flesh and bone under a different name. Surely, on anybody's understanding of rubber, rubber can exist as rubber outside living organisms. Further, if the question is whether humans could be made of rubber *extra vivo*, the answer is "no," unless a case can be made that there are two kinds of rubber, organic and inorganic.[13]

Of course the foregoing musings can be boiled down to the following. If the form MAN is to admit of the compositional plasticity of artifacts and other functional kinds, then the different materials in which this form is multiply realizable must be capable of existing on their own as the materials they are without being thus enformed. But the flesh and bones of an animal only exist as such when ensouled. A dead dog is only homonymously a dog, its flesh and bones, homonymously flesh and bones. After all, if a dead dog is only a body homonymously, surely its parts, that is, its flesh and bones, are as well.[14] If this is right and a corpse is only a heap of flesh and bones homonymously, then the forms of animals and plants do not admit of the sort of compositional plasticity apparently entertained in Aristotle's question at 1036b3-7. The issue to be argued is whether flesh and bone and other homoiomerous tissues are form-dependent in just this way.

There is, however, a question of compositional plasticity that does not immediately run up against this problem. Since the elements, earth, air, fire, and water, are, presumably, not form dependent in the way, I claim, the homoiomerous tissues of plants and animals are, and since the elements constitute the ultimate material of which these tissues are made, why not just retrench and raise the question of compositional plasticity at the level of the elements?[15] So to complete the exercise, let's just ask whether men and other animals could have been composed ultimately of materials other than earth, air, fire, and water. But, assuming the unity of nature, this is to raise the question of whether, for Aristotle, there could have been different elements to be the ultimate materials of everything else in the sublunary sphere. Now I think we have to assume that the alternative elements must include the primitive powers that characterize the familiar four, however else they differ, because it is hard to see, given the work to be done by the hot, the cold, the wet, and the dry, how the functional kinds there are could supervene on elements that lacked these powers. Now it seems there are two strategies for distinguishing the alternative elements from the actual ones: either add to them other arbitrary powers which would not inhibit the work of the original powers and would not give rise to novel functional kinds directly or indirectly by changing the climate or some other factor or ground the original powers on real constitutions which would of course ground numerous other powers, with the same proviso as above: no new kinds that might threaten the identity of the old kinds. We can dismiss the latter, Lockean[16] suggestion, on the grounds that it violates Aristotle's conception of an element as something that is either an aggregate of some of the primitive powers or prime matter plus some of the primitive powers, which in any event is regularly transformed into the other elements. So what we are left with is a conception of an alternative element characterized by non-contrary pairs of primitive powers and other powers that do no discernible work. But this is no real alternative at all.

3 A Reading of Z.11 1036a-b32

So if Aristotle were raising the question of compositional plasticity of interest to functionalists, I think he would have ample reason in his own views for answering in the negative. However, I do not think he is raising that question in Z.11. The explicit concern, as in Z.10, is with the parts of a form and the parts of its definition and not with whether the form of concrete substances can be realized in different materials. Consider the opening sentences of Z.11 immediately preceding the passage at issue.

> The question is naturally raised, what sort of parts belong to the form and what sort not to the form, but to the concrete thing. Yet if this is not plain it is not possible to define anything; for definition is of the universal and form. If then it is not evident which of the parts are of the nature of matter and which are not, neither will the formula of the thing be evident. (Z.11 1036a 26-31)

Aristotle does imply an answer of "no" to the question whether flesh and bones are parts of the form and account of man (because they are matter), and then goes on to explain the failure to grasp this point, our inability to separate this form from its matter, as being due to the exceptionless coupling of this form with flesh and bones. But clearly, whether we are able to separate x from y is a matter of whether we are able to define y without mention of x, and not a matter of whether y can exist without x, as compositional plasticity requires. The inference Aristotle is questioning is the move from "men are always of flesh and bones" to "flesh and bones are parts of the form/definition of man." In order for Aristotle to be committed to the possibility of men who are not composed of flesh and bones, one would have to argue that, for Aristotle, if G is not included in the definition of the form F, something could be an F without being G. (It is certainly not true in the case of the *idia* that definitional non-inclusion entails contingency of the sort at issue. Risibility does not occur in the definition of the form MAN [Met. Z.10 1036a9].) And it also looks as though the definition of the pure universal CIRCLE does not mention matter, while individual circles necessarily have intelligible matter.

Aristotle next takes up the excesses of the Pythagoreans and some members of the Academy who go in for definitional separation without limit. They, apparently encouraged by the slippage between man and flesh and bronze and statue, go so far as to define geometrical forms without mention of line or continuous magnitude. It is not clear whether Aristotle thinks that the Pythagoreans or the Platonists also believe in or are committed to nonspatial triangles and lines (triangles and lines whose matter is a nonspatial continuum) or in materially unrealized forms of triangle and line. It does not matter, nor do his specific complaints. He dismisses the whole enterprise (that of reducing everything to pure form and abstracting matter) as pointless (*periergon*). His reason is that, notwithstanding the acknowledged difficulties in fixing on a rule, some things just are "thises in thises, or thises disposed in particular ways" (1036b22-4). This could mean either that matter is mentioned in some definitions or that some kinds of thing (not just individuals) are necessarily, though perhaps not definitionally, made of what they are made of.

He then continues this theme by rebuking Socrates the Younger for speaking in ways that make one suppose that a man could exist without parts just as a circle without bronze:

> And the comparison that Socrates the Younger used to make in the case of the animal is not good; for it leads away from the truth, and makes one suppose that man can possibly exist without his parts, as the circle can without bronze. (*Met* Z.11 1036b24-8)

I am going to follow Ross,[17] who appears to take it that the form MAN includes no reference to (material) parts just as the form CIRCLE includes no reference to bronze, and suppose that the man without parts is the object of definition for these further reasons: (1) concern here with the parts of the definition of man would maintain what seems to be intended contact with the earlier question regarding the suggested exclusion of flesh and bones from the form/definition of man,[18] as well as continued contact with the immediately preceding discussion of unprincipled abstractionism in definition, and (2) Aristotle responds to the analogy at issue with remarks at the level of definition and not at the level of concrete individuals. And at any rate, since whatever (material) parts, if any, Aristotle thinks belong to the form MAN will be necessarily true of individual men, no content is lost by construing the man without parts as the form.

The form MAN can exist without parts just as CIRCLE without bronze according to Socrates the Younger. This is an odd-sounding analogy because one expects mention of specific material on par with bronze, say flesh and bones. Nor may we supply an implicit reference to such specific materials. Aristotle's rejection of the analogy and the inference built upon it makes it clear that the reference to parts is a generalized reference to concrete parts that move in space (or are subject to change in general) and not materials of a specific sort. Because animals necessarily move in space (are subject to change), they must have parts that move in space (are subject to change). In that case it would seem that "circle without bronze" is elliptical for "circle made neither of bronze, nor wood, nor any concrete material." And thus the man without parts would presumably be a Platonic Form whose definition made no reference to material parts and whose existence did not depend on concrete spatial exemplars.

In any case, whether or not the parts are strictly parts of the form/definition of man, they do belong necessarily to humans and not only to that:

> For an animal is something perceptible, and it is not possible to define it without reference to movement—nor, therefore without reference to the parts and to their being in a certain

state. For it is not a hand in *any* state that is a part of a man, but the hand that can fulfill its work, which therefore must be alive. (1036 b28-32)

These parts are only the parts they are when possessed of form-borne capacities, that is, when they are parts of living human beings. And so taken by itself without regard to how it bears on the earlier question at 1036b3-5, Aristotle's criticism of Socrates the Younger establishes more than that the form MAN must be realized in some matter or other. Man cannot be defined without change and therefore not without parts fitly disposed. But, to reiterate, for the parts to be fitly disposed, they must be parts of what already has the form. (This does not mean, I think, that hand is part of the form/definition of man, although it probably does mean that "sensible material parts fitly disposed to enable a man to do and suffer what a man does and suffer" does belong in the definition of man.) The parts in question here then are ontologically form dependent.[19]

What bearing does this passage have on the earlier one? On the face of it, Aristotle here seems intent on drawing a contrast between, on the one hand, mathematical items like circles, which, while capable of informing a variety of circle-independent sensible materials, are, strictly speaking, realized in intelligible matter, and, on the other hand, sensible objects like humans and other animals, which must have sensible material parts. Yet, this contrast looks like it might restrict if not undermine the initial abstraction question at 1036b3-5. For, on one reading at any rate, if the parts which Socrates the Younger suggests a man need not have and which Aristotle insists a man must have are just stand-ins for the parts mentioned in the earlier question at 1036b3-5, then humans, as a matter of definition, will be made of flesh and bones after all. But I agree this seems forced. Moreover, it appears to contradict Aristotle's earlier willingness to exclude flesh and bones from the form/definition of man.

What I think is going on is a typical exercise in Aristotelian dialectic. He begins by observing that one might rashly conclude that flesh and bones are parts of the form/definition of man, because, unlike the variety of materials in which circles are found, humans are everywhere composed of flesh and bones. At the other extreme, there are abstractionists who, in the absence of a rule for determining where abstraction is warranted and to what extent, would exclude any and every manner of matter from form and definition. One might even go so far as to suppose that the form MAN can be defined without mention of material parts on the model of circle whose definition makes no mention of bronze or wood or any other sensible material that can be shaped into a circle. However, this is to go too far. The analogy breaks down because the form MAN or that of any other animal cannot be defined without reference to change, that is, characteristic ways of acting and being acted on, and this implies having sensible material parts fitly disposed to support these characteristic ways of acting and being acted on. And for the parts to be fitly disposed, they must be parts of what already has the form. So while it is unclear just how specifically these parts are to be mentioned in the definition, some generalized mention must be made.[20] We may, however, safely conclude that even if Aristotle were dialectically entertaining the idea of the human form realized in materials other than flesh and bone, there is no evidence in the passage that he endorses it as a metaphysical possibility. His interest is in what goes into a definition of the form, not in the possible compositional plasticity of the forms of animals, human, or otherwise.

4 Aristotle and Common-Sense Realism

Commentators have understandably been attracted to the nondualism of Aristotle's hylomorphism. But it is carefully positioned between two forms of reductionism: Platonism/Cartesianism, on the one hand, and materialism on the other. Each in its own way threatens the integrity of individual organisms and more particularly the agency of humans. Accordingly, Aristotle's view is more suited to a defense of commonsense realism about familiar everyday objects. Just as he takes ordinary individual organisms as basic, so too does he take ordinary sensible features of objects to be basic. Consider his views about perception. He claims that the exercise of the power of vision is a case of taking on the sensible form of an object without its matter. The fact that it is the same form is a way of indicating that in sense perception objects reveal themselves in their actual features.[21] It is in part because of this commitment to the manifest image[22] of the world that seventeenth-century philosophers took aim at him. Aristotle is an impediment to the project of relocating the apparent features of things in the structure of their physical constitutions. Aristotle's distinction between common and proper sensibles[23] would have to be remade into the primary/secondary quality distinction. As for minds, Aristotle's hylomorphism represents the worst of all possible worlds, however otherwise useful Leibniz found the idea of a soul as an entelechy. By making animal bodies essentially psychological in his sense and finite psychological subjects material in his sense, Aristotle provokes Cartesians into distinguishing minds and matter as ontological kinds and removing the former from the latter so that the new science of matter can proceed uncluttered. Materialists taking one half of the distinction have been trying ever since to relocate and naturalize the mental within the physical. Rather than misappropriate Aristotle's hylomorphism as a materialist solution to the seventeenth-century mind-body problem within the narrow physicalist framework, it would be better to try to reconcile his metaphysics of common sense and our current physicalist framework within a single comprehensive framework.

Notes

1. For ease of exposition I will assume that there is a Platonic Form of Tree.
2. When Aristotle at *An* I.1 403a25-b9 considers the role of the student of nature who studies the matter of psychological phenomena such as anger, the matter in question is blood boiling around the heart. But for Aristotle the latter is still psychological in his sense insofar as it is a process that necessarily only occurs in a living organism.
3. John Dupré (1993, pp. 99–106) links this sort of reductionism to what he calls the thesis of causal completeness.

4. The fact that each of the elementary bodies also admits of a form-matter distinction poses another, perhaps the ultimate, difficulty for materialist functionalist interpretations of Aristotle. Consider the following inconsistent set of propositions:

   (1) Every compound individual of the form F is F, e.g., every dog is a dog.
   (2) Every compound individual of the form F is F only if its compositional matter is contingently F and essentially something else.
   (3) Every determinate individual member of the kind F is a compound of the form F and matter.
   (4) Portions of earth are determinate individuals of the kind earth.
   (5) The matter of a portion of earth isn't anything essentially.

   Aristotle is clearly committed to (1) and (3). (5) calls for brief comment. Either (i) the matter of a portion of earth is prime matter or (ii) it is some other substratum surviving the change from earth to water and the change from earth to fire (*GC* I.2 329a25-b2, I.4, 5). If the matter of a portion of earth is prime matter, then it isn't anything essentially. According to (ii) since the surviving substratum is a different contrary depending on which of the two transformations occurs, the matter of a portion of earth won't be anything essentially, unless the disjunctive property of being either cold or dry can be an essential property.

   Whiting's (1992) functionalist Aristotle is also committed to (4) and more crucially to (2).

5. Burnyeat (1992) is an extreme version of this in that he argues that there is not even a physical change in the sense organs in the transition from not perceiving to perceiving. All there is to the act of seeing is the activation of the psychic power of sight to take on sensible form without matter.
6. Code and Moravcsik (1992) represent this strategy. There is no Cartesian/Galilean matter contingently to instantiate mental states.
7. Whiting (1992) tries to show that the elements can play the role of soul-independent categorical base by distinguishing between the inorganic matter of an animal body and its organic soul-dependent matter. (Shields (1999, p. 150ff.) makes a similar move.) On her view, as I understand it, it is a contingent fact that portions of earth, air, fire, and water regularly find themselves in the essentially ensouled tissues of living organisms. The question then is whether for Aristotle a world of unwrought heaps of earth, air, fire, and water with no further prospects would be radically incomplete and unintelligible. There is also the further question of whether the form is contingently predicated of the inorganic body and whether this would render an individual substance an accidental unity.
8. As Shields (1999, p. 150) appears to note, compositional plasticity (multiple realizability) implies that material states realize functional states only contingently.
9. See, for example, *An* I.1 403a3-b9 and I.4 408b10-15.
10. Williams (1986) is not among them. In a footnote (p. 192 n. 2) he says that the passage "might be taken to mean that the human *form* could be realized in something other than flesh and bones," but then immediately dismisses such a reading as doubtful on the grounds that "Aristotle thinks it necessary that they go together...."
11. Shields (1999) argues in a footnote (p. 151) that the necessity Williams must have in mind, on pain of inconsistency, is nomological necessity in which case multiple realizability is not precluded. I discuss this below.
12. Translations are from W. D. Ross (1924) and revised *from* Barnes (1984).
13. This is precisely what Whiting (1992) and Shields (1999) try to do. But this requires that members of animal species are accidental unities of a species form and an inorganic body.
14. *Met* Z.10 1035b 22-25 is relevant here as casting its shadow on the passage in Z.11. "For they [the parts of a concrete thing] cannot even exist if severed from the whole; for it is not a finger in *any* state that is the finger of a living thing, but the dead finger is a finger only homonymously." There's no reason to think that this doesn't also apply to such homoiomerous tissues of an animal as flesh and bone. More importantly, Aristotle makes the same point in the

passage at 1036b 30-32 in connection with the condition of the parts to which there must be general reference made in the definition of the form. The parts must be alive.
15. I have already offered some reasons for thinking that the elemental bodies of earth, air, fire, and water are unsuitable candidates for the role of physical kinds that contingently instantiate psychological states. I have also suggested that if they were, the consequences would be unacceptable to Aristotle, namely, that individual substances would turn out to be accidental unities. Here I consider the more exotic suggestion of alternative elemental bodies.
16. Here I am invoking Locke not as a defender of nominal essences but as one who acknowledges that the features of a sample of kind K are grounded in the unknown real constitution of that sample.
17. Ross (1924, Vol. 2, p. 201) is apparently led to this conclusion in part by the *ton anthrôpon* in the absence of the indefinitely particularizing *tina anthrôpon*.
18. This is presumably Ross's reason.
19. It is worth noting that Aristotle no longer seems to care about flesh and bones as putative parts of the form as he draws his conclusion regarding the generalized reference to parts in the definition of a form. He is now content to talk about fingers. This shows, I think, that the earlier provocative implication that humans might be made of something other than flesh was a dialectical ploy. The role of flesh can be taken over by fingers.
20. In the next section, 1037a5-20, Aristotle considers another way of including matter in the definition. Rather than focusing on the form exclusively, he considers a universal corresponding to concrete individuals like Callias or a particular snub nose. The formula of such a universal would mention matter—flesh and bones in the case of a man and nose in the case of a snub nose. There is still nothing in the parallel between human soul and concavity, the respective forms, to suggest that Aristotle is endorsing the possibility that the human soul is the form of a concrete individual of different matter, not to mention a different matter that is not form dependent. If anything, the suggestion is that MAN is parallel to SNUBNESS with the implication that no individual man could exist without flesh and bones.
21. See *An* I.5 418a3-4, II.12 424a17.
22. The expression is due to Sellars (1963).
23. The distinction is drawn in *An* II.6 418a9-11.

Bibliography

Barnes, Jonathan (ed.). 1984. *The complete works of Aristotle: Revised Oxford translation.* Princeton: Princeton University Press.
Burnyeat, Myles. 1992. *Is an Aristotelian philosophy of mind still credible?* ed. Martha C. Nussbaum and Amelie Oksenberg Rorty, 15–26. New York: Oxford University Press.
Code, Alan, and Julius Moravcsik. 1992. *Explaining various forms of living,* ed. Martha C. Nussbaum and Amelie Oksenberg Rorty, 129–146. New York: Oxford University Press.
Dupré, John. 1993. *The disorder of things.* Cambridge, MA: Harvard University Press.
Mineo-Paluello, L. (ed.). 1956. *Aristotelis Categoriae et De Interpretatione.* Oxford: Oxford University Press.
Nussbaum, Martha, and Amelie O. Rorty (eds.). 1992. *Essays on Aristotle's De Anima.* New York: Oxford University Press.
Ross, W.D. (ed.). 1924. *Metaphysics: A revised text with introduction and commentary.* Oxford: Clarendon.
Ross, W.D. (ed.). 1961. *De Anima.* Oxford: Oxford University Press.
Sellars, Wilfrid. 1963. Philosophy and scientific image of man. In *Science, perception, and reality.* London: Routledge and Kegan Paul.

Shields, Christopher. 1999. *Order in multiplicity*. New York: Oxford University Press.
Whiting, Jennifer. 1992. *Living bodies*, ed. Martha C. Nussbaum and Amelie Oksenberg Rorty, 93–108. New York: Oxford University Press.
Williams, Bernard. 1986. Hylomorphism. *Oxford Studies in Ancient Philosophy* 4: 189–199.

Aristotle on Belief and Knowledge

Fred D. Miller, Jr.

Aristotle is "the master of them that know" in Dante's *Divine Comedy* (I.4.31). His *Metaphysics* begins with the stirring declaration that "All men by nature desire to know" (A.1 980a21). As Werner Jaeger (1962, p. 68) observes, "Knowledge has never been understood more purely, more earnestly, or more sublimely." Aristotle agrees with Plato that knowledge is superior to belief: "He who has beliefs is, in comparison with the man who knows, not in a healthy state as far as the truth is concerned" (*Met* Γ.4 1008b27-31; cf. Plato *Rep.* VI 508d4-9). Aristotle's remarks concerning belief are scattered throughout his works, none of which contains a systematic discussion of this topic. Not surprisingly, commentators have tended to give his account of belief short shrift.

Yet belief (*doxa*) has an important place in Aristotle's philosophy.[1] His *Nicomachean Ethics* VI.5 1140b26 characterizes practical wisdom (*phronêsis*) as an intellectual virtue of the capacity for belief (*doxastikon, NE* VI.5 1140b26). Scholars in recent years have come increasingly to appreciate the crucial role of a privileged class of beliefs called "reputable" (*endoxa*), not only in his ethical writings but also in treatises such as the *Physics* and *Metaphysics*. Myles Burnyeat (1986, p. 11) observes that

> Aristotle is unique among ancient philosophers in his respect for people's opinions: both the opinions of other philosophers and the opinions of the ordinary man. He does not defend

---

This essay joyfully revisits issues that I explored in my Ph.D. dissertation, *Aristotle's Account of Being and Truth*, under the direction of David Keyt. I am indebted to Taylor Vaughn, a graduate student who aroused my interest in this particular topic when he wrote an interesting paper on it in my seminar in 2000. Pamela Phillips made helpful corrections on an earlier draft. I also benefited from comments on earlier drafts by audiences at the American Philosophical Association Central Division, the University of Alabama at Tuscaloosa, the University of Washington at Seattle, the University of Arizona at Tucson, and the University of Kansas at Lawrence.

F.D. Miller, Jr. (✉)
Social Philosophy and Policy Foundation, 1616 E. Wooster St., Ste. 24,
Bowling Green, OH 43402, USA
e-mail: fmiller@sppfbg.org

a "common sense" philosophy in the manner of G. E. Moore, but if something is believed by absolutely everyone, then, he holds, it must be true. Aristotle also does something that a 20th-century philosopher like Moore could never have dared. He establishes *science* on the basis of the opinions of "the majority" and of "the wise."

This essay tries to prepare the ground for a reconstruction of Aristotle's account of belief and its relationship to knowledge by considering his solutions to four related difficulties.

1   Four Problems Concerning Belief

Belief differs from knowledge in that belief can be false as well as true (cf. *NE* VI.3 1139b17-18). This basic fact presents a number of difficulties concerning belief:

(1) *How is false belief or error possible?*

Aristotle complains that many earlier natural philosophers failed to answer this question, because they viewed thinking (*noein*) as a bodily process like perceiving, and they also held that like is known by like. He quotes Empedocles:

By Earth we see Earth, by Water Water,
By Ether divine Ether, again by Fire ruinous Fire,
By Love Love, and Hate by baneful Hate. (DK 31B109; apud *An* I.2 404b13-15)

Aristotle objects that these theorists faced a dilemma: "either all appearances are true (as some say) or contact with the unlike is error (*apatê*); for this is the opposite of being aware of like by like" (*An* III.3 427a21-b6). Aristotle should take this problem seriously because he also compares thinking with touching an object.[2] Granted that he can explain how error is possible, another problem arises:

(2) *If belief can be false, how is knowledge possible?*

One answer would be that knowledge and belief have essentially different domains, as argued in Plato's *Republic*: "If a different capacity is naturally over something different, and belief and knowledge are different powers, then the knowable (*gnôston*) and the believable (*doxaston*) cannot be the same" (V 478a12-b2). On this view, knowledge has its own special object, such as the Form of Beauty, and belief has its own special object, such as a particular beautiful thing. There is therefore an unbridgeable divide between knowledge and belief.[3] The attempt to grasp knowable objects such as the Forms by means of belief would be futile and fundamentally misguided, because belief is prone to error and falsehood in a way that knowledge is not. Aristotle cannot of course accept Plato's solution, insofar as it presupposes the theory of Forms rejected by Aristotle (cf. *An. Post* I.22 83a32-5). But he does seem to endorse a similar view: the object of knowledge (*epistêton*) is necessary and cannot be otherwise, whereas the object of belief (*doxaston*) is possible but can be otherwise.[4] Thus, knowledge has necessary objects, whereas belief has contingent objects. But this seems to present yet another problem:

(3) *How is it possible to believe and know the same objects?*

If the objects of knowledge are necessary and the objects of belief are not, it would seem to be impossible to know and believe the same things. Yet, as Aristotle reports, we believe that we have beliefs about eternal objects such as mathematical objects and gods (*NE* III.2 1111b31-3). Aristotle seems right that we can hold beliefs about necessary objects. But how can we do so, if belief is of contingent rather than necessary objects? The dichotomy between knowledge and belief raises another problem concerning Aristotle's philosophical method:

(4) *How could beliefs be of any use for philosophy?*

Aristotle sometimes suggests that knowledge and belief belong to different types of inquiry: knowledge is the province of first philosophy (metaphysics) and second philosophy (natural science such as physics), whereas belief is the concern of dialectic. Dialectic involves the kind of reasoning found in a Platonic dialogue, when Socrates asks questions and then reasons on the basis of answers another person gives to his questions. Unlike scientific demonstration, which proceeds from first principles known with certainty, a dialectical deduction reasons correctly from reputable beliefs (*endoxa*). In this it differs from contentious or eristic deduction, which reasons fallaciously or which uses only apparently reputable beliefs as premises (*Top* I.1 100a21-101b4).

Aristotle seems to be of two minds about the relation of dialectic to philosophy. If there is a radical dichotomy between knowledge and belief, it would seem that the philosopher and scientist should have no use for dialectic. Aristotle sometimes says as much: "For the purposes of philosophy these things should be handled according to truth, but dialectically according to belief" (*Top* I.14 105b30-1; cf. *Met* Γ.2 1004b25-6). Yet he also indicates that dialectic can be of service to science and philosophy, because we can use it to detect truth and falsity more easily by going through difficulties on both sides of an issue, and because dialectic enables us to discuss the principles common to all the sciences: "it is necessary to discuss them by means of particular reputable beliefs" (*Top* I.2 101a34-b4). In fact the reputable beliefs make an appearance in his philosophical treatises, most notably the ethical works, but also those devoted to natural science.[5] Hopefully, a fuller understanding of Aristotle's theory of belief will clarify his stand on the reputable beliefs employed by dialectic.

2 Aristotle's Basic Account of Belief

Before examining Aristotle's solutions to the foregoing problems, we should consider the place of belief and knowledge in his psychology. Aristotle distinguishes different kinds of capacities of the soul by which human beings think and act. First, in contrast to plants, which possess only a nutritive faculty, animals also have the faculties of locomotion and awareness. Awareness (*gnôristikon*) involves two different capacities, sense-perception (*aisthêtikon*) and thought (*noêtikon*). "By these alone are we aware (*gnôrizomen*) of anything" (*Insomn* 1 458b1-3). The capacity of thought (*noêtikon*) or mind (*nous*) enables us to cognize (*dianoesthai*) and to judge (*hupolambanein*).[6]

The cognitive faculty (*dianoêtikon*) is exercised in the process of discursive thought or reasoning which terminates in cognitive states (*hexeis peri dianoian*), for example, judgments.[7] Although Aristotle does not offer a systematic treatment of ratiocination, he frequently mentions two main forms: inference and inquiry, which are essential to teaching and learning. Inference (*sullogismos*), the process of deriving judgments from other judgments, can be inductive (reasoning from the particular judgment to universal) or deductive (reasoning from universal judgments to particular judgments or other universal judgments).[8] Inquiry (*zêtêsis*) is the process of rationally forming judgments in the first place. Aristotle mentions different types of inquiry: analysis, for example, of a geometrical diagram, deliberation (*bouleusis*) or calculation (*logismos*) concerning means to ends, and the going through puzzles or problems (*diaporein*). Inquiry and inference, understood as cognitive processes, must be distinguished from contemplation (*theôria*) in the narrow sense, which involves the exercise or activation of a judgment already in one's possession, for example, knowledge of a rule of grammar.[9]

Cognition culminates in judgment (*hupolêpsis*), which is a state of the mind that stands in relation to things (*pragmata*) independent of the mind.[10] Aristotle compares judgment to assertion (*phasis*) which can be true or false.[11] Because it is essentially related to an object, a judgment is in a good or bad condition depending on whether it is true or false (*NE* VI.2 1139a28-9, 9 1142b10-11). Although belief is a judgment that can be mistaken, "correctness of belief is truth" (*NE* VI.3 1139b17-18, 9 1142b11).[12] In contrast, knowledge is a judgment which is necessarily true: it does not make sense to ask where an instance of knowledge is correct, because "there is no such thing as error of knowledge" (*NE* VI.3 1142b10). Knowledge is thus relative to facts in a stronger sense than belief, because destruction of what is knowable results in the destruction of knowledge, whereas destruction of the object of belief merely makes the belief false.[13] The difference between knowledge and belief is so fundamental for Aristotle that he distinguishes between two judgmental capacities: the faculty of knowledge (*epistêmonikon*) and the faculty of belief (*doxastikon*).[14]

Belief shares a number of features with other conscious states. Like perception, belief is a mode by which the soul discriminates (*krinei*) between and is aware (*gnôrizei*) of entities (*An* III.3 427a19-21). Belief differs from perception insofar as it has a universal object (II.5 417b22-3). States of belief are reflexive as well as intentional: Along with knowledge, perception, and cognition, belief "appears to be always of something else and of itself by the way" (*Met* Λ.9 1074b35-6; cf. *NE* IX.9 1170a31-2). That is, if I believe that I believe, I must first believe something else (e.g., that Aristotle was a citizen of Stagira). Further, a single act of thinking and perceiving must be performed by a single thinker or perceiver, just as a single speech act must be performed by a single speaker (*An* III.2 426b21-2, 6 430b5-6). Finally, among animals, only human beings are capable of belief and other forms of judgment which require persuasion and hence a rational capacity.[15]

3 How Is False Belief or Error Possible?

Aristotle's explanation of false belief includes three main points: First and foremost, our judgments involve a combination of thoughts: "In those things where there is the false and true, there is a sort of combination of thoughts (*sunthesis tis noêmatôn*) as if they were one thing" (*An* III.6 430a27-8, b5-6).[16] For example, we combine the thoughts of diagonal and incommensurate to judge that the diagonal is incommensurate. One can also combine a negative thought with another thought, for example, to say that Cleon is not white. "Even if you assert that the white [i.e., Cleon] is not white you have combined not-white [with Cleon]. It is also possible to call all these cases division" (430b2-4). Although here and in other places Aristotle describes negative judgment as a sort of division, he also treats any judgment (negative or affirmative) as a combination.[17] True and false judgment are defined accordingly: "One who thinks (*oiomenos*) the divided is divided and the conjoined is conjoined has the truth, while one who is in a condition contrary to that of the things is in error" (*Met* Θ.10 1051b3-5).[18]

Aristotle's account of truth involves many complications and difficulties which cannot be explored in this essay.[19] One fundamental distinction, however, is important: that between individual judgments and universal judgments (see *Met* A.1 981a5-12). An individual judgment—for example, that Bucephelas is a horse—is true or false just in case the corresponding individual—the horse Bucephelas—and the universal (horse) are conjoined or divided in the appropriate way. A universal judgment—for example, that all horses are animals—is true or false just in case the corresponding universals—horse and animal—are conjoined or divided in the appropriate way.[20] It is noteworthy that both forms of judgment involve a universal predicate.

The second point in Aristotle's explanation of error is that the truth or falsity of a judgment depends upon the corresponding fact: "for it is not because we think (*oiesthai*) that you are white that you are white, but because you are white we who say this have the truth" (*Met* Θ.10 1051b6-9). Thus, the corresponding object seems in a way to be the cause (*pôs aition*) of the truth or falsity of the judgment.[21] The basis for this claim of dependence seems to be this: things are what they are regardless of what we think. We form judgments, which are combinations of thoughts, in order to be aware of these things. Whether or not the combinations in thought succeed depends on whether they stand in the proper relation to things. Aristotle concludes, then, that truth and falsity exist in thought rather than in things, but they depend on things (*Met* E.4 1027b25-7, K.8 1065a21-3).

The third point in Aristotle's explanation of error is that we may not realize that our judgments are at variance with the facts. This can happen for various reasons; for example, the facts may change. "Suppose you hold a belief (*doxazoi*) truly that somebody is sitting; after he has got up you will believe falsely if you have the same belief (*doxa*) about him" (*Cat* 5 4a26-8). Thus, a true belief can become false, if the thing changes without the believer noticing it.[22] This assumes that a belief exists over time and that it can have different truth values at different times. One may also believe, for example, that Coriscus is present because one does not realize that Coriscus is appearing in a dream (*Insomn* 3 462a7-8). Or one might be mistaken about whether some members of a group possess a property and some do not, for example, about whether some even numbers are prime and some are not (*Met* Θ.10 1052a8-9). In conclusion, then, our judgments can be false, because the way we combine our thoughts may disagree with the facts. But why is this not true of all judgment?

4 If Belief Can Be False, How Is Knowledge Possible?

Aristotle's answer, as suggested earlier, is to distinguish between objects of belief and objects of knowledge: "Regarding contingent things (*ta endechomena*), then, the same belief or the same statement comes to be false and true, and it is possible at one time to have the truth and at another to be in error; but regarding things that cannot be otherwise the same things are not at one time true and at another false, but are always true or always false" (*Met* Θ.10 1051b14-17). Each judgment corresponds to a combination of things, and knowledge is a judgment corresponding to a universal and necessary combination (e.g., all ravens are birds).[23] In contrast, belief is a judgment corresponding to a combination which is not both universal and necessary. This includes judgments about the combinations of an individual and a universal (e.g., that is a raven) and judgments about contingent combinations of universals (e.g., all ravens are black).

Aristotle is very strict about what he recognizes as knowledge (*epistêmê*), especially in the *Posterior Analytics*. He says, "We think (*oiometh'*) that we know (*epistasthai*) each thing without qualification … whenever we think that we know (*ginôskein*) that the cause on which the thing depends is its cause, and that it is not possible for this to be otherwise" (*An. Post* I.2 71b9-12).[24] In order to have this knowledge, we must be able to demonstrate what we claim to know. A demonstration (*apodeixis*) is thus a deduction (*sullogismos*) that results in knowledge. Therefore, "it is necessary for demonstrative knowledge to depend on [premises] which are true and primary and immediate and more familiar than and prior to and the causes of the conclusion" (*An. Post* I.2 71b20-2).

This leads to the central problem of the *Posterior Analytics*: How do we secure these premises? The answer in brief is that they are the object of non-demonstrable knowledge (*anapodeiktos epistêmê*) or comprehension (*nous*), which is itself the result of induction (*epagôgê*).[25] Comprehension is always true and even more precise than knowledge, because its objects are more familiar principles. But Aristotle distinguishes two different ways in which a thing may be familiar: familiar to us or familiar by nature (i.e., without qualification or according to reason). "I call prior and more familiar in relation to us what is nearer to perception, prior and more familiar without qualification what is further away. What is most universal is furthest away, and the individuals are nearest" (*An. Post* I.2 71b33-72a5).[26] It is in the latter sense that the objects of comprehension are more familiar, that is, without qualification or by nature.

In the *Posterior Analytics,* Aristotle distinguishes the three main forms of judgment in terms of their objects as follows:

Knowledge is about a demonstrable necessary proposition. (I.4 73a21-4)
Comprehension is about an immediate necessary proposition. (I.33 88b37)
Belief is about an immediate contingent proposition. (89a3-4)

An immediate contingent proposition—for example, that all ravens are black—may be familiar to us through perception and induction. An immediate necessary proposition—for example, that the shortest distance between two points is a straight line—is familiar by nature: once we comprehend it, we realize that it must be true. Therefore, belief is concerned with propositions which are merely familiar to us, whereas comprehension is of propositions which are familiar by nature. But according to Aristotle, "when a person is convinced (*pisteuêi*) in a certain way and the principles are familiar (*gnôrimoi*) to him, he knows (*epistatai*); for if they are not more familiar than the conclusion, he will have knowledge accidentally" (*NE* VI.3 1139b33-5; cf. *An Post* I.2 72a36-7, 25 86b27). A judgment constitutes knowledge only if it is demonstrated from a judgment concerning a proposition which is familiar by nature. Hence, knowledge cannot be derived from belief, because belief and its objects are unstable (*abebaion*), since the objects of belief are only familiar to us and not familiar without qualification (cf. *An. Post* I.33 89a5). Knowledge derived from beliefs would only be accidental knowledge. Aristotle claims that this analysis agrees with what people ordinarily think about believing and knowing: "no one thinks (*oietai*) that he holds a belief (*doxazein*) when it is impossible for it to be otherwise, but that he knows (*epistatai*); but when he thinks that it is so but nothing prevents it from being otherwise, then he holds a belief, on the grounds that belief (*doxa*) is about this sort of thing while knowledge (*epistêmê*) is about the necessary" (89a6-10).

The thesis that one can know only necessary truths demonstrated from principles which are familiar by nature and not merely familiar to us requires qualification. For Aristotle also distinguishes between knowing *that* something is the case and knowing *why* it is the case. For example, someone may know that the planets (in contrast to stars) are near to the earth because he has learned through perception and induction that objects like planets that do not twinkle are nearby. However, he may not be able to explain *why* nearby objects do not twinkle.[27] But, as Aristotle remarks, "we do not think we do know (*eidenai*) a thing until we have grasped the *why* of it" (*Phys* II.3 194b17-20). How then can we have knowledge *that* (*to hoti*) without knowledge of the reason why (*to dioti*)? Aristotle's solution is evidently to distinguish between degrees of knowledge: A person knows better (*mallon*) insofar as his knowledge is based on higher causes or reasons, and knows best (*malista*) if he relies on causes or reasons which themselves have no prior causes or reasons (*An. Post* I.9 76a18-22). The person who can explain why nearby objects do not twinkle knows this better than the person who merely knows it through induction but cannot explain it.

A related puzzle is how it is possible for the knowledge *that* something is the case belongs to one science (i.e., organized body of knowledge) and the knowledge *why* to another science. For example, the doctor knows that circular wounds heal more slowly, and the geometer knows why this is so. Presumably this is because a circular wound has a greater area relative to its perimeter and the parts are farther apart from each other.[28] In such a case it belongs to empirical scientists (*aisthêtikoi*) to know the fact and to mathematicians (*mathêmatikoi*) to know the reason why. Mathematicians study the universal truth but may not know particular applications due to lack of observation. Aristotle's explanation is that mathematics treats certain attributes of material bodies (e.g., edges, surfaces, volumes) in abstraction from their other attributes (e.g., the material stuff composing them). The less abstract science depends on the more abstract. Aristotle distinguishes three levels of science: pure mathematics (e.g., geometry), applied mathematical science (e.g., optics), and empirical science (e.g., theory of the rainbow) (*An. Post* I.13 78b32-79a13).

The claim that knowledge concerns necessary truth also needs to be qualified in order to accommodate Aristotle's threefold classification of the sciences: natural science studies natural objects which are material, perceptible, and mutable; mathematical science studies immutable objects which are inseparable from matter; and first philosophy (or theology) studies substances which are immutable and separable from matter (*Met* E.1 1025b18-1026a10; *An* I.1 403b7-19). However, natural science lacks the precision of mathematics and theology, because it deals with material objects and hence with truths that hold for the most part (*hôs epi to polu*). Indeed, Aristotle suggests that the natural (*pephukenai*) is convertible with what usually occurs; for example, a human being turns gray naturally or for the most part.[29] Had Aristotle not made this qualification, the sublunary realm would be largely inaccessible to scientific knowledge.

In spite of these qualifications, however, there are problems with some of Aristotle's pet examples: for example, I know (*oida*) Coriscus and I know the man approaching, but I do not know that the approaching man is Coriscus (*SE* 24 179b2-3, 27-33). Aristotle may have beliefs about Coriscus and the man approaching, but knowledge of either is out of the question, unless it is knowledge in a homonymous sense. As Aristotle remarks, "it is difficult to be aware (*gnônai*) of whether one knows (*oiden*) or not. For it is difficult to be aware of whether we know (*ismen*) from the principles of a thing or not—and that is what it is to know (*eidenai*)" (*An. Post* I.9 76a26-8, cf. *Met* α.1 993a30-b11). This is such a stringent account of knowledge that some commentators argue that Aristotle is talking about scientific explanation and understanding rather than knowledge.[30] However, it seems that Aristotle in fact holds that a judgment fully qualifies as knowledge only if it is proven by induction or demonstration. This helps to explain why he uses the same term *epistêmê* for "science": an organized body of judgments that are known to be true (*Met* E.1 1025b19, K.7 1064b1-3; *Top* VI.6 145a15). If this is his view of knowledge, then a great deal of what we claim to be knowledge will turn out to be mere belief. But Aristotle's way of distinguishing belief from knowledge seems to have an even more paradoxical consequence.

5 How Is It Possible to Believe and Know the Same Objects?

If belief and knowledge are judgments about fundamentally different sorts of objects, it is impossible for us to believe and know the same things. But this seems to conflict with Aristotle's own observation that the task of learning or inquiry is "to start from what is more familiar to oneself and to make what is familiar by nature familiar to oneself" (*Met* Z.3 1029b7-8; cf. *Phys* I.1 184a18-21, *NE* I.4 1095b2-4). Typically, we start from the belief that something is the case and then try to get to the point where we know why it is the case by providing a demonstration of it. Yet, if we can also believe every step of the demonstration, does not the distinction between belief and knowledge collapse?

Aristotle's (typically Aristotelian) solution is that in a sense we can have knowledge and belief about the same thing, but in another sense we cannot. He offers the following example:

> For [knowledge] is of an animal in such a way that it cannot not be an animal, while [belief] <is of it> in such a way that it can <not be an animal>; for example, if the former is of what man essentially is (*hoper anthrôpou estin*), and the latter is of man but not of what man essentially <is>. For <the object> is the same because <it is> a man, but the manner is not the same. (*An. Post* I.33 89a33-7)[31]

The point of this highly compressed argument seems to be the following:

If X knows that S is P, then S cannot not be P.
If X believes that S is P, then it does not follow that S cannot not be P.
The judgment that S is P entails that S cannot not be P if, and only if, it is a judgment about what S essentially is.
Judgments about S and about what S essentially is are about the same thing but in a different manner.
Therefore, knowledge and belief are about the same thing but in a different manner.

Knowledge unlike belief involves an awareness of man's essence—man's form (*eidos*) or substance (*ousia*)—and hence an awareness of what being a man necessarily entails (cf. 89a20). Nevertheless, belief and knowledge can be about the same object.

Aristotle maintains, however, that it is not possible to both believe and know the same thing *at the same time*, arguing as follows:

> For one would at the same time have the judgment (*hupolêpsin*) that the same thing can be otherwise and not otherwise, which is not possible. For in different persons it is possible for there to be each of these <states> with regard to the same thing, as has been said; but in the same person it is not possible even in this way; for he will at the same time have a judgment, e.g., that a man is essentially an animal (for in this case it was not possible for <man> not to be an animal) and that man is not essentially an animal (for in this case it will be possible). (89a37-b6)[32]

In this passage, Aristotle again uses the term "judgment" (*hupolêpsis*) for the genus of which knowledge and belief are species.[33] The argument is that knowledge and belief involve conflicting judgments:

If at t X knows that S is P, then at t X judges that S cannot be not-P.
If at t X believes that S is P, then at t X judges that S can be not-P.

One cannot make contradictory judgments at the same time (cf. *Met* Γ.3 1005b29). Therefore, if at *t* X knows that S is P, then at *t* X does not believe that S is P.

The point of the argument is that I cannot simultaneously know and believe the same proposition, because knowledge and belief involve contradictory judgments. It is, however, perfectly possible for me to believe a proposition first and later come to know it.

Aristotle's argument here seems problematic. This is evident from one of his own examples. I might believe that the moon is always full when it rises in the east in the early evening because it has been full every time I observed it rising at this time and place, but I may have no explanation of this, so that I do not know it to be true. But if I figured out that the moon always has its bright side toward the sun because it receives its light from the sun, I would *know* that the moon is always full when it rises in the east in the early evening. Aristotle seems correct to say that if I know that this is the case, I also judge that it cannot be otherwise. But he does not seem correct to say that if I merely believe this is the case, I also judge that it is possible that the moon will not be full when it rises. In this case I might instead say that I believe the moon will be full the next time, but I am uncertain whether or not things could be otherwise. It is evident, then, that the judgment that things could not be otherwise is not a component or entailment of belief. It may be possible however to remedy this difficulty. Aristotle might have argued instead that I know that *p* only if my judgment that *p* is the result of a demonstration or induction which also enables me to judge that it could not be the case that not-*p*, but if I merely believe that *p* then my judgment that *p* is not the result of such a probative process. This would suffice to show that I cannot simultaneously know and believe that *p*.[34]

How can we reconcile this account of how we can believe and know the same things with the claim that knowledge and belief are distinct faculties with distinct objects? One answer would be to distinguish between the primary and secondary uses of the faculty of belief. The primary use of belief is the awareness of variable and contingent things, for example, that Coriscus is approaching or that all ravens are black. These facts are proper objects of belief because none of them are knowable in the strict sense. But belief also has a secondary use, as applied to invariable and necessary facts that we do not know: for example, Goldbach's conjecture that every even integer greater than two is the sum of two prime numbers. In such cases we resort to belief *faute de mieux*. This also helps to explain Aristotle's analogy between belief and illness. A person who believes rather than knows is in a privative condition insofar as he lacks what the knowing person has: the ability to prove that things could not be otherwise.

6 How Could Belief Be of Any Use to Philosophy?

As noted earlier, Aristotle seems to be of two minds about dialectic. Unlike science and philosophy, dialectic reasons from premises about what is believed to be the case, which may not be the same as the truth (*An. Post* I.19 81b18-23). Whereas a demonstrative deduction proceeds from premises that can be known with certainty because they are universal, necessarily true, and primitive, a dialectical deduction is based merely on reputable beliefs (*endoxa*; *Top* I.1 100a25-30; cf. *An. Post* I.6 74b21-6). Yet, Aristotle also maintains that dialectic can be useful for the "philosophical sciences" (*Top* I.2 101a34-b4). Can his theory of belief support this claim of usefulness for dialectic?

Some light seems to be shed on this issue by the introduction to Aristotle's *Rhetoric*: "Rhetoric is the counterpart to dialectic. Both are concerned with the sorts of things which are common (*koina*) in a certain way to everyone to be aware (*gnôrizein*) of and which require no specialized knowledge (*epistêmê*)." Aristotle goes on to say that everyone partakes of these although some do so at random and others through practice and habit (*Rhet* I.1 1354a1-7). Later he remarks,

> To discern (*idein*) what is true and what is like the truth belong to the same capacity, and at the same time also human beings are, sufficiently, naturally inclined to the truth and they reach it most of the time. That is why anyone who is capable of aiming at the truth is similarly capable of aiming at reputable beliefs. (1355a14-18)[35]

Aristotle adds that "things that are true and things that are just are by nature stronger than their opposites."[36] Thus, according to Aristotle, human beings have a natural tendency to believe what is true rather than what is false. This is in keeping with the aforementioned declaration, "All human beings desire by nature to know" (*Met* A.1 980a21). Our natural desire for knowledge is also expressed in the impulse to believe what is true rather than what is false.

This seems to be related to Aristotle's claim that imagination is voluntary in a way that belief is not. We are free, for example, to imagine that a lion just entered the room, but "it is not up to us to hold a belief." Aristotle thus espouses a version of *doxastic involuntarism*, the thesis that belief and disbelief are not subject to our direct control. (As a thought experiment, ask whether you could suddenly believe at will that Aristotle was a Roman, if you were offered a million dollars to do so.[37]) Unfortunately Aristotle's argument for this seems incomplete: "it is not up to us to hold a belief; for it is necessary either to be mistaken or have the truth" (*An* III.3 427b16-21). The premise seems to mean: if we have a particular belief, it is not up to us whether it is true or false (because that would depend on the facts). But it does not follow from this alone that it is up to us whether we hold that particular belief or not. Perhaps, however, Aristotle is tacitly assuming that beliefs essentially aim at the truth, and that they could not perform their essential function if they were under our direct control. As Robert Bolton (2003, p. 157) suggests, Aristotle has a conception of "true belief generated by a certain natural process that reliably leads to true belief." The idea that belief is essentially truth directed makes sense in Aristotle's teleological framework. Our ability to survive and flourish depends on our capacity to respond appropriately to the particular contingent events which occur around us.[38] Realism (i.e., the disposition to have correct beliefs) about oneself and one's circumstances is central to our mental health and indispensable for our survival and flourishing.[39] This line of argument seems promising, although the argument would need to be fleshed out and the thesis appropriately qualified, in order to deal with apparent counterexamples such as prejudice, willful ignorance, self-deception, and leaps of faith.[40] Arguably in these cases, belief and disbelief are subject at least to our indirect control, in that whether or not we form a belief or make a judgment can depend on factors under our direct control: for example, whether or not we pay attention, or whether or not we manage our emotions and appetites properly.

Even if beliefs naturally aim at the truth, they often miss the mark. In *Metaphysics* α.1 993a30-b12, Aristotle compares our mind (*nous*) to the eyes of bats which fail to grasp objects in the blaze of day. However, earlier in this same passage, he likens the truth to the proverbial door that no one can fail to hit but no one can grasp in its entirety.[41] This provides a rationale for Aristotle's conception of reputable beliefs, that is, beliefs which have already undergone a process of screening.[42] For they are "believed (*dokounta*) by everyone or by the majority or by the wise—i.e., by all, or the majority, or by the most notable and reputable (*endoxois*) of them" (*Top* I.1 100b21-3; cf. 10.104a8-11).[43] This capacious definition of "reputable beliefs" obviously allows incompatible beliefs to qualify as "reputable."[44] The Socratic paradoxes provide striking examples of this: the wise Socrates believes that incontinence is impossible, and the many disagree. Such a collision between reputable beliefs presents a puzzle (*aporia*) which is a kind of intellectual impasse or knot: "for cognition (*dianoia*) is tied up, when it is unwilling to rest because the conclusion does not satisfy it but it cannot progress because it cannot refute the [puzzling] argument" (*NE* VII.2 1146a24-7; cf. *Met* B.1 995a29-31). A person who is perplexed is in a state of wonder and thinks that he is ignorant; he engages in philosophy in order to escape from ignorance (*Met* A.2 982b11-21, 983a11-21).

In his ethical works Aristotle prescribes a method for resolving such difficulties. First, in the *Nicomachean Ethics*:

> We ought, as in all other cases, to set the appearances (*phainomena*) before us and, after first presenting the puzzles go on to prove, if possible, the truth of all the reputable beliefs (*endoxa*) about these affections or, failing this, of the greatest number and the most authoritative; for if we both resolve the difficulties and leave the reputable beliefs undisturbed, we shall have proved the case sufficiently. (*NE* VII.1 1145b2-7)[45]

The aim of the method seems, then, to produce a consistent set of beliefs which include most of the reputable beliefs, including those which are most authoritative, that is, those which have been most rigorously examined.[46] Aristotle's favorite way of resolving apparent conflicts is to make appropriate distinctions, as described in the *Eudemian Ethics*:

> A method must be obtained that will best explain the beliefs (*dokounta*) concerning these things, and resolve the puzzles (*aporias*) and contrary views. This will be the case if the contrary views are seen to be believed in a well reasoned way; for such an account will be most in agreement with the appearances. The contradictory views will consequently stand, if what is said is true in one sense but not in another sense. (*EE* VII.2 1235b13-18)

Aristotle calls the solution to such a puzzle a discovery (*heuresis*, *NE* VII.3 1146b7-8).

The foregoing remarks imply an *Aristotelian doxastic method*, including the following dictum: We ought to form the belief B if it agrees with how things appear to us and does not conflict with any reputable belief; but if B agrees with some reputable beliefs but not with others, thus resulting in puzzlement (*aporia*), we should try to reconcile these beliefs by making appropriate distinctions; and if we cannot do that, we should try to form the belief B´ that agrees with the greatest number of reputable beliefs and the most authoritative of these.[47] Although Aristotle does not provide clear guidance on how to weigh the beliefs in terms of quantity (how many people hold them) and quality (the authority of the believer), he is emphatic in the *Physics* that we should eschew paradoxical theories that conflict with well-nigh universal beliefs and appearances based on sense-perception. Thus, he rejects the theory of Melissus that being is entirely motionless:

> To claim that all things are at rest and to disregard sense-perception and seeking argument for this thesis is a kind of weakness of thought; and it is to dispute the whole<of physics> and not <merely> a part, in opposition not only to the physicist but to almost all cases of knowledge and all beliefs, since they all make use of motion. (*Phys* VIII.3 253a32-b2)

Aristotle adds a more fundamental methodological point:

> To inquire about this, and to seek an argument for that which we are too well off to need an argument is to judge badly about what is better and worse, about what is convincing and unconvincing, and what is a principle and what is not. (254a30-3)

Philosophical theorizing is called for when there is no consensus, are no reputable beliefs, or when our beliefs are unclear. It is misguided, Aristotle maintains, to try to prove the obvious or, even worse, to defend paradoxical theses that defy the overwhelming verdict of reputable belief (cf. *EE* I.6 1216b26-35 and *Phys* II.1 193a4-9). Rather, a theory will be confirmed if it harmonizes with "the views of many people and those of old or with the views of the few and the reputable; for it is reasonable not that either of these be mistaken, but that they are correct in one respect or even in many" (*NE* I.8 1098b26-9).

In order to appreciate Aristotle's doxastic method, it is useful to contrast it with the procedure adopted by Descartes in his *Meditations on First Philosophy* (published in 1641):

> Some years ago I was struck by the large number of falsehoods that I had accepted as true in my childhood, and by the highly doubtful nature of the whole edifice that I had subsequently based on them. I realized that it was necessary, once in the course of my life, to demolish everything completely and start again right from the foundations if I wanted to establish anything at all in the sciences that was stable and likely to last. (Meditation I, Descartes 1985, II, p. 12 = AT VII.17)

Descartes makes a similar remark in his *Discourse on the Method* (published in 1637):

> [R]egarding the opinions to which I had hitherto given credence, I thought that I could not do better than undertake to get rid of them, all at one go, in order to replace them afterwards with better ones, or with the same ones once I had squared them with the standards of reason. (Part 2, Descartes 1985, I, p. 117 = AT VI.13-14)

In the *Objections and Replies* (appended to the *Meditations* in 1647), Descartes responds to the objection that his procedure is too extreme with two apt analogies.

> Suppose [my critic] had a basket full of apples and, being worried that some of the apples were rotten, wanted to take out the rotten ones to prevent the rot spreading. How would he proceed? Would he not begin by tipping the whole lot out of the basket? And would not the next step be to cast his eye over each apple in turn, and pick up and put back in the basket only those he saw to be sound leaving the others? (Set VII, Descartes 1985, II, p. 324 = AT VII.481)

Likewise for those who have never philosophized correctly and who have many beliefs which they have accumulated since childhood; the best way for them to separate the true from the false is "to reject all their beliefs in one go, as if they were all uncertain and false. They can then go over each belief in turn and readopt only those which they recognize to be true and indubitable." Descartes offers a second analogy with architecture:

> [M]y method imitates that of the architect. When an architect wants to build a house which is stable on ground where there is a sandy topsoil over underlying rock, or clay, or some other firm base, he begins by digging out a set of trenches from which he removes the sand, and anything resting on or mixed in with the sand, so that he can lay his foundations on firm soil. (Ibid., p. 366 = AT VII.537)

Similarly Descartes began by throwing out any questionable beliefs, until he discovered that it is impossible to doubt that a doubting or thinking substance exists. "I took this as the bedrock on which I could lay the foundations of my philosophy."

Descartes' two analogies are telling, for they underscore the danger of holding false beliefs. Because a false premise may undermine the entire edifice of science, it is better to discard every dubious belief rather than run the risk of accepting a mistaken one. In defense of Aristotle's reliance on reputable beliefs, however, it might be pointed out that there are also perils in rejecting opinions that may be true. The point of Aristotle's comparison of truth to the proverbial door which nobody fails to hit is that our beliefs can reveal parts of the way the world is, even when they misrepresent other parts and even when they miss the big picture.

This methodological dispute can be brought into sharper relief by distinguishing between two types of doxastic failure: a type I failure is accepting a false belief, and a type II failure is failing to accept a true belief.[48] For example, believing that a spouse is unfaithful when the spouse is really innocent is a type I failure, while failing to believe this about a cheating spouse is a type II error. A doubtful or indecisive person is more inclined to avoid type I errors but also more prone to fall into type II failure, while a credulous or suspicious person is more inclined to avoid type II failure at the price of greater type I failure. Carried to extremes these habits become doxastic vices. A gullible or paranoid person leaps to conclusions and harbors preposterous and even inconsistent beliefs, while a doubting Thomas withholds judgment and is loath to venture any opinion. Doxastic virtue presumably involves finding an appropriate mean between these two extremes.[49]

Where does the mean lie? On this issue Descartes and Aristotle disagree. Descartes defends a skeptical method by emphasizing the dangers of type I doxastic failure with his analogies of a rotten apple spoiling the basketful and a house built on sand. Type I failure can indeed be hazardous, as Shakespeare's *Othello* illustrates. But, on the other hand, Hamlet illustrates the converse as he persistently insists upon "grounds more relative than this" for taking action. Aristotle might object that Descartes' method is overly skeptical, because it can be very costly to reject beliefs that may in fact be veridical. A lot of valuable information may be lost in the inflexible insistence on irrefragable opinions. In order to avoid excessive type II failure, more beliefs should be accepted. But won't this open the floodgates of credulity as Descartes fears? Aristotle tries to avoid this problem by prescreening and critically evaluating beliefs. He admits only reputable beliefs, he presents puzzles arising out of conflicting beliefs, and he tries to preserve those that are most credible. Consider, for example, a police detective who questions a number of eyewitnesses about a shooting. The investigator would be well advised to use Aristotle's method here, namely, to discount obviously silly or idiosyncratic reports and to give serious consideration to the beliefs shared by all or most of the witnesses and to those of expert or privileged witnesses (e.g., a police officer who reports the make of pistol carried by the perpetrator). If there are apparent disagreements, the detective should try to determine whether the reported beliefs can be reconciled, but, if not, to determine which reports have the greatest authority. Descartes' method of rejecting any belief about which a doubt can be raised would seem to be inappropriate in such a case. It is of course a matter of debate which is the superior method for scientific inquiry: Aristotle's or Descartes'?

Aristotle's doxastic method is in keeping with his general policy of *teleological approximism*: "While it is clearly best for any being to attain the real end, yet, if that cannot be, the nearer it is to the best the better will be its state" (*Cael* II.12 292b17-19; cf. *GC* II.10 336b25-34). For example, health is the best condition for a human body, and those who are not already healthy can become so by reducing their weight or by exercising and thereby reducing their weight. Even someone who can never become entirely fit (due, e.g., to having suffered a stroke) should strive for a condition that resembles health by exercising as much as possible under the circumstances. Teleological approximism may be applied to knowledge and belief in an analogous way. Knowledge of the truth is a natural end of human beings (cf. *Met* A.1 980a21). If we cannot achieve knowledge, the closest we can come is to true belief, and we are most likely to believe truly if our beliefs are in agreement with beliefs that are reputable. In this way we can attain doxastic virtue, which is an approximation of the intellectual virtue of wisdom (*sophia*), a condition incapable of error.

Such a process of testing our beliefs would be a valuable preliminary to scientific demonstration, since it could help us to pick out and eliminate mistaken generalizations, to clarify and reconcile seemingly inconsistent observations, and to establish the logical order between beliefs. By analyzing and criticizing our beliefs, we can make gradual progress from what is "plain and clear to us in a confused way" toward knowledge of primary causes and first principles (*Phys* I.1 184a21-6, b10-14).

A critic might object, however, that Aristotle's doxastic method would incline toward a conservative (if not reactionary) deference to popular opinion and a resistance to the theoretical leaps and "paradigm shifts" required for scientific progress. Such a critic might add the ad hominem remark that Aristotle's writings are rife with erroneous opinions and that he rejected scientific theories that turned out be true such as the atomic theory, the heliocentric theory of the solar system, and the theory of evolution. Now it is undeniable that Aristotle made many mistakes. It is debatable, however, whether these are due to his doxastic method or to the way he applied this method. In the scientific realm a number of his errors (e.g., that the heart has only three chambers, *PA* III.4 666b21) might be attributed to the limitations of equipment and observational technique, since he also made accurate observations such as his detailed study of the development of a chick embryo (*GA* III.1-2). Admittedly, there are less excusable gaffes (e.g., that women have fewer teeth than men, *HA* II.3.501b19-20) and even seeming instances of prejudice (e.g., that women have an inefficacious deliberative capacity and that Greeks are more rational than Europeans, *Pol* I.13 1260a13, VII.7 1327b23-31). Arguably, however, these mistakes are corrigible by means of Aristotle's own method. It must also be kept in mind that Aristotle did not intend for his doxastic method to guide scientific demonstration, as described in the *Posterior Analytics*. The doxastic method was intended instead to identify the prescientific data that were to be explained by the special sciences and the basic principles presupposed by scientific explanations. Aristotle's own theory of celestial spheres (*Met* XII.8) is clear evidence that he was prepared to endorse a new theory if it provided a convincing causal explanation of reliable beliefs.

7 Conclusion

Belief is an important concept for Aristotle. He recognizes a distinct capacity to form beliefs and offers careful accounts of how false belief occurs, how belief differs from knowledge, and how we can believe and know the same things. Although knowledge is clearly superior to belief, our beliefs form the starting point for the pursuit of knowledge. Although human beings can achieve genuine knowledge, even if temporarily and on specific topics, we must remain content with beliefs when the objects of judgment are inconstant or obscure, and our quest for certainty is all too often frustrated by our human limitations.[50] An understanding of the place of belief in his philosophy helps to explain why Aristotle places a premium on dialectic even though it is concerned with reputable beliefs. For belief can have epistemic value even if it is not knowledge. This is in accord with Aristotle's contextual approach to cognitive awareness:

> One must not demand that for every problem the deductions should be equally reputable and convincing; for it belongs directly by nature to some objects of inquiry to be easier and to others to be harder, so that if a man reached a conclusion from the most reputable beliefs possible, he has argued soundly. (*Top* VIII.11 161b34-8)

Some commentators have wanted to go further and attribute to Aristotle the view that we can acquire a "common knowledge" by means of dialectic (e.g., Bolton 2003, p. 154). We should, however, note that Aristotle in the *Rhetoric* only says that everyone is aware (*gnôrizein*) of certain common things (I.1 1354a3). As we have seen, Aristotle speaks of awareness quite widely, for perception as well as knowledge, and of objects familiar to us and familiar in nature.[51] We should not suppose that Aristotle views dialectic as a foundation for knowledge.[52] Aristotle can vindicate dialectic without collapsing the distinction between knowledge and generally accepted belief. At the beginning, I remarked how Dante memorialized "the master of them that know." If I have argued soundly here, we should also celebrate Aristotle as the master of them that believe.

Notes

1. The translation of *epistêmê* as "knowledge" and *doxa* as "belief" is potentially misleading because Aristotle does not regard *epistêmê* as a species of *doxa*. They are, as will be seen, mutually exclusive types. Hence, "belief" as used in this essay corresponds to what many modern epistemologists might call "mere belief." See the appendix on the translation of Aristotle's terms for belief. All translations of Aristotle are by the author.
2. *Phys* VII.3 247b8-9, *Met* Λ.7 1072b20-1; cf. Rosen (1961).
3. Aristotle cites an argument like this at *Met* B.4 999b1-3: "If nothing exists apart from individual things, nothing will be thinkable (*noêton*) but all things will be perceptible, and there will be knowledge (*epistêmê*) of nothing, unless we say perception is knowledge."
4. *An. Post* I.33 88b30-2; cf. *An* III.3 428a19, *Met* Z.15 1039b34-1040a1.
5. Cf. *NE* VII.2 1145b8; cf. 3 1146b6-8, 14 1154a22-5; cf. *EE* VII.2 1235b13-18, Phys IV.4 211a7-11. Useful discussions of this notion include Owen (1961) and Pritzl (1994).
6. Nutritive capacity: *An* III.12 434a26, *GA* II.7 745b24; awareness: *An* I.2 404b28, III.3 427a17-19; sense-perception: *GA* I.23 731a31-3; thought: *An* II.3 414b18, III.4 429a23.
7. *An. Post* II.19 100b6; cf. *NE* VI.9 1142b12-14. This brief summary requires qualifications which cannot be elaborated here. First, Aristotle often uses these terms more freely than this summary suggests. For example, he uses the term *dianoêtikon* for the entire capacity of thought (equivalent to *noêtikon*) at *An* II.3 414a32, 2 413b12, *NE* IX.4 1166a17, and at *MM* I.1 1182a18-20 (where it is equivalent to *logistikon*). Second, Aristotle denies that these cognitive states "come to be" (*gignetai*) in the strict sense: "There is no coming-to-be of the use and activity [of these states] ... And the original acquisition of knowledge is not a coming-to-be; for we say that we know and comprehend because cognition comes to rest and takes a stand. And there is no coming-to-be of being at rest, for generally there is no coming-to-be of change.... [S]omething becomes understanding and knowing because it settles down from its natural restlessness" (*Phys* VII.3 247b7-8, 9-13, 17-18).
8. *An. Pr* II.23 68b13-14, *An. Post* I.3 72b29, *Top* I.12 105a10-19.
9. Analysis: *NE* III.3 1112b20; deliberation: *NE* III.3 1112b21-3, VI.1 1139a12-13, 9 1142b2, 15; problem solving: *Meteor* II.2 355b20, *Pol* III.4 1276b36, 13 1283b35, 16 1287b20; contemplation: *An* II.1 412a22-7, 5 417a22-9. It should be noted that Aristotle often uses the terms *sullogismos*, *zêtêsis*, *theôria*, and so forth in broader senses, in which case the fine distinctions noted in this paragraph become blurred. For example, he describes recollection (in distinction from memory) as both a kind of *sullogismos* and a kind of *zêtêsis* (*Mem* 2 453a11-12). Here he compares recollection to deliberation, and he seems to be using *sullogismos* in a broad sense.
10. See *Phys* VII.3 247a1-2, b1-3. Cf. *Cat* 7 7b22-35 where Aristotle treats knowledge (a form of judgment) as a kind of relation: the knowable object is prior to knowledge. For the *pragma* as object, see *Cat* 5 4a34-b10 and 12 14b15-22.
11. *NE* VI.9 1142b13; cf. *Met* Γ.4 1008b10, *Insomn* 1 458b11-12. In *Int* 14 23a32-3, 24a1-2, Aristotle says that spoken affirmation (*kataphasis*) and negation (*apophasis*) are symbols of things in cognition (*dianoia*), i.e., presumably, judgments; cf. *Int* 1 16a4. *Hupolêpsis*, like "judgment," can refer either to an occurrent mental act or to a state or disposition to perform such an act. In the *Nicomachean Ethics* passage Aristotle uses *phasis* in a generic sense covering both affirmative and negative assertions, but he sometimes contrasts *phasis* and *kataphasis*, e.g., *Int* 4 16b27-8 and *Met*. Θ.10 1051b24-5. On the latter passage cf. note 19.

12. Cf. *MM* I.34 1197a30-2: "It is judgment (*hupolêpsis*) by which we are ambivalent about all things as to whether they are in a particular condition or not." *Hupolêpsis* here is equivalent to *doxa* and opposed to *epistêmê* (cf. *Cat* 7 8b11). We may compare in English the guarded phrase "in my judgment...."
13. On knowledge, see *Cat* 7 7b22-35 and *Phys* VII.3 247b2-3; on belief, see *Cat* 5 4a35-b13.
14. The objects of *epistêmonikon* are "things whose principles cannot be otherwise," while *doxastikon* "is about what can be otherwise" (*NE* VI.1 1139a6-8, 5 1140b26; cf. *An. Post* I.33 89b3-5, *Top* V.3 131b23, *Phys* V.4 227b13). The *doxastikon* corresponds to the calculative faculty (*logistikon*) at *NE* VI.1 1139a12 and deliberative faculty (*bouleutikon*) at *MM* I.34 1196b15. Deliberation belongs to the doxastic faculty because we can only deliberate about perceptual objects which involve change and are subject to generation and destruction (*MM* I.34 1196b27-9, cf. *NE* VI.1 1139a13-14).
15. *An* III.3 427b13-14, 428a19-22, 429a5, *Mem.*1 450a14, *PA* I.1 641b7, *NE* VII.5 1147b4-5. Flora (2010) discusses the relationship of belief to persuasion and reason. Aristotle believes that higher beings also have the power of thought (*An* III.2 414b18, *Met* Λ.7, *NE* X.8), but it is questionable whether this would include belief.
16. Cf. *An* III.8 432a11-12, *Cat* 4 2a4-10 and *Int* 1 16a12-13. The final clause "as if they were one" touches on the problem of predication. As Barnes (2007, pp. 111–12, 192–3) points out, ancient commentators viewed the copula as the key to solving this problem. The copulative use of "is" is adumbrated at *Int* 3 16b24-5, 5 17a11-12, and 12 21b9-10. It should be noted that Aristotle recognizes that not all combinations are true or false: an *assertive* (*apophantikos*) statement is true or false, but a prayer, command, threat, or question is not (cf. *Int* 4 17a1-6, *Poet* 19 1456b8-17).
17. Cf. *Met* Γ.7 1012a4-5 and *An* III.6 430b1-2. For the sake of clarity, I shall use "combination" for the wider relation and "conjunction" for the narrow relation contrasted with "division." Aristotle uses the terms *sunthêkê* and *sumplokê* interchangeably.
18. Cf. Δ.29 1024b17-21, E.4 1027b20-3. Crivelli (2004, ch. 4) argues that the things conjoined or divided are states of affairs, so that Aristotle holds a correspondence theory of truth, while Barnes (2007, pp. 64–6) ascribes a deflationary theory to him.
19. One notorious problem involves beliefs about the future, e.g., that there will be a sea battle tomorrow (see *Int* 9). Another complication concerns simple (*hapla*) objects. *Met* E.4 1027b27-8 (cf. *Cat* 10.13b10-11) states, "with regard to simple things and essences they [namely, falsity and truth] do not exist even in thought," and promises further discussion. But *Met* Θ.10 1051b22-32 distinguishes assertion (*phasis*) of an essence or non-composite substance from subject-predicate affirmation (*kataphasis*) and argues that an assertion can be true but not false. About simple objects "it is not possible to be in error, but only to know (*noein*) them or not." But he does allow that there can be error about them "accidentally." What exactly Aristotle means in this context by an assertion (*phasis*) and by the corresponding simple object is controversial. Different interpretations of this enigmatic passage are offered by Wedin (1988, pp. 125–36), Butler and Rubenstein (2004), Crivelli (2004, pp. 100–16), and Makin (2006, pp. 258–60). By an "accidental" error Aristotle may mean a case in which the essence is involved in a false predicative belief, e.g. the belief that every *man* is uneducated—an example due to Crivelli (2004, p.111).
20. For example, *An* III.6 430b1, 5 notes that time may be combined as well through the tense of the verb. *De Interpretatione* and *Prior Analytics* provide extensive and systematic accounts of the way in which terms can be combined in judgments.
21. Cf. *Cat* 12 14b18-22. This concerns true and false statements, but these are, in Aristotle's view, symbols of judgments in the soul: cf. *Int* 1 16a3-4.
22. *Cat* 5 4a21-b13 argues that the belief or statement undergoes no change in the strict sense but has contrary truth values due to a change in the facts. Cf. *An* III.3 428b8-9, *NE* VI.3 1139b21-2. *Met* Θ.10 1052a5 also mentions "error in respect of time," but does not say explicitly that the numerically same belief has different truth values.
23. *NE* VI.6 1140b31; cf. *An. Post* I.33 89b3-5, *Top* V.3 131a23, *Phys* V.4 227b13.

24. Cf. 72a30-2; 25 86b5, 27-30. Aristotle makes similar claims in other works: "We think (*oiometha*) that we know (*ginôskein*) a thing whenever we have become aware (*gnôrisômen*) of its primary causes or first principles up to its elements" (*Phys* I.1 184a12-14; cf. II.3 194b18-20, *Met* A.3 983a25-6, α.2 994b29-30, B.2,996b14-16). See Burnyeat (1981, p. 106) on Aristotle's subtle variations of epistemic verbs.
25. *An. Post* I.3 72b18-22, II.19 100b3-15. I follow Barnes (1994, p. 268): "the method by which we gain knowledge of the principles ... is, in a word, inductive." Other commentators understand by *nous* a special act of intuition, e.g., Irwin (1988, pp. 134–37).
26. Cf. *Phys* I.5 188b32-3, *An* II.2 413a12, *Top* VIII.1 156a6-7. The word *gnôrimos* is translated as "familiar," "knowable," "known," "intelligible," "notable," and so forth. Translators and commentators sometimes shift confusingly between these; for example, Taylor (1990, pp. 119–20) shifts between "known" and "familiar." Burnyeat (1981, pp. 128–29) defends "knowable" or "familiar" as a translation. Of the two, "familiar" seems better because *gnôrimos* is closely related to *gnôrizein*, which Aristotle uses widely for perceptual awareness as well as strict knowledge (cf. *An. Post* II.19 99b18).
27. *An. Post* I.13 78a22-38. Aristotle attempts to explain this phenomenon at *Cael* II.8 290a17-24.
28. *An. Post* I.13 79a13-16. This is the interpretation of Philoponus, *Commentary to Aristotle's Posterior Analytics* 182.21-3.
29. *An. Pr.* I.3 25b14, 13 32b6-22, 27 43b33-6, *An. Post*. I.14 79a21, 27 87a31-4, *Top* II.6 112b1-20.
30. See, e.g., Burnyeat (1981) and Taylor (1990).
31. On the phrase *hoper anthrôpou estin*, see Ross (1965, p. 608). Diamond brackets indicate additions that seem necessary to make sense of Aristotle's highly compressed text.
32. Reading *estai* at b6 with Bekker and ms. A2.
33. Barnes (1994, p. 202) comments that Aristotle would have done better to use the "obvious suggestion" that belief might be *defined* as a judgment which is not knowledge. However, although this stipulative definition would trivially entail that one cannot believe and know the same objects at the same time, it would not have shown *why* what we (nonstipulatively) call belief and knowledge are incompatible.
34. This agrees with the account in *NE* VI.3 1139b26-35. Cf. also *An. Post* II.19 100b3-12. See note 25 for the interpretation that comprehension (*nous*) is an epistemic state resulting from induction. If comprehension is assumed instead to be an act of intuition, the solution suggested in the text would need to be modified accordingly.
35. The translation in Bolton (2003, p. 157) is somewhat misleading: "Therefore, anyone who can proceed effectively on the basis of what is generally accredited (*ta endoxa*) does so equally on the basis of the truth." *Homoiôs* is translated more precisely as "similarly" than as "equally," and *stochastikôs echein pros* means to "be capable of aiming at" or "skilled at aiming at." Cf. Cooper (1994, p. 203 n. 15).
36. *Rhet* I.1 1355a21-2. Aristotle also speaks of thinkers as being "guided" or "forced" by the facts to abandon mistaken for correct views: see *PA* I.1 642a19-21, 24-8, *Met* I.3 984b8-11. See Wians (2008, pp. 58–60).
37. See Alston (1988, p. 263) for a similar example.
38. Aristotle offers a teleological explanation like this of sense-perception: "Any body capable of locomotion would, if it lacked sense-perception, perish and fail to reach its end, which is the function of nature" (*An* III.12 434a31-b1). Although sense-perception is for the sake of a self-moving creature's survival, in rational animals it exists for the sake of living well, "for they report many differences of things, from which arises knowledge of the intellectual and the practical" (*Sens* 1 436b18-417a3). Again, if we believe that something is frightening or threatening, we have an immediate emotional response, but this does not happen if we merely imagine it (*An* III.3 427b21-4). This natural connection between belief and emotion can be explained teleologically if belief is naturally directed to the truth.
39. Although this thesis is widely accepted by philosophers and psychologists, there are some theorists who argue that we may be better off if we are under certain illusions about ourselves

and the world around us. Badhwar (2008) criticizes these arguments and argues a persuasive defense of psychological realism.

40. On the thesis that "beliefs aim at truth," see recent discussions by Williams (1973) and Velleman (2000).
41. Cf. *EE* I.6 1216b30-2. According to Alexander of Aphrodisias (*Commentary to Aristotle's Metaphysics* 140.12-18, trans. William E. Dooley), the proverb, "'Who could fail to hit a door?'... refers to simple tasks involving nothing difficult or hard to discover; the figure is borrowed from archers shooting at a target. For if the target before them is narrow, they do not find it easy to hit the mark, but if the target is broad, it is not difficult for them to hit it, and hence all of them shoot successfully." The point of the passage is that it is easy to arrive at a true belief (in the sense that beliefs generally contain some truth) but hard to arrive at comprehensive or thorough knowledge of the truth.
42. Barnes (1981) argues persuasively that *endoxos* means "reputable." On the contrary Nussbaum (1982) argues that *ta endoxa* are "our most common beliefs," but Cooper (1999) offers a convincing critique, noting that "our" corresponds to nothing in the Greek. Reeve (1998, pp. 238–40) defends the even stricter interpretation that an *endoxos* proposition must be "deeply unproblematic." However, *Top* I.10 104a8-11, which he cites, says only that a *dialectical* proposition is *endoxos* "provided that it is not paradoxical"; it does not say that every *endoxos* proposition is non-paradoxical.
43. Note that the adjective *endoxos* in 100b21-3 is applied to persons as well as beliefs. As applied to persons, *endoxos* has a positive connotation, suggestive of virtue (cf. *NE* IV.2 1122b32, 13 1127a21, *Rhet* I.9 1368a21). *Top* I.1 100b21-3 presents a problem for Smith (1997) who translates the two occurrences of the adjective inconsistently in the same sentence: as "acceptable" for beliefs and as "esteemed" for persons. This is also awkward for Irwin and Fine (1995), who translate *endoxon* as "common belief" (which would be more apt for *koinê doxa*); their solution is to translate *endoxos* as "commonly recognized" when it is applied to a person.
44. As remarked by Evans (1977, pp. 80–84), *Top* VIII.5 159a39-b1 distinguishes between *endoxon* (or *adoxon*) without qualification (*haplôs*) and in a restricted sense (*hôrismenôs*), i.e., relative to someone. Presumably the *endoxon* without qualification satisfies the canonical account at *Top* I.1 100b21-3, while the restricted sense pertains to what is reputable to a particular speaker or writer. A dialectical argument may proceed from what is *endoxon* in either sense but should do so consistently: i.e., one might try to defend Heraclitus' thesis that good and evil are one and the same, appealing exclusively to beliefs that would have seemed reputable to Heraclitus.
45. Cf. *EE* I.6 1216b26-35 and *Top* I.2 101a34-6: dialectic enables us to detect truth and falsity more easily by going through difficulties (*diaporêsai*) on both sides of an issue. Here and often elsewhere Aristotle evidently uses *phainomena* interchangeably with *endoxa*, which leads Nussbaum (1982) to view *phainomena* and *endoxa* as coextensive. Irwin (1988, p. 494 n. 42) also appeals to the alleged near equivalence of *endoxon* and *phainomena* in rejecting "reputable" as a translation of *endoxon*. However, Aristotle implies that an *endoxon* may be at variance with the *phainomena* when he says that Socrates' belief that nobody acts against what he judges best "contradicts the plain appearances" (*NE* VII.2 1145b26-8; cf. Cooper 1999). Again, *Top* I.1 100b26 warns that not every *phainomenon endoxon* (apparently reputable belief) is an *endoxon*. (Note that this sentence is mistranslated by Reeve [1992, p. 35] as "Not every *phainomenon* is an *endoxon*." Reeve seemingly ascribes to Aristotle the questionable view that *endoxa* are a subclass of *phainomena*.) Belief (*doxa*) and appearance (*phantasiai*) are distinguished at *An* III.3 428b2-4, *Insomn* 2 460b18-20, 3 462a2-7, and *EE* VII.2 1235b25-9.
46. Aristotle compares this method of testing beliefs to Socrates' method of elenchus (*SE* 34 183a37-b9).
47. This is to be distinguished from the converse principle enunciated by W. K. Clifford and criticized by William James: "It is wrong always, everywhere, and for anyone, to believe anything on insufficient evidence." Aristotle's prescription concerns not how we ought to believe

directly (since he holds that belief and disbelief are not "up to us"), but how we ought to go about forming beliefs. For a recent discussion of this distinction, see Chrisman (2008).
48. This distinction resembles to some extent the familiar distinction between two sorts of statistical error: A type I statistical error (or "false positive") consists in failing to reject the null hypothesis (the hypothesis that there is no statistically significant difference), while a type II statistical error (or "false negative") consists in mistakenly accepting the null hypothesis (i.e., in thinking that there is no difference where in fact there is one). For example, there is a type I error if a patient after biopsy is judged to have a disease even though the person does not have the disease. A type II error occurs if the patient is deemed to be free of the disease even though it is present. As described in the text, the doxastic distinction differs slightly: Believing falsely that the patient is sick would be a type I doxastic failure; failing to believe truly that the patient is sick would be a type II doxastic failure.
49. Zagzebski (1996, p. 216) complains that Aristotle does not recognize a virtue corresponding to "opinions about contingent matters other than those concerning what is to be done"; cf. Régis (1935, p. 61). However, Aristotle leaves room for such an intellectual virtue. In addition to the virtues of the scientific part of the rational faculty (*epistêmê*, *nous*, and *sophia*), he mentions a virtue of the doxastic part that forms beliefs, namely, prudence (*phronêsis*). But Aristotle adds that prudence is not merely a state "involving reason (*meta logou*)" (*NE* VI.5 1140b25-30), because it also involves habits of action. Theoretical doxastic virtue would be the corresponding virtue not involving habits of action. Both practical and theoretical doxastic virtue would be species of correct thinking (*orthotês dianoias*) or correctness of thought (cf. 10 1142b12-13). In addition to Zagzebski (1996), see Greco (2001) for modern discussions of epistemic virtue along neo-Aristotelian lines.
50. See Wians (2008) for a valuable discussion of Aristotle on the limits of human knowledge.
51. In support of this view, Bolton (2003) also cites *Phys* I.2 185a2-3, but the common knowledge (*koinê epistêmê*) tentatively mentioned there is not the same as in *Rhet* I.1 1354a3. It is a much narrower discipline that attempts to prove the first principles such as the law of noncontradiction; cf. *An. Post* I.11 77a26-31. Also problematic is the interpretation of Irwin (1988) that Aristotle employs a "strong" form of dialectic in order to overcome skeptical objections. Aristotle does not himself distinguish between different types of dialectic. See Striker (1991) for a critique of Irwin's claim that Aristotle tries to defend his first principles by means of a nonempirical, proto-Kantian version of dialectic.
52. Bolton (2003, p. 157) insightfully observes that the validity and value of dialectic depend on the fact that "we are *naturally set up* so that it comes about that our items of most common agreement on ordinary matters are true, or sufficiently so." But it is hard to accept Bolton's further claim that "Aristotle equates reasoning from *common knowledge*, in rhetoric and dialectic, with reasoning from certain *generally accredited beliefs* or *endoxa*."

Appendix on Translation

Many of Aristotle's key terms are hard to translate, but the topic of belief presents exceptional challenges especially for Greekless readers, because Aristotle uses a wide variety of terms for belief, each of which is translated in different ways. The problem is compounded by the fact that he wields a panoply of terms for knowledge as well. Nonetheless, by using plausible translations for Aristotle's terms and following them consistently wherever possible, we can show that Aristotle's discussions of belief in different works exhibit impressive coherence. I should also mention that I prefer "belief" to "opinion" for the simple reason that the related verb "believe" is more manageable in English than the verb "opine." Aristotle's vocabulary for belief may be divided into three main groups.

First and foremost is a family of words associated with the verb *dokein*. Although *dokein* is often translated as "believe," the two verbs play different grammatical roles. For example, although *Sôkratês dokei moi einai sophos* can be translated "I believe that Socrates is wise," the subject of the Greek sentence is *Sôkratês*. The grammatical form of the Greek sentence is much closer to "Socrates seems to me to be wise." Indeed *dokei* is often translated as "seems," and *dokei* frequently seems equivalent to *phainetai*, which may be translated as "appears." The participle *dokounta* (sometimes used interchangeably with *phainomena*) is used for the objects of belief: what are believed or what seem to be. Related to the verb *dokei* is the important noun *doxa* which I shall translate "belief" and the verb *doxazein*, "to have a belief," which unlike *dokein* does take the believer as the subject. Also related is the noun *dogma*, for which "opinion" will serve. Finally, there are two related adjectives: The first, *endoxos*, as applied to a person means "reputable" or "of good repute"—for the noun *doxa* can also mean "reputation." The second adjective, its opposite, *adoxos* means "disreputable" or "of ill repute." Aristotle uses the neuter substantive *endoxon* translated here as "reputable belief." (The expression *koinê doxa*, "common belief," is sometimes equivalent to *endoxon*.) He also uses the neuter substantive *adoxon* for a "disreputable belief," which may also be translated "unbelievable" or "incredible."

Second is a family related to the verb *lambanein*, which may be translated as "grasp" or "apprehend." In connection with belief, the most important verb is *hupolambanein*, which I translate as "judge" (because it can refer to knowing as well as believing). However, other translators also render it as "believe" or "suppose," and in some contexts, *hupolambanein* is equivalent to *doxazein*. The related noun is *hupolêpsis*, which I translate as "judgment," although it is sometimes equivalent to *doxa*.

Third is a heterogeneous group of verbs which are often translated as "believe." These include *oiesthai* as well as *hêgesthai* and *nomizein* (often used for religious belief). These terms are frequently used instead of, and seemingly in the same sense as, forms of *hupolambanein* and *dokein*. I translate *oiesthai* as "think" (noting the Greek verb to avoid confusion with *noein*).

Bibliography

Alston, William. 1988. The deontological conception of epistemic justification. *Philosophical Perspectives* 2: 257–299.
Badhwar, Neera K. 2008. Is realism really bad for you? A realistic response. *Journal of Philosophy* 105: 85–107.
Barnes, Jonathan. 1981. Aristotle and the methods of ethics. *Revue Internationale de Philosophie* 34: 490–511.
Barnes, Jonathan. 1994. *Aristotle's Posterior Analytics*, 2nd ed. Oxford: Clarendon Press.
Barnes, Jonathan. 2007. *Truth, etc.* Oxford: Clarendon Press.
Bolton, Robert. 2003. Aristotle: Epistemology and methodology. In *Blackwell guide to ancient philosophy*, ed. Christopher Shields, 151–162. Oxford: Blackwell Publishing.
Burnyeat, Myles F. 1981. Aristotle on understanding knowledge. In *Aristotle on science: The Posterior Analytics: Proceedings of the eighth symposium Aristotelicum*, ed. Enrico Berti, 97–139. Padua: Editrice Antenore.

Burnyeat, Myles F. 1986. Good repute. *London Review of Books* 8(19): 11–13.
Butler, Travis, and Eric Rubenstein. 2004. Aristotle on *nous* of simples. *Canadian Journal of Philosophy* 34: 355–374.
Chrisman, Matthew. 2008. Ought to believe. *The Journal of Philosophy* 105: 346–370.
Cooper, John M. 1994. Ethical-political theory in Aristotle's *Rhetoric*. In *Aristotle's Rhetoric: Philosophical essays*, ed. David J. Furley and Alexander Nehamas, 193–210. Princeton: Princeton University Press.
Cooper, John M. 1999. Aristotle on the authority of "appearances.". In *Reason and emotion*, 281–291. Princeton: Princeton University Press.
Crivelli, Paolo. 2004. *Aristotle on truth*. Cambridge: Cambridge University Press.
Descartes, Réné. 1985. *The philosophical writings of Descartes*. 2 vols. Trans. John Cottingham, Robert Stroothoff, and Dugald Murdoch. Cambridge: Cambridge University Press. [AT = *Oeuvres de Descartes*, ed. Charles Adam and Paul Tannery, 1964–1976. Paris: Vrin, Centre National de la Recherché Scientifique.]
Evans, J.D.G. 1977. *Aristotle's concept of dialectic*. Cambridge: Cambridge University Press.
Flora, Ian C. 2010. Human reason as persuasion: Aristotle on belief and rationality. Presented at American Philosophical Association, Central Division (unpublished).
Greco, John. 2001. Virtues and rules in epistemology. In *Virtue epistemology: Essays on epistemic virtue and responsibility*, ed. Abrol Fairweather and Linda Zagzebski, 117–141. New York: Oxford University Press.
Irwin, Terence. 1988. *Aristotle's first principles*. Oxford: Clarendon Press.
Irwin, Terence, and Gail Fine. 1995. *Aristotle selections*. Indianapolis: Hackett Publishing Company.
Jaeger, Werner. 1962. *Aristotle: Fundamentals of the history of his development*, 2nd ed. Trans. Richard Robinson. London: Oxford University Press.
Makin, Stephen. 2006. *Aristotle Metaphysics book Theta*. Oxford: Clarendon Press.
Nussbaum, Martha C. 1982. Saving Aristotle's appearances. In *Language and logos*, ed. Malcolm Schofield and Martha C. Nussbaum, 267–293. Cambridge: Cambridge University Press.
Owen, G.E.L. 1961. Tithenai ta phainomena. In *Aristote et les problemes de méthode*, ed. S. Mansion, 83–103. Louvain: Publications Universitaires de Louvain. [Reprinted in Owen, G.E.L. 1986. *Logic, science, and dialectic*, 239–251. Ithaca: Cornell University Press.]
Pritzl, Kurt. 1994. Opinions as appearances: *Endoxa* in Aristotle. *Ancient Philosophy* 14: 41–50.
Reeve, C.D.C. 1992. *Practices of reason: Aristotle's* Nicomachean Ethics. Oxford: Clarendon Press.
Reeve, C.D.C. 1998. Dialectic and philosophy in Aristotle. In *Method in ancient philosophy*, ed. Jyl Gentzler, 227–252. Oxford: Clarendon Press.
Régis, L.M. 1935. *L'Opinion selon Aristote*. Ottawa: Institut d'Étude Médiévales d'Ottawa.
Rosen, S.H. 1961. Thought and touch: A note on Aristotle's *De Anima*. *Phronesis* 6: 127–137.
Ross, W.D. 1965. *Aristotle* Prior *and* Posterior Analytics. Oxford: Clarendon Press.
Smith, Robin. 1997. *Aristotle's* Topics *books I and VIII*. Oxford: Clarendon Press.
Striker, Gisela. 1991. Review of Irwin (1988). *Journal of Philosophy* 88: 489–496.
Taylor, C.C.W. 1990. Aristotle's epistemology. In *Epistemology*, ed. Stephen Everson, 116–142. Cambridge: Cambridge University Press.
Velleman, J. David. 2000. On the aim of belief. In *The possibility of practical reason*, ed. J. David Velleman, 244–281. New York: Oxford University Press.
Wedin, Michael V. 1988. *Mind and imagination in Aristotle*. New Haven: Yale University Press.
Wedin, Michael V. 1993. Content and cause in the Aristotelian mind. *Southern Journal of Philosophy* 31(Supplement): 49–105.
Wians, William. 2008. Aristotle and the problem of human knowledge. *The International Journal of the Platonic Tradition* 2: 41–64.
Williams, Bernard. 1973. Deciding to believe. In *problems of the self*, ed. Bernard Williams, 136–151. Cambridge: Cambridge University Press.
Zagzebski, Linda T. 1996. *Virtues of the mind: An inquiry into the nature of virtue and the ethical foundations of knowledge*. Cambridge: Cambridge University Press.

Aristotelian Grace

Charles M. Young

1 Introduction

In *Nicomachean Ethics* V.5 Aristotle says this about the importance of reciprocity to the political community:

> The city is maintained by proportionate reciprocity. For people seek to return both evil for evil (if they cannot, it seems to be slavery) and good for good, since otherwise exchange does not occur, and exchange is what keeps them together. (V.5 1132b33-1134a2)[1]

He then takes the opportunity to append a footnote, as it were, on grace and the Graces:

> This is why people put up shrines to the Graces in prominent places: so that favors done shall be returned. For what is special about grace is that it's gracious for one who has been shown favor to do a kindness in return, and for him to go first in showing favor next time out. (a2-5)

For some years I have discussed the ideas in this paper with anyone who was willing to listen and even with a few who really weren't; there is little chance that I will remember all or even most of them. Special thanks, though, are due to discussions with Jay Atlas, Paul Hurley, Debra Nails, Dion Scott-Kakures, Rivka Weinberg, and Nancy Young, among others, and to written comments from Kirk Fitzpatrick, Gabrielle Lear, and Suzanne Obdrzalek. I presented earlier versions of the paper at KeytFest, a conference honoring David Keyt at the University of Washington in May 2006, at the Northwest Philosophy Conference Seattle University in October 2006 (where Harald Thorsrud commented), at the Midsouth Philosophy Conference at Memphis University in February 2005, at the Ninth Annual Southern California Philosophy Conference at UC Irvine in October 2004, and at the Conference on Value Inquiry at the University of North Dakota in April 2003; I am grateful to those audiences and commentators for helpful discussion.

I am pleased to offer this chapter to David Keyt, to thank him for his many estimable contributions over the years to ancient philosophy and to those who work in the field.

C.M. Young (✉)
Department of Philosophy, Claremont Graduate University,
121 E. Tenth Street, Claremont, CA 91711, USA
e-mail: Charles.Young@cgu.edu

Aristotelian grace thus involves doing good in return when good has been done to one.[2] I shall begin with that idea and take up the notion of "going first ... next time out" later on, in Sect. 8.

2 Examples

It will be useful to have some illustrations of the phenomenon on the table. I think I know the first time I fully appreciated an instance of grace in operation. Grace is a common phenomenon in life, of course, and I knew about it, but I think that this was the first time I took official—professional—notice. I had occasion to give copies of a draft of a paper I had written to two of my colleagues for comment. Shortly thereafter, my colleagues got back to me to arrange a lunch to talk about my paper. If you are an academic, you will recognize that as perfectly normal behavior on their part. People often give papers they have written to their colleagues to read. It's fun, it promotes collegiality, and it decreases one's chances of saying something stupid in print. Also, those who read the papers typically respond, and often enough lunch plans are made to talk about them.

In the case at hand, what is hard to explain is the *timing*. Each of my colleagues — independently of each other—got back to me within a couple of hours of receiving my paper. Usually people take a good couple of weeks to respond. Sometimes a couple of months. A couple of days, in the very best case. But a couple of hours? What was going on? Well, as it happens, I had read two or three papers by each of my two colleagues previously. We had discussed those efforts over lunch, and, I believe, the discussions improved the papers. This was the first time, though, that I had given them work of mine to read and talk about. It was the first chance they had to do something by way of paying me back. That is why they did it so quickly: Aristotelian grace at work.

I do not know whether my colleagues saw things that way or not. That is, I do not know whether, for example, they said to themselves, "Here's a chance, at last, to pay him back," or whether they simply acted. The following case is one in which I am confident that the agents of grace simply acted. I work a lot on Aristotle's accounts of the individual virtues of character. And a minor industry called "virtue ethics" has burgeoned in philosophy in recent years. However, there are some experiments in social psychology that, in the view of some—among them Gilbert Harman (1999, 2000), no less—threaten to disprove the very existence of states of character and, therewith, the existence of virtues of character themselves. In one such experiment (Isen and Levin 1972), people who had just completed a telephone call in a shopping mall were confronted with a woman mildly in need of assistance. Some people offered to help the woman; other people did not. It turned out that, with only a few exceptions, the people in question helped or not depending on whether they got their dime back when they checked the slot of the pay phone when they finished their call. If they got their dime back, they helped; if they did not get their dime back, they did not help.

Here is one version of the line of thought that some think leads to the nonexistence of character traits. If kindness exists, then surely the no-dime-back group included some kind people. It strains probability, not to mention poetic justice, to suppose that all the kind people just happened to be in the dime-back group. But if there were kind people in the no-dime-back group, they surely would have helped the woman. Since the woman's need was mild, the costs of helping would have been insignificant; so *any* kind person would surely have helped. But no one in that group helped. Hence, there were no kind people in that group, and there is no such thing as kindness. Mind you, I am not endorsing this line of thought; I am just rehearsing it. But it is not without its appeal.

Of course that is just one way of understanding what is going on in the experiment. Alternatively, we might note that the default response to this particular case of mild distress is apparently *not to help* and seek to explain why those who got their dime back did help. I suggest that what is going on is this: Something good happened to those who got their dime back, and they were moved to do good in return. In other words, what was at play in this instance was not kindness but grace. The dime-back people could not do anything for the pay phone, except maybe dust it off. So they took the first chance they had to do something good for someone else: the woman in mild distress, provided for them by their friendly neighborhood social psychologists. Again, grace in operation. And if that is right, we do not have to say that with the pay phone experiment, social psychologists established the nonexistence of kindness. We can say instead that they established the existence of grace.

Further proof of the existence of grace is that it has been discovered—and corrupted—by direct mail solicitors. I am sure all of you have received solicitations from charitable and other groups in which a request for a contribution is accompanied by a nickel, sometimes even a quarter, a calendar, or a sheet of return address labels. Once I myself received a small packet of chicken bouillon from the Los Angeles Mission, which needs contributions each year to enable them to provide meals for the homeless at Thanksgiving. These solicitors are confident that we are more likely to send them money in response to a small gift from them than if they simply ask for the money. And we can be sure that this confidence is supported by studies in which both types of solicitations are used.

So that is Aristotelian grace: the impulse to return good that has been done to one. More exactly, Aristotelian grace is the natural force that takes the good that we do to and for one another and returns, magnifies, and ramifies it. This essay is an effort to begin to write its natural history.

3 Other Forms of Grace

Aristotelian grace is to be sharply distinguished both from the grace of God—that is, forgiveness—and from what Ernest Hemingway called "guts"—that is, grace under pressure.[3] Aristotelian grace is a response to goodness. The grace of God and the grace of guts are, in contrast, responses to evil. The grace of God is God's response, if we are fortunate, to the evil that we do to one another. Grace under pressure is our response, again if we are fortunate, to the evil that God—the world, or other people, if you prefer—does to us. Aristotelian grace is different. It is, again, a response not to evil but to goodness.

4 Grace as a Natural Force

In speaking of the natural history of Aristotelian grace, and in calling grace a force in nature, I have several things in mind. In the first place, as I just noted, grace has in addition a supernatural history and a visceral history, so to say, and I want to mark my subject off from both of those.

Second, and more importantly, I think that there is something wrong—warped, distorted, or unnatural—in people who are not moved to return good for good, in much the same way that there is something wrong—warped, distorted, or unnatural—in a child who does not return the love of his or her parents. Indeed, if I knew how to prove it, I would say that the natural impulse in mature humans to return good for good received is what the natural impulse in children to return love for love received develops into.

Be that as it may, as I say, I cannot prove it. But remember, among the Lilliputians in Jonathan Swift's *Gulliver's Travels*, lack of gratitude—gratitude is the daughter of grace, as I will explain in the next section—is a capital offense. In the Lilliputians' view, the inability to feel gratitude expels one out of the human realm. And even Ben in Doris Lessing's *Fifth Child* is capable of gratitude.[4] Indeed, Ben's capacity for gratitude is one thing that makes it possible for us to recognize him as human, even if he is overwhelmed by the feeling of gratitude when it comes, so inexperienced is he with occasions in which the feeling is in order.

A final point on grace as a natural force. I call it a force because I think its operation is, or can be, independent of the will and even independent of consciousness. The graciousness of those who helped the woman in the pay phone experiment, if what I said about it is convincing, was unconscious and unaware. So too, probably, was the graciousness of my colleagues in getting to my paper so quickly. And surely the exploitation of grace by our marketers depends on grace's operating below the level of consciousness. Aristotelian grace is a force operating in and through people, often without their even knowing it.

5 Gratitude and Grace

I said a moment ago that gratitude is the daughter of grace, and I will say what I mean by that, and prove it, in a moment. But first I want to make the point that gratitude is not the same as grace. Gratitude involves the *acknowledgment* of good received. Grace involves the *return* of good for good received. And acknowledgment and return are different things.

A couple of summers ago, a graduate student in English who knew some Greek asked if I would be willing to read parts of Euripides' *Bacchae* with her. I agreed. Among other things, the play has everybody's favorite emendation—*hedeôs* for *hedeôn* in line 188—and I would enjoy discussing that and other things about the play. I had other reasons for agreeing too, as I will soon explain. In any case, we spent some weeks that summer working through the play. Afterward, the English student of course thanked me for being willing to read the play with her: That is gratitude. If there were something in which she were more expert than I that she might be willing to read with me, that would be grace. But there is nothing that really fills that bill. She could give $1,000 to Oxfam in my name, I suppose, and that would be a good thing, at least if she could afford it. But even that would not count as paying me back directly for what I did for her. Something can count as payback only if there is some appropriate connection between the original good done and the good done in return—some form of repayment in kind—and there is nothing she can do for me directly that has that connection.

There is something, though, that she can do by way of paying me back indirectly. Thirty-five years from now, perhaps, a graduate student in philosophy will want to read Shakespeare's *King Lear* with her. Perhaps he will be interested in the severance imagery or all those monosyllables. My English student will be moved to comply with the student's request. She may not be able, but she will be moved to do it. And she will be moved to do it in part because 35 years before, I had been willing to read Euripides' *Bacchae* with her. And of course part of the reason that I had been willing to read Euripides' *Bacchae* with her, back then, was that 35 years before that, Russ Dancy had been willing to read Plato's *Protagoras* with me. So my English student cannot pay *me* back directly, but she can pay the human community back down the line, just as I did.

So it is, too, with what is an appropriate response to those responsible for one's training in philosophy. "For such gifts the only proper return is the endeavor to make worthy use of what one has learned," as Myles Burnyeat says, apropos of Bernard Williams,[5] in his gloss on *to endechomenon* ("what one can") at *Nicomachean Ethics* IX.1 1164b5-6 (Burnyeat 1982, p. 40 n. 40).[6]

6 "Lafayette, We Are Here"

The English student case is one in which the author of the original favor is not the recipient of the favor done in return. I did the original favor. When my English student returns the favor, she will return it not to me but to a counterpart, some graduate student, some years from now. Sometimes it's even the case that both the author and the recipient of the returned favor are different from the author and the recipient of the original favor.

A few weeks after the death of the Marquis de Lafayette in 1834, an American flag was raised over his grave in Paris, where it has flown ever since—it was not removed even by the Germans in World War II—as an expression of our gratitude to him and to France for their assistance to us in the Revolutionary War. Lafayette, in particular, had won the battle of Yorktown for us. On the Fourth of July in 1917, shortly after the arrival in Paris of the American Expeditionary Force in World War I, the flag was reinstalled at Lafayette's grave in an official ceremony. Colonel Charles E. Stanton, General J. J. Pershing's deputy, saluted the reinstalled flag and announced, "Lafayette, we are here." With these words, he represented our presence in France in 1917 as a payback for France's presence, summed up in the figure of Lafayette, in America 141 years earlier. Grace across generations.

7 The Daughter of Grace

As we saw earlier, gratitude is different from grace. Gratitude is the acknowledgment of a good received, while grace is the repayment of a good received. But there is an element of grace in gratitude. Imagine this. I am on a crowded bus. All the seats are taken. An older woman gets on. I rise and offer her my seat. She thanks me and sits down. A simple story. A favor is extended. Gratitude is expressed.

But my offering her my seat involves my recognition of her as another human being with needs and interests of her own that draw my attention, here and now, in this respect, to her: She needs that seat. Likewise, her thanking me for the seat involves her recognition of me as another human being with needs and interests of my own that I am willing to sacrifice, here and now, in this respect, for her: I want that seat, too, although I am prepared to give it up. So the acknowledgment of common humanity that I express in offering her my seat she returns to me, in kind, in thanking me for it. Her expression of thanks is as much an acknowledgment of my humanity and my needs and interests as my giving her my seat was an acknowledgment of her humanity, needs, and interests. Thus, her thanking me counts in this respect as repayment in kind. That is the element of grace in gratitude, and that is why gratitude is the daughter of grace.

8 A Regress

Let me now return to Aristotle's idea that it is gracious for one who has received a kindness "to go first ... next time out." If you have invited me to dinner, you've done me the kindness of the invitation. You've also done me the kindness of extending an invitation that is not a response to a previous invitation. It is gracious for me to return both kindnesses. Thus, it is gracious for me to reciprocate the kindness of your original invitation by inviting you to dinner. It is also gracious for me to reciprocate the kindness of your extending an invitation that is not a response to a previous invitation by extending a similar invitation to you.

There is an appealing regress here: A gracious regress, if I may. You invite me to dinner (Y). It is gracious for me to reciprocate (M). That's a cycle, YM. It is also gracious for me to initiate the next cycle, MY. But now we have a larger cycle, YMMY, that you initiated. So it is gracious for me to initiate a second larger cycle, MYYM. And so on, and on. It is thus a theorem of Aristotelian grace that if you do me a kindness, I will be forever in your debt.

Aristotle may think that by "going first … next time out," I square things with my benefactor. If so, our gracious regress is vicious against this thought. Kant goes straight to the heart of the matter: "For even if I repay my benefactor tenfold, I am still not even with him, because he has done me a kindness that he did not owe. He was the first in the field … and I can never be beforehand with him" (1930, p. 222).

9 Lafayette Revisited

I conclude with one more point about "our Marquis." In 1824, Lafayette returned to the United States to receive our thanks as part of a 13-month (!) celebration of the fiftieth anniversary of the American Revolution. He made a grand tour of all 24 states, at the end of which he said farewell to America with these words:

> God bless you, Sir, and all who surround you. God bless the American people, each of the states, and the federal government. Accept this patriotic farewell of a heart that will overflow with gratitude until the moment it ceases to beat.

What is going on? We had just spent 13 months expressing our gratitude to him. Why is *he* grateful to *us*?

Aristotle knows why. In *Nicomachean Ethics* IX.7, he offers several explanations for why benefactors love their beneficiaries more than beneficiaries love their benefactors, something that seems, he says, "contrary to reason." (And so it still seems to some: see Elster 1999, p. 313.) Aristotle's deepest explanation has it that the love that benefactors feel toward their beneficiaries is a form of self-love. Benefactors love their beneficiaries in the way parents love their own children and poets love their own poems: as expressions of themselves, of who they are. And they love those expressions because they love themselves. "What a thing is potentially, its work reveals in actuality" (1168a8-9). So too with Lafayette. Lafayette tried to bring democracy to America and succeeded. He also tried to bring democracy to his native France and failed. So he is grateful to us for giving him an opportunity that France could not: We gave him the chance to be Lafayette.[7]

Notes

1. I follow the text of Bywater (1894). Translations are my own.
2. I call the phenomenon "Aristotelian" grace to mark its provenance in Aristotle and to mark it off from other forms of grace (see Sect. 3). What I say about the phenomenon goes well beyond what little Aristotle himself has to say about it.

3. Dorothy Parker (1929, p. 31) reports this exchange in a "Profile" in *The New Yorker*:

    - "Now just a minute. Listen. Look here a minute. Exactly what do you mean by 'guts'?"
    - "I mean," Ernest Hemingway responded, "'grace under pressure'."

4. "'You're a good boy, Ben,' she said, and tears came into his eyes and she heard him give a sort of bark, which meant he wanted to say thank you to her, expressing his love and gratitude for those words, but he had never heard them, except from her" (Lessing 2000, pp. 33–34; a sequel to Lessing 1988).
5. Compare Lear (2000, pp. 184–5).
6. I have not made a thorough study of the phenomenon of "table grace." But it is perhaps worth mentioning that two specimens that I remember from my (mostly Presbyterian) childhood—"Bless us, O Lord, for these thy gifts which we are about to receive through thy bounty ..." and "Bless these gifts to our use and thus to thy service, and keep us ever mindful of the needs of others ..."—exemplify, respectively, *gratitude* and *worthy use*.
7. A wonderful biography of Lafayette is Unger (2002). It is unremitting hagiography; it should perhaps be read in conjunction with the relentlessly postmodern Beard (2000), on the classicist Jane Harrison, inter alia. Two biographies could not be more different.

Bibliography

Beard, Mary. 2000. *The invention of Jane Harrison*. Cambridge, MA: Harvard University Press.
Burnyeat, Myles. 1982. Idealism and Greek philosophy: What Descartes saw and Berkeley missed. *The Philosophical Review* 91: 3–40.
Bywater, Ingram (ed.). 1894. *Aristotelis: Ethica Nicomachea*. Oxford: Clarendon.
Elster, Jon. 1999. *Alchemies of the mind: Rationality and the emotions*. Cambridge, UK: Cambridge University Press.
Harman, Gilbert. 1999. Moral philosophy meets social psychology: Virtue ethics and the fundamental attribution error. *Proceedings of the Aristotelian Society* 99: 315–332.
Harman, Gilbert. 2000. The nonexistence of character traits. *Proceedings of the Aristotelian Society* 100: 223–226.
Isen, Alice M., and Paula F. Levin. 1972. Effect of feeling good on helping: Cookies and kindness. *Journal of Personality and Social Psychology* 21: 384–388.
Kant, Immanuel. 1930. *Lectures on ethics*. London: Methuen.
Lear, Jonathan. 2000. *Happiness, death, and the remainder of life*. Cambridge, MA: Harvard University Press.
Lessing, Doris. 1988. *The fifth child*. New York: A. A. Knopf.
Lessing, Doris. 2000. *Ben, in the world*. New York: Harper Collins.
Parker, Dorothy. 1929. The artist's reward. *The New Yorker.* November 30, 1929, 28–31.
Unger, Harlow Giles. 2002. *Lafayette*. New York: Wiley.

The Works of David Keyt

1951. The problem of immortality from an atheistic point of view. *Hika* 16:3–6.
1955. C.I. Lewis's theory of meaning. Dissertation. Cornell University.
1961. Aristotle on Plato's receptacle. *American Journal of Philology* 82:291–300.
1963. Singer's generalization argument. *Philosophical Review* 72:466–476.
1963. The fallacies in *Phaedo* 102A-107B. *Phronesis* 8:167–172.
1963. Wittgenstein's notion of an object. *Philosophical Quarterly* 13:13–25.
1964. Wittgenstein's picture theory of language. *Philosophical Review* 73:493–511.
1965. A new interpretation of the *Tractatus* examined. *Philosophical Review* 74:229–39.
1966. Wittgenstein's notion of an object. In *Essays on Wittgenstein's Tractatus*, ed. Irving M. Copi and Robert W. Beard, 289–303. New York: Macmillan. (Reprint of original published 1963.)
1966. Wittgenstein's picture theory of language. In *Essays on Wittgenstein's Tractatus*, ed. Irving M. Copi and Robert W. Beard, 377–392. (Reprint of original published 1964.)
1968. Wittgenstein, the Vienna Circle, and precise concepts. *Proceedings of the XIVth International Congress of Philosophy.* 2:237–246. Vienna.
1969. Plato's paradox that the immutable is unknowable. *Philosophical Quarterly* 19:1–14.
1969. Review of *Letters from Ludwig Wittgenstein with a memoir* by Paul Englemann. *Dialogue* 8:128–131.
1969. Review of *Material objects* by W. D. Joske. *Philosophical Review* 78:110–113.
1971. The mad craftsman of the *Timaeus*. *Philosophical Review* 80:230–235.
1973. Plato on falsity: *Sophist* 263B. In *Exegesis and argument: studies in Greek philosophy presented to Gregory Vlastos*, ed. Edward N. Lee, Alexander P. D. Mourelatos, and Richard Rorty, 285–305. Assen: Van Gorcum.
1973. The philosophy of C. I. Lewis. *Philosophical Review* 82:491–516.
1974. The social contract as an analytic, justificatory, and polemic device. *Canadian Journal of Philosophy* 4:241–252.

1978. Intellectualism in Aristotle. In the Special Aristotle Issue of *Paideia*: 138–157.
1981. Review of *Aristotle's political theory* by R. G. Mulgan and of *Aristotle* by John B. Morrall. *Philosophical Quarterly* 31:68–69.
1983. Intellectualism in Aristotle. In *Essays in Ancient Greek Philosophy* (Vol. II), ed. John P. Anton and Anthony Preus, 364–387. Albany: SUNY Press. (Revision of 1978.)
1983. Review of *Plato's theory of understanding* by John Moline. *Journal of the History of Philosophy* 21:551–552.
1984. Review of *Plato's Arguments for Forms* by Robert William Jordan. *Ancient Philosophy* 4:241–46.
1985. Distributive justice in Aristotle's *Ethics* and *Politics*. *Topoi* 4:23–45.
1985. Review of *An introduction to Plato's Laws* by R. F. Stalley. *Journal of the History of Philosophy* 23:249–250.
1987. Three fundamental theorems in Aristotle's *Politics*. *Phronesis* 32:54–79.
1987. Review of *The Dialogues of Plato* (Vol. 1), trans. with analysis by R. E. Allan. *Ancient Philosophy* 7:222–227.
1988. Injustice and pleonexia in Aristotle: a reply to Charles Young. In *Aristotle's Ethics*, ed. Timothy D. Roche. Supplementary volume of *The Southern Journal of Philosophy* 27:251–257.
1989. The meaning of *BIOS* in Aristotle's *Ethics* and *Politics*. *Ancient Philosophy* 9:15–21.
1991. *A companion to Aristotle's Politics*, co-edited with Fred D. Miller, Jr. Oxford: Blackwell Publishing.
1991. Aristotle's theory of distributive justice. In *A companion to Aristotle's Politics*, ed. Keyt and Miller, 238–278. (Substantial revision of 1985a.)
1991. Three basic theorems in Aristotle's *Politics*. In *A companion to Aristotle's Politics*, ed. Keyt and Miller, 118–141. (Revision of original published 1987.)
1992. Analyzing Plato's arguments: Plato and platonism. With S. Marc Cohen. In *Methods of interpreting Plato and his Dialogues*, ed. James C. Klagge and Nicholas D. Smith, 173–200. Supplementary volume of *Oxford Studies in Ancient Philosophy*. Oxford: Clarendon Press.
1992. Review of *Forms in Plato's Philebus* by E. E. Benitez. *Ancient Philosophy* 12:190–193.
1992. Review of *Plato on the self-predication of Forms* by John Malcolm. *Bryn Mawr Classical Review*. http://bmcr.brynmawr.edu/1992/03.01.08.html.
1993. Aristotle and anarchism. *Reason Papers* 18:137–157. (Abridged version of original published 1996.)
1994. Review of *Parmenides, Plato, and the semantics of not-being* by Francis Jeffry Pelletier. *Noûs* 28:117–119.
1995. Supplementary Essay. To the reissue of *Aristotle's Politics, Books III and IV*, trans. with a commentary by Richard Robinson, 125–152. Oxford: Clarendon Press.
1995. The four causes in Aristotle's *Politics*. In *Aristotelian political philosophy*, (Vol. 1), ed. K. I. Boudouris, 101–107. Athens: International Center for Greek Philosophy and Culture.

1996. Aristotle and the ancient roots of anarchism. *Topoi* 15:129–142.
1996. Fred Miller on Aristotle's political naturalism. *Ancient Philosophy* 16:425–30.
1998. Analyzing Plato's arguments: Plato and platonism. In *Plato: Critical Assessments*, ed. Nicholas D. Smith (Vol. I), 357–381. London: Routledge. (Reprint of original published 1992.)
1998. Review of *Aristotle's criticism of Plato's Republic* by Robert Mayhew. *Ancient Philosophy* 18:486–492.
1999. *Aristotle Politics Books V and VI*. Translation with introduction and commentary. Oxford: Clarendon Press.
1999. Three fundamental theorems in Aristotle's *Politics*. In *Aristotle: Critical Assessments* (Vol. IV), ed. Lloyd P. Gerson, 83–107. London: Routledge. (Reprint of original published 1987.)
2003. Review of *Aristotle: political philosophy* by Richard Kraut. *Bryn Mawr Classical Review*. http://bmcr.brynmawr.edu/2003/2003-02-07.html.
2004. Ancient Greek political thought. With Fred Miller. In *Handbook of political theory*, ed. Gerald Gaus and Chandran Kukathas, 303–319. London: Sage Publications.
2005. Aristotle and anarchism. In *Aristotle's Politics: critical essays*, ed. Richard Kraut and Steven Skultety, 203–222. Lanham: Rowman & Littlefield. (Reprint of 1993.)
2006. Aristotle's political philosophy. In *A companion to ancient philosophy*, ed. Mary Louise Gill and Pierre Pellegrin, 393–412. Oxford: Blackwell Publishing.
2006. Plato and the ship of state. In *The Blackwell guide to Plato's Republic*, ed. Gerasimos Santas, 189–213. Oxford: Blackwell Publishing.
2006. Plato on justice. In *The Blackwell companion to the philosophy of Plato*, ed. Hugh H. Benson, 341–355. Oxford: Blackwell Publishing.
2006. Review of *Political authority and obligation in Aristotle* by Andrés Rosler. *Journal of Hellenic Studies* 126:213–214.
2007. *Freedom, reason, and the polis: essays in ancient Greek political philosophy*, co-edited with Fred D. Miller, Jr. Cambridge: Cambridge University Press. Published simultaneously as *Social Philosophy & Policy: Ancient Greek Political Philosophy*, 24.
2007. The good man and the upright citizen in Aristotle's *Ethics* and *Politics*. In *Freedom, reason, and the polis: essays in ancient Greek political philosophy*, ed. Keyt and Miller, 220–240. Cambridge: Cambridge University Press.
2008. Plato on justice. *Philosophical Inquiry* 30—In Honor of Gerasimos Santas: 37–53. (Reprint of original published 2006.)
2009. Deductive logic. In *A companion to Aristotle*, ed. Georgios Anagnostopoulos, 31–50. Oxford: Wiley-Blackwell.
2010. Review of *The virtue of Aristotle's ethics* by Paula Gottlieb. *Ethics* 120:855–859.
2011. Plato on justice. In *Socratic, Platonic and Aristotelian studies: essays in honor of Gerasimos Santas*, ed. Georgios Anagnostopoulos, 255–270. Dordrecht: Springer. (Reprint of original published 2006.)
2013. A life in the academy. In *Reason and analysis in ancient Greek philosophy: essays in honor of David Keyt*, ed. Georgios Anagnostopoulos and Fred D. Miller, Jr., 11–44. Dordrecht: Springer.

Index

A
Accidents, 14, 19, 32, 63, 231, 232, 236, 237, 239, 241
Ackrill, J., 2, 23, 33, 34, 214, 217–222, 227, 228
Adeimantus, 137, 139, 197
Aeschylus, 91, 207
Afterlife, 111, 171, 197, 201, 205, 206, 208
Agency, 46, 192, 206, 280
Agents, 3, 5, 36, 45, 46, 51, 59, 61, 66, 99, 142, 159, 172, 176–183, 185, 192, 193, 201, 310
Agreements, 4, 58–66, 91, 93–95, 107, 151, 179, 194, 220, 267, 296, 299, 305
Akrasia, 45, 97. *See also* Weakness of will
Alcibiades, 4, 5, 109, 113–122
Aldrich, V., 12–14
Allen, R.E., 91, 102, 107
American Expeditionary Force, 314
An Analysis of Knowledge and Valuation (Lewis), 16
Anarchy, State, and Utopia (Nozick), 27
Anaxagoras, 245
Anger, 48, 49, 51, 151, 155, 158, 159, 161, 163, 170, 177–179, 192, 280
An Introduction to Logic and Scientific Method (Cohen and Nagel), 38
Annas, J., 192, 198, 199, 207, 208
Answerability, 84
Antisthenes, 220, 228
Apology (Plato), 3, 45–52, 55, 56, 66, 69, 73, 98, 99, 111
Appearance, 7, 19, 20, 26, 67, 70, 113, 118, 151, 152, 156, 201, 214, 227, 245, 259, 262, 274–277, 286, 287, 296, 297, 304

Appetites, 3, 46, 47, 51, 52, 119, 147, 149–165, 168–170, 176–181, 184, 186, 192, 193, 201, 203, 205, 296
Aristides, 80
Aristophanes, 112, 118, 227
Aristotle, 271, 278, 279, 281, 295
 on belief and knowledge, 286–294, 301, 302
 and distributive justice, 26, 27, 29
 doxastic method of, 293–300
 and the elements, 274–276
 on form and matter, 272, 273, 280, 282
 and grace, 315–318
 and teleological explanation 303, 304
 theory of substance, 268
 on virtue, 310
Aristotle and the Politics (Roberts), 32
Aristotle's Criticism of Plato and the Academy (Cherniss), 18
Artifacts, 172, 173, 271, 272, 274, 276
Assembly, 69, 80, 81, 87, 200
Athena, 205
Athenagoras, 83
Athens, 3, 4, 21, 23, 48, 49, 55–65, 68, 69, 83, 91–93, 104–107, 131, 133, 137, 141, 144, 170
Atlas, J., 28, 309
Authoritarianism, 73–76, 84, 87
Authority, 21, 24, 26, 56, 60–62, 72, 75, 86, 88, 128, 202, 247, 297, 299
Autonomy, 40, 72, 84, 131, 273
Awareness, 144, 215, 287, 293, 294, 300, 301, 303
Ayer, A.J., 21

B

Barnes, J., 27, 240, 241, 281, 302–304
Being, 167, 214, 220, 221, 252–268
    accidental, 231–239
Belief, 50–52, 57, 110, 111, 138, 151, 152,
    162, 175–177, 185, 187, 188, 194, 223,
    287, 291–293, 299, 300, 306
    false, 46, 288–290
    and motivation, 45
    about Platonic Forms, 142
    reputable, 285, 286, 296–298
    true, 294, 295
Bennett, J., 70, 239
Bentham, J., 97, 98
Black, M., 14, 16
Blondell, R., 120
Blue Book, 14
Bobonich, C., 142, 177, 179, 182–185, 192, 193
The Body of a Person (Aldrich), 12
Bolton, R., 295, 300, 303, 305
Bonitz. H., 18, 256–259, 266
Bostock, D., 241, 256, 262–264, 266
Brickhouse, T., 3, 45–52, 65, 76, 88
Brown, L., 66, 223, 228
Buckner, B., 32
Burnyeat, M., 130, 131, 138, 144, 169, 246,
    250, 251, 260–264, 266, 267, 281,
    285, 303, 313

C

Callias, 235, 239, 255, 282
Callicles, 47, 174
Calling, 5, 52, 107, 121, 126, 128, 155, 165,
    178, 312
Capacities, 6, 52, 68, 84, 88, 136, 137, 155,
    156, 162, 165–167, 207, 254, 271, 272,
    279, 285–288, 295, 300, 301, 312
Carnap, R., 19
Categories (Aristotle), 7, 52, 83, 233–241,
    245, 251, 255, 265, 272
Causal determinism, 202
Causality, 201, 207, 273
Chance, 15, 87, 99, 116, 122, 137, 138, 198,
    200, 202, 203, 206, 207, 309–311, 315
Character traits, 85, 111–113, 311
Charity, principle of, 25, 31, 73
Charmides (Plato), 52, 112
Cherniss, H., 18, 27, 28, 144, 206, 250, 251, 262
Choice, 6, 16, 52, 115, 142, 143, 154,
    166–168, 193, 194, 197–208, 250, 251,
    257, 258, 266
Churchill, W., 85
Citizenship, 60, 61, 64, 65
City of Pigs, 139, 141
Civil disobedience, 94, 194
Clatterbaugh, K, 39, 41
Code, A., 241, 253, 258, 261, 262,
    264–267, 281
Coercion, 27, 107, 163
Cognition, 46, 177, 271, 288, 296, 301
Cohen, M., 6, 7, 31, 37, 38, 41, 171, 231–241
Communist Party, 17
Compositional plasticity, 7, 271, 274–277,
    280, 281
Comprehension, 290, 291, 303
Consent, 34, 61, 62, 65, 166
Consequences, 4, 29, 57, 63, 77, 92, 95,
    104–106, 149, 167, 177, 185, 186,
    199–201, 206, 208, 217, 222, 224,
    238, 244, 248, 252, 253, 255, 257,
    272, 282, 292
Constitution, 2, 26, 27, 83, 169, 189, 191, 276,
    280, 282
Contemplation, 114, 154, 288, 301
Cooper, J., 25, 29, 52, 88, 183, 185, 303, 304
Coriscus, 233–235, 238, 290, 292, 294
Cornell University, 14–16
Cornford, F., 18, 192, 211–213, 216, 217, 219,
    222, 223, 225, 226, 228
Courage, 27, 39, 68, 111, 160, 162, 175, 185,
    187–189, 194
Craft, 73, 77, 80, 81, 129, 132, 140
Crito (Plato), 3, 4, 52, 55–61, 63, 64, 73,
    91–108
Cuban Missile Crisis, 19
Custom, 19, 35, 128

D

Dante, 285, 301
Davidson, D., 31
De Anima (Aristotle), 245, 271, 272, 274
Death, 6, 22, 33, 37, 49, 50, 57, 65, 68, 69, 77,
    98, 99, 111, 166, 168, 198, 200, 201,
    205, 208, 314
Deduction, 287, 290, 295, 300
Definition, 1, 19, 77, 100–104, 110, 127, 140,
    171, 172, 175, 178, 182–188, 190, 191,
    193, 194, 205, 213, 236, 243, 253, 261,
    265, 268, 277–280, 282, 296, 303
de Lafayette, M., 313–316
Deliberation, 56, 57, 192, 201, 204, 288,
    301, 302
Delium, 114, 118, 122
Delphic Oracle, 47
Democracy, 2, 28, 29, 50, 71, 72, 74–77, 79,
    83–85, 87, 89, 130, 315

Democritus, 207, 245
Demonstration, 1, 21, 22, 287, 290, 292–294, 299, 300
Depew, D.J., 26
Descartes, R., 8, 272, 273, 297–299
Desire, 3, 22, 25, 28, 40, 85, 103, 105, 109, 113, 119, 121, 122, 126, 134, 137, 141, 144, 152–159, 164, 166, 167, 171, 177, 179–181, 183, 188, 189, 192, 201, 263, 272, 273, 285, 295
De Sophisticis Elenchis (Aristotle), 245
Dharmakirti, 25
Dialectic, 8, 34, 129, 133, 143, 199, 222, 279, 287, 294, 295, 300, 301, 304, 305
Dietrichson, P., 17
Diotima, 13, 115, 122
Disconnect Paradox, 68, 69, 71, 76
Discourse on the Method (Descartes), 297
Discreteness contention, 220, 225
Disobedience, 55, 60, 65, 94, 194
Dispositions, 110, 132, 135, 152, 272, 276, 295, 301
Divine Comedy (Dante), 285
Divine, the, 19, 41, 73, 115, 126, 137, 149–151, 164–166, 169, 198, 202, 207, 286
Division, 12, 15, 19, 31, 36, 129, 132, 151, 160, 173, 176–179, 181, 182, 186, 190–194, 213, 231, 285, 289, 302
Doctorow, E., 13
Doubt, 30, 33, 45, 46, 59, 61, 73, 84, 88, 103, 113, 118, 129, 130, 132, 147, 154, 171, 186, 189, 194, 200, 202, 211, 232, 263, 298, 299
Dover, K., 114
Doxastic involuntarism, 295
Duty, 16, 17, 60–62, 82

E

Education, 5, 13, 18, 29, 46, 60, 62, 85, 86, 89, 115, 122, 126, 130–136, 138, 152, 156, 157, 160, 162, 171, 173, 175, 176, 179, 180, 183–186, 188–190, 192, 193
Eleatic stranger, 223
Elections, 85, 89
Elenchus, 50, 110, 117, 122, 304
Elitism, 72, 76, 81, 172, 183, 184, 186, 187, 190, 193
Emerson, R.W., 11
Emotion, 3, 49, 51, 52, 95, 296, 303
Empedocles, 286
Engagement Paradox, 69
Eros, 5, 109, 113–117, 120–122, 176

Essence, 7, 76, 183, 238, 243–268, 272, 274, 282, 293, 302
Eudemian Ethics (Aristotle), 296
Eudoxus, 135, 142
Euripides, 207, 313
Eurycles, 212, 220, 227
Event, 7, 15, 19, 21–23, 27, 29, 32, 39, 46, 48, 142, 158, 168, 197, 203, 207, 217, 218, 239–241, 273, 277, 295
Evil, 8, 12, 159–161, 166, 197, 199, 203, 204, 206, 304, 309, 311, 312
Existence, 6, 11, 61, 114, 150, 163, 164, 205, 206, 212–214, 217, 218, 222, 225, 226, 232, 234–239, 250, 258, 268, 272, 278, 310, 311

F

Faculties, 5, 172, 176–183, 192, 287, 294
Falsity, 2, 23, 215, 217, 219, 223, 226, 251, 287, 289, 302, 304
Fear, 46, 49–51, 74, 86, 98, 99, 111, 153, 157, 160, 165, 166, 175, 182, 185, 187, 188, 192–194, 203, 208, 299
Fields, W.C., 30
Fifth Child (Lessing), 312
Fine, A., 35
Fisher, D., 39
Force, 2, 8, 12, 17, 24, 32, 55, 83, 86, 115, 122, 128, 131, 143, 158, 162, 202, 208, 212, 221, 265, 267, 311, 312, 314
Form, Aristotelian, 248, 258, 260, 261, 271–280
Forms, Platonic theory of, 20, 115, 129, 130, 136, 140, 142, 148–150, 153, 162, 163, 167–169, 177, 179, 181, 183, 188, 189, 211–226, 243–245, 250–257
  and essence, 247
  and the Good, 186, 187
Foundational Paradox, 70
Frede, M., 29, 228, 259, 262–267
Freedom, 3, 83, 87, 180
Freud, S., 12, 13, 193
Friedländer, P., 19
Function, 7, 29, 96, 99, 127, 143, 147, 152, 164, 172–176, 178, 180–182, 184–187, 189–191, 205, 272, 273, 295, 303
Functionalism, 7, 271–282
Furley, D., 23

G

Gardiner, S.M., 4, 67–89
Gass, W., 14, 15, 34, 40

Gaus, G., 32
Gettier, E., 16
Glaucon, 62, 129, 149, 157, 159, 160, 178, 183, 184, 189, 194, 205
Glaucus, 149, 150
Goldstein, L., 28
Goodness, 8, 69, 142, 148, 149, 156, 192, 200, 264, 311, 312
Gorgias (Plato), 45, 47, 52, 73, 88, 97, 227
Gotthelf, A., 26
Government, 27, 50, 75, 85, 87, 98, 99, 191, 200, 315
Grace, 8, 14, 16, 35, 128, 160, 309–316
Gratitude, 36, 211, 312–316
Grice, P., 26
Guardians, 132, 134, 137, 141, 157–159, 163, 164, 179, 190, 200, 207
Gulliver's Travels (Swift), 312
Guts, as a character trait, 8, 311, 316

H
Habit, 149, 157, 174, 198, 203, 205, 207, 295, 298, 305
Habituation, 152, 158, 179
Hades, 111, 165
Harm, 58, 65, 87, 93, 94, 102–107, 156, 194
Harman, G., 310
Hedonism, 112
Hemingway, E., 8, 311, 316
Herodotus, 30, 77–79
Hobbes, T., 2, 27, 143
Holocaust, 17
Homer, 78, 82, 83
Homonoia, 136, 138
Honor, 48, 49, 60, 82, 86, 148, 153, 154, 158, 160–164, 176, 178, 180, 185, 204
Humiliation, 48, 49, 51
Humor, 4, 30, 109–120

I
Identity, 6, 7, 15, 62, 106, 201, 217, 232, 235, 239, 243–255, 260, 261, 263, 266–268, 273, 275, 277
Ignorance, 45, 48, 70, 73, 76, 78, 88, 89, 116, 203, 205, 296
Immortality, 1, 11, 13, 197
Incontinence, 156, 159, 296
Index Aristotelicus (Bonitz), 18
Individualism, 84, 88
Induction, 16, 19, 290–292, 294
Injury, 58–60, 63, 65, 101–106
Injustice, 4, 57–59, 61, 63–65, 68, 73, 77, 107, 149, 158–160, 183, 184

Intellectualism, 2, 3, 45–52
Intellectual wisdom, 115
Intention, 6, 94, 97, 105–107, 171, 233, 251
Introduction to Logical Theory (Strawson), 38
Introduction to Metamathematics (Kleene), 38
Irony, 4–5, 57, 109, 117–120, 127
Isolationism, 71–84
Izzing, 7, 253–255, 260, 265, 266

J
Jaeger, W., 144, 248, 285
Jäkel, P.S., 24
Johnston, M., 14, 29
Judgment, 4, 51, 60, 68, 84, 104, 110, 126, 171, 206, 208, 220, 222, 228, 288–294, 296, 298, 300–303, 306
Judson, L., 34
Justice, 5, 6, 55–57, 59, 60, 65, 73, 77, 136, 148, 171, 184
  distributive, 2, 26, 27, 134
  equalitarian, 71
  and happiness, 183
  as a Platonic Form, 217
  psychic, 172–174, 182
  rewards of, 197–199
  and spirit, 158, 160, 190
  as a virtue, 178, 179
  and wisdom, 186, 187

K
Kallipolis, 5, 126–128, 130, 132, 133, 136–138, 141, 144, 164, 200, 205–207
Kamtekar, R., 36, 67–71, 75–85, 88, 89
Kant, I., 12, 26, 84, 92, 315
Kenyon College, 12–14
Keyt, C., 25
Keyt, D., 1–3, 5, 8, 13–16, 18, 20, 21, 23, 25, 27, 30–32, 34, 36, 37, 89, 174–176, 179, 182, 191–194, 222, 228, 266
Kim, J., 239
Kindness, 309, 311, 314, 315
King, M.L. Jr., 21, 78, 168
Kinship, 60, 61, 149, 160
Kleene, S., 38
Kneale, M., 216
Kneale, W., 216
Knowledge, 6, 8, 16, 17, 31, 34, 45, 52, 68, 73, 82, 85, 86, 88, 105, 106, 119, 129, 133, 134, 136–138, 142, 144, 147, 148, 153, 157, 160, 162, 167, 172, 181, 183, 185–188, 191, 194, 203, 211, 252, 255, 259, 266, 285–306
Knox, B., 24, 25

Kooky objects, 7, 232, 233, 241
Korean War, 16, 40
Kraft, Victor, 21
Kraut, R., 33, 66, 67, 70, 73, 74, 76, 88, 102, 103, 107, 108
Kreisel, G., 19
Kripke, S., 29
Kukathas, C., 32

L

Laches (Plato), 52, 112, 118, 193, 199
Language, 2, 6, 11, 12, 21, 33–35, 59, 167, 174, 180, 185, 193, 194, 211–213, 215, 221, 223–227, 246
Larkin, P., 33
Laughter Down the Centuries (Jäkel), 24
Law, 55, 62, 69
  and agreement, 64, 93
  and forethought, 194
  and justice, 50, 65
  obedience to, 56, 57, 63
  and obligation, 91
Leadership, 73, 85, 86, 127, 128
Lear, J., 122, 144, 197, 205, 316
Legitimacy, 15, 56, 62, 80, 93, 103
Leon of Salamis, 98
Leontius, 158–161, 164, 170
Lessing, D., 312, 316
Lewis, C. I., 16
Lewis, F., 7, 23, 235–237, 239, 241, 243–268
Liberalism, 89
Lobbying, 81–84
Logic for Mathematicians (Rosser), 38
Logos, 6, 211–229
Los Angeles Mission, 311
Love, 12, 38, 80, 109, 115, 116, 120–122, 149, 154–157, 160–164, 168, 170, 176, 178, 204, 227, 286, 312, 315, 316
Luck, 6, 40, 197–208
Lucretius, 21, 207
Lyceum, 238

M

Malcolm, N., 14–16
Malcolm X, 21
Manipulation, 84, 85
Marlowe, C., 38
Materialism, 37, 272, 280
Matter, 8, 11, 23, 25, 50, 51, 56, 58, 59, 61–64, 66, 69–73, 79, 81, 84, 88, 91–93, 95–97, 99–102, 107–109, 111, 117, 122, 132, 135, 141, 144, 152, 163, 165, 166, 168, 189, 193, 206, 215, 216, 222, 224, 225, 233, 235, 237, 257, 258, 263, 264, 271–274, 277–282, 292, 299, 305, 315
Matthews, G.B., 7, 231–233, 240, 263
McCarthy era, 17
McGonigle, T., 29
McPherran, M., 6, 39, 89, 197–208
Meaning, 2, 13, 16, 22, 47, 59, 125, 200, 202, 211–213, 215, 216, 219, 221–228, 243, 261
Meditations on First Philosophy, 297
Melden, A., 17
Melissus, 297
Mellon, P., 24
Meno (Plato), 45, 70, 88, 97, 193, 205
Metaphysics (Aristotle), 7, 32, 41, 137, 143, 172, 213, 221, 234, 236, 237, 241, 243, 245, 251, 255, 261–263, 265, 271–282, 285, 287, 296, 304
Methods of Logic (Quine), 38
Meyerhoff, H., 19
Miller, F.D., 285–306
Mill, J.S., 84
Milo, R., 34
Milton, J., 33
Minds, 12, 13, 23, 25, 37, 49, 58, 61, 64, 75, 82, 83, 87, 102, 104, 114, 115, 118–120, 126, 135, 140, 142, 149, 152, 154, 159–161, 169, 179, 185, 192, 206, 208, 220, 222, 238, 245, 259, 262, 263, 271, 272, 280, 281, 287, 288, 294, 296, 300, 311, 312
Moderation, 132
Monarchy, 77, 89
Money, 18, 35, 39, 49, 63, 83, 85, 92, 148, 153–158, 162–164, 176, 180, 181, 311
Montague, R., 19
Moore, G.E., 103, 286
Moral expertise, 56, 73
Moral principles, 59, 92, 96, 97, 102
Moral progress, 74
Moral psychology, 3, 45–52, 112
Mores, 128
Motivation, 45, 46, 52, 105, 170, 183, 184, 199, 202, 219, 225
Myth of Er, 6, 30, 198, 200, 205–208
Myth of the metals, 137, 138, 141, 192

N

Nagel, E., 38
Natural aptitude, 135, 140–142
Natural kinds, 174, 271, 273

Nature, 178, 207, 236, 290, 291, 300
  antecedent, 126, 131, 132, 134–140, 142, 179, 180
  and functions, 172, 173, 184
  human, 96, 97, 155, 156, 169, 182
  and Platonic Forms, 246–249
  unity of, 276
Neutrality, 83
Newman, P., 13
Nicomachean Ethics (Aristotle), 8, 15, 16, 24, 25, 30, 40, 285, 296, 301, 309, 313, 315
Noble lie, 138, 192
Nozick, R., 27
Nussbaum, M., 115, 116, 121, 304

O

Obedience, 3, 56, 61, 62, 74, 93, 128, 194
Ober, J., 130, 144
Objections and Replies (Descartes), 297
Obligation, 3, 4, 58, 61–66, 91, 93, 223
Odysseus, 158–161, 164, 170, 177, 178, 204–206, 208
The Old Fashioned Way (Fields), 30
Oligarchy, 50, 68, 75, 77–79, 83, 84, 89, 159
On the Knowledge of Good and Evil (Rice), 12
Open society, 71–73, 85
Oresteia (Aeschylus), 91, 96
Orpheus, 166, 201
Othello (Shakespeare), 298
Owen, G.E.L., 23, 31, 233, 301
Oxfam, 313

P

Pain, 65, 98, 106, 160, 166, 188, 198, 201, 206, 232, 234, 236, 246, 281
Palme, O., 13
Paradise Lost (Milton), 33
Parker, R., 35, 39
Parmenides (Plato), 15, 31, 202, 253
Partisanship, 79, 80
Passions, 3, 36, 45–49, 51, 52, 115, 116, 153, 155, 159
Perfection, 72
Pericles, 52, 69, 78, 118
Pershing, J. J., 314
Persuasion, 82, 84, 157, 163, 288, 302
Pessimism, 4, 67, 70, 76, 84–87, 89, 142, 205
Phaedo (Plato), 1, 5, 18, 112, 153, 165, 208
Philebus (Plato), 20, 148
Philia, 176, 192
Phillips, H., 17, 18
Philosopher-ruler, 126, 127, 129, 140, 142, 184

Philosophical Investigations (Wittgenstein), 15, 21, 129
Philosophy of Art (Aldrich), 12
Physics (Aristotle), 7, 11, 207, 232, 236, 245, 272, 285, 287, 297
Plato, 1, 11, 45–52, 55, 67, 107, 109, 125–144, 147–169, 171–194, 197, 211, 243–268, 285, 313
Plato's Earlier Dialectic (Robinson), 34
Plato's Progress (Ryle), 20
Plato's Universe (Vlastos), 24
Pleasure, 16, 18, 98, 121, 138, 148, 149, 153–155, 157, 158, 160, 163, 166, 171, 177, 179, 184, 188, 192, 193, 198, 201, 203, 211, 243
Plutarch, 80
Polis, 2, 3, 5, 27, 35, 84, 87, 91, 94, 104, 105, 129–132, 141, 143, 184, 191
Political speech, 77, 79, 80
Politics (Aristotle), 2, 3, 23, 24, 26, 29, 30, 32, 35, 37, 45, 147
Politics als Beruf (Weber), 125
Politicus (Plato), 20
Popper, K., 67, 70–76, 84, 85, 88
Poseidon, 205
Posterior Analytics (Aristotle), 290, 291, 300, 303
Potidaea, 114
Power, 13, 36, 50, 51, 62, 68, 69, 71, 74, 76–78, 80, 85–87, 131, 136, 137, 143, 149, 151, 165, 168, 174, 177–182, 185, 200, 203, 205, 227, 273, 276, 277, 280, 281, 286, 302
Predication, 2, 213, 214, 217, 223, 265, 302
Pride, 48, 49, 164, 170
Principia Mathematica (Whitehead and Russell), 38
Principles, 37, 58, 59, 68, 70, 91–93, 95, 96, 99, 101, 138, 258, 266
  of justice, 15, 189, 192
  and knowledge, 287, 291, 292
Prior Analytics (Aristotle), 37, 302
Problem of Evil, 199
Profession, 76, 77, 81–85, 128, 142
Project Archelogos, 35
Properties, 2, 7, 20, 22, 142, 161, 163, 182, 193, 194, 223, 227, 228, 231, 232, 234–241, 257, 258, 260, 266, 267, 272, 273, 281, 290
Protagoras (Plato), 52, 77, 97, 98, 118, 120, 193, 313
Protection, 4, 68, 71, 72, 74, 82–84, 87, 89, 154
Pseudo-Xenophon, 79, 82, 83, 89

Psyche, 37, 110, 171, 172, 174, 177, 178, 180, 185, 191–194
Punishment, 46, 65, 98, 102, 103, 117, 158, 197, 198, 201, 205
Puzzlement, 297
Pythagoreans, 206, 277

R

Rader, M., 17
Ransom, J.C., 13
Rationality, 4, 26, 158, 169, 226
Rauhut, N., 4, 5, 34, 35, 39, 109–122
Rawls, J., 15, 16, 84, 88, 110, 189, 192–194
Reason, 57, 71, 147, 177, 178, 182, 188, 290, 291, 297, 302, 305. *See also* Soul
  and appetite, 156, 157, 180
  and choice, 205
  and Forms, 153, 154, 193
  rule of, 152, 179, 181, 182, 184–186
  and the soul, 148–151, 164–167, 201, 204
  and spirit, 158–163
  and wisdom, 187
Reasonable politics, 4, 67–89
Reason and Human Good in Aristotle (Cooper), 25
Reasoning, 6, 46, 68, 80, 101, 103, 171, 177–179, 182, 186, 192, 193, 215, 227, 243, 287, 288, 305
Reciprocity, 193, 309
Reductionism, 273, 280
Reeve, C.D.C., 5, 36, 144, 147–170, 304
Reference, 47, 49, 51, 61, 94, 139, 149, 172, 180–182, 187, 207, 227, 228, 232, 243, 245, 247, 250, 251, 253, 261, 263, 264, 274, 278, 279, 282
Reform, 72, 73, 86
Reincarnation, 137, 166, 168, 205, 208
Republic (Plato), 5, 6, 13, 28–30, 34, 36, 37, 52, 58, 59, 62, 63, 73, 74, 88, 101, 111, 121, 125–144, 147, 156, 157, 159, 165, 168, 169, 171–194, 197–208, 286
Reputable beliefs, 8, 287, 295–300, 304, 306
Reputation, 47, 49, 57, 92, 148, 154, 157, 197, 306
Respect, 17, 20, 33, 56, 60, 62, 69, 71, 73, 75, 78, 82, 83, 92, 94, 98, 112, 116, 118, 126, 129, 135, 137, 143, 151, 162, 164, 165, 174, 184, 191, 193, 214, 216, 218, 224, 225, 228, 239, 241, 250, 257, 263, 265, 266, 268, 285, 297, 302, 314
Responsibility, 6, 94, 138, 198–202, 204, 205
Retaliation, 4, 58, 64, 65, 91–108
Revolutionary War, 314

Rhetoric (Aristotle), 82, 84–87, 134, 207, 295, 300, 305
Rice, P.B., 12–14, 16
Ring, M., 4, 91–108
River of Forgetfulness, 199
River of Unheeding, 201, 203, 207
Roberts, J., 3, 32, 55–66, 89
Robinson, R., 23, 33, 34
Roochnik, D., 111
Rorty, R., 23
Rosser, B., 38
Ross, W.D., 18, 216, 217, 241, 243, 245, 256, 258, 259, 262–264, 266, 267, 278, 281, 282, 303
Rudebusch, G., 111
Rule, 28, 29, 45, 65, 68, 71–80, 82, 83, 88, 89, 105, 106, 127–129, 131, 134, 136, 142, 148, 151–153, 155, 157, 159, 163, 164, 170, 177, 179, 180, 182–188, 194, 204, 208, 217, 256, 257, 278, 279, 288
Russell, B., 109
Ryle, G., 19, 20

S

Sachs, D., 184, 190, 191
Salamis, 50, 55, 98
Santas, G., 5, 6, 52, 107, 171–194
Santayana, G., 12
Satyr drama, 116
Scaltsas, T., 35
Schleiermacher, F., 114–116
Schlick, M., 21
Schopenhauer, A., 11, 12
Science, 8, 23, 24, 32, 128, 129, 131–134, 140, 142, 143, 272, 273, 280, 286, 287, 292, 294, 295, 297, 298, 300
Seattle Liberation Front, 21
Seattle Seven, 21
Self-defense, 21, 102, 103
Sense-perception, 110, 166, 273, 280, 281, 287, 297, 303
Sensibles, 1, 85, 177, 180, 181, 187, 188, 193, 198, 253, 254, 262, 264, 265, 279–281
Service, 23, 77, 80–83, 89, 128, 147, 153, 287, 316
Shakespeare, W., 298, 313
Shame, 49–51, 58, 74, 162, 164
Sheffield, F., 115, 116, 121
Shields, C., 6, 33, 211–229, 274, 281
Silverman, A., 5, 32, 125–144, 226
Slavery, 26, 69, 122, 309
Smith, N., 3, 26, 45–52, 65, 76, 88, 208
Smullyan, A., 17

Social contract, 15, 62
Social psychology, 138, 310, 311
Society, 32, 67, 82, 83, 86, 87, 89, 139, 171, 189, 190, 193, 194, 208
Socrates, 3, 20, 45, 55–89, 91, 109–122, 129, 147, 174, 198, 232, 255, 272, 287
Socrates in Sichuan (Vernezze), 34
Socratic problem, 112, 113
Solmsen, F., 16, 20, 28
Solon, 78, 217
Sophist (Plato), 2, 6, 20, 23, 47, 48, 77, 81, 82, 85, 91, 155, 168, 211–214, 218–222, 226–228
Sophistry, 82
Sophocles, 11, 162, 207
Soul, 58, 111, 129, 131, 143, 176, 273–275.
 See also Justice, Reason
 and appetites, 153–158, 287
 and city analogy, 175–183
 complexity of, 151, 180
 and justice, 171, 173, 174, 178, 184, 188–191
 rational elements of, 126, 137, 148, 149, 166–169, 202
 rule of, 152, 163, 164, 185–187, 203, 204
 and spirit, 159–162
 tripartite, 13, 147, 150, 172, 181, 182, 201
 and virtue, 150, 179, 194
Sovereignty, 68, 72, 76
Spanish Civil War, 24
Specialization, 125, 126, 129–131, 134, 135, 139–143
Spinoza, B., 11
Spirit, 132, 147, 150–152, 158–167, 169, 176–180, 184–186, 192–194, 203, 245
Stability, 126, 136–138, 183, 194
Stanton, C.E., 314
State (political), 68, 71, 82, 83, 85, 105, 106, 126, 129, 131, 134, 135, 137, 138
 definition of, 127, 128
 limits of, 72
 obligations to, 93
 and specialization of citizen vocations, 139, 141, 143
 and stability, 136
Statements, 6, 55, 63–65, 85, 88, 105, 107, 129, 171, 174, 179, 193, 211, 213–223, 225, 226, 228, 250, 261, 263, 290, 302
Stern, L., 17, 199, 205
Substance, 231, 233, 234, 243, 248, 267, 268, 272, 293
 and accidental properties, 239, 240, 281
 and essence, 245–247, 249, 261
 parent, 235
 and Platonic Forms, 250, 251
 primary, 252, 258
 and priority, 236
Superiority, 77, 80, 81, 89, 197
Surviving Death (Johnston), 14
Sutcliffe, D., 39
Swift, J., 312
Symposium (Plato), 4, 13, 109, 112–115, 117–122, 176, 226

T
Tapscott, B., 35, 41
Taraska, G., 35
Teleological approximism, 8, 299
Theaetetus (Plato), 77, 112, 214–217, 220, 222–229
Theia moira, 205
Themistocles, 80
Theory of Justice (Rawls), 15, 192
Thesaurus Linguae Graecae, 28
Third man argument, 15, 31
Thirty Tyrants, 68, 98
Thoreau, H.D., 11
Thought, 211, 212, 214, 215, 274, 287–289, 301, 302, 305
 and language, 223, 225
 and Platonic Forms, 213, 226
Thrasymachus, 154, 183, 189, 194, 205
Throne of Necessity, 204
Thucydides, 20, 36, 52, 69, 78, 83, 207
Timaeus (Plato), 2, 5, 24, 166, 167, 192, 193, 204, 206, 208
Tractatus Logico-Philosophicus (Wittgenstein), 14
Trope, 233, 239, 241
Truth, 8, 16, 31, 37, 40, 47–49, 77, 84, 86, 95, 115, 117–119, 134, 144, 148, 149, 153, 162, 163, 169, 178, 181, 186, 215, 220, 225, 226, 228, 255, 278, 285, 287–292, 294–296, 298, 299, 302–304
The Tunnel (Gass), 34
Tweedale, M., 31
Tyranny, 75, 122, 202

U
Uniformity, 7, 255–261, 266
Unity, 3, 136, 144, 149–151, 155–157, 161–163, 166, 178, 182, 193, 232, 276, 281, 282
Universals, 7, 171, 228, 233–235, 238–241, 256, 257, 259, 264–266, 277, 282, 288–290, 292, 295, 297

University of Washington, 17–19, 24, 28, 31, 38–40, 231, 285, 309
Upbringing, 61, 63, 137, 156, 158, 161, 204

V
Value, 16, 40, 49, 57, 58, 70, 72, 83, 85–87, 110, 119, 126, 128, 130, 131, 142, 181, 184, 185, 193, 200, 201, 211, 223, 225, 263, 289, 300, 302, 305, 309
Vengeance, 91, 93
Vernezze, P., 34
Vienna Circle, 19, 21
Virtue, 4–6, 8, 49, 52, 59, 69, 76, 85, 86, 89, 109, 110, 114, 116, 122, 127, 130, 132, 137, 141, 142, 149, 150, 157, 160, 162, 163, 166, 171–175, 179, 182, 185–191, 193, 197–208, 217, 227, 244, 247, 248, 250, 258, 263, 285, 298, 299, 304, 305, 310
Vlastos, G., 15, 23, 24, 26, 29, 33, 34, 66, 69, 87, 89, 202
Vocation, 1, 5, 125–144
von Wilamowitz-Moellendorff, U., 20

W
War, 2, 11, 12, 16, 17, 21, 24, 30, 36, 40, 55, 69, 102, 103, 132, 136, 143, 153, 314
Washington State Un-American Activities Committee, 17
Weakness of will, 70
Wealth, 131, 153, 178–180, 194, 200, 203, 204

Weber, M., 5, 34, 125–131, 135, 142–144
Weiss, R., 92
Well-being, 67, 73, 75, 83, 88, 89, 155, 156
Weller, C., 7, 8, 18, 271–282
White, M., 26
Whiteman, R., 13
Williams, B., 23, 170, 192, 281, 304, 313
Willingness, 68, 126, 198, 279
Winters, J., 13
Wisdom, 38, 47, 49, 69, 72, 73, 85, 88, 115, 149–151, 153–156, 183–189, 193, 194, 198, 205, 206, 285, 299
Wittgenstein, 2, 14, 15, 19, 21, 27, 41
Wolin, S., 5, 125–131, 142, 143
Woodruff, P., 49, 50, 89
Woozley, A.D., 98, 99, 107
The World as Will and Idea (Schopenhauer), 11
Wright, J., 13
Wrongdoing, 57, 58, 95, 96, 102, 103, 107, 199

X
Xenophon, 83, 112

Y
Young, C., 8, 39, 116, 194, 309–316

Z
Zeller, E., 110
Zeus, 139, 157, 170, 205, 207

CPSIA information can be obtained at www.ICGtesting.com
Printed in the USA
LVOW102130200613

339618LV00005B/69/P